THE SILENCE OF
PIUS XII

THE SILENCE OF
PIUS XII

by Carlo Falconi

Translated by Bernard Wall

LITTLE, BROWN AND COMPANY
Boston — Toronto

CONTENTS

FOREWORD

This book is the outcome of a well-known polemical argument. But it is not a polemical work. And still less a pamphlet aimed against Pius XII.

If such it were, it would not have taken so long to see the light. Though I was continually urged to write such a work, I had no ambition to join in the chorus of dissonant voices merely so as not to be absent from the records.

I was convinced then—as, of course, I still am—that the only chance of objective and constructive discussion lay in getting right away from the ever more pointless whirlpool of loud-voiced accusations made from set positions and interested lines of defence, and concentrating on the search for documents—to which the outcome of the increasingly publicized trial would in all impartiality be entrusted. So, as I had other work on hand, and as I was persuaded that I would thereby discourage the polite if insistent overtures of publishers, I told them that I would only consider their offers if sufficient means were put at my disposal for long and patient research in the most important European archives. Quite unexpectedly two publishers—Sugar (of Italy) and the Editions du Rocher (of the Principality of Monaco)—took me at my word, and so I had no choice but to accept.

The trips I originally planned were to France, Holland, Great Britain, Austria, Poland, Yugoslavia and Israel. By pure chance my first expeditions were to Yugoslavia and Poland. I set out with feelings of distrust and scepticism—it would be hard to say which was predominant—but there, as with the publishers, my facile conjectures were proved wrong. For after only two visits—to Warsaw and

11

Zagreb (Croatia)—I came back with spoils more than adequate to satisfy the hopes placed in my investigations.

Of course even in these countries my study of all the existing archives was not exhaustive. Far from it: when I did not merely reap the fruit of research made with astonishing disinterestedness on my behalf, I did little more than go straight ahead on the basis of precise indications that I had been given. I feel I ought to confess that at the outset I was afraid I would have to be on my guard against tendentious material (there is no need to say of what kind). But my mind was soon put at rest.

In Poland, for example, all I came across were a few publications of minor importance, and not a single historical essay on Pius XII and his relations with that country during the wartime occupation. As for the material that proved useful for my research, it came from the information services and the archives of the clandestine Polish government in Warsaw representing the government in exile in London: and it is common knowledge how un-Communist both these were.

In Yugoslavia the situation was certainly very different. The anticlerical polemics of the immediate post-war period had produced a type of pamphleteering that hardly inspired confidence—even when it resulted in massive tomes such as Viktor Novak's *Magnum Crimen* or semi-official publications with revelations from secret documents. No great perspicacity was needed to see that often, if not always, these documents were quoted only in extract, or with suspect omissions. But when I asked for access to the original texts my request was hospitably granted, though after some understandable hesitation.

As for their contents, despite the fact that they referred to geographically limited and specific situations, the two groups of documents that I collected proved to complement each other in a remarkable way, and were also an unexpected and valuable contribution to solving the general problem. And in any case, each particular orbit is only relatively restricted, especially in the case of Poland which, as is well known, was the tragic theatre for the sacrifice of six million Jews (over half of them living in the country, and the remainder coming from all parts of Europe) as well as about a third of its territory being used as a testing ground for forced Germanization. In addition, the German occupation of Poland was the first and most long-lasting of all the occupations in the Second World War; and was marked by an attempt to establish an autonomous ecclesiastical policy totally outside the control of the Holy See.

The evidence from Croatia (or more specifically from the independent Croat State—known as NDH—administered by the Ustaše between 1941 and 1945 with the help of the Axis powers) was altogether less sensational than the evidence from Poland, even though, from some points of view, it was even more disturbing. For the Ustaše, who lagged behind their Nazi colleagues in the massacre of the Jews and Gypsies (but this was mainly for lack of 'human material'), unquestionably surpassed them in anti-religious racism—for when they struck out at the Serbs it was not only at a rival and erstwhile oppressive people, but also at a schismatic and 'traitorous' people who had betrayed the true faith. Only in Croatia was the extermination of at least half a million human beings due more, perhaps, to hatred of their religion than of their race, and was sacrilegiously bound up with a campaign for forced 're-baptism' (from Orthodoxy to Catholicism). There had been no precedent for centuries for the scale or violence of this operation.

Nor was it only the contents of the two groups of documents that turned out to be so exceptional, but also—so to put it—their formal characteristics. For most of the Polish documents consisted of secret reports (mainly in cipher, as shown in several illustrations in this book) assembled by the information service of the 'Delegatura' (the clandestine delegate government) and the clandestine National Army, and destined to be transmitted to the government in exile in London; of valuable digests of the clandestine press; and of analyses and reports on the home situation and the attitude of the Church drawn up during the Nazi occupation with unremitting determination. Of no less appreciable importance are the documents, especially the diplomatic ones, sent 'for information' from London to Warsaw. There is no need to emphasize that the Polish government in London drew on this material both to illustrate Nazi atrocities to the Allied governments (as well as to the Vatican, as we shall see), and to give momentum to anti-German propaganda.

The central core of the Croatian documents, on the other hand, consisted in surviving accounts sent to the Ustaši foreign ministry at Zagreb by its two *de facto* representatives at the Vatican from the beginning of 1942 to the summer of 1943. These minute and often even pedantic accounts brought to light an entirely new and unsuspected harvest of revelations on the men and the mysterious world of the Secretariat of State, the Roman Curia, the Sacred College of Cardinals and the Pontifical Court during the central period of the war. So much so that it could be said that they present a positive gallery of portraits hitherto unrivalled.

Of course all this mass of information had to be situated in the respective contexts of the two historical 'cases', and, above all, the 'state of the question' had to be explored—that is to say the true meaning of the problem of 'Pius XII's silence', in a broad and universal sense, not a particular and polemical one. This task was even harder and more complicated than the tracking down and interpretation of the documents—but it is not for the author to force his difficulties on the reader.

Though I am not entirely dissatisfied with the results I obtained, these are not of a kind to delude me into thinking that I have written a definitive work. They were merely strokes of luck as I probed a field that still holds unpredictable secrets. And I sincerely hope that very soon others will follow and profit by the threads I have discovered—and with even better results.

As for the conclusions I reached—namely that the Vatican was very well informed and that the Pope was continually being urged to speak out, etc.—they certainly do not favour a justification of Pius XII's caution and silence. This judgment will probably be shared by my readers. And, if they are Catholics, they will certainly not be in bad company. For on 8 March 1964 in St. Michael's church in Munich—the very church in which, before the war, Cardinal Faulhaber had attacked the Nazi ideology on more than one occasion, and especially for its basic anti-Semitic ideas—his successor, Cardinal Julius Doepfner, did not hesitate to say in a sermon commemorating Pope Pacelli: 'The retrospective judgment of history provides every ground for the view that Pius XII should have protested with greater firmness.'[1] And there is no need to recall that other Catholic spokesmen, especially those in the world of culture, expressed the same conviction both before and after Cardinal Doepfner.[2]

And that this happened is surely no cause for surprise. For it was Pius XII himself who taught us how the behaviour of a Pontiff can and should be evaluated with honest impartiality, even when his fame and greatness are generally admitted. He did this, by a significant though obviously unintentional coincidence, only a few weeks before he died when he wrote a detailed commemoration of Benedict XIV (the greatest pope of the eighteenth century) which became known only after his death. In this he had no hesitation in joining the ranks of those critics who maintain that the conduct of Pope Lambertini (i.e. Benedict XIV) was 'too conciliatory and docile . . . in face of the vehement and excessive claims of the secular courts.' In Pius's view, if 'his compliance towards the King of Prussia can be explained by the higher aim of not wishing to worsen the situation of the Catholics in that State,' the concessions accepted in his Concordats with the courts of Sardinia-Piedmont, Naples and Spain 'seem really extraordinary and outside all tradition'.[3]

In some of his other writings the author of the present work has laid rather a heavy hand on certain aspects of Pope Pacelli's pontificate—*et pour cause*. But, as in 1950 I refused outright a publisher who asked me for a book aimed at proving the absurd theory that Pius XII wanted the war, so in this book I did not wish to set out from any predetermined position: my sole purpose has been to put before the reader some explanation of why Pope Pacelli did not dare to adopt a decisive position against the civilian misdeeds of the Nazis and their allies—in spite of ardently wishing to do so. The fact that, in my belief, Pius XII was silent not out of fear, but for respectable if inadequate motives, means that we cannot brand him with infamy, even if it does not absolve him from undoubted responsibility. In any case, a severe judgment on his silence does not exclude an open-minded and unconditional recognition of all that he did to prevent the outbreak of war, to discourage its spreading, and to alleviate the sufferings of its victims.

Finally I would like to express my personal gratitude for the courage and generosity of the publishers, Sugar, of Milan, and du Rocher of the Principality of Monaco; as well as for the encouragement of friends encountered during my successive stays in Poland and Yugoslavia, in particular Woiciech Pomykalo and his editorial colleagues on the Warsaw *Wychowanie*, Frane Barbieri, Ivan Lazić, Ive Mihovilović of Zagreb, and others.

C. F.

THE SILENCE OF PIUS XII
THE PROBLEM: ITS SIGNIFICANCE AND LIMITS

The office of Sovereign Pontiff throughout the centuries has served nothing if not the truth; the truth, let us say, which is total and sincere, not obscured by any shadow, nor subject to any weakness, nor ever separate from the love of Jesus Christ. During every Pontificate, in fact, and particularly in Ours which is called upon to fulfil its mission towards the human community at a time of such discord and conflict, there predominates, as a sacred command, the word of the Apostle: 'to do the truth in charity.'[1]

As Vicar of Him who in a decisive hour pronounced before the highest earthly authority of that day the great words, 'For this was I born and for this came I into the world; that I should give testimony to the truth. Everyone that is of the truth heareth my voice' (St. John xviii: 37), We feel We owe no greater debt to Our office and our time than to testify to the truth with Apostolic firmness: *testimonium perhibere veritati*, 'to give testimony to the truth'. This duty necessarily entails the exposition and confutation of errors and human faults; for these must be made known before it is possible to tend and to heal them: 'You shall know the truth and the truth shall make you free' (St. John viii: 32). In the fulfilment of this our duty We shall not let ourselves be influenced by earthly considerations nor be held back by mistrust or opposition, by rebuffs or lack of appreciation of Our works, nor yet by fear of misconceptions and misinterpretations. We shall fulfil Our duty, animated ever with that paternal charity which, while it suffers from the evils which afflict Our children, at the same time poinst out to them the remedy: We shall strive to imitate the Divine Model of shepherds, Jesus the Good Shepherd, Who is light as well as love, 'doing the truth in charity'. (Eph. iv: 15.)[2]

It was Pius XII himself who offered himself to the tribunal of history when he pronounced the foregoing words on two solemn occasions early in his pontificate. It was he himself who spoke of duty, of what was demanded of his high office, of how this should necessarily be carried through whatever fears or difficulties or hostile influences might arise. So, if he really drew back from his task and duty of condemning the unspeakable forms of violence that were perpetrated with the war—but especially under the cloak of war—the accusation that he broke down over what was precisely his function is not one either morally unjustified or juridically baseless. A pope who remains silent when serious errors in dogma or morals are spreading all around him is a pope who betrays his own mission.

In admitting this, if only implicitly, Pius XII did no more than repeat the traditional Catholic doctrine common to all his predecessors: a doctrine that comes straight down from a conception of the Church which, far from being weakened and toned down during the preceding centuries, and least of all in the last one, had been reinforced and given fresh vigour. We need only recall the statements made by Pius XI in *Ubi arcano Dei* and *Quas primas* (December 1922 and 1925 respectively).

In *Ubi arcano Dei*, the encyclical in which he laid down his programme, Pope Ratti went so far as to define the Church as follows:

> a divine institution able to safeguard the sanctity of the law of nations; an institution both belonging to and at the same time superior to all nations, endowed with supreme authority and venerable for the perfection of its magisterium.

Only the Church, the document went on, has

> the capacity of making itself the teacher and the peacemaker in full charity: the capacity also to unite among themselves all classes of citizens, and indeed the whole people, in a sentiment of higher benevolence and *quadem quasi fraternitate* (St. Aug.: De Moribus Eccl. Cath., i, 30) and lead up to God Himself the dignity of man, with its right recognized; the capacity, lastly, to see that, when public and private morals have been reformed and established on more holy principles, all things shall be fully subjected to God who 'beholdeth the heart' (1 Kings xvi: 7), and shall be inwardly informed by His teaching and laws, with the result that all things, the minds of all men, private individuals and rulers, even the public institutions of civil society, shall be penetrated by the sense of religious duty and 'Christ shall be all in all' (Col. iii: 11).

And naturally the Church is:

> teacher and head of all other societies, in such a way, of course, as
> not to diminish their power—for all in their own order are legiti-
> mate—but opportunely to perfect them as grace perfects nature, so
> that in very truth these societies may be of great help to man for
> the attainment of his supreme end of eternal happiness, and may
> bring happiness, too, and prosperity, in this mortal life.[3]

For non-Catholics, whether religious or not, such claims imply a
presumption, not to say a medieval anachronism, beyond all imagination. The fact remains, however, that they are still the official basis of
the ecclesiology and credo of Catholicism. As Pope Pius XI (Ratti)
admitted, the programme of his pontificate, 'Pax Christi in Regno
Christi', took over the programmes of his two immediate predecessors, Pius X and Benedict XV. Moreover Pius XII, at the beginning of his first encyclical, *Summi Pontificatus*, promulgated on
the feast of Christ the King in 1939 and placed under the sign of
Christ's Kingship, returned to the 'consecration of mankind to the
Most Sacred Heart of the Redeemer proclaimed by Leo XIII at the
end of the last century to inaugurate the Holy Year', and to the
devotion to the 'King of kings and Lord of lords' sanctioned by
Pius XI; indeed, Pius XII was precisely referring to the relations
between the Church and public authority when he reconfirmed in
full what his predecessor had taught in his encyclical *Quas Primas*
'concerning the power of Christ the King and of his Church'.

So the words quoted at the beginning of this chapter have to be
interpreted in the light of an ecclesiology adapted to modern needs by
Leo XIII, developed by his successors, brought to completion by
Pius XI, and solemnly taken up and made his own by Pope Pacelli.
And, in this light, the obligations claimed by Pius XII before the
Church and before mankind, at the very moment when the Second
World War broke out, take on even vaster and deeper dimensions.

Nevertheless we must still define, always within the context of this
doctrine, what the real function of a pope consists in, and what are
his rights and duties both towards his Church and towards the non-
Catholic world. The fierce arguments that have been raging for the
last two years about Pius XII's silence have caused such confusion of
ideas (rather than of facts) that we have no option but to clarify the
terms of the debate as a necessary point of order.

To keep to essentials, we must remember that, in Catholic theology, the pope as Vicar of Christ is the visible head of the Church, an absolute monarch with full, universal and immediate jurisdiction over all its members: bishops, priests and the faithful. On this unrestricted authoritarian basis his primary function is that of teacher: that is of guardian, interpreter (on the one hand) and propagator (on the other) of the dogmatic and moral truths contained in the so-called deposit of revelation. As such, he is given an additional protection and guarantee by his exceptional personal privilege: that of infallibility, by which he safeguards the Church from all error.

In addition the pope is the lawgiver, the judge and the supreme ruler of the entire ecclesiastical community. In these further capacities he is not, however, infallible—though, as the First Vatican Council laid down:

> priests and faithful of every rite and time, individually and collectively, are held in obligation to hierarchical subordination and true obedience, not only in matters of faith and morals, but also in those of discipline and Church government.

To conclude—always according to Catholic ecclesiology—the power of the pope is absolutely autonomous, that is to say it is not only independent of, but superior to, any earthly power: in a word, it is supreme in an absolute sense. The Church, like the State, is a society complete unto itself, but it surpasses the State owing to the pre-eminence of its end. And as, in view of its catholicity or potential universality—its attribute as essential dowry of Christ—it also stands above the totality of States and any international organization that they may eventually achieve, the pope is the supreme authority on earth in the spiritual order.

With regard to the problem we are discussing—namely, Pius XII's presumed responsibility in the matter of war crimes and crimes committed under cover of war by the Nazis and their allies—the aspects of the papal function relevant to the situation are those of 'teacher' and, still more, of 'judge'.[4] As moral teacher, the Pope is accused of treating the war almost exclusively as a social and juridical event, leaving the individual problem (the problem of individual consciences) entirely on one side; while it is argued that the Pope as judge withheld his condemnation of the worst and most wanton crimes, or condemned them only in general terms and without explicit reference by name to those responsible.

But what, in practice, are the specific duties of a pope with regard to war? If we leave aside his duty to give the abstract teaching on the morality of war (that is to say the elaboration of an organic doctrine of war and the responsibilities that it involves for heads of State as for private individuals, whether in the services or in civil life), it is obvious that in the case of actual armed conflict the functions of moral guide and judge proper to the Papacy—as, incidentally, to any other spiritual leader—operate in different ways according to the various stages of the conflict: its preparations and outbreak, its development, its conclusion.

In the initial stages, when the war is still incubating, the pope's main intervention can only be as admonisher, peacemaker and mediator. Once the war has broken out, however, he must set himself to examine whether it is opportune or necessary to make a pronouncement on the responsibilities of the parties concerned (leaders and followers), distinguishing the provoker and aggressor from the provoked and attacked. Safeguarding the moral conduct of the war as waged is the task that falls to him during the development of the struggle; while in the final phase he must devote himself to preparing the most advantageous conditions for the achievement of a just peace.

In practice the two most delicate and demanding tasks are (1) identifying and condemning the aggressor, and (2) safeguarding the moral conduct of the conflict. In the matter of condemning the aggressor, the situation of a pope is unlike that of any other religious leader unless that other leader be invested with sovereign characteristics equal to those of the head of the Roman Church. Even for a pope, however, the situation today is substantially different from that of his predecessors in the age of the 'temporal power'. The pope-kings (the last of them was Pius IX who held his position until 20 September 1870, when Italian troops entered Rome and made it the capital of Italy) could on occasion operate as peace-makers and judges in exceptional controversies between Christian States and communities. But more often they were contestants rather than arbiters—allies of the side that coincided better with the interests of their States as against the side inimical to them. 'The Papacy, even before being a tribunal of arbitration, a high court of international justice and an oracle of morality, is (in reality) an institution directed by the inner laws of its own conservation and growth.'[5]

It was Benedict XV in 1914 (Pius X having died a few days after Austria declared war on Serbia) who was the first modern pope able, when confronted with war, to adopt an attitude of total detachment from a temporal sovereign's 'reasons of State'. By choosing neutrality, Benedict skilfully brought the requirements of the Holy See's new status (a status still ill-defined juridically in international law, and in fact extremely precarious owing to the long-lasting 'Roman question') into line with the ideal requirements of a higher and spiritual form of detachment, narrowly linked to the Church's mission.

Subsequently the neutrality of the Holy See was ratified at Pius XI's wish by Article 24 of the Lateran Treaty (11 February 1929) in the eventuality of war between Italy and other nations. But in the first paragraph of that Article the Holy See reserved to itself the right 'to bring its moral and spiritual pressure to bear in all circumstances' in accord with its mission of peace. Since 1929, therefore, the juridical side of papal neutrality has not been in question, but only the moral side. As a Catholic theologian has written, 'Where truth and justice are concerned, and the distinction between good and evil, the pope neither wishes nor is able to remain indifferent. A neutrality in that sense . . . would not accord with the high duty felt by the pope towards the divine mandate entrusted to him. It was for this reason that in his Easter message (of 1941) Pius XII spoke of the share of fighting he was doing among the nations at war, though with arms "not of might or blood".'[6]

Precisely because the Roman pontiffs are no longer entangled by their sovereign interests, and because their political neutrality does not necessarily involve any moral neutrality, the problem of making a statement on war and its responsibilities can be tackled in substantially favourable conditions. Yet the fact remains that from another point of view we are dealing with an extremely difficult task. The theologian quoted above, who was writing in defence of Pius XII near the beginning of the Second World War—for even at that early date he was accused of irresolution regarding the warring parties—was hardly exaggerating when he said that:

to define the general character of the present conflict in relation to religion would require a gigantic stature and what I would call an age-old maturity—such as individual Catholics, however zealous, are incapable of possessing. Nor should we use the recent Spanish War as an example, for there the conflicting parties were sufficiently clearly identifiable in terms of religion to merit approval or condemnation on the part of the highest ecclesiastical authority. . . .

Every time that the Roman Pontiffs intervened in civil society . . . the first thing they had to bear in mind was *the object* of their intervention, so as to judge whether or not the matter was—at least indirectly—within their competence; then the *personalities* with whom they had to negotiate; and finally *the climate of the times* and the social and religious milieu.

All this represents difficulties of a complexity never experienced by even the most powerful monarchs on earth, for there is the need to harmonize heaven and earth, and time and eternity; the need to answer to God and to man, to the present and to history; the need to nourish equal affection and respect for different and rival countries, and to distribute justice to governments and peoples. If we remember the ill-will, distrust, garrulity and insincerity of certain elements, then we may begin to form a just estimate of the Holy See's arduous and complex task.[7]

No less are the difficulties that arise in the second sector: that concerned with the moral conduct of the war. The fact remains however, that some deeds—or rather misdeeds—are not and never can be justified or protected by any reason of political or military necessity. Here we must refer explicitly to the mass extermination of ethnic minorities, of entire governing establishments, of prisoners and civil deportees, as well as the transference of whole populations from their lands of origin to other lands so as to denaturalize them and favour their assimilation, etc. The existence of such monstrous evils causes such an upheaval of the criteria of good and evil, and such a challenge to the dignity of the human person and society as a whole, that it cannot fail to fasten the duty of condemnation on all those who have the possibility of influencing public opinion, whether they be private citizens or public authorities. To remain silent before such excesses would in fact correspond to actual collaboration, inasmuch as it would encourage the savagery of the criminals and excite their arrogance and vanity. But if anyone has a moral duty to react before crimes of this kind—crimes on the level of sheer wantonness—a still more compelling and unconditional duty falls to religious societies and their heads, in accordance, of course, with their power and efficacity: hence, first and foremost, to the head of the Catholic Church.

When we come to such extreme violations of the natural law, obviously all objections that could reasonably be raised on grounds of war have to give way. This applies above all to political expediency, but also to the charitable precautions rightly invoked by Pius XII in every normal situation. For charity itself, as even Catholic moral theology admits, obeys a hierarchy of order, and no one can doubt that charity for innocent and unprotected victims should prevail over charity for their butchers.

But it is now time to try to formulate, however summarily, the rules regarding a pope's conduct in face of war. Here it is:

1. The imminence of a war, or its unexpected outbreak, do not necessarily call for a public condemnation of those responsible, even in the (somewhat rare) case when there can be little or no doubt as to where the responsibility lies and there is thus no need for the usual laborious inquiries. An intervention of this kind would in fact impede, and in all likelihood definitively block, recourse to those means —diplomatic or otherwise—favouring a suspension of hostilities or a patched-up peace. And there is no doubt that the achievement of peace is an immeasurably greater good than an abstract condemnation of the aggressor.

It is also obvious that in exploring the various ways of peace-making there is no *a priori* dateline, and that it is perfectly possible to extend the period of patient and realistic endeavour granting that this extension is not used as an alibi to escape from moral responsibility and the consequences of condemnation.

Condemnation *can* (but still *need* not) be made when all legitimately-based hopes of achieving a settlement by other means have failed. But even in this case it should be able to be motivated—if it comes from a religious authority—exclusively by reasons in the moral order, once the responsibility of the side that provoked the conflict has been verified with a reasonable degree of certainty.

In no case, however, is a Church bound to adopt this sort of position when its followers are wholly outside the disturbance in question. For a Church's task is exclusively that of illuminating the consciences of its followers as to the behaviour they must adopt in accord with the principles of their faith—indeed, should a Church behave in any other way its action would lack proper motivation and would inevitably be viewed as superfluous or self-interested and hence provocative.

In calculating the consequences that a condemnation of the aggressor would inevitably entail both for the faithful and for its own organization and institution, a Church should not let itself be held back by earthly considerations. Whatever the material loss, or even the loss in human lives, encountered in the defence of the natural and divine ideals of justice and freedom, such loss would end up by bequeathing a matchless inheritance on this Church, and a prestige which, once the ordeal was over, would be translated into further positive affirmations. Yet it is also true that such a grave decision should not be taken with too bold a disregard for the consequences nor with too pure and uncalculating an idealism.

The obligation to intervene, though not absolutely imperative in a limited conflict when good and convincing reasons show that it is more opportune (for religious and social ends) to abstain, becomes ever increasingly pressing and inescapable, however, when the provocation is so reiterated and shamelessly wilful that it leaves no doubt as to the existence of an organic plan worked out down to the last detail. Yet even in this eventuality, especially when it is difficult to foresee where the consequences of this chain of provocations will lead, there is no way of establishing *a priori* the moment for intervening. This must be chosen with extreme prudence, by measuring on the one hand its necessity for the faithful, and on the other its usefulness to the cause of good.

2. When dealing with crimes of genocide—that is to say crimes neither justified nor justifiable by the exigencies of war or politics—it would be absurd to deny that it is legitimate to explore the possibilities of securing their abandonment before proceeding to a solemn condemnation such as would be made by a pope. Without previous recourse to persuasion and, should the opportunity arise at

a second stage, to threats arranged through private and secret channels, the act of condemnation would seem almost treacherous and pointlessly provocative and hostile; and rather than facilitating a suspension of the crimes it would tend to make them worse.

Yet procrastination at the preliminary stage, so to speak, should be much shorter in this case than in the previous one, as we are dealing with a situation that allows of no possible mitigation or accommodation. The sheer unjustifiability of such inhuman actions renders temporization unendurable, the more so if it has been verified that any delay would only increase the proportions of the holocaust.

Another stage, the final one, could consist in a generalized and impersonal condemnation of such monstrous deeds; but if even this bears no fruit, the duty of resorting to the decisive exposure, to the cry of horror and indignation, in short to the total and explicit condemnation, cannot tolerably be delayed any longer.

The belief that one can satisfy one's duty with the first type of condemnation (i.e. the generalized one) is an illusion that cannot stand out for long against the uneasiness of an honest conscience. The duty to bear witness to the truth and to tear the veils from any sort of tampering with it, and the duty to affirm the demands of justice and goodness as against every kind of baseness and every kind of falsification and oppression, cannot be aquitted by formal and generalized interventions, attenuated still more by ambiguous and hesitant formulas. This applies especially when we are dealing with the extremes of savage violence on the most unheard-of scale; unless one wants to make an absurd and grotesque parody, graver than the very evil that it should strike down. If, when confronted with the worst, most wanton and most provocative outrages, the mission of a Church or a religion is satisfied with interventions from which any possibility of efficacity has been deliberately and fastidiously removed, then we are obliged to say that that Church and that religion are the most repulsive parody of faith and of the need to believe.

It is in the light of these premises, about which we maintain that it is anything but difficult to agree, that we shall examine Pope Pius XII's behaviour in face of the unleashing of the war and the great Nazi perversions. We shall examine, we shall not judge. The true and proper judgment must be for the reader himself to deduce.

PART ONE

The Problem in General

THE PROBLEM IN GENERAL

An objective examination of the documents known so far (i.e. up to December 1964) concerning the attitude taken by the Holy See in general, and by Pope Pius XII in particular, towards the Nazi war and the planned extermination carried out under cover of war-operations by Hitler and his allies, calls for three observations—all irrefutable in the present state of our knowledge:

1. Pius XII never promulgated an explicit and direct condemnation of the war of aggression, and still less of the unspeakable acts of violence carried out by the Germans and their accomplices under cover of the war;

2. Pius XII's silence cannot be attributed to ignorance of events. He had full knowledge of the gravity of the facts from the earliest stages—a knowledge possibly greater than that of any other head of State in the world;

3. Pius XII continued to remain silent even though he himself felt urged to make a stand and even though he received ceaseless appeals from victims and governments asking him to 'speak out'.

As we have said, we are dealing solely with authenticated facts and objective verifications based on documents so far known: hence these data, taken alone, are insufficient; they require further careful evaluation if we are to put forward any considered judgment as to the Pope's responsibility. In order to reach such a judgment we need to assess, first, whether the events in themselves, and the circumstances in which they occurred, were genuinely of a kind to demand the Pontiff's 'witness to the truth' required by his office; and, secondly, if the answer be yes, whether the reasons adopted by Pius XII to justify his reserve are really sufficient to win our approval of his choice.

Chapter 1

THE FACT OF THE POPE'S SILENCE

Those who hold the Pope to be guilty, and those who hold him to be innocent, do not usually distinguish between (1) the evidence concerning his attitude towards the war, and (2) the evidence concerning those crimes which were not necessarily related to the war. We ourselves, however, on the premises laid down in the Introduction, will distinguish very carefully between the two categories of evidence. This will help us to clarify how Pope Pacelli's attitude differed towards the two types of event, and that in its turn should enable us to make a more exact statement about the moral responsibility in which he was involved.

Silence about the War

The most surprising fact for anyone who looks back over the early stages of Pius XII's pontificate is unquestionably the unexpected silence in which the Pope immured himself almost as soon as he heard of the outbreak of hostilities between Germany and Poland. Up to the day before, up to the last hours of 31 August 1939, his activity in diplomacy and oratory had been on a feverish level. Even today when we read his radio appeal from Castel Gandolfo on 24 August we feel a deep emotion, and the impression it produced at the time was enormous; there was even a widespread rumour that the Pope was to set off from Rome by air to face Hitler and his henchmen and try to make them change their minds. But the interminable first day of the war, 1 September, passed with no declaration or message from him. The same happened on 2 September, and the same again on the days that followed. The rooms of the Secretariat of State at the Vatican were hardly big enough to contain the ambassadors and officials of the diplomatic missions accredited to the Holy See, all waiting for the Pope to utter a solemn protest if not

31

an outright declaration of an anti-Nazi crusade. The various governments pressed the Holy See to extract promises and did all they
could to prevent even an hour's postponement of the inevitable intervention that the Pope would make. 'The facts speak for themselves,' Cardinal Maglione, Secretary of State, answered with brusque
politeness, 'so let them speak.'[1] While day after day all the facts told
was of the German army and air force tearing their way into the
heart of Poland with fire and sword. The aggressor was trium-
phant.

Not a single note of protest left the Vatican for the Wilhelmstrasse
even in secret, and neither then nor thereafter did the Secretariat of
State or the Pope make any statement about Germany's responsibility for the war. Instead the Pope waited until the last minute before
addressing invaded Poland, and then it was to lament her harsh
destiny. Whereas when two new ambassadors went to present their
letters of credit to him, he eagerly seized the opportunity to define
his absolute neutrality as regards the war for its duration.[2] If such a
proclamation was not formally superfluous, the Lateran agreements
made it quite out of date. Of course nobody expected the Pope to
side openly with one of the two opposing sides, but they did expect
him to avail himself of the freedom of his 'moral and spiritual
power'. Whereas Pius XII not only made it clear that unless he was
appealed to as mediator he would not be involved 'in the purely
temporal controversies and territorial rivalries between States', but
also insisted on declaring that his real preoccupations extended beyond the initial circumstances of the conflict and were concerned
with quite other dangers of a 'new and immeasurable' kind. These
preoccupations were bound up with the appearance on the horizon
of Christian Europe of the 'sinister shadow, becoming daily closer
and more threatening, of the ideas and activity of God's enemies.'[3] It
was the first and far-from-obscure allusion—which he was to follow
up with a dozen or so more in the years to come—to the Communist
menace (the day before he spoke the Soviet Union had advanced its
forces over the eastern frontier of Poland). Such anxiety was doubtless only too legitimate in a religious leader; but surely it was imprudent on his part to give the impression that the war between
Germany and Poland was serious, not so much in itself, as because

it was opening up a way by which atheistic Communism could enter Europe.

But Pius XII's pastoral silence could not go on for ever, and on 30 September, when the dividing-up of the Polish spoils had already been ratified by the aggressors,[4] he consented to receive the Polish colony in Rome—now, suddenly, a colony of refugees. Those who expected anything like Pius XI's address to the Spaniards in 1936 were to suffer bitter disappointment. With infinite caution Pope Pacelli selected the most moderate terms of condolence he could find, and put all his energies into counselling resignation. He did not permit himself even the vaguest reference to those responsible for the new partition of Poland.

His caution remained unchanged with the publication of his first encyclical. Pius XII had begun writing it before hostilities broke out. When overtaken by the 'horrifying news' all he could find to say was:

> . . . when We think of the wave of suffering that has come on countless people who, but yesterday, enjoyed in the environment of their homes some little degree of well-being, We are tempted to lay down Our pen. Our paternal heart is torn by anguish as We look ahead to all that will yet come forth from the baneful seed of violence and hatred for which the sword today ploughs the blood-drenched furrow. But precisely because of this apocalyptic fore-sight of disaster, imminent and remote, We feel We have a duty to raise with still greater insistence the eyes and hearts of those in whom there yet remains good will to the One from Whom alone comes the salvation of the world. . . .[5]

And he immediately went on to find comfort in the thought that for many people 'hours of such painful distress are often hours of grace'—a thought that seems deliberately calculated to justify those who maintain that religion inevitably deadens sensitivity and makes its followers less than men. In the same way we find this further consideration as remote and cold as the stars:

> . . . safety does not come to peoples from external means, from the sword, which can impose conditions of peace but not create peace. Forces that are to renew the face of the earth should proceed from within, from the spirit.[6]

These last words, true enough, were not without a polemical thrust

directed at the Axis powers, as being powers that preached the necessity of a 'new order' for the world while taking the destruction of the
old order as their starting-point. But with what caution was his
insinuation made! Surely the statement that the present moment was
'a real "Hour of Darkness" (St. Luke xxii: 53) in which the spirit of
violence and discord brings indescribable suffering on mankind'
could hardly be viewed as an explicit condemnation of those who had
provoked the outbreak of hostilities. There is no need to stress that
words like 'the spirit of violence and discord' are as generalized and
futilely rhetorical as could be imagined; while the hope that Poland
would soon experience 'the hour of a resurrection in harmony with
the principles of justice and true peace'[7] was hardly calculated to
offend the Germans, who had not yet officially decided on Poland's
destiny and were unquestionably preparing their own idea of a just
and peaceful place for that country within the 'new order'.[8]

So, in a word, Pius XII could find nothing more to say about the
war, then in full swing, than that he should hold before his eyes:

> 'the image of the Good Shepherd' . . . and it seems as though We
> ought to repeat to the world in His Name: 'If thou . . . hadst
> known . . . the things that are to thy peace, but now they are
> hidden from thine eyes.' (St. Luke xix: 42.)[9]

A few weeks later, on the occasion of his first Christmas radio-
message, Pius XII once more faced the question of the war—indeed
of 'the unspeakable horror of the war'. His pontifical heart felt
'immense bitterness' at the thought that that Christmas would be
celebrated 'to the funereal roar of cannons and under the terror of
flying missiles, in the midst of the menaces and dangers of armed
navies'. The more so in that the war, 'initiated and waged in such
unusual circumstances', had led to a whole series of excesses—foreseeable enough, as they were the inevitable product 'of the political
doctrines and arts which ignore the laws of God', but no less deplorable for that. They were more deplorable still owing to their
future consequences, destined to come to fruition after the end of
the war: 'an exhausted or weakened economy' would then have great
difficulty in finding the means of reconstruction, and 'the forces and
artifices of disorder, lying in wait, will seek to make use (of the
difficulties) in the hope of giving the final blow to Christian Europe'.

In other words Pius XII confirmed his point that the real gravity of the conflict, unleashed through a lack of any serious desire for conciliation on the part of the opposing sides, would only show itself later—with the calculated intervention of the Communists who would reap the harvest. At the time he could cite (but in the first case refrained from doing so) not only the annexation of eastern Poland by the USSR, but also the ultimatum to Finland, immediately followed by the Soviet invasion of that country.[10]

This is not to say, of course, that Pius XII's forebodings were wrong, nor his far-sighted assessment of the situation; but to attribute the real danger almost exclusively to the threat of atheistic Communism seemed to render Nazi Germany's responsibility almost negligible—whereas it was the Nazis who were the first real enemies not only of civilized Europe but of Christian Europe. Moreover the fact that he made a public condemnation—and without his usual laborious circumlocutions—of the aggression against Finland seemed to savour of clear-cut partiality, when he had not dared to intervene even vaguely at the time of the attack on Poland.

But Pius XII was soon to become almost stubborn in this partiality. In the spring of 1940, on 10 April, Germany occupied Denmark and Norway—naturally without any warning and justifying this decision on grounds of strategic necessity.[11] Though the violation of international law was blatant, the Pope avoided pointing it out. A month later Belgium, Holland and Luxembourg experienced the same fate, and now at last three telegrams were despatched from the Vatican to the respective sovereigns. The expressions of sympathy and solidarity (which were not reserved only for Catholic Belgium and Luxembourg but included Calvinist Holland) for the first time contained some vigorous expression about the wrongs that had been inflicted on them. Yet here again judgment fell only indirectly on the country really responsible for their fate—Nazi Germany. And it is worth recalling the Holy See's silence that thenceforth regularly recurred—first about the Baltic States (Latvia, Esthonia and Lithuania), and Bessarabia and Bukovina which were devoured by Russia (15 and 26 June 1940), then about the Italian aggression against Greece (28 October 1940), and finally about the invasion of Yugoslavia by Axis troops (7 April 1941). With none of these countries—any more than

with Russia, attacked by Germany on 22 June of the same year—
did either the Pope or his Secretary of State declare their solidarity
even in the most general terms. We may well wonder, at this point,
whether the criterion of political neutrality had not evolved into a
pretext to cover up a nameless moral neutrality. Aggression, in fact,
was no longer an exceptional phenomenon—as, despite peace-time
precedents (Austria, Czechoslovakia, Ethiopia and Albania), even
the attack on Poland could have been viewed—but had become an
endemic practice or, if the phrase be preferred, a systematic method.
Or were all the outrages perpetrated with horrifying reiteration by
the Nazis to be grouped together under the convenient label of 'pre-
cautionary measures of a strategic character'? It was in this way that
the Holy See chose to view things. To remove all doubt, Pius XII's
Christmas broadcast of 1941 confirmed his rule of intransigent
neutrality:

> As God is Our witness, We love all peoples without exception
> with equal affection; and up till now We have imposed the maxi-
> mum reserve on Ourselves so as to avoid even the appearance of
> being contaminated by the Party spirit. . . .

Of course we are not forgetting the noble if rather obvious principles to which Pius XII's wartime writings and messages bear witness. These documents included his first encyclical which recalled the
common origins and hence the universal equality of all peoples and
condemned the totalitarian State. It is never too late for either individuals or nations to admit their errors, but it was surely rather naïve
(though obligatory for a religious leader) to appeal to these principles
(which, incidentally, the Holy See itself did not adhere to properly as
can be seen by its indulgent attitude to Catholic totalitarian States
such as Spain and Portugal) when their very antithesis had reached
its point of culmination and was already reaping a vast and successful
harvest.[12]

Thus his confirmation of the rights of ethnic minorities to existence
and to the means that guaranteed their existence (but did Pius XII
raise his voice over the aggression against Albania a few days after
his election?), and his condemnation of the predatory behaviour of
the great States towards them etc., had their importance and necessity. But the powers that had unleashed war[13] were the least likely to

appreciate his teaching (and they aroused the passions of minorities or lesser peoples so as to make them allies). It must be added that for the head of a Church and his followers the problems of war were religious rather than political and juridical—and for all honest men driven into the struggle by the implacable mechanism of general mobilization, they were moral problems.

It would be a mistake to assume that Pius XII's neutral attitude implied lack of feeling or interest regarding the tragedy of the war. At a very early stage, as is well known, he lent his support to a German plot to depose Hitler; and he also gave his protection to daring diplomatic moves to reach peace by conciliation. Pius XII never gave up hope that sooner or later he could bring the war to an end. The severest blow to his hopes came with the Casablanca conference (January 1943) which laid down 'unconditional surrender'[14] as the only acceptable form of surrender. For he knew very well that the Germans would never capitulate without fighting to the last man— which is in fact what happened.

Yet as the war proceeded his diplomatic activity became more and more confined within a closed circle of ecclesiastic interest: the preservation of Italy and above all of Rome from the war. Not even after Italy had entered the war despite his efforts and the pressure he brought to bear on her (and here once again Pius XII seemed on the verge of bold action in his effort to separate Fascism from the monarchy) could he accept the situation. Henceforward all his effort was aimed at finding a way of getting her out of the war as soon as possible. There is no denying that his love for his motherland motivated his action. And yet for him a neutral Italy meant more than preserving his country from chaos and hence from Communism; it meant a protective buffer around the Vatican. When it proved impossible to achieve this aim, his last ditch was the protection of Rome —which was not only his native city but above all the capital of the Catholic world.

To sum up: Pius XII never formally condemned the outbreak of war, its development, nor all that it finally involved. Indeed he systematically avoided pronouncements about who was responsible for the war. His preaching, even when aimed at a wider audience than Catholics, was always confined to upholding the Church's preference for peace by illustrating ways of achieving this either within individual States or in international relations. As regards the war proper, he went on deploring the pointless disasters and horrors which it inevitably produced. Yet he avoided dealing with how believers should behave in conscience when faced with the obligation to take part in it, despite their possible disgust at its aims or at the means used to attain them.

Yet the day came when a decisive tone of condemnation for a war of aggression passed his lips—a condemnation that he at last recognized as an urgent duty to be put off no longer:

> There is a duty binding on everyone, a duty which can tolerate no delay, postponement, hesitation or reversal: namely, to do everything possible to prohibit and outlaw definitively aggressive war as a lawful solution to international disagreements and as an instrument of national aspiration. We have seen many attempts made to this end in the past. All have failed. And they always will fail until the healthiest element in the human race desires stubbornly, steadfastly, holily, and as an obligation in conscience, to fulfil the mission which has formerly been tackled with insufficient seriousness and resolution. If ever a generation has been forced to hear in the depths of its conscience the cry, 'Make war on war', that generation is the present one. It has passed through an ocean of blood and tears perhaps never before experienced; it has lived through unspeakable atrocities of war so intensely that . . . the horrors must remain engraved on its memory and in the depths of its soul like an image of hell—an image on which everyone whose heart has feelings of humanity must hunger . . . to close the doors for ever.

But Pius XII pronounced these words on Christmas Eve 1944[15] when Rome had been liberated for six months, when the Germans were on the Gothic line, when Paris had been reconquered, and the outcome of the war was decided. Even then there was no hint of to whom they were directed. In the judgment rendered by the highest religious tribunal of mankind, the aggressor remained for ever unnamed.

Silence about civilian atrocities

If we drew on the official and pastoral attitudes of Pius XII alone, our history of the Second World War would be a patchy one, as it might be if derived from the notes of a rather inattentive neutral, or, better, of a philosopher of history and society more concerned with general abstract problems than with concrete detail. It is certain that if we made use of Papal sources alone we would have no idea that, aside from the war, equally or more wicked and hair-raising events were taking place. Or at most we would note a few indications pointing to excesses occurring here and there, but viewed as the more or less inevitable outcome of war and occupation.

During the Second World War (and in accord with plans laid down in advance if only on general lines) there occurred, in Europe occupied by the Nazis or their allies, the massacre of:

1. 6,000,000 Jews of Polish, German, Hungarian, Slovakian, Rumanian, French, Italian, etc., nationality;

2. Over 3,000,000 Russian prisoners;[16]

3. 500,000–700,000 Orthodox Serbs;

4. More than 200,000 gypsies;

5. 200,000 Germans incurably ill and sacrificed to the programme of euthanasia.[17]

In addition tens of millions of peaceful people had to do forced labour, and tens of thousands of children were victims of the round-ups.[18]

It is true that whereas the soldiers who fell in military operations were recorded in the bulletins of the various nations at war, and even the civilian victims of bombing were recorded as dead, the Jews, the Russian prisoners, the Polish intellectuals and the incurably sick (whether German or not) died without their deaths being made public. Yet the massacre of so many millions of men, though unpublicized at least for a while, was never unknown and became better known as the information services of the civil authorities and especially, as we shall see, of the Vatican, were improved.

Yet this organized and scientific genocide, involving ignominies of every kind and reaching such gigantic proportions that acts of barbarism in the past pale beside it, had only a fragmentary or generalized echo in Papal documents. Not a single document dealt with it explicitly or exclusively, and the rare and limited hints were made in summary allusions. Moreover these were drafted not in a language of outrage but consistently in a cold and juridical style. We look in vain among the hundreds of pages of Pius XII's allocutions, messages and writings for the angry, fiery words that would brand such horrible acts for ever.

It is this silence that has caused the most scandal. Pius XII only referred to the Jews once, and then without actually naming them. Yet at an early stage there were vague hints at a condemnation that never came. In his Christmas message of 1939 we read:

Alas, We have been forced to witness a series of acts which cannot be reconciled either with what is explicitly laid down by international law, or with the principles of natural law, or even with the most elementary feelings of humanity. These acts show the vicious circle to which the sense of juridical rights has been perverted by purely utilitarian considerations. These acts include: premeditated aggression against a small, hard-working and peaceful nation on the pretext of a threat that neither existed, nor was intended, nor was even possible; atrocities (committed by whatever side), and the forbidden use of weapons of destruction against non-combatants, refugees, old people, women and children; a disregard for dignity, freedom and human life that has brought about acts that cry to heaven for vengeance: *vox sanguinis fratris tui clamat ad me de terra*; and an ever-growing, methodical, anti-Christian, even atheistic propaganda especially among the young.[19]

If we set aside the aggression against Finland and anti-religious propaganda, which do not concern our problem, we find that the acts deplored and condemned by Pius in the above message are referred to in his usual vague and generalized style, thus enabling the adversaries to lay the blame on each other. Such a list of lamentations could nevertheless give grounds for hoping that greater courage might be shown as time went on and as needs required it.

And this hope seemed confirmed by the following extract from Pius' allocution to the Sacred College of 2 June 1940:

On this occasion it would not be permissible for Us to withhold the expression of Our sorrow at the sight of non-combatants in more than one region being treated without regard to the rules of humanity. . . . Hence it is fitting . . . that as the area of battle spreads there should be no lack of that calm dignity of reason which dictates the supreme principles of promoting good and restricting evil, principles that strengthen and honour the orders of those in command and make those subject to command more ready and inclined to bow their will and work for the common interest. Hence the wider the extent of territories subject to foreign domination, the more urgent it becomes to harmonize the juridical order applied to them with the dispositions of the rights of the peoples and above all with the requirements of humanity and equity. Nor must there be any failure to recognize that, alongside the safety precautions justified by the real necessities of war, the good of the peoples that have fallen under Occupation in no way ceases to be an obligation in the exercise of public power. Justice and equity demand that they should be treated as the Occupying Power would wish to see its own nationals treated in similar circumstances.

It is not difficult for those who want to rise above human actions to deduce the consequences of these elementary principles of right reason and lay down a ruling for special issues concerning the Occupied countries in accord with the Christian and human conscience and with real wisdom about the affairs of State: respect for the life, honour and property of citizens, respect for the family and its rights; and, on the religious side, freedom for the private and public exercise of divine worship and spiritual assistance in a manner fitting the people in question and its language, freedom for religious instruction and education, the safe-guarding of ecclesiastical property and of facilities for bishops to correspond with their clergy and faithful in matters involving the care of souls. . . .

Though highly juridical, the tone is also noble. What we find irritating is the emphasis laid on ecclesiastical privileges in an otherwise valuable ruling. Yet what was really happening, though referred to only obscurely and fleetingly in the Papal text, was far more serious than anything that could be imagined; and within another year and a half no one could delude themselves any longer, least of all the Vatican. By the end of 1941 no one could have any doubt of Germany's intention to destroy Poland. The first mass-deportations of the Jews had begun (1941 also brought the well-known Jewish statute into Vichy France and to Monsignor Tiso's Slovakia), and in Croatia the first hundreds of thousands of Orthodox Serbs had been killed on grounds of religious rather than racial intolerance. Yet, in his Christmas message, Pius XII found time to express only stupefaction and distress at the continuing obstacles put in the way of the Catholic Church's activity:

It is inexplicable to Us that in certain regions numerous regulations block the way to the message of the Christian faith though they allow wide and free passage to a propaganda that militates against it. They withhold the youth from the beneficial influence of the Christian family and estrange it from the Church; they bring it up in a spirit at enmity with Christ by diffusing anti-Christian ideas, maxims and practices; they militate against the work of the Church in her care for souls and her actions of charity; they ignore or reject her moral influence on the individual and society. . . . That all this and more can be carried on amid the sufferings of the present hour is a sad sign of the spirit in which the enemies of the Church are imposing on the faithful—among all their other heavy sacrifices—a sorrowful load of bitter anxiety which weighs on consciences.[20]

Pius XII was right to complain about this, though it is rather surprising that he of all people should have expected anything different from the Nazis and Communists. Whereas what fills us with amazement is that immediately afterwards he made so bold as to threaten a solemn protest against the obstacles set in the way of the Church:

In order to avoid even the appearance of being contaminated by Party spirit, We have so far imposed a maximum reserve on Ourselves, but the regulations against the Church and the aims they have in view compel Us in the name of truth to give utterance, if only to avoid the faithful being misled.[21]

A solemn protest of this kind was of course within his rights, but surely it also came within the scope of his duties to do as much to put an end to the crimes committed against hundreds of thousands of innocent victims who were being persecuted simply because of their race or because it was politically convenient to the victor.

The Christmas message of 1942—which coincided with the approaching peak of the various anti-Semitic and genocidal campaigns—contains the announcement of a positive crusade. By that time those who had been secretly murdered by Nazi barbarism could be estimated at some two and a half million. But the Pope pointed to quite different horizons:

The best and most elect Christians, inspired by a crusading enthusiasm, must gather together in the spirit of truth, justice and love, and rally to the cry 'God wills it!'—prepared to serve and sacrifice themselves like the crusaders of old. Whereas in those days they were freeing the land sanctified by the life of the Word, today, if We may so express Ourselves, they must . . . overcome the sea of contemporary errors so as to free the spiritual holy land destined to be the basis and foundation of unchangeable laws for solid and consistent social constructions.

It is with this high aim that, from the cradle of the Prince of Peace and trusting that his grace will be diffused in all hearts, We turn Ourselves to you, beloved sons, who recognize and adore Christ as your Saviour, to all those who are united with Us at least with a spiritual link of faith in God, to all those who are eager to free themselves from doubts and errors and are hungry for light and guidance; and We exhort and entreat you with fatherly insistence not only to seek to understand the anguished society of this hour, but also to meditate on a possible beneficent and supernatural dawn, and to work for the renewal of society in spirit and in truth.

The essential aim of this necessary and holy Crusade is that the star of Peace, the star of Bethlehem, should burst forth once again in its shining light, in its pacifying comfort, as promise and augury of a better, more fruitful and happier future.[22]

The gas chambers were burning systematically in the Polish and German camps, whole villages with their Orthodox churches and faithful were being set alight in Croatia, preparations were being made for deportations in Slovakia, three hundred thousand Jews had already been secretly liquidated in Bessarabia and Bukovina, millions of future victims were living in the ghettoes, the concentration camps and at home, awaiting the hour of extermination, and Pius XII announced the 'star of Peace' as the essential aim of the 'necessary and holy Crusade'!

Happily he found a new tone and a more solid level of argument towards the end of the document:

What has been held in in time of peace has burst forth in war in a tragic series of actions that contradict the human and Christian spirit. International conventions to make war less inhuman by restricting it to combatants, and to lay down rules for Occupation and for the imprisonment of the conquered, have been ignored as a dead letter in various places. Who can see the end of this progressive deterioration?[23]

Though the Pope remained silent about the enormities crying out for vengeance, he went on:

Do the peoples really wish to look on in apathy at this disastrous progress? Ought they not rather to gather together, on the ruins of a social order that has given such tragic proof of its ineptitude for bringing about the good of peoples, all those with generous

and honest hearts in a solemn vow to take no rest until the ranks
of those determined to lead society towards the unshakeable centre
of gravity of divine law, of those zealous to serve the person and its
community as ennobled by God, become legion within the peoples
and nations of the earth?

This is a vow that mankind owes to the countless dead lying
buried on the battlefields; the sacrifice of their lives in the fulfilment of their duty is their offering for a new and better social
order. This is a vow that mankind owes to the infinite host of
mourning widows and orphans who have seen the support, the
light and the comfort of their lives snatched from them. This is a
vow that mankind owes to the innumerable exiles whom the
hurricane of war has torn from their homeland and scattered
abroad. This is a vow that mankind owes to the hundreds of
thousands of people who, through no fault of their own, and
sometimes only on grounds of nationality or origin, are destined
for death or slow deterioration. . . .[24]

Now the Pope had begun to talk. But, alas, he had also finished.
This allusion in a few cautious lines was not only to be the strongest,
but also the first and last allusion that he was to allow himself to
make to the mass murders. Why then, one wonders, announce such
a solemn and fierce crusade if he did not dare unmask the real, if not
the only, objectives that justified it? Perhaps, as the plan remained
at the stage of a mere exercise in rhetoric and there was no effort to
give it concrete form, we would not be far from the truth in supposing that it was aimed at intimidating the Nazi leaders into putting
an end to their mass murders.

However this may be, henceforward Pius XII did not allow himself
even to glance at the unspeakable atrocities of the Nazis and their
allies.[25] Until the war was over, save for the speech he made on 5
June 1945 from which we shall quote later, he was never willing to
throw light on the mystery of that silence. If we consider all the
propaganda made during the war by the Holy See to publicize its
acts of pacification and relief (that was the time that the review
Ecclesia was born, and the yearly *L'Attività della Santa Sede* and
other publications on specific subjects)[25 bis], and above all if we
recall Pius XII's constant reiteration of the fact that he always tried
to do all he possibly could, we cannot help suspecting that it all
came from a need to react to a dramatic guilt complex. Moreover,

nothing except a complex of this kind could account for Pius XII's subsequent breathless search for temporal prestige for himself and the Church, as if only the temporal glories of his peace-time pontificate could distract the eyes of the indiscreet from the still so recent war-time period, and thereby prevent them from uncovering his enormous sin of omission.

Chapter 2

PIUS XII KNEW

But did Pius XII really know about the unspeakable atrocities carried out by the Nazis and their allies under the cover of war?

Here we have the crucial question by which Pius XII's silence may be judged blameworthy or excusable. Hence it is not surprising that his official defenders should cling to a negative answer—at least in the early stages.

When the Jesuit, Robert Leiber,[26] who had been Pacelli's secretary for thirty-four years (from 1924 until the Pope's death) was asked by the *Frankfürter Allgemeine Zeitung* to comment on Hochhuth's *The Representative*, which had been put on in Berlin on 17 February 1963, he answered with a long article (27 March 1963) in which he said:

Pius XII did not know what was really happening. Nor did the allies. It was not until after the war that they were able to realize the extent of the Nazi crimes.

At about the same time the Secretariat of State mobilized its official historian, Mgr. Alberto Giovannetti, author of *Il Vaticano e la Guerra, 1939–1940*[27] (The Vatican and the War, 1939–1940) and *Roma Città Aperta* (Rome, Open City),[28] who also compiled and wrote a commentary on the Pacellian documentation about the Church of Silence.[29] And in the *Osservatore Romano* of 5 April 1963 there appeared a substantial article entitled *Storia, Teatro e Storie* (History, Theatre and Gossip) by the permanent representative of the Holy See at the United Nations who maintained the following thesis:

With the conflict there began the systematic deportation and the scientifically organized extermination of Jews and other categories of citizens (the reader will recall how the Polish clergy was decimated). The tragedy reached its peak with the first military setbacks of the Nazis, but its immense dimensions, and the monstrous cruelties that accompanied it, appeared in all their sinister light only after the war was over. Even the great majority of the German population only knew of these appalling crimes after the war. . . .

Information about these crimes reaching the Vatican itself was scarce and vague. For the most part it originated from one belligerent side (the Allied powers) and was based on revelations and news whose certainty could not be guaranteed even by those who divulged them. . . . The absence of Vatican representatives in German-occupied countries, the isolation and inactivity to which the nuncio in Berlin was condemned, the answers he received when he dared refer to various rumours, the general lack of accurate detail about the information available, suggested that it was inadvisable to adopt a public position which might give the Nazis an excuse for accusing the Holy See of violating its neutrality.

In the spring of 1963 no one could have foreseen that the polemics regarding the thesis put forward in *The Representative* would have lasted beyond, say, a few weeks. And this would probably have been the case had not the Catholic press, and subsequently the attitude of Paul VI, stirred up a wasps' nest. With a short view in mind, it was not considered too dangerous to force the facts, disregard the cost, and substitute apologetics for a more measured and persuasive historical judgment. But as time went by the 'excessive' defence began to run down and came to a point where it could no longer be maintained. In June 1964 *Civiltà Cattolica*[30] felt obliged to ask one of its experts, Fr. Angelo Martini, to re-examine the question.[31] Here follows the new position as expounded by Martini:

So Pius XII spoke. According to his duty and his knowledge of the facts. We must emphasize to what extent and in what way he knew of the nature and method of exterminations. As regards the Jews, the full figure of six million dead was established and known only at the end of the war. The decision to adopt the final solution (*Endlösung*) was *suspected* from the middle of 1942, but the details were clear only when the extermination was completed, i.e. after the defeat. The World Jewish Congress, with the help of its centres for information and checking, was able to obtain approximate figures which, beginning with hundreds of thousands, reached the estimate of four million by 1944. The Jewish agencies set about publishing the news at the same time as other sources, one of the principal of these being the Polish Government in Exile which drew on information from Poland. This latter documentation was substantially accurate as regards the positions of the concentration camps, exact descriptions of the methods of extermination, and approximate estimates of the number of victims. The Pope also received news, though not as often nor as accurately as could have been desired. This came from the clergy in the Occupied countries, army chaplains passing through, and members of the armed forces or civilians. Unfortunately this data lacked the verification needed to provide grounds for denouncing it as fact. Here we must point out that there existed no international agreement dealing with civilian internees and political prisoners, and even when the International Committee of the Red Cross (Geneva) carried out its intensive work for prisoners of war (wherever and on whatever terms it was allowed to do so) it always found the gates of the civilian prison camps barred. . . .

The language is still rather cautious but, despite the obvious reservations, it is different indeed from that of the earlier apologists. For all his minor reservations (and they were obviously irrelevant to the *Endlösung* of the Jews: planned or not, what mattered was that this was happening and with an ever-increasing rhythm), Martini ended up by admitting that the Pope was 'aware of the facts'. Yet as Martini was only discussing the Jewish question, for him 'the facts' meant the extermination of non-Aryans. Whereas the problem of Pius XII's silence goes much further than this. It involves the extermination of the Polish intelligentsia, the acts of violence against the Serbs, the assassinations in the name of euthanasia, and so on. But for all that Martini gave implicit credit in too summary a way to arguments supporting the inadequate documentation of the Holy See, and above all to the argument about the isolation of the Vatican.

This last legend came from Vladimir d'Ormesson, French ambassador in Rome up till October 1940.[32] As d'Ormesson had direct experience, having spent four months as compulsory guest in the Vatican after Italy entered the war, many people swallowed his bait. Here are his words:

Those who were shut up in the Vatican City during the last war . . . can testify to the total isolation of the Holy See. Fascism, followed by Hitler's armies, raised a real 'wall' between the tiny pontifical city and the rest of the world. The telegraphic service was under Fascist control. The foreign radio was infuriatingly jammed. While the less said about the telephone the better. . . . The Fascist police was soon doubled by Hitler's police and never loosened its grip. . . . Upon my soul and conscience, I am absolutely convinced that, like everyone else, Pius XII was uninformed about the monstrous refinements of cruelty of which the Jews were the secret victims.[33]

Despite this impassioned appeal, there was no such thing as the 'total isolation' of the Vatican; even its partial isolation was very relative. We have no cause to disagree with what d'Ormesson goes on to say immediately afterwards, namely that 'the Vatican is far indeed from being the best informed centre in the world'. But we must make a distinction. In normal circumstances this is true; but in time of war, and particularly during the Second World War, the very opposite was the case.

How can we prove it? Our only difficulty is which evidence to select. We can appeal to the authority of a cardinal whose name will often crop up in this book, Eugène Tisserant. In a speech he made in Paris on 13 December 1944, he said:

In the course of this war the Papacy was not entirely free. Yet we must not exaggerate or pretend that the Lateran agreements were an inadequate guarantee of Papal freedom.

These words are all the more telling in that (as the reader will see in due course) they came from a man who was anything but an italophile.

But the facts speak even clearer. We can begin with the asylum offered by the Vatican City first to the Allied diplomatic representatives, then, after the liberation of Rome, to those of the Axis. On the outbreak of war the representatives of France, Belgium, Great Britain and Poland found refuge in Santa Marta, followed by others as their respective States joined in the struggle for democracy: Brazil, Chile, China, Columbia, Cuba, Ecuador, Italy, Yugoslavia, Peru, Uruguay, the United States and Venezuela. At one time a hundred-odd people were crowded in there.[34]

True, these compulsory guests lived in close confinement and even their recreation was rationed to a short car drive, a game of tennis in the grounds of the Ethiopian College, or else a stroll, though only in the mornings, in the Vatican Gardens. But their main task was to carry out their particular functions and, given their circumstances, these consisted mainly in providing and obtaining news. In other words, besides gleaning information from the Secretariat of State and those Roman ecclesiastical circles most active in political affairs, they had to try to influence the Holy See by transmitting the news they received from their respective governments. Furthermore, as it was possible for them to meet diplomats living in Rome and people concerned to visit them in the precincts of the Sacred Palaces, their relationships extended to a notable part of the diplomatic world living in the city, above all that of the neutral countries.

As for communication with their own governments, the diplomatic bags were either forwarded through neutrals or with the help of the Papal diplomatic organization, at least as far as the nearest representatives of their countries. The Vatican radio worked regularly at fixed hours for the transmission of reports. The publication of the correspondence between Roosevelt and Pius XII is sufficient proof of how the American president's personal representative (or, in his absence, his assistant Harold Tittman) communicated with his government either directly by radio or through the United States legation in Berne.

In any case it is untrue that the diplomats who were the Vatican's guests in their capacity as representatives accredited to the Holy See could not leave the Vatican[34 bis] or Rome to reach their own countries, even though this was obviously not the general rule. Sir Francis D'Arcy Osborne, for instance, the British Minister, left for London on 8 April 1945 and remained there until 29 June. Roosevelt's personal representative, Myron Taylor, made three visits to Rome before Mussolini deprived him of authorization to cross the Italian frontier; namely, from 27 February to 22 August 1940, from 5 to 21 September 1941, and from 17 to 28 September 1942. He subsequently returned with the victorious Allies on 10 June 1944.

As regards the Holy See itself, it was always able to communicate with the various countries of the world through its own normal diplomatic channels even when the difficulties arising from the war made relations harder. The events of war tended to eliminate a certain number of Papal diplomatic offices. Those in Warsaw were suppressed in September 1939, those in Belgium and Holland closed down in July 1940, those in Lithuania and Latvia in August of the same year, and those in Belgrade in June 1941. Already in 1938 the nunciature in Vienna had been suppressed after the *Anschluss*, while in the spring of 1939 the nunciature in Prague was to some extent taken over by the legation at Bratislavia, the capital of the new Republic of Slovakia.

But hostilities also led to the setting-up of new diplomatic relations: with Finland (though the Finnish representation was not reciprocated by the Holy See) with China and Japan.[35] Moreover we must not forget *de facto* relations such as those with the new Kingdom of Croatia. And it can be said that the Berlin nunciature, against the will of the German Government, replaced the three sister representations that had disappeared from the centre of Europe: Warsaw, Brussels[36] and The Hague. And in any case the diplomatic network of the Vatican could always rely on a considerable number of nunciatures and Apostolic Delegations.

The nunciatures were those in Berlin (though it gradually became paralysed, it was still the most important of them all), Rome, Vichy (taking the place of the Paris nunciature), Budapest, Bucharest, Bratislava, Berne, Madrid and Lisbon. There can be no need to emphasize the importance of the three last which were in neutral countries. Berne was especially important in view of its position in the heart of Europe, and it leant towards the Allies, whereas the two Iberian capitals tended towards the Axis. And it would be a great mistake to underestimate the part played by the Vatican representatives in Hungary, Slovakia and Rumania merely because those countries were allies of the Axis, for in the matter of defending the Jews their interventions were notably efficacious. As for Vichy, the Papal nuncio, Valeri (who remained *en poste* up till the liberation, i.e. until the end of 1944, when his place was taken by the former Apostolic Delegate to Istanbul and Athens, Giuseppe Roncalli) had freedom of movement backwards and forwards to Rome; and until the Allied landings in North Africa (November 1942) he had wide facilities for contacts with the European and extra-European world through his American and Canadian colleagues.

As is well known, Apostolic Delegations are almost invariably nunciatures either secret or *in fieri*. During the Second World War the Holy See had five Apostolic Delegations at its disposal in European territory, two of them of first-grade importance (not to mention

the Delegations to the United States and Canada and two nearer
non-European ones, in Syria and Egypt). Though the importance of
the Delegations at Sofia, Athens and Scutari was only relative,
those in London and Istanbul were of first-class significance. Istanbul
was considered so important that Germany kept a man of von
Papen's ability there; as for London, it housed not only the government of one of the greatest Allied powers, but also many of the
exiled governments, for instance the Polish, Belgian, Dutch and
Yugoslav, with all of which the Papal Delegation was in touch.

Even Catholic historians took this situation for granted. For instance, in an article appearing in *Civiltà Cattolica* on 30 June 1961,
the Jesuit Fr. Fiorello Cavalli wrote concerning the spring of 1942:

In those days (of March) anguished appeals for help reached the
Vatican from the Jews and their governments in many countries,
through the British Minister to the Holy See, President Roosevelt's
personal representative to Pius XII, the Apostolic Delegations in
Great Britain, the United States and Turkey, and the Nunciatures
in Rumania, Hungary and Switzerland.

Moreover quite often the Vatican received and despatched abroad
lay or religious persons whose active part in politics was well known.
To give an example: from 20 February to 4 March 1943 the Vatican
had as guest Francis Spellman, Archbishop of New York ([36] *bis*).
Now the Archbishop of New York was no pacifist bishop, such as
many were, but the United States Archbishop to the forces, no less,
whose military visits to the front, or diplomatic visits to sound the
ground, or visits in the interest of relief work (to help prisoners and
war victims) were the object of close scrutiny by the Axis powers
(between April and May of that year he also spent several weeks in
Turkey). In November 1941, and subsequently in August 1943 (after
the fall of the Fascist regime but while Italy was still allied to Germany and at war with the Allies) the *ingegnere* Enrico Pietro
Galeazzi (to take another example) left the Vatican for two short
visits to the United States. Galeazzi had been in Pacelli's suite when
he made his famous trip to the United States as Secretary of State in
1936.[37]

Naturally, the Fascist police, helped by the German Secret Service,
kept a close watch on the Vatican. It appears that the main task of

the Italian police was to watch the postal and telegraphic services, while as early as April 1940 the Gestapo had taken over surveillance of the diplomatic bags of the nunciatures, having been told that the bishops in the occupied countries were making use of them to send news to the Holy See. But this sort of thing is anything but extraordinary in wartime.

The Vatican's operative freedom during the Second World War can be divided into periods as follows:

1. Between 1 September 1939 and 10 June 1940 (i.e. as long as Italy remained non-belligerent) the Vatican City had absolute freedom.

2. Between 10 June 1940 and 8 September 1943 the conditions of control were endurable.

3. Between 8 September 1943 and 3 June 1944 (i.e. during the German occupation of Rome) the control was intensified.

4. After the liberation (4 June 1944) complete freedom was restored to the Vatican.

To sum up, then, the period of greatest hardship lasted for a maximum of ten months. But if we admit, as now seems to be established, that precisely in that period the relations between the Holy See and the German authorities in Rome improved considerably, then even in this period we should speak rather of watch than of measures attempting to achieve isolation but failing to do so.[38]

It is in any case an established fact that the emergency services set up by the Vatican on the one side, and by the episcopates concerned on the other, guaranteed—though in a way that was inevitably discontinuous—what the obstacles were set up to prevent. And there is nothing surprising about this. Even private individuals, and persecuted ones at that, managed in much worse circumstances to set up almost unbelievable systems of communication. During 1943 Gisi Fleischmann, an unknown Jewess from Bratislava, managed to send messages to the highest authorities in the world (and probably to the Pope himself). She also managed, through a chain of messengers, to get into.touch with the 'American Jewish Joint' [*sic* Trs.], one of the most powerful Jewish organizations, and to work out a complicated plan for the financial ransom of the Jews. The 'Europa-Plan', it appears, was on the point of being approved by Himmler and only

broke down owing to Eichmann's intransigence. It was taken up
again a year later in Budapest by the journalist Rudolf Kästner and
had a partial success. Kästner, too, was able to establish relations
with several Jewish organizations on the other side of the Atlantic
and bring about negotiations in Lisbon and Italy.[39]

Obviously the problem was much easier for the Vatican. Even
apart from all the nunciatures, there were bishops, priests, religious
and laymen who could be mobilized, having been carefully selected
with a view to their suitability and trustworthiness. When we come
to deal with Poland we shall see a fairly detailed picture of the network that kept the Holy See in secret communication with that
country. For the time being let us quote the statement made by Fr.
Paul Duclos in his study, *Le Vatican et la seconde guerre mondiale*:

> . . . Almost all the Pope's messages reached the bishops in the
> Occupied countries. . . . Probably private individuals were en-
> trusted with transmitting them to the bishops. Recourse to a
> clandestine network became more and more necessary. Bold,
> devoted men, above all priests and religious, always managed to
> infiltrate through the Gestapo net.[40]

Only someone with a very superficial knowledge of Catholic
ecclesiastical organization could suppose that the opposite was true.
But what has been said is already more than enough to show that
'despite all the material obstacles, the Vatican had the means for
being heard and making itself heard'.[41]

And we must not overlook the fact that a quantity of valuable
data was handed to the Holy See, directly or indirectly, by political
men in the various countries (even by Germans who were anti-
Nazi in ideology or had ceased to be Nazi) who were often placed in
exceptionally favourable conditions to do this. The most typical example was that of Admiral Canaris, head of the Third Reich's secret
service, who on two notable occasions appears to have spoken in the
Vatican about the extermination of the Jews.[42] In all likelihood a
fairly generous source of indiscretion must have been von Papen
both before and during his assignment in Istanbul. This could be the
only justification for the gratitude shown him by Mgr. Giuseppe
Roncalli.[43]

However, the fact that the Vatican was not isolated but only held under check, that it disposed of its normal and highly efficient network of diplomatic representatives as well as the diplomatic services accredited to the Holy See, that a clandestine emergency system existed over and above these, only proves that the Vatican *could* obtain knowledge of the Nazi exterminations, not that it *did*. Given the difficulty of communications, it would not be surprising, for instance, had the nuncios confined themselves to informing Rome of the religious and politico-military situations in the territories to which they were assigned, and only referred marginally to other questions such as the persecution of the Jews and the treatment of prisoners. But surely it would be very surprising had the diplomats of the Allied countries made no attempt to bring to the Pope's notice documentation confirming Nazi barbarities, given that it was their aim from the very beginning of hostilities to wrest from him a condemnation of Hitler's Germany. And it would be equally surprising had the countless Jewish organizations spread across the world refrained from bringing pressure to bear on the Vatican. But it is precisely this point that is to be demonstrated in a historical study of Pius XII's responsibility towards the civilian victims of Nazism.

And an answer to all these questions does exist despite the fact that we are still at the beginning of our inquiries and despite the understandable motives of certain governments today to withhold information about their relations with the Holy See during the war.

But before proving that the Holy See was adequately informed we still have to face the objection made by the Secretary of State's official historian, Mgr. Giovanetti; namely, that there was no means for other than vague or irrelevant news to reach Rome because during the war no one knew of, or wanted to believe in, the monstrous acts whose documentation was only completed later.

If by 'no one' he means the mass of people involved in the war it would be difficult to contravert the statement, except as regards Germany and Poland. After the war, when the hour of *redde rationem* came, it was to be expected that the Germans would maintain that they had never known of these events. But leaving aside that certain camps (Dachau, Buchenwald, etc.)[44] were already notorious before the war, we only need consider the millions of soldiers in the

Wehrmacht and the SS who were witnesses of, and sometimes collaborators in, the public massacres of prisoners, civilians and Jews, to deduce that this ignorance could only have been very relative.[45]

Moreover, news about the camps spread and infiltrated. A witness at the Frankfurt trial (which began in December 1963) mentioned the name of a Catholic nurse who managed to smuggle abroad the secrets of Auschwitz. Shortly afterwards her account was broadcast to the whole world by the BBC.[46]

As for countries like Poland, Croatia and Rumania—all theatres of enormous massacres—obviously their inhabitants could hardly have remained in complete ignorance of what was happening before their eyes, and as they were victims they had every inducement to talk: their only problem lay in finding the means to get such explosive news outside their frontiers.

As for the remaining countries in the Europe of 1940–45, i.e. the Axis countries, the Axis allies and those occupied by the Axis forces (hence only excluding Switzerland, Great Britain, Sweden and Ireland: Spain and Portugal were totalitarian and neutral States and therefore anxious not to irritate the Nazi powers) plainly what was known there was what Nazi-Fascist propaganda allowed to be known, and even that only in part, considering the handicaps of war, the inadequate circulation of the press, the interruptions and jammings of broadcasts, etc.

True, there was a clandestine way of finding out, based on stories told by soldiers on leave, BBC broadcasts from London, and broadcasts from other 'illegal' stations, but evidence was not always convincing as it came from people listening to fragments of jammed news which could then be whispered among friends but not repeated too casually without running the risk of facing the consequences.

Whereas when we are dealing with the Holy See we are dealing with a world organization, admittedly with a good third of its adherents in Europe, but with the rest scattered throughout the countries and continents of the world, some involved in the war, some outside it; we are dealing with an organization solidly centralized on various levels, horizontal and vertical, right up to the apex in Rome; an organization in diplomatic relations with various States

through its own and their representatives, benefiting from all necessary means and all the guarantees of protection; an organization
supranational owing to its religious and moral aims, and viewed by
all as a point of reference. Hence conceptions that would be valid for
ordinary nations or political powers of modest proportions cannot
be applied to the Vatican.

When we come to governments, ministers, military leaders and so
on, obviously ignorance cannot possibly be ascribed to them. For
either they knew because they were the immediate planners and
promoters of the atrocities (consider the trials for collaboration
mounted pretty well everywhere once the war was over), or because
they rose in rebellion and attempted to get away from them, or because they were clandestine in character—such as governments in
exile—and had every interest to develop information services so as to
despatch documentary evidence on German atrocities to the free
world, or, finally, because they were at war with the Axis powers and
the revelation of atrocities formed part of so-called psychological
warfare.

So it is perfectly obvious that they would see to it that news of the
kind reached the Holy See. For as it held a neutral position, or was
anyway outside the struggle, the Vatican was regarded as a presump-
tive ally. Several of these governments published a series of official
booklets on the German atrocities; indeed the first of these publications appeared in the autumn of 1939.[47] And who could suppose that
they failed to send them to the Vatican Secretariat of State?

In any case the secret documentary information presented from
time to time to the authorities of the Holy See was far more volumi-
nous than the official reports. This came through diplomatic channels.
There is unquestionable evidence of this in official publications and
in the personal war memoirs of politicians. It would seem that 1942
provided a striking example of this, as will be apparent when we
come to deal with Poland. And we find yet another example in the
Roosevelt-Pius XII correspondence. The President referred to the
civilian atrocities committed by the Germans on a number of occasions, especially in the note he sent to the Cardinal Secretary of
State on 22 October 1941, when he referred to the massacres of Jews
carried out behind the German front in Russia and described them

as 'surpassing everything known since the most brutal and bestial epochs of mankind'.

Even apart from the information received from governments the Holy See was kept in close touch with the situation by its own diplomatic corps (nuncios and Apostolic Delegates). In 1961, before the polemics surrounding *The Representative* started, *Civiltà Cattolica* began publishing a series of articles on the activity of the Holy See on behalf of the Jews during the war. Publication of the articles ceased without explanation after the third of the series. On 4 March Fr. R. Leiber dealt with the Jews in Rome between 1943 and 1944; on 1 July Fr. F. Cavalli evoked the Vatican's opposition to the deportation of Jews from Slovakia; and on 2 September Fr. A. Martini wrote of the experiences of the Jews in Rumania. These articles owed their importance to the fact that they were patently written on the basis of an exceptional access to the secret archives of the Secretariat of State. Now the last two of the articles in particular provide a sufficiently detailed documentation on the frequency and tenor of the communications that took place between the Nuncios and the Secretariat during those years to establish the view that these communications were extraordinarily regular. Here are a few examples drawn from the second article:

(a) The Slovakian *Jewish Code*, running to 270 paragraphs and drafted in accordance with the famous Nuremberg anti-Jewish laws, was promulgated on 9 September 1941. The Holy See's representative, Mgr. Giuseppe Burzio, who had had wind of it some time earlier and had called on the President of the Republic, Mgr. Tiso, to ask for clarifications, sent an accurate account of it (and almost certainly the original text of the document) to the Secretariat of State, which, in the November of that same year, was in a position to hand the Slovakian Minister to the Holy See, Carlo Sidor, a carefully-drafted note on the situation in which the 'Catholic Jews' were placed.

(b) On 9 March 1942 Mgr. Burzio, having learnt that a mass-deportation of Slovakian Jews to Galicia and the Lublin district was in preparation (without distinction of age, sex or religion), hastened to inform his superiors in Rome of the fact and added that the first consignment was planned for the following April.

The deportation of eighty thousand persons to Poland, to the
mercy of the Nazis, amounts to condemning a large proportion of
them to certain death [these were the Papal diplomat's very
words].

Exactly five days later, on 14 March, Sidor was summoned to the
Secretariat of State and handed a note which expressed the hope that
the news of the deportation of the Slovakian Jews was unfounded.

On 25 March Mgr. Burzio confirmed from Bratislava that the first
contingent of Jews to be deported would amount to ten thousand
people.

Thereupon [writes Fr. Cavalli] the Minister of Slovakia was summoned on direct orders from Pius XII and asked to influence his
government against carrying out these proposals. At the same
time an urgent telegram was sent to the Papal representative in
Bratislava informing him of the step that had been taken and
charging him to address himself personally to the President of the
Republic.

(c) Despite the Holy See's intervention some seventy thousand
Jews were evacuated from Slovakia between the end of 1942 and the
beginning of 1943. Nevertheless on 7 February 1943 the Minister of
the Interior announced that, in view of a law passed on 15 May 1942,
it was necessary to finish off with the remaining sixteen to twenty
thousand non-Aryan persons still remaining in the country. The
news reached Rome by the normal channel and by return Mgr.
Burzio received orders from the Secretariat of State to call on the
Prime Minister and Foreign Minister to try to dissuade them from
taking this step:

Your Excellency [these were the words used by the Papal representative according to his report back to Rome on the 'stormy
interview'] is doubtless aware of the sad news circulating about the
atrocious fate of the Jews deported to Poland and the Ukraine.
Everyone is talking about it. . . .

Of course it would not be prudent to indulge in generalizations
and assume that all relations between Papal diplomatic representatives and the Holy See took place under the same conditions. As
regards Rumania it is well known that Mgr. Andrea Cassulo, the
nuncio in Bucharest, who was perhaps the most fortunate of his
colleagues in view of his success with Marshal Antonescu's government over protecting the Jews, managed to visit all the camps for

prisoners and civil internees in the country in the course of a journey undertaken with that intention between 27 April and 5 May 1943. And there are grounds for believing that equal freedom was enjoyed by the nuncios at Vichy and Budapest, the Papal Legate to the New Independent State of Croatia in Zagreb, and the Apostolic Delegate in Istanbul (in the neutral States).

Possibly the most hindered and unfree Papal representative in the whole of Europe was Mgr. Orsenigo in Berlin. He was very closely watched at home (Rauchstrasse 21) and as time went on had to endure the consequences of the ever-increasing friction characteristic of relations between the Holy See and the Third Reich following on the Concordat—friction that grew more acute during the war, above all after the Vatican had refused to recognize the war against Russia as a crusade. When his colleagues in Warsaw, Brussels and the Hague had been withdrawn, the Holy See entrusted the nuncio in Berlin with the task of extending his activities to their areas. And this was a further reason for the precariousness of his situation, for the German government put up a firm opposition to his carrying out Vatican instructions.

The isolation of the nuncio in Berlin brings to mind the well-known Gerstein episode. But it also raises the question of the sources of information available to Papal representatives in other countries. As a discussion of this would take up too much space, we shall restrict ourselves to drawing attention to cases when information was provided by volunteers such as, precisely, Kurt Gerstein. Gerstein had deliberately joined the Waffen-SS so as to be able to unmask its monstrous activities in the extermination camps. When he had collected enough data on the Treblinka camp he managed to enter the Berlin Nunciature in the summer of 1942 so as to present them to Mgr. Orsenigo. But he was apparently turned back by Orsenigo's secretary—who, incidentally, was quite capable of withholding the document.[48] But two prisoners—Rudolf Wrba and Alfred Wetzler, who had escaped from the Auschwitz-Birkenau camp in April 1944 and whose aim was the same as Gerstein's—succeeded with the Papal representative in Bratislava, Mgr. Burzio. The conversation that they were able to have in June 1944 lasted five hours. They were able to give the Papal delegate a detailed report with geographical maps showing the measurements and plan of the camp, the position of the gas-chambers and the railway leading to it.[49]

Besides the documentary evidence provided by the various governments and the Papal diplomatic service, the Vatican was constantly besieged by reports and appeals from organizations of all kinds, especially Jewish. At one point in his article on the Holy See and the Rumanian Jews, Fr. Martini quotes examples of this sort of thing in the year 1942 alone.

> In June 1942 Pope Pius XII received a pressing appeal written in Latin from a group of Jews in Cernauti imploring his protection so as to avoid deportation across the Dniester and the Bug and gain mitigation of the punishments in the ghetto; and drew his special attention to the thousands of orphaned children who were deprived of all aid.
>
> In October the nuncio in Switzerland, Mgr. Bernardini, sent to the Holy See a report by the president of the Israelite Communities in Switzerland asking for a speedy intervention of the Holy Father not only on behalf of the Rumanian Jews across the Dniester but also on behalf of the others threatened with mass-deportation to those regions.
>
> A similar memorandum was presented at that time on behalf of the Jews of the Banat who were also threatened with deportation.[50]

We should add the telegram sent by Mgr. Roncalli, then Apostolic Delegate in Istanbul, to the Secretariat of State on 28 February 1944: 'Chief Rabbi of Jerusalem Herzog came personally Apostolic Delegation to thank officially Holy Father and Holy See for manifold acts of charity on behalf of Jews in these years; he made heartfelt appeal for effective concern for 55 thousand Jews concentrated beyond Dniester under Rumanian occupation facing grave danger in view eventual withdrawal German troops. Appears welfare action can be exercised Government Bucharest which could . . . at least allow their evacuation.'

All that we have said, though so briefly, seems to support our contention that the Holy See was more than adequately informed both about the massacres of civilians and about the legislation that prepared the way for them (at least in the case of the Jews). This legislation was on foot from the second half of 1940 onwards. The first decrees were made in July of that year. On 3 October the Vichy government promulgated its 'Statute for the Jews'. The spring of

1941 saw the laws and ordinances of the Ustaši of the new Independent State of Croatia. And on 9 September 1941 came the Slovak Statute. These provisions were all known to the Holy See; indeed, they provoked the Holy See to protest. These protests were in no way dangerous for they were made to governments relatively autonomous in home affairs and with cordial diplomatic relations with the Holy See—indeed sometimes Concordats.[51]

So the evidence we have brought forward seems more than conclusive. Nevertheless, as all things are possible and as there would be nothing new in this, we cannot overlook the fact that—even supposing the Secretariat of State to have been informed of all that was going on down to the smallest detail—there could have been a filter system or even a real blockage which prevented the documentation from reaching the Pope. Such a suspicion could have generalized foundation in the fact that after the death of Luigi Maglione, his first and only Secretary of State, Pius XII never wanted to hear of having another. 'I do not need collaborators but executives'.[51 *bis*]

Yet the known documents of Pius XII's private correspondence remove all doubt on this score. He was continually and peremptorily bearing witness to his awareness of the conditions in the countries he was addressing. This will be seen in his correspondence with the Polish hierarchy. The only other document recently released is his letter of 30 April 1943 to Mgr. Konrad von Preysing, Bishop of Berlin. There we read this open admission:

> Day after day We hear of inhuman acts which have nothing to do with the real necessities of war, and they fill us with stupefaction and bitterness. Only a recourse to prayer . . . etc.[52]

In a letter to another German bishop, Cardinal Adolf Bertram of Breslau (which we came across in a book by a Polish priest on the priests in the Nazi camps), Pius XII was no less explicit. But we shall be quoting it later on.

And these self-admissions were sealed by Pius XII in his address to the Sacred College of Cardinals on 2 June 1945:

> During the war we never stopped, especially in our messages, and in accordance with the unfailing requirements and rules of humanity and the Christian faith, opposing the ruinous and ruthless application of National-Socialist doctrines, which ended

up by using the most exquisite scientific methods to torture and suppress people who were often innocent.

The war had come to an end twenty days previously, and no official disclosures had yet been made concerning the macabre discoveries in the camps that had escaped the destruction ordained by Himmler in early 1944 so as to prevent the Allies from seeing the proofs of the enormous massacres that had been carried out. Yet the Pope was already talking about exquisite scientific methods. Not only that; but he went so far as to display 'copious' information on the subject:

> Though We are not yet in possession of complete statistics, We cannot refrain from mentioning . . . at least something of the copius information that has come to Us of priests and laymen interned in the Dachau camp and made to endure contumely for the name of Jesus (Acts v: 41).
>
> First and foremost, both from the point of view of their number and the harshness of the treatment they endured, come the Polish priests. Between 1940 and 1945, 2,800 Polish priests and religious were imprisoned in that camp, including the auxiliary Bishop of Wladislaw who died of typhus there. Last April only 816 remained; all the others were dead save for several who were transferred to another camp. . . .

Even if we accepted the hypothesis about the inadequacy of his means of obtaining information, or about the withholding of documents by those in charge of, or working in, the Secretariat of State, the Pope would have been able to obtain news—at least in a general sense—from the press and the radio. As regards German newspapers, anyone who was in Germany or took a look at the German press in the years 1942 and 1943 will recall their obsessive flow of anti-Semitic propaganda. The space devoted to articles against 'non-Aryans' was only surpassed by news of war operations on the different fronts— and not always even then. As for the future in store for the Jews there was certainly no element of mystery in the ferocious editorials dictated by Dr. Goebbels in *Das Reich* and echoed in all the other German papers.[53] And over and above the Nazi press, there was a neutral press, small though it was. Jacques Nobécourt has quoted the article published on 5 November 1941 by the *Neue Zürcher*

Zeitung on the deportations of the Berlin Jews to the east. And that was by no means the only voice raised on the subject.

As is well known, Pius XII had a daily habit of looking through the press digests put at his service by his own secretaries and the special offices of the Secretariat of State; but he preferred to read the newspapers for himself. And, as report has it, he had a special preference for the German papers. Hence he could not remain in ignorance. Moreover, the Vatican radio provided him with adequate information material. This it did by its own news summaries and comments (these were particularly well supplied in the first weeks after war broke out and in several other periods); but even more by its monitoring service for foreign radios, particularly the BBC. And no prelate in the Secretariat of State, however meddlesome he might be, could prevent Pius XII from turning the knob of his radio or looking through the pages of the newspapers.

On finding themselves confronted with such an array of evidence, the official defenders of Pius XII's silence take refuge in a final explanation. The news that reached the Vatican—so they argue—might seem substantial taken as a whole because it was spread over so many years; but in fact it was not sufficient as to quantity or quality to justify a solemn protest such as was asked of the Pope; for detailed descriptions were often lacking, the information was vague and generalized, and—more serious—came from suspect sources, namely Germany's political and military enemies or victims. Moreover it was unverifiable.

The real argument the apologists rely on is the last, that the facts were unverifiable, and this depended exclusively on the German's veto on their verification. What was their motive for refusing from the first to allow a Papal representative, even if not a diplomat, into Polish territory? Merely so as to prevent the Holy See from having at its disposal its own observer in the area lying on the nerve of the extermination operation for the whole Continent. Naturally they did everything they could to prevent inspections by the International Red Cross; and when they had to submit to such inspections they established model camps like Theresienstadt in Czechoslovakia.

But a little reflection leads us to see that the other arguments quoted above are faulty too. The forms the documentary evidence took may have left a lot to be desired; but the documentary evidence provided by governments and several of the big organizations had not the defect mentioned. Moreover, the sifting and comparing of evidence, the study of divergent and coinciding elements, if carried out with special regard to their origins, would easily have led to certainty as to the substantial truth of the accusations.

No one would be inclined to dispute that the documentary evidence provided by Allied governments needed to be treated with greater caution. The Holy See could not forget, and would have done wrong to do so, the resounding lies told by Allied propaganda during the First World War about cutting off the hands of Belgian children. Yet the Holy See had the means for comparing the data provided by interested governments with the reports coming from its own official or clandestine informers.

But the most obvious proof that the Holy See was convinced of the substantial objectivity of the facts was afforded, as we shall see, by the decision taken in June 1942 to prepare the famous 'terrible document', and also by the Pope's oft-repeated resolves (whether he kept them or not has no bearing) 'to raise his voice at last'.

Chapter 3

PIUS XII WAS CONSTANTLY IMPLORED TO INTERVENE

Pius XII's official defenders argue that if he did not speak it was because the victims of Nazi barbarity themselves asked him to remain silent so that their situation should not be made worse and further reprisals brought down on their heads.

This statement is not without foundation, provided we do not exaggerate it by generalizing it. For the proofs adduced boil down to a letter from Archbishop Sapieha of Cracow as regards Poland; a resolution made by the assembly of German bishops at Fulda in 1943;[54] and several requests from groups of Jews. And it must be noted that in the case of Archbishop Sapieha and that of the German bishops' Conference the decision to suppress publication of papal documents occurred only after these had been requested, i.e. in an obvious state of perplexity.

There is nothing surprising about this. Several times a papal intervention had led to local recrudescences of violence, because some commanders of isolated camps thought such intervention might favour a return of morale in their communities. But this phenomenon had parallels elsewhere but with quite different causes—as with the announcement in a war-bulletin that squadrons of the Polish air force had taken part in the bombardment of Reich territory. Pretty well anything served as a pretext for the concentration camp butchers— or, on a wider scale, for the German governors of occupied areas—to terrorize their victims.

Whereas the very rarity of the cases we have mentioned shows that they were exceptions mainly due to personal initiatives or estimates of the situation, and were plainly confined to particular categories such as Catholic prisoners, priests, etc., and the fear that what the Pope said might have a particular effect on them. Moreover the futility of the argument is manifest—for where were these words uttered by the Pope that were capable of unleashing a rebellion and exacerbating feelings against the oppressor?

Besides, the recommendations made by groups here and there to avoid action that might make their condition worse may well have been suggested by the very natural panic of people who had already had experience of countless outrages. And it would be hard to find anyone who would dream of blaming them for being in such a state of anguish and terror that they even refused to accept the hand outstretched to help them. The fact remains, however, that the decision on whether papal intervention was opportune or not should not have been left to the weakest and most timorous. Quite apart from the fact that an intervention such as that of the Pope should never have been judged primarily and exclusively in terms of what was useful and efficacious.

In any case the few occasions on which the Pope was begged not to provoke reprisals by taking up anti-Nazi attitudes were overwhelmingly outweighed by the number of appeals he received to speak out in solemn condemnation. Nowadays Pius XII's more prudent defenders, such as Father Martini, admit this. They recognize that 'appeals for help were often addressed to the Pope' either by international Jewish organizations or by Jewish victims themselves. For instance (and here we quote from the Jesuit historian himself) the representative of the Jewish Agency for Palestine, C. Baclas, wrote from Istanbul to the Apostolic Delegate for Egypt and Palestine on 20 January 1943:

> May I venture to suggest that a declaration might be made by means of the radio or some other suitable channel saying that the Church views helping the persecuted Jews as a good work. This would certainly strengthen the activity of those Catholics who, as we know and appreciate, are helping Jews condemned to extermination in the occupied territories of Europe.[55]

As for the entreaties made by governments it is not yet possible to make a definitive estimate, but the documentation already published suggests that the number was large. In 1942 alone, as we have already pointed out, diplomatic steps were repeatedly taken for this purpose, either to the Secretariat of State or to the Supreme Pontiff directly, by individual powers or by groups of powers acting in co-ordination to give greater weight to their initiative.

Among the States that took individual steps in this sense on a number of occasions were Great Britain and the United States. Our witness for Great Britain is the well-known banker Angelo Donati who was tireless in his attempts to save the Jews who had taken refuge in the part of southern France occupied by the Italians. According to one of his declarations, Sir D'Arcy Osborne asked the Pope on a number of occasions 'to pronounce a formal condemnation of the German atrocities'.[56] If we bear in mind that Sir D'Arcy Osborne visited England between April and June of that year (1942) we may assume that he returned to Rome with first-class documentary evidence to justify this step.

As for the United States, the assistant to President Roosevelt's personal representative to Pius XII, Tittman, telegraphed in the same sense to the State Department through the legation in Berne, signifying that in recent reports to the Department he had drawn attention to the view that the failure of the Holy See to protest publicly against Nazi atrocities was endangering its moral prestige and compromising trust both in the Church and in the Holy Father himself. On a number of occasions he had, like some of his colleagues, officially brought the matter to the notice of the Vatican, but without result. The answer invariably was that the Pope had already condemned crimes against morality in war and that a specific condemnation would in present circumstances make things worse.[57]

The President's personal representative, Myron Taylor, returned to Rome in September and on the 26th he formally renewed the request in Roosevelt's name and with a detailed memorandum on the persecutions of the Jews in Poland and other Nazi-occupied areas. On this occasion the Pope delayed his answer so that when he made it (10 October) Taylor had already returned to the United States. So Tittman again had to telegraph Washington to the effect that the Holy See had received similar reports but had no means of verifying their authenticity, and that in any case the Pope never let slip an opportunity 'to mitigate the sufferings of the non-Aryans'.[58]

Earlier in September the Brazilian ambassador to the Holy See had taken the initiative of presenting a collective appeal to the Pope (his co-signatories were the diplomatic representatives of Great Britain, Poland, Yugoslavia and various South American countries) asking him to break his reserve about Nazi atrocities. But though this step was 'much encouraged by the Jesuits' it had no better out-come than its predecessors. The answer can hardly have differed much from the one sent to Roosevelt by Tittman.

That Pius XII was subjected to this sort of insistent hammering for over five years without being substantially deflected from his line leaves us amazed at the sheer tenacity of his powers of resistance. Yet it is not difficult to understand that pressures from the political world would not necessarily be of a kind to shake him despite their carefully worked-out wording. Governments that appealed to transcendent values were the first to ignore or even spurn these when it suited them; and, also, there could be no denying that their main aim was to ex-ploit a papal proclamation politically, whether it was confined to ethical considerations or went beyond them. Pius XII had every reason to be wary of the political snares that might be laid for him.

But this certainly would not apply to requests made by the faithful, especially when they were members of the hierarchy. There is not the slightest doubt that the faithful, with or without titles, tried to arouse the Vatican, just as there is not the faintest doubt that their appeals were fated not to come to the knowledge of their exalted addressee or to receive, at the most, a blessing as answer—sent, vicariously of course, from the offices of the Maestro di Camera or the Secretariat of State. This was certainly the only answer Edith Stein received when, in April 1933, she had to give up teaching because she was Jewish, and wrote a long letter to Pius XI with the idea that this might provoke an encyclical on the Jewish question. But it must be supposed, if only because of the high esteem in which we hold many responsible members of the Church, that from time to time impor-tant personalities in the hierarchy sent similar appeals. If such mes-sages have been preserved, their secret has been jealously kept within the Vatican archives. Yet one or two secrets have emerged.

The appeals of Sapieha and Bertram have already been men-tioned. Then, apart from Cardinal Hlond—perhaps the first member of the Sacred College to ask Pius XII for such a delicate intervention —there was Cardinal Suhard with his somewhat different appeal.

Immediately after the collapse of France the Archbishop of Paris asked Pius to write a message of comfort not only to French Catholics but to all Frenchmen who had been laid low by the humiliation of defeat. Obviously he had no fear that he might involve the Pope in an action irritating to the Germans. Yet this incident perplexes us in that the Pope evidently felt no personal impulse to communicate his sympathy to 'the eldest daughter of the Church' but had to be expressly asked to do so.

Recently, in early 1964, the existence of a document of greater relevance was revealed: the famous letter sent by Cardinal Tisserant to Cardinal Suhard on 11 June 1940.[59] It is not so much a letter as an outburst, and its sensational character derives less from what it confirms about the Curia and its Fascist affections than from its lamentations regarding the Pope's silence. And it is unexpected to find the ultra-political and *avant tout* Frenchman, Tisserant, less pained by the Pope's reserve about his own country (though he was writing immediately after Italy had stabbed France in the back)—i.e. by his political reserve—than by his moral reserve as to the ethical choice imposed on everyone when faced with the inadmissability of German violence.[60]

> Tisserant confided to his colleague and compatriot that he had:
> urgently asked the Pope as early as December to issue an Encyclical about the individual duty to obey the imperatives of conscience, as this is the most vital point of Christianity.

The mention of December suggests an ever graver judgment on all the events that followed thereafter. Yet Tisserant omits any reference to the occupation of Denmark and Norway or to the violation of Belgian and Dutch neutrality (predominantly political and juridical events with a greater or less margin for argument) and concentrates on the radical reason why an ethical revolt of people's consciences cannot in his view be delayed; i.e. on the fact that the Nazi-Fascist ideology had unleashed a war apparently of a traditional kind but really a war of systematically planned destruction inspired by the principles of racism, a war whose aim was to substitute the German and Italian races for all others on the European continent as a preliminary to realizing Axis supremacy over the whole world.

The French must cherish no illusions: what their enemies want is their destruction. The Italian newspapers have been full of texts by His Excellency Mussolini stating that Italy has a large population and needs more land. So Germany and Italy will set about destroying the inhabitants in the occupied areas as has been done in Poland. . . . Our rulers do not want to understand the real nature of the conflict and insist on supposing that this is a war like wars in the past. But the Fascist and Hitlerite ideology has transformed the consciences of the young, and all those under thirty-five are ready to commit any crime granted they can attain the goal set by their leaders.

Tisserant was doubtless exaggerating where Fascism and the Italian Fascists were concerned—as was shown by the different way the war was waged by the Nazis and the Fascists, and, incidentally, by their frequent friction. And this outburst shows over-simplification. But there can be no denying that he had put his finger on the substance of the situation. The letter goes on:

I'm afraid that history may be obliged in time to come to blame the Holy See for a policy accommodated to its own advantage and little more. And that is extremely sad—above all when one has lived under Pius XI.

We can be sure that on the occasions when Tisserant made his requests to Pius XII he did not remain silent regarding these fears, and he must have made a deep impression on Pius XII—so deep an impression, perhaps, that the Pope discouraged his collaborator from returning to the subject, suggesting that he should only talk to him in a way in harmony with his own ideas.[61]

Whether appeals like Tisserant's were frequent or not (and it is hardly possible that the American episcopate should have remained silent either before or during the war; after all the American bishops had issued a tough collective anti-Nazi pastoral in 1937 which had provoked deeply-felt protests from the German government to the Holy See),[62] they soon confronted Pius XII with the true measure of the struggle. These protests were more than political, military or charitable in character; they were above all moral. They reminded him that the war victims had material needs, yes—and as a result he organized the seeking-out of prisoners and displaced persons and promoted the despatch of food and clothes to the prisoners and civil populations who were victims of bombardment or fighting, etc.—but above all they urged him to concern himself with the anguish and uneasy conscience of those who did not want to collaborate in the unspeakable crimes of the Nazis and still less let themselves be subjects and dependants of the Nazis, and were therefore expecting precise directives and suitable encouragement. He had not, after all, been elevated to the dignities of Head of the Church merely to carry out duties of material charity, but first and foremost to give witness to the truth that the faithful should believe and practise. Had he concerned himself with the true relations between the State and its subjects, with the limits of civil power regarding the natural rights of the human person, he would have done much more than alleviate occasional distress and dry the occasional tear; he would have got to the root of the social disorder. Indeed, had he done so, he would have prevented the evil from getting the upper hand and spreading beyond all bounds.

But to meet this duty he would have had to eschew his generalized pronouncements condemning totalitarianism, or his pronouncements of abstract principles about the equality of peoples. He would have had to descend from the generalized plane of moral and social duties to the plane of individual duties, exactly as Cardinal Tisserant had suggested when he expounded the concrete duties of individuals in the context of civil and military obligations, both when authority was acting within the limits of its rights and duties and above all when it went outside them.

So, to sum up, the challenge was not only one of speaking out so as to fulfil a duty towards his office, but of speaking out as a duty to Christianity and mankind. His refusal to speak out played into the hands of evil as this grew bolder and fiercer and became more provocative. Silence amounted to complicity with iniquity. And this supreme omission was not redeemed by multiple acts of charity (always and inevitably inadequate) towards the victims (which incidentally meant little more than making other people's donations available).[63] The Church is not the International Red Cross. For the faithful the Church is the supreme organism whose vocation it is to testify to the message of the Gospels and to bring the faithful to live in accord with that message; it is the guide of their consciences. As a

Protestant pastor pointed out in the course of the recent polemics: a Church which has done all it should have done has done nothing if it has agreed to remain silent.

Chapter 4

THE OFFICIAL JUSTIFICATIONS

If Pius XII knew what was going on by the middle of 1942, and if he avoided condemning Nazi atrocities in the face of every kind of pressure, then how can we explain behaviour so at variance with his mission as moral and religious guide of four hundred million Catholics?

It was dangerous to speak out

If we listen to his defenders, there were two reasons: speaking out would have been dangerous for the victims; and in any case it would have been useless. In his letter to *The Tablet*[64] Cardinal Montini put the reasons concisely when he said that an attitude of condemnation and protest would have been both useless and harmful. And this seems to have been Pius's genuine conviction.[65] We are left in no doubt on the point if we consider two documents of 1943, one private, the other public. On 30 April Pius XII explained in a letter to the Bishop of Berlin that the difference between his own behaviour and that of individual bishops was not a matter of chance:

> As regards episcopal declarations, We leave to the pastors in office on the spot the responsibility of judging whether and to what extent the danger of reprisals and pressures and other possible circumstances due to the length of the war and war psychology counsel reserve—despite possible reasons for intervention—in the interests of avoiding greater evils. This is one of the reasons why We ourselves impose limits on Our declarations. Our experience in 1942 when We allowed free publication for the use of the faithful of various pontifical documents justifies Our attitude at least insofar as We can see things.[66]

Not long afterwards, in the customary allocution of 2 June when the Cardinals presented their good wishes (2 June was his feast-day, that of St. Eugenio), he did not hesitate to say, although the speech would be published:

74

You will not expect Us to explound in detail all We have tried and undertaken to do to lighten their sufferings, improve their moral and juridical conditions of life, protect their basic religious rights, and help them in their necessity and needs. All the words that We address to the competent authorities, and every public declaration, has to be seriously worked out and weighed by Us in the interests of the victims so as not to make their situation more grievous and insupportable and contrary to Our intentions.

The importance of these statements derives from the fact that they date back to the period before the war had entered its most dramatic phase with the Allied landings in Italy and the fall of Mussolini. As regards the second statement, we should point out that Piux XII had never before been so explicit; while the significance of the first lies in his reference to this particular reason as being one among others which, alas, he does not enumerate. He does not seem to attach pre-eminent importance to it.

Far from being a reason it might, of course, have been a pretext— but at that rate it would be naïve to look for an admission of this, even by a slip of the pen. All that we can express is our bewilderment at the firmness of his motive. For, as we have seen, the appeals addressed to him to refrain from a solemn condemnation were many fewer (at least as far as we can ascertain) than the urgent appeals made to him to speak out. And what worse evils could lie in store for victims destined for massacre than—at the most—massacre at an earlier date?

So all that remains for us to do is to proceed to an attentive examination of the texts we have quoted and thus convince ourselves that the Pope's horizon did not extend to victims generally, but was confined to Catholic victims and, to be more precise, Catholic communities seen primarily in the structural complex of their organizations and their influence on their surroundings. For in his war writings and addresses Pius XII never referred to the Protestants and Orthodox or, indeed, the Jews, who were, after all, in at least as bad a predicament as his own followers. For them there were only rare and vague allusions. And not only that. It was no accident that Pius XII gave no more than a glance at the war in progress in his Christmas broadcasts but devoted them almost entirely to post-war problems. He was really much more preoccupied by thoughts of the future than of the present. It was his nightmare that any interference of his would be viewed on some occasion as excessive, and that the Nazi backlash would fall inexorably on the Churches in the various countries and would peel away the organisms which he saw as foundational for the post-war period—either so as to achieve the Church's hegemony in the conquered countries by seizing the opportunity provided by the vacuum of power following on defeat, or alternatively to confront the arrogance of the conquerors whenever these should attempt to prevail at the expense of the Church. Any more general and universal reference to war victims (as in the second text quoted above with its public and hence in some way propagandist tone) was no more than an extension of this deep anxiety—besides being an obvious manifestation of feelings of human solidarity.

It could even be said that Pius XII's preoccupation with any weakening of ecclesiastical structures in Europe reached a point of positive psychosis as war went on. For it was based almost exclusively on the theory that some such annihilation of the Church could occur, not on any concrete proof of an intention to bring it about. At the present stage of historical research it is beyond question that the Nazis had amongst their objectives the *Endlösung* of the Churches, particularly of the Catholic Church, and it is equally certain that they intended to postpone the 'settling up' until after the war. During the war they contented themselves with isolating the Vatican mainly by diplomatic methods, keeping the German Catholic organization in a state of alarm but avoiding exasperating it to danger point, and keeping the Polish Church—which was too dangerous owing to its influence over the people—in a ghetto.

It is a fact that in no part of Europe save Poland was a Catholic bishop ever touched. In Germany the bishop most detested was Graf von Galen, Bishop of Munster. The Nazis considered the possibility of arresting him but never went further than ignoring the letters of protest he sent to the government.[67] And on one occasion when a canon of the Olmütz chapter, who was a prisoner in Buchenwald, was elected suffragan bishop of his city, the SS immediately released him.[68]

In France, between July and August 1941, two cardinals (Suhard of Paris and Gerlier of Lyons) and numbers of archbishops and bishops led by the future Cardinal Saliège (then Archbishop of Toulouse), rose in revolt against the deportation of the Jews, but despite many provocative statements made by the Nazi- or Vichy-controlled press, none of them was touched. It was only on the eve of liberation that someone thought of taking revenge on the Archbishop of Toulouse. But when two German officers called at the Archbishop's residence to arrest him (it was 9 June 1944) they found a half-paralysed man incapable of speech. It was enough to make them turn round and get out of the orders they had been given.[69]

On 28 July of the same year the Dutch episcopate made a public protest to the *Reichshalter*, Seyss-Inquart, against the plan for deporting the Jews, though as early as the end of 1941 they had been assured that the Catholic Jews would be spared. The Nazis' reply was to withdraw this concession and they even went so far as to begin with the Catholic Jews in their deportation plans. But they carried out no reprisals against the Aryan Catholic communities or their leaders.

The same occurred in Nazi-allied Slovakia. The bishops of that country sent the government a whole series of collective protests against the rounding-up of the Jews and the plans to send them to Galicia and the Lublin region. But despite the number and grave tone of their protests, not a hair of their heads was touched.[70]

But if the Nazis avoided open conflict with the local hierarchies, still more did they avoid attacking the Church in its central stronghold, however great was their secret desire to do so. Proof of this—besides the evidence of the facts—can be found in Goebbels's *Diary* and Hitler's *Table Talk*. In any case the only period in which such an attack would have been possible was between 25 July 1943 and 4 June 1944. Directly after Mussolini's arrest on the first of these dates, a project for an attack on the Vatican (held co-responsible with King Victor Emmanuel for the arrest) so as to capture the diplomats in refuge there, make a haul of documents, and 'take the Pope into safe custody' in Germany, was really entertained. But common sense soon prevailed over such a harmful plan. In any case the German occupation of Rome which followed the Italian armistice (8 September 1943) made it out of the question, for the Pope's presence helped to keep Rome quiet—and not only Rome. It is true that there were intermittent subsequent alarms within the Sacred Palaces (on one occasion members of the Secretariat of State packed their bags because they were afraid of deportation, and on another diplomats accredited to the Holy See destroyed documents so as to prevent them falling into Nazi hands), but it would not surprise us if it emerged in time to come that these alarms and excursions originated in the double game of the German ambassador to the Holy See, Ernst von Weizsäcker, who was already preoccupied about his own safety when the final reckoning came.[71] Anyone could see through the absurdity of a second Avignon or, better, a second Fontainebleau. And no one could pretend that they wanted to protect the Pope from the Allies when the Pope had hailed as a great achievement the arrival of a special representative of the American President at the Holy See, and when he had formally refused to turn the attack on Soviet Russia into a crusade.

Moreover the Nazis' political line as regards the Vatican had always been extremely cautious, even in situations much less critical than those of wartime. We need only recall the very controlled reaction to the Encyclical *Mit Brennender Sorge* in 1937. True, that papal document did not explicitly involve the supreme heads of the Third Reich and avoided any formal judgment as regards the regime; but it remained nonetheless a document grave enough to provide the German government with an excuse for throwing over the Concordat. And of course there was no lack of leaders impulsive enough to want that; but in the end nothing happened. The Church would have been the winner had the Concordat been abrogated, for she would have had her autonomy restored whereas the State would have risked alienating the sympathies of twenty-two million German Catholics— not to mention the crisis of conscience of those Austrians who wanted the *Anschluss* and might have ceased to opt for Germany.

It was therefore only natural that the Nazis should content themselves with vague threats and whispering campaigns, to which they lent a certain semblance of reality with an occasional act of violence (such as the violation of the extra-territoriality of St.-Paul's-Without-the-Walls which was entrusted to the Fascists; or the irruption into the Pontifical Eastern Institute). The threats were not so much aimed at occupying the Vatican and taking the Pope to 'safe custody' as at

silencing the Vatican radio (which could have been done by an aircraft of unknown origin like the one that dropped a few bombs on
the area of the Vatican City on 5 November 1943)[72] and breaking off
diplomatic relations with the Holy See.

Mgr. Giovannetti, in the article from which we have already
quoted and which was accorded the honour of high praise from
Cardinal Montini, gives these two threats as decisive motives for
viewing a solemn papal condemnation as dangerous and hence
impracticable. For at that time the Vatican radio was:

> the only possible link between the Holy See and the outer world
> (and hence the only means of governing the Church); and the
> breaking-off of diplomatic relations would have made it impossible
> to communicate with the German government and hence with at
> least half (i.e. occupied) Europe, and would have led to the com-
> plete paralysis of every charitable activity for the aid of war vic-
> tims.

Of course anything was possible; but as things were the German
government was satisfied with using much less drastic means to discourage the Pope's intervention. In Ribbentrop's instructions to
ambassador von Bergen, given on 13 January 1943 and discovered
at the end of the war in the Wilhelmstrasse archives, we read:

> If the Vatican should threaten or try out any political or propa-
> gandist action against Germany, the Reich would obviously have
> to retaliate in an appropriate manner. In that eventuality the
> Reich would have no lack of effective means or possibilities for
> taking concrete measures against the Catholic Church.[72 bis]

This warning sounds more like blackmail than a real threat; but
blackmail which, though apparently of a generalized kind, would
indeed have become concrete and very grave if fully implemented
(and no one can be so naïve as to suppose that von Weizsäcker, who
succeeded von Bergen, kept quiet about it to Vatican authorities,
whether or not he was playing a double game). What matters is that
though this threat may not have been the primary reason for the
Pope's silence, it was certainly one of the reasons and probably not
the weakest.

But an explanation of the lack of a papal condemnation in terms
of this type of fear hardly increases our respect for the disinterestedness of the Pope's silence. Moreover, in her struggle with 'the world',

with the hostile powers of 'the world' (and God knows Nazism was a personification of such powers), the Church, any Christian Church, but above all the Church most intransigent and peremptory about her claims to uniqueness and truth, should have no doubt of final victory. After all it is written in the Gospel that the gates of hell shall not prevail against her—and Pius XII recalled this in paragraph 38 of his *Summi Pontificatus*. How then are we to explain such a serious incongruity except by saying that 'for the Church, belief is not dependent on her existence, but her existence is dependent on belief'.

It was useless to speak out

We shall now consider the second official justification for Pius XII's silence, namely that it was useless to speak out.

On 20 July 1955 an unusual article appeared in the *Osservatore Romano*. Written by the editor, and entitled *Un Magistero e un Testamento* (A Teaching and a Testament), it contrasted the sensation Einstein's Testament had caused throughout the world with the slight interest aroused by Pope Pacelli's teaching:

> Einstein's posthumous message has been presented as more than a grave warning; it has appeared as a moral communication. Either we must abolish war for ever, or it will be the end of mankind. His message is scientific and materialistic, and specifies the end of the human species. Now we wonder why an equally deep and universal impression was not made on 21 February 1943 when Pius XII spoke to the Academy of Sciences about the natural laws of the inorganic world, and vegetative and animate life, and issued a warning about the 'disastrous catastrophe' that nuclear discoveries would bring about if used as instruments of war: and not five years later, on 8 February 1948 . . ., and in his Easter messages of 1954 and 1955. These warnings naturally met with unanimous agreement. We are not disputing that. But we are saying that these warnings did not arouse that horror and perturbation which even made the voice of the 'frigid' Lord Russell tremble . . . and vibrated through the newspaper headlines and comment that publicized the news. . . .

After describing his sense of bewilderment at this, the writer continues:

> What is the reason for this contrast? Are we to look for it in the psychology of the world audience which is not accustomed or

prepared to recognize in a papal utterance words that are valid for all periods of history and all human consciences? Or are we to suppose that the human mind is so distracted by . . . experiments and facts that it only meditates on material things and things expressed in materialistic language with material egoism as its aim?

And the editorial rather irritably ends up on the side of the second hypothesis, that of the prevailing materialism of contemporary man: 'Pius XII spoke as a Father, he spoke of mankind. Einstein spoke as a member of the "human race"; he spoke of a "biological species" like the director of a zoo or a wild game preserve. . . .'

But can the climate of 1955 be said to have been the same as the climate of 1943? Was 'the psychology of the world audience' unprepared to heed what the Pope said in 1943? In our view the opposite was the case. During the war the Pope's words—this means, of course, words of genuine liberation—were awaited far beyond the confines of the countries at war (we would even be so bold as to include Russia, whether Soviet or Orthodox); they were awaited by all honest and conscientious men who wanted confirmation for what they held to be their duty, and were left in anguish when they waited in vain. The situation was made worse because the shepherds of lower rank (from bishops downwards) usually remained in a state of humiliated and tormented reserve, for they, too, lacked directives and encouragement from on high. And the greater the expectation of the Pope's words the greater the disappointment or bitter resignation at his silence.[75]

We get another if belated answer to our problem concerning the Pope's silence in an *Osservatore Romano* article of 19 March 1964.

A Pope's silences, when they occur, are not his silences but ours, that is to say they are imposed on him by Christians whose filial unreceptiveness seals the lips of the father and master. It is written in the Gospel that 'Jesus was silent'. Similarly the Vicar of Jesus may want, and need, to be silent.

This may seem a sibylline answer, but it is not. What it says, though with diplomatic reticence, is that it was useless for Pius XII to speak out for the simple reason that his words would have been powerless to win over enough people to the sort of crusade that was needed. In other words, given the psychological conditions prevailing, it would have been sheer folly to pronounce an anathema against

Hitler. 'Catholic *maquis* organizations flying the Pope's white and yellow colours would not have sprung up over Europe from one day to the next.'[74]

Since the experience of Pope John, however, we may have to moderate our scepticism regarding the efficacity of a Pope's words. For by means of words—and note, they were written words and written at a time unquestionably more distracted than that of wartime—Pope John shook the world. True, the Catholic Church had to wait two thousand years to have a Pope John, and there is no guarantee as to the future. Yet Pius XII, acting at the level of a realist politician, must have made a cool estimate of the concrete possibilities of such a serious step, he must have calculated the reaction such a step would cause in the German Catholic world. And the results of his calculation undoubtedly lay behind his pessimism.[75] In Greater Germany there were forty-five million Catholics who, by and large, adhered to the regime or at least to the mirage of it; forty-five million Catholics already impregnated with anti-Semitism and convinced that other countries were abusing their country; forty-five million Catholics labouring under the delusion that they were benefiting the Church by collaborating with the New Order set up by the Axis Powers in which the massive Catholicism of Italy and that of the other Latin countries was bound to play a determining part.

But German Catholicism was not the only consideration. And in any case only a recognition of error in its midst could thinkably have provided the proverbial grain of sand that would have smashed the cogs of the German war machine. Surely there were men in the German ruling class itself, beginning with the army, who were ready to overthrow the handful of criminal lunatics who were ruining their country. And it should be remembered that Axis Europe was an occupied and humiliated Europe which would have leapt to its feet had there been an opportune call to revolt. But Pius XII had a timid and negative temperament to whom actions not circumscribed by a clearly-defined horizon were foreign, and the very thought of repeating Pius IX's easy and laughable 'miracle' appalled him. Yet the turning-points of history are made by men who believe without too much calculation; men like John XXIII whose faith forced events so irresistibly that it seemed to be supporting them and yielding to them.

Moreover, whatever the appearances, it would not have been so utterly exceptional had Nazism been halted. Psychology is not outraged at the thought of an unarmed man, Pope Leo the Great, halting a man like Attila the Hun. Terrorism, to be effective, must carry conviction; it needs to feed on the weakness of those on whom it is perpetrated; they must yield without a struggle. If confronted with unexpected resistance, it collapses. All sadists have weak characters.

And we must not forget the essential characteristic of Nazi terrorism—that it was planned and bureaucratically administered, and could hardly have been otherwise given the colossal repressions at which it aimed. The comparatively recent trials at Frankfurt and Munich, like the personal inquiries of Simon Wiesenthal,[76] help us to get a precise picture of the organizational apparatus of the German terror machine and its schools of graduate butchers.[77] But this was observable even during the war. Obviously the agents were carefully selected. Yet the resistance of human nature to such ruthless activities could only be weakened, if not strangled, by exceptional psychological education, by iron discipline, by a sense of one's own power— or, better, by that of the omnipotence of the group. It was an acquired rather than a spontaneous terrorism, dependent on brute potentialities that had been anaesthetized by agelong traditions of self-control and revulsion. Moreover, in the case of members of the specialized terroristic bodies, the best guarantee for production lay in secrecy both about their membership of these organizations and about these organizations' very existence. For however much the Third Reich prided itself on forming butchers' consciences, it could hardly suppose itself capable of conferring prestige on the executioner's profession. Hence had the existence and organization of the death camps (including even the exterminations imposed on the regular army) been suddenly unmasked to the whole world, the victims would have been stimulated to rise against their butchers and all honest God-fearing men would have been filled with shame and disgust.

Of course a show-down of this nature could have been made by the Allies—and it was. But what good did it do? Every German was bound to view it as an invention of enemy psychological warfare. The only authorities who could carry conviction were religious authorities outside and above the struggle.

What if they failed? What if an attempt of the sort had turned out to be useless or dangerous? Even so—let us say again—the world of religion has dimensions and laws all its own. We only have to re-read the Gospels and the Sermon on the Mount to realize this. Success is not enumerated in the list of Beatitudes, whereas failure is implicit throughout (Blessed are those who hunger and thirst after justice ... blessed are the poor in spirit ... blessed are the meek ...).

But this apart, the Gospels, like every other sacred book of mankind, have ruthlessly and explicitly condemned silence in face of moral evil, whatever justifications may be found: 'You are the salt of the earth, but if the salt has lost its savour, wherewith shall it be salted? ... You are the light of the world; a city that is set on a hill cannot be hid. Neither do men light a candle and put it under a bushel, but on a candlestick and it giveth light unto all that are in the house ...'.

Chapter 5

THE MOST PROBABLE EXPLANATION

Did Pius XII's silence come from fear—or, in the last analysis, from religious sterility? The acceptance of either verdict would imply a total failure to understand Pius XII's personality, besides imputing monstrous deceit to him. No, as the author sees things, the truth lies in neither of these extremes. Personal fear, at any rate, can be immediately ruled out.

Pius XII's character and temperament were the opposite of cowardly. He lived his whole life in a tense state of interior exaltation and sometimes (particularly in the last ten years) the symptoms were rather alarming. His exaltation was essentially and predominantly a form of self-exaltation, and this explains his isolation and solitude—though these also derived from timidity (timid people sometimes compensate for their incapacity to communicate by developing a cult of the ego so as to distinguish themselves and bring themselves out). This was also the explanation of the Pope's ascetic austerity, which was naturalistic and formalistic rather than religious in inspiration (though as a priest he had felt deep religious urges). And finally this was the explanation of his amazing round of activity which he pushed to an extreme as regards method, zeal and duration.

Fear of the shadow and shame of defeat, especially as a result of cowardice, was unthinkable in a superman type such as Eugenio Pacelli. He despised cowardice as he despised compromise and devious manœuvres. He wished to be, and succeeded in being, an integrated personality. He always wanted to be first—but this had to be due to personal merit and with no debt to anyone else. Similarly he would rather have been broken than bent.

During the First World War, Benedict XV gave him two unusual diplomatic missions—one to the Austrian Emperor in Vienna,[78] the other to the Kaiser's general headquarters at Kreuznach.[79] We know nothing about the impression he made on Franz Josef; but the Kaiser—though it looks as though he wanted to give a different impression of Pacelli in his Memoirs—was forced (in a way unusual with him) to praise the Papal Legate.

But it was in defeated Germany after the First World War, during the famous period of the 'Red' government, that the symbolic episode took place. One April day in 1919 the armed Spartakist Guards broke into the Apostolic Nunciature in Munich. Mgr. Pacelli insisted on facing them alone, and by impressing them with his dignified, decisive and immovable protest he forced them to withdraw without daring to commit violence. It was a magnificent victory for him, but it was also a genuine shock to his system. His private doctor recounted later that the Pope often relived it in his dreams even when he was nearly eighty.[80] But it acted on him as a stimulant rather than a depressant, and many of his challenges to the Communists after the Second World War were inspired subconsciously by that remote incident.

During the Second World War he faced the possibility that he might be seized and sent to a concentration camp long before the situation involving threats against his person could have been envisaged.[81] Even if he had been seized he would never have been sent to an ordinary camp, but the prospect of this gave him such feelings of exaltation that he might thinkably have been led to provoke its occurrence had it not been for the agony of the violation of the Vatican and the dispersal of the Curia.

Although some such provision undeniably existed, we do not know how true the rumour is that, in the event of his being seized, Pius XII had given precise directions and authority to Cardinal Cerejeira, Archbishop of Lisbon, to take command of the Church. The answer Pius is reported to have given to someone who mentioned the possibility of his arrest by the Nazis—'They would not take the Pope, only Cardinal Eugenio Pacelli'—may be equally apocryphal. But the spirit these stories display is undoubtedly true.

His subordinates at the Secretariat of State and the other Vatican offices may have felt fear (we can imagine how much he must have enjoyed the drama of convening the members of the Sacred College on 9 February 1944 to tell them that if the Holy See's neutrality were violated he would free them from the obligation to remain with him in Rome); the diplomatic corps may have quailed at the fate awaiting it if the Nazis occupied the Vatican Palaces,[82] but we can be very sure that Pius XII was not afraid. It would probably have been his finest hour if he could have provoked his own captivity by denouncing Nazi atrocities or by calling on Catholics all over the world to unite in a crusade against the worst barbarities in history.

The most unexpected and improbable proof of Pius' courage and even boldness both as man and Pope (in the most habit-ridden and methodical temperaments there often lurks a nostalgia for adventure) occurred a few months after the beginning of war, in the Spring of 1940, when he supported a German officers' plot to depose Hitler.[83] Though he later kept away from such exploits as this, there is no denying that on more than one occasion he seemed determined to raise his voice, and always backed down at the last minute.[84]

We already know of one of his specific threats: the 1941 Christmas broadcast against religious persecution. It was a threat that leaves us rather puzzled when we consider its neglect of the massacres, forced deportations and cruelties of every sort then being perpetrated by the Germans and Russians; he concentrated his protests against the measures being taken 'against the Church and the aims she pursues.' True, many of the protests by ecclesiastical authorities on behalf of the Jews make us equally uneasy, for they either referred only to Catholic Jews or showed a marked preference for them; but these were mainly diplomatic protests, and obviously papal representatives were restricted by the need to respect juridical norms in their notes. But in a public and non-diplomatic document the situation was quite different, and such sectarian egotism is deeply disturbing.

Cardinal Tardini, then under-secretary for Extraordinary Ecclesiastical Affairs and Chief of the First Section of the Secretariat of State, who later became pro-secretary under Pius XII and finally Secretary of State under John XXIII, has revealed the story behind the three telegrams that Pius XII sent to the sovereigns of Belgium, Holland and Luxembourg the day those countries were invaded by Germany.[85] The moment he was told the news, which was only a few hours after the event, Pius decided that Cardinal Maglione should compose a brief memorandum for the *Osservatore Romano* while

Mgr. Tardini should prepare an open letter which, following papal custom, he would address to his Cardinal Secretary of State. The letter, restrained but severe, had to be carefully planned and had to await publication until the next day at least. Thus in order to avoid delay in taking a stand, Pius XII decided to send three telegrams to the countries involved—telegrams with full and significant references to the situation. Unfortunately no sooner had they been sent (and their texts made known) than Pius XII decided that the letter itself would be interpreted as a serious provocation, so he abandoned the idea of publishing it.[86]

According to disclosures from an unknown source,[87] another document was planned and drawn up, only to be abandoned and destroyed by Pius XII. It was a speech to be delivered in August 1942; the occasion, one of the usual general audiences. The Pope had been advised that a number of the German armed forces would be present, and after some hesitation he apparently decided to take advantage of their presence to express his deep displeasure at all the violations against the human person for which Nazism had been responsible in the various theatres of war. The text was to have been unusually vigorous. Then an hour before the audience Pius XII re-read it and was assailed by such grave doubts that he threw it into the waste-paper basket. The story goes that he said to the unknown witness: 'My duty is to simplify things, not to complicate them.'

Whether or not this episode be true, Pius XII never came closer to intervening than towards the middle of 1942. So much so that he ordered the Secretariat of State to begin drafting a document of 'terrible' portent (destined to a grotesque end, as we shall see). That year his Christmas broadcast included a romantic peroration about a crusade of all honest and generous men—a purely rhetorical figure of speech probably aimed at intimidating all those who had reason to fear that the Pope was about to turn from words to action.[88]

These incidents are a clear indication of Pius XII's inner struggle, and his correspondence with the leaders of the various national communities is just as explicit. In his private letters, too, he expressed his desire to speak out with a vehemence that would carry conviction. For instance, writing to the Bishop of Berlin:

The path that the Vicar of Christ has to follow so as to steer a just course between the conflicting demands of his pastoral office is more and more twisted and beset with thorns.

In this letter Pius XII came near to abandoning his role of politician and diplomat and revealed his feelings as pastor of his flock— we can see his deep concern about the spread of the Nazi 'mentality' among young people:

> Of all the questions for which We feel concern and hope, by far the gravest as regards the future is this: how can Catholic youth—after total subjection to the influence and education of a closed system, foreign to Christianity, and deriving from party organization and the notorious regulations of the future *Volksgesetzbuch*—how can the rising Catholic generation be custodians of their own Catholic faith and transmit it intact?[89]

This statement, in anyone else, might be interpreted as wishful-thinking or a clever lie. But not so in Pius XII. The impression he left on most of the diplomats accredited to the Holy See, and especially on those who were there during the war,[90] was that of a man of deep integrity who stood far above the murky mêlée of diplomacy. Whether or not he was mistaken both during the war and afterwards (and he made serious mistakes on more than one occasion), we have no reason to doubt his honesty and good intentions.

Unfortunately this image deteriorated and for many people became blurred during the last ten years of his pontificate. The Pope whose eloquence was pentecostal (in the words of his predecessor), the triumphalist Pope of the Holy Year, the belligerent Pope of the Italian Civic Committees, the Pope of the West and the Cold War, are all images which have been superimposed on the image of the Pope of the war years. They have deformed that earlier image which was diaphanous and emaciated, but above all compassionate and deeply, humanly sad, as we still see in the faded photographs of the time.

In an official commemoration in 1961, Cardinal Tardini recalled how during the war the Pope reduced his food and increased his penances to the point, for instance, of refusing to heat his private apartments in winter. By the end of the war he was so thin and emaciated that he weighed under nine stone though nearly six feet tall.[91] But his transparent thinness and above all the look of suffering on his face were due less to his penances (though these were discussed endlessly in 1939 and 1940 by people who frequented the house of his sister, Donna Elisabetta Rossignani) than to his tormented striving after a solution to the dilemma gnawing at his very being: the dilemma of whether or not to speak. Deep in his austere conscience, Pius XII underwent a daily struggle to find the answer.

His tormented vacillations are revealed in the admissions and episodes referred to above; but there is also the fact that from time to time he did urge the official propaganda vehicles of the Holy See— the *Osservatore Romano* and Vatican Radio—to speak on his behalf. But while Vatican Radio was perfectly explicit about the Polish situation, especially in the first months of the war, the *Osservatore Romano* never mentioned the war crimes of the Nazis and their allies. The farthest it went towards disconcerting the Axis countries, and Germany in particular, was a reference to the illegality of the invasion of neutral countries (Poland, Finland, Denmark, Norway and the three Benelux countries), and an expression of regret at the lack of religious freedom, and actual religious persecution, in Germany and some of the occupied countries.[92] As regards the Jews, as the editor Della Torre himself pointed out in an interview,[93] the Vatican daily newspaper only intervened with three articles, all concerned with the SS raid of October 1943 in Rome.

Though interventions by the *Osservatore* and Vatican Radio were naturally no substitute for the voice of the Pope, they at least suggested that any position they adopted had his approval. If they failed to satisfy even half the people who unremittingly hoped that sooner or later the Pope would throw off his reserve, still less must they have appeased Pius' own anxiety and possibly even remorse (he is said to have admitted at least once in private that he had only one regret: to have kept silent about Poland).[94]

The problem of whether or not to speak out was sub-divided into other secondary problems, such as the manner and means and the opportune moment for doing so. All this was complicated by the fact that Pius XII never gave up his attempts to influence the course of events through diplomacy.[95]

The fluidity of the war situation, and its continual surprises, obliged the Pope to abandon or alter over and over again the method and content of his diplomatic moves, and the confusion caused by what he planned to do on the one hand, and what he had to do on the other, made any intervention not strictly based on the war's development increasingly difficult. Moreover the success of any diplomatic move on his part kindled his hopes and made him feel that an intervention over war crimes would be untimely—for a halt in the war itself would end them anyway.

Only a detached observer of the various diplomatic and military phases of the war could ever understand the complex situation in which Pius XII was enmeshed. But such an observer would benefit from hindsight and from the psychological calm and objectivity ideal for retrospective analysis. Whereas the Pope had to act in the heat of events that were either hurtling from one horrible explosion to the next, or stagnating in insidious tension within which unforeseen anxieties were brewing.

But the ideal time for an intervention, taking all in all, could have been the second half of 1942. Before that time, the plans for the extermination of the Jews and other peoples were not yet known—with the exception of the Polish massacres—and at most the Pope could have issued a solemn condemnation of Germany for her repeated aggressions. There was certainly no lack of grounds for a condemnation of the sort, but could (and can) one really blame Pius for avoiding this step in the hope of ending the conflict by milder methods?[06]

During the second half of 1941, after the German attack on the Soviet Union, a papal intervention became even less probable. In whatever way German double-dealing might be judged on a political and ethical level, it was bound to appear to the Vatican as one of those curious undertakings so dear to divine Providence which resolves things in mysterious ways.

But by 1942, and especially in the second half of that year, the situation had undergone a major alteration. This was not only from the military point of view, in that the chances of final success had become more and more equal—with the Allied landings in North Africa, the battle of El Alamein, the deadlock on the Russian front and the beginning of the Stalingrad resistance. No, the main alteration was the outburst of homicidal lunacy that had spread through all the occupied countries, transforming them—above all in the East

—into theatres for extermination, massacre and execution. The end of 1941 had already seen the slaughter of hundreds of thousands of Jews and Russian prisoners at the hands of the *Einsatzgruppen* operating behind the lines as the German army advanced into the heart of the USSR. Tens of thousands of Serbs had been killed in Croatia, two or three hundred thousand Jews had been massacred in Bessarabia and Bukovina, and the same number deported from Germany. During the first months of 1942 the mass extermination of local 'non-Aryans' had begun in Poland, as well as the extermination of those despatched from France, Holland, Germany and Slovakia.

The duty to intervene against gratuitous crimes of genocide precludes, at least theoretically, any considerations of how, when and where. The Holy See was sufficiently informed to intervene, and it should have done so. But Pius XII was held back out of fear (as he himself confided) that once the war was over the Germans would blame him for stabbing them in the back at the most dramatic hour in their history when they were falling like flies before the walls of Stalingrad.[97] It is hard to accept this excuse. First of all, the real consequences of the Russian barricade at Stalingrad were only revealed later; and secondly, the Pope's opposition to the massacres would not have been directed against Germany itself but against Nazism and the Nazi hierarchy. Whatever the German armed forces were suffering, this was no more terrible than the victimization of innocent Poles, Jews and Russians.

During the subsequent period, Pius XII became literally paralysed by the drama of advancing Communism. Not even the fact of being free at last—after 4 June 1944 when the Allies entered Rome—could persuade him to criticize Germany when her soldiers were so desperately resisting the irresistible Red armies.

Why, then, did Pius XII not speak?

For various reasons, which had nothing to do with his character or with utilitarian motives, such as Hochhuth made out.[98]

—There was his pessimistic analysis of the situation—i.e. the psychological unreadiness of Catholics, especially German Catholics;

—There was his conviction that Communism would derive encouragement from any weakening of Nazism, particularly in view of the blind faith the Allied leaders placed in Russia;

—Most important of all, there was his preoccupation with guaranteeing the Church's survival all over Europe, and guaranteeing it sufficient energy to exercise a decisive influence on the future of the Continent and the whole world, once the war was over.

Added to these reasons, which could be called situational, are other intimate but no less important ones of a sentimental-psychological nature: the Pope's Germanophilia; his inability to shed his professional training as a diplomat, and his genuine feeling of repulsion, in the earlier period of his pontificate, for noisy gestures. We have already dicussed the situational reasons; much has already been written, and very persuasively, about Pius XII's Germanophilia;[99] so we shall now concentrate on the most neglected of the reasons mentioned above.

There was something pathetic in Pius XII's blind trust in diplomacy, for he continued to believe in it tenaciously to the end, and his absurd faith was never ruffled by the innumerable setbacks. The root of such disconcerting obstinacy must have lain in some infantile fixation which, in my view, can be identified with his limitless cult of Leo XIII. For a Catholic, particularly for an ecclesiastic, and above all for a Roman, the first Pope that makes an impression on him is 'the' Pope (happily reigning), and all the more so if this Pope happens to be an outstanding figure. Leo XIII not only revived Vatican prestige, which had reached its lowest ebb under Pius IX, but under him it reached a peak unattained for centuries.

Pius XII grew up in the school of Rampolla, Leo XIII's Secretary of State. He had been the pupil of Gasparri and Della Chiesa, and the political disillusionment in the reign of Pius X had, by violent contrast, made his ardour even more intransigent. And then, after Pius X, Benedict XV and Pius XI had unexpectedly regained lost ground, so that by the time Eugenio Pacelli reached the centre of Vatican diplomacy he had direct personal acquaintance with the heights and depths—acquaintance that would have been enough to exhaust weaker and less idealistic natures. And he had definitely come to believe that the seesaw of alternatives was an inevitable part of the relativity of human undertakings.

Another of his rooted convictions was that Roman ecclesiastical diplomacy had so many resources (a thousand years of experience, a coherence based on extra-political ideals which were immutable under any circumstances and therefore certain to be continuous, etc.) that it was bound to emerge victorious even from the direst predicaments. From this came his concern to continue and strengthen Vatican diplomacy at all costs, and this was also why he unhesitatingly adopted the line of political neutrality as chosen by Benedict XV at the beginning of the First World War, and added to it the moral neutrality which in the course of the following twenty years Pius XI had adopted with incredible lack of prejudice.

Throughout the recent polemics it has become fashionable to contrast the ambiguity and reticence of Pius XII with Pius XI's tough and determined outspokenness. Now it is true that in the last years of his pontificate Pius XI underwent a certain re-orientation in his policy towards the totalitarian regimes and even managed to utter compassionate words about the Jews. But these extreme *retractationes* on his part were more verbal than real, and they were usually confidential rather than public and programmatic.[100] The famous speech about Catholics being the 'spiritual heirs of the Jews', for instance, was made behind closed doors and went unrecorded by the *Osservatore Romano*.[101]

Pius XI said nothing on 7 April 1933 when the first two anti-Semitic laws were passed in Germany excluding non-Aryans from public office and the bar (the Concordat with Hitler was then being prepared—in record time).[102] He said nothing after the promulgation of the Nuremburg race laws on 15 September 1935 which, among other things, prohibited sexual relations between Germans and Jews 'so as to protect German blood and honour'—though this touched the question of 'mixed marriages' (incidentally, between 1 July 1933 and 15 September 1935, fifty thousand Jews had had to leave Germany and many had committed suicide). He even said nothing after the *Anschluss* in 1938 when anti-Semitic measures were redoubled and it was made obligatory, for example, to declare all Jewish property so that it could be expropriated, and the letter 'J' (*Jude*— Jew) was put on passports and identity cards. Nor did he say anything after the night of 9–10 November when revenge was wreaked on German Jews for the murder of Ernst von Rath, counsellor at the Paris Embassy, by a Jewish boy. This revenge involved the destruction of 7,500 shops, the setting fire to some 200 synagogues, the arrival at Buchenwald (within four days) of 10,454 Jews, and the elimination of 'non-Aryans' from commercial activity, with the imposition of a thousand-mark fine and the restriction of their movements.

'The day the first synagogue was burned,' wrote a well-known German Catholic writer, Reinhold Schneider, 'the Church should have risen up like a sister on the side of the Synagogue.' But Pius XI made no mention whatever of these crimes, any more than of the persecution of the evangelical sects. There was not even a reference to them in the famous *Mit Brennender Sorge*.[103] This encyclical is famous without reason, for far from being an anti-Nazi document (as it is reputed to be) it did not even dare lay at Nazism's door the errors in dogma and morality then spreading throughout Germany; it confined itself to laying the blame on certain currents in Nazism. The one reproach made by Pius XI (and with all due respect) against the Nazi leaders, the one reason why the encyclical was written at all, was that the Concordat had been violated. Nothing else struck the Pope as urgent or important. And so as to obtain a modest guarantee that there would be no further violations, he scrupulously avoided making any clear judgment on a concept of the State inspired by the most brutal and grotesque racial theories. The only aspect of Nazism criticized in the encyclical was its totalitarianism, and that only because it was in the name of State totalitarianism that the German authorities were staking their claims over the education of the young and abolishing church schools. And Pius XI ended up by offering Hitler the olive branch of reconciliation so as to win back for the German Catholic Church its exorbitant bureaucratic and organizational prosperity.

In his encyclical *Non Abbiamo Bisogno*, six years earlier, his attitude to Italian Fascism had been no different. But between 1937 and 1938 there was a rumour that he had decided to put an end to compromise and was even going to denounce the Lateran Treaty. This was reputedly the contents of his legendary speech to the Italian episcopate gathered in Rome for the tenth anniversary of the Treaty, but the address was never delivered because the Pope suddenly died. But when John XXIII published the text[104] all illusions vanished. Once

again Pius XI had confined himself to protesting against the continuing obstacles to the Church's freedom and activity in areas where
she was most susceptible; and his boldness only consisted in a
vigorous and caustic choice of language.

But even this seems to have been enough to persuade Pius XII to
pass over his predecessor's last utterance in silence and to return to
the sinuous methods of diplomacy. His long experience should have
deterred him, particularly as he knew the deep hostility the Axis
leaders felt for him and his advisers;[105] and he certainly should have
perceived the incongruity of insisting on diplomatic methods with
statesmen who openly scorned diplomacy, or only made use of it
when it was the best means for playing on the good faith of their
adversaries. Not that Pius XII should have abandoned all contact
and formal negotiations, for at least these provided a bond of non-
violent relationships and could always offer the possibility of understanding, but he should never have looked on them as his only hope.

The total inadequacy of diplomacy to meet the situation presented
the problem of finding some new means to combat the impositions of
the totalitarian regimes and neutralize their abuse of power. For the
democratic nations this was no easy task, but it should have been
easy enough for the Church. After all, for the Church diplomacy is
a sort of superfluous politeness—a residue from the temporal power
—and she can always do without it, for she has at her disposal the
weapons guaranteed to bring about the inevitable and final victory
of all spiritual power when assailed by brute force.

On the eve of war, therefore, the Church should have put her trust
in a deeply religious Pope rather than a diplomatic one. In other
words, the Catholic Senate, gathered for the conclave after Pius XI's
death, should have risen above the temporal demands of the moment,
however pressing—and the conviction to do this was tragically
lacking. But this is not to say that a religious statement would have
been anachronistic and hence impossible given the climate of the
Church from 1939 onwards. It was in the very arid period of 1903
that the Sacred College chose Pius X, a man altogether foreign to
politics, and his pontificate would certainly have left a deep imprint
on the history of Catholic spirituality had its achievements not been
upset by the sudden and blind anti-Modernist reaction. But Pacelli's

election could be regarded as a fatal error of judgment from yet another point of view. As Pius XI seemed to have designed him as his successor, the majority of the cardinals might well have thought that they were voting for an heir to the policy of re-orientation that had marked the last months of Pius XI's reign.

Whatever the intentions of the electors, or those of the man they chose, the world situation finally overwhelmed the willing and generous new Pope, so that, try as he might, he could only seek a solution to the conflict within the terms of the conflict itself, rather than outside it. No one, I think, can question Pacelli's religious sincerity. Unlike some of his predecessors—and indeed some of his contemporaries in the Curia—Pius XII was a true believer. Unfortunately his piety was not visionary and prophetic, that is, it enshrined not the fire of immediate experience but the reflected light deriving from a theological-juridical view of life, and into this his profession as diplomat fitted harmoniously. In other words, as often happens with believers, his piety, while permeating his ideal conception of existence and his main field of activity, was also conditioned and restricted by these. There was no direct or conscious conflict between his religion and a profession bound to a particular outlook, in fact there seemed to be the maximum harmony between them; but in fact there was that latent contradiction that realities bring to the surface when they try to co-exist without the necessary subordination of the lesser to the greater. This is the deepest reason, though certainly not the only one, why Pius XII's tireless activity during the war was condemned to sterility, and it is also the truest and innermost reason for his disconcerting silence about the Nazi crimes.

The fact that his lofty and austere conscience was racked throughout the whole war as to whether or not to speak out implies no contradiction to these assertions but confirms them and is illuminated by them. While the sincerity and depth of Pius XII's piety lie behind his moral torment, his unconscious professional deformation explains the final victory of the diplomat over the man of God.

In Fr. Leiber's interesting profile of the Pope[106] written a few weeks after he died, mention is made of two very significant characteristics: his keen sense of 'power' and his instinctive dislike of all forms of hyper-spirituality or isolation in a purely religious sphere. The Jesuit

Fr. Leiber, who regarded Pius XII as a hero, naturally viewed these among his most admirable characteristics. Unfortunately it took the revolutionary advent of Pope John XXIII to convince at least one section of Catholics that a papacy based on the 'Constantinian' spirit of power was in dangerous contradiction to the true mission of all religious movements and of a Christian Church.

Chapter 6

WHAT SHOULD HE HAVE DONE?

What should Pius XII have done? Vladimir d'Ormesson's opinion was: 'above all, no theatrical gestures . . .'.

> . . . I am convinced that everything he said and did was dictated, after a torment of inner struggle, by the certainty that he was doing his duty as Pope. To complain that he failed to do this or that, make gestures, pronounce anathemas, would be to confuse theatre with reality. Theatre is mere fiction, but we live in reality.[107]

But when the Germans wanted to introduce the yellow star into Denmark, having imposed it on Jews in every other country, King Christian threatened that he would be the first to wear it. Was it a theatrical gesture? However this may be, the Germans forgot their decree. Would it have been a theatrical gesture if Pius XII had declared publicly what Theodor Haecker wrote in his diary on 13 September 1941, the day the same decree was passed in Germany: 'There may come a time when Germans abroad will be forced to wear the swastika, sign of the Anti-Christ, on the left lapel of their coats'?

Was it a theatrical gesture when the Pope appeared in the bombed areas of Rome on 19 July and 13 August 1943, his white robes visibly spattered with blood (no one has ever known how that happened)? It was surely a precedent which moved the world.

It has been said that he should at least have denounced the Concordat with the Reich. But would that have really been the most appropriate gesture—something so typically political? Official apologists such as Fr. Martini are not completely wrong when they say:

> . . . leaving aside the fact . . . that the Concordat referred to conditions in the life and activity of the German Church, its denunciation by the Holy See would have given Hitler two immediate advantages: a very effective propaganda weapon and an absolutely

free hand in liquidating Catholicism wherever his power extended.
Hitler and the Goebbels propaganda machine had always represented universal Jewry as leading the struggle against Germany
ever since the Treaty of Versailles. The rupture of the Concordat
would have been a clear demonstration of the intimate union and
criminal pact between the Catholic Church and—not an oppressed
people—but an oppressor to whom the worst intentions of domination and exploitation were ascribed. A denunciation of the
Concordat would have led not only to a break-off of diplomatic
relations, but to all contact, direct or indirect, between the
Catholic hierarchy and faithful, and Rome.[108]

Should Pius XII, then, have thundered anathemas and interdicts?
Probably not. Not because this would have been a recourse to old
and rusty weapons—for though Pius IX's excommunication of the
House of Savoy did nothing to prevent the unification of Italy, it
would be imprudent to say absolutely and *a priori* that censures from
Rome are powerless (witness, among others, the case of Peròn). Yet
we cannot help wondering about the reaction which such a course of
action would have aroused among German Catholics. No procedure
of the kind, let us add, could have come suddenly like a bolt from the
blue; it would have had to follow on from some solemn denunciation
which had had no result; so that even in this case the really sensational event would have been not the anathema but the denunciation.

The denunciation could have been strong and yet loving, with none
of the hatred that inevitably colours excommunications and interdicts. And it could have been accompanied by a threat to release
the Catholic citizens of Germany and her allies from their national
obedience. This would not have been a novelty, for *Mit Brennender
Sorge*, though so meek and mute in its denunciation of political
Nazism, had incited German Catholics to a sort of civil disobedience
by recommending 'generous heroism' to anyone in public office who
was put under pressure to abandon the Church, and by urging
parents who were forced to send their children to non-Catholic
schools to 'disengage their own responsibility' from decisions made
by God's enemies.

Mit Brennender Sorge ended up by exhorting all Catholics to have
faith in their final victory, because 'the arm of God has not shrunk
even today'. Did the 'arm of God' shrink or weaken subsequently

with the much graver crimes the leaders of Hitler's regime initiated and pursued with ever accelerated rhythm under cover of war? Should the Church have demanded less 'generous heroism' and less courageous 'disengagement' from people exposed to these criminal tragedies?

It is only too natural to ask what would have been the outcome if the Pope had taken up such a position himself, directly, personally. If he had done so at the right moment, it would probably have been very effective indeed—possibly even a determining factor in the war. By this I do not mean that the Pope should have acted imprudently or inopportunely. The more serious, the more extreme, his gesture, his overture, his move, was to be, the more realistic and well-considered had to be the measures to ensure its effectiveness and forestall any untoward consequences. But precisely for this reason, why waste time in diplomatic activity? Why not set about reinforcing the scope of the gesture by seeking solidarity with other religious organizations, and above all with the separated Christian Churches—Protestant and Orthodox? Why, in other words, not relegate inconclusive secular machinations to a secondary level, and begin developing religious alliances on an open ecumenical level so as to build up a solid religious bloc that would give greater authority to the coming denunciation? If the Holy See saw itself as equal to any individual nation in its right to exercise diplomacy, why should it not feel a greater need and duty to be on cordial and collaborative terms with the other Christian faiths with a view to safeguarding the basic rights of man, international solidarity, and common spiritual progress the world over? Should not a Pope devote himself first to achieving that sort of brotherly mobilization of forces before giving his time to tasks incompatible with the true spirit and aims of the Church?

The most obvious objection that will be raised to this argument is that it is anachronistic, based on a situation which only arose later (at least in official circles in the Catholic Church), with the 'scandal' of Pope John—as a few of his qualified representatives in the hierarchy defined it. At the beginning of Pius XII's pontificate nothing could have been so unforeseeable and beyond the pale of the general outlook—alike at the summit and the base of Catholicism—as an appeal to the Separated Churches. Up to that time, and especially under Pius XI, the ecumenical movement had met with nothing but suspicion and mockery; how, without any serious ideological motive-force, could Pius XII suddenly reverse an official and established attitude?

The answer is simple. To form a united religious front against the Nazis, Pius XII had no need to pioneer with this idea but merely to agree to it. For on 20 March 1939, in the British House of Lords, after Lord Halifax, the Foreign Minister, had commented on the recent annexation of Bohemia and Moravia by the Third Reich, the Archbishop of Canterbury, primate of the Anglican Church, rose to speak. Everyone expected an official routine discourse, but suddenly Dr. Lang proposed something which left many of his listeners breathless:

> This seems to me to be the nearest approach which in the circumstances we can get to collective security, and if it be made plain that there are a sufficient number of peoples possessed of sufficient collective resources then I think that even Herr Hitler would be induced to call in and put a leash upon his inordinate ambitions.
>
> But is there any other force that can be brought in for the defence of justice and freedom? I think there is. Not a political force, but a spiritual force. There are multitudes of people in every country, most loyal to their own States, and yet members, citizens, of another society, the Christian Church, using that term in its widest sense, and through it of the Kingdom of God. Nothing has been more remarkable than the proof in recent years that, in a manner which I think has never hitherto been displayed, Christian people in spite of differences of doctrine and denomination, are willing to unite together for the setting forward of those principles which are their common heritage and responsibility. . . . Now it occurs to me to ask whether in this present grave situation it may not be possible to give Christendom a voice. I have it in mind to renew once again (as in 1935, on the occasion of the Italo-Ethiopian war) this invitation to the leaders of all Christian communions throughout Europe and possibly in the United States. *Much of course must depend on whether His Holiness the Pope would be willing to give his leadership.* His recent election has given rise to the highest hopes. It is possible he may feel that he has come to his spiritual kingdom for such a time as this. Is it inconceivable that under his leadership other leaders would be unwilling to make a declaration to the effect that the new exaltation of the State at

the expense of human personality, the new exaltation of force as a means of adjusting international questions, is inconsistent with Christian principles? It may be so. *It is obvious that His Holiness would be entitled to choose his own time and his own way, but, if moved by the present state of the world, he were willing to make some declaration, I think I can safely promise that all the leaders of the Anglican and Orthodox and Protestant Churches would give simultaneous support.* . . . It may prove that what I have suggested is impracticable, but at least I am willing, so far as I can, to do my best. Meanwhile I am convinced that I am speaking for multitudes, without distinction of Church or political Party, who are certain that now it is the concern not only of statesmen but of all who care for the Christian ordering of society, to do their utmost to see that justice and good faith among nations, freedom of thought, of speech, of conscience, of worship, freedom for the full development of human personality, shall not be further imperilled.[109]

This bombshell proposal was not taken up by Pius XII because (as with incredible lack of comprehension it was said) 'well-known reasons of a theological nature forbid the Catholic Church, and forbade it on that occasion, to join its voice on matters of faith and morals with that of other Christian confessions under the form of *Common Declarations*'.[110] The following 24 May, disillusioned but undaunted, Dr. Lang spoke again in the House of Lords on the prospects of the possibility of some joint action on the part of the Christian Churches, though he admitted, with reference to the proposed 'Conference of Christianity' that 'it would be discourteous and useless to invite the Pope to convoke such a meeting when it would be impossible for him to accept'. Obviously these circumspect words were intended to re-introduce the bold proposal to Pius XII in the form of an extreme appeal. A few days earlier he had explicitly referred to the example of the Pope's appeal for special prayers for peace during the month of May, and had associated himself with the initiative. But it was all in vain.[111]

One would like to believe that the Pope's refusal had not been dictated by a desire to win for himself and the Holy See the exclusive credit for any eventual success in the various diplomatic negotiations then under way, or even for the success of future negotiations which, somewhat ingenuously, he tried to encourage by offering the Vatican Palaces as a meeting-ground. We are certainly puzzled by such an

inexplicable and unjustifiable 'No', above all when we recall the
cordial words—unusual among his papal predecessors—spoken by
Pius XII about the Separated Churches at the time of his election,
and later confirmed in the encyclical *Summi Pontificatus*[112] and subsequent documents. True, he had been prompted, so to speak, by the
consensus of sympathy which many of the schismatic hierarchies
showed him on his election, but we would have thought that whatever he said was more than a mere exchange of compliments.

The abyss towards which the world was sliding was not a rhetorical
abyss, but the abyss of the Second World War. Faced with such a
prospect a pope whose spirituality was total and open would not
have cared about differences between sects. He would have felt an
overriding need to set an example by bringing peace to the world of
religion which had for so long been separated by age-old rivalries.
Then, with increased strength from this new solidarity, and the feeling
that he could act in concert with his new colleagues, he would have
tried all possible ways to stop the oncoming menace of war. Unfortunately Pius XII preferred to continue his tragic and pathetic
monologue. His Christmas broadcast of 1941 declaimed at length:

O Christian Rome . . . you are great and even the ancient ruins of
your pagan greatness are seen in a new light. . . . You are the
mother of higher and more human justice . . . you are the beacon
of civilization . . . etc.

and then ended by invoking God's blessing also upon 'those who,
though not members of the visible body of the Catholic Church, are
near to Us in their faith in God and Jesus Christ, and share Our view
with regard to the provisions for peace and its fundamental aims'.

One cannot even say that an alliance such as Dr. Lang proposed
would have amounted to a shock for the Catholic world. After all,
it was not a question of initiating a completely new form of existence
ex abrupto among the followers of the various faiths—something for
which they would have been absolutely unprepared. For years, in
Germany itself, persecution had not only brought Catholics and
Protestants closer and necessitated a sort of mutual assistance, but
it had even led to a sense of co-existence (which the war must have
strengthened—with the exchange of churches for religious services,
for instance). The ecumenical crusade which John XXIII accepted

and made his own produced no scandal in time of peace, but only warm admiration; so how could it have produced disturbance and upheaval for the faith in time of war?

Once more, then, the key to the mystery of Pius XII's silence can be found in the theological-bureaucratic narrowness with which he envisaged relations between the Church and the world; in his need to isolate himself and hold himself distinct, as Pope, instead of throwing himself open to the service of all.[113] Today we shudder as we read his radio-message of 3 May 1939, the day after his election:

We see before Us a world afflicted by immense evils; to its help the Lord now sends Us, unarmed but unafraid. . . .

In a different style, but with similar exaltation, another leader was simultaneously announcing that he had been sent by Providence to offer the world a new order, destined to last at least a thousand years: on his banner and on the uniforms of his soldiers he had inscribed, 'God is with us'. Hitler's blasphemy lay in identifying God with the land and blood of the German race. But when Pius XII identified God with his Church alone, his illusion, surely, was just as disastrous.

PART TWO

The Case of Poland

Chapter 1

THE OCCUPATION OF POLAND

It was 4 o'clock in the afternoon of 31 August 1939. In Gleiwitz, a small Silesian town on the Polish frontier, a hotel porter switched the telephone to an occupant's bedroom. The commercial traveller who had taken up residence in the hotel a few days earlier listened impassively to the voice repeating twice: 'Grandmother is dead.' Four hours later, at exactly 8 o'clock, a 'commando' of six or seven armed men in Polish military uniforms entered the local radio station, fired a few rounds to frighten the occupants, locked in the basement the few people working there, interrupted the programme and seized the microphones. One of the men repeated in a stentorian voice and a perfect Polish accent, 'This evening Gleiwitz radio is in our hands', while the others kept on firing at ghosts: then all withdrew. Five seconds later a Gestapo car quickly deposited in front of the same building 'a tin of food' (Secret Service slang for the body of a prisoner from a concentration camp killed by a shower of bullets in the face to make him unrecognizable)—and left. A few minutes later again and it was the turn of the police to arrive to register what had happened. Less than an hour later all the German radios were already denouncing the 'provocation' in all its details, including that of the 'aggressor' killed in the exchange of shots.

The operation was perfectly mounted. Helmut Naujoks—the SS colonel who later, among other things, devised the Bernhard plan for manufacturing and distributing forged English pound notes on a large scale—had carried out his mission laudably.[1] At 4.45 next morning the first detachments of the Wehrmacht penetrated Polish territory without a declaration of war.

Only two weeks later the *Blitzkrieg* had already passed into history. There were still some pockets of resistance to be mopped up, but with the capital surrounded that would be a mere matter of days.[2]

The fate of the troops that had escaped encirclement was sealed by the Russians whose divisions crossed the Polish frontier on 17 September. In Moscow on the 28th the Nazis and Communists signed their treaty and agreement for the partition of Poland—a partition that was only going to last until the summer of 1941 when the Germans attacked their Soviet allies, incorporated into Greater Germany the province of Białystok, and turned Eastern Galicia, with Lwów as capital, into the fifth district of the General Governorship of Poland.

Hence the most lasting partition was the one the Nazis made on 19 October 1939 as it lasted until the autumn of 1944 or more, that is to say for more than five years. This partition cut off the western provinces of Poland—Poznania, Polish Pomerania and Silesia—involving over ten million inhabitants, of whom only six hundred thousand were German, and annexed them to the Great Reich; and left to Poland, administered as conquered territory and called the General Governorship, the central provinces, i.e. the districts of Cracow, Warsaw, Lublin and Radom, comprising some twelve million inhabitants.[3]

The territory annexed to the Great Reich was destined to ruthless Germanization by the systematic uprooting (*Ausrottung*) of all that remained Polish, and the gradual substitution of Aryan citizens of the Third Reich in place of the original population.

As for the General Governorship, its purpose was to serve as a labour reserve (agricultural and industrial) for the war. Its final destiny would be decided later. As long as the war lasted, the order was for it to be denationalized and disarticulated as far as possible, and—in the words of Hans Frank who was Governor-General from 1940 until the collapse—made into an 'intellectual desert'.

Obviously the territorial and administrative partition of Poland affected the Catholic Church as well as the Poles.[4] In 1939 the Church included six ecclesiastical provinces each governed by a metropolitan: five of the Latin rite (Gniezno and Poznań, Warsaw, Wilno, Lwów and Cracow) and one of Greco-Ruthenian rite (Lwów) plus an Armenian-rite archbishopric also centred on Lwów. So all told six archbishoprics, an autonomous archbishopric and eighteen suffragan dioceses.

The demarcation line between the areas annexed to the Reich and the General Governorship not only separated various metropolitan sees from their respective suffragans but cut many dioceses in half according to whim[5]—as can be seen from the following survey:

Area Incorporated into the Reich
(a) Whole dioceses:
    The archdiocese of Gniezno and Poznań (including Poznania),
    The diocese of Chełmno (Polish Pomerania),
    The diocese of Katowice (Polish Silesia),
    The diocese of Włocławek;
(b) The greater part of the dioceses of Łódź, and Plock;
(c) Part of the archdiocese of Warsaw;
(d) Part of the dioceses of Lomza
    and Częstochowa;
(e) And a small part of the archdiocese of Cracow
    and the diocese of Kielce.

The General Governorship
(a) Whole dioceses:
    Sandomierz,
    Siedlce,
    Lublin,
    Tarnów;
(b) The greater part of the archdiocese of Cracow
    and the diocese of Kielce;
(c) Part of the archdiocese of Warsaw;
(d) Part of the dioceses of Częstochowa
    and Przemyśl;
(e) And a small part of the dioceses of Łódź
    and Plock.

(The remaining dioceses, and the remaining parts of those already mentioned, were included, until August 1941, in the Soviet-occupied area.)

The consequences of a partition such as this would have perhaps been endurable had the criteria adopted for the two areas not been so opposite to each other. As regards the area annexed to Germany, the Germans intent on Germanizing it were obviously unable to accept the survival of the pre-established ecclesiastical organization —especially as they were fully aware of the extent to which the Church supported Polish nationalism during the oppression of the country. And this meant nothing more nor less than the destruction of the original zones of ecclesiastical administration; it was not enough merely to change the personnel (by the removal of the Polish bishops and priests, the annihilation of the diocesan curias, the closing of the seminaries and religious houses, the suppression of organizations involved in the apostolate, charitable work, and so on). As for the General Governorship where the Polish Church could have carried on its traditions, all it could expect was vigilant control of its activities, especially those not directly concerned with religious practices, and the deployment of other impediments so as to restrict the efficiency and moderate the influence of individual people or of works.

And so it was. Just at first the Germans appeared to be uncertain of what they wanted. This was in the weeks immediately before and after 19 October, a kind of 'no man's time' when things were left to the will of the strongest, i.e., as usual, to the Gestapo. Then their plan of campaign became clearer. There is an account of considerable value on all points which for the time being we shall call Document A; it dates back to the end of December 1939 and shows the Nazi aims in a clear light, at least as regards two of the oldest and most historic Polish dioceses within the territory annexed to the Reich, the archdioceses of Gniezno and Poznań, on the very nerve of Polish Catholic life and including a good two million of the faithful. We quote it almost in its entirety:[6]

DOCUMENT A

1. *Archdiocese of Gniezno*

(1) The Vicar Generalship of Gniezno is in the hands of Canon Edward van Blericq of the metropolitan see, and a doctor in canon law.

When the Germans occupied the area they forbade him to carry out any acts of ecclesiastical jurisdiction. This prohibition remained in force until the middle of November. The Curia of the Archdiocese was closed by the Gestapo. The Vicar General carries out his office from his home as he is forbidden access to the registers and archives in process of being searched by the police. The only priests he can receive are those obtaining permission to go to Gniezno; he himself is forbidden to visit parishes outside the city. The Curia's money has been confiscated as well as the fund amounting to 80 thousand złoty. Similarly the Gestapo has closed and occupied the metropolitan courts of first and second instance. The keys of both Curia and tribunal are in the hands of the Gestapo.

The metropolitan chapter has been dispersed. The Vicar General and Mgr. Krzeszkiewicz stay in their houses. The other canons have been expelled from their homes and Canon Brasse has been deported to Central Poland [the Governorship].

The metropolitan basilica which has been restored and re-decorated in the last few years has been declared uninhabitable and closed by the police who have taken possession of it. But behind closed doors, concerts and meetings have been held. As it has been used for various activities without any higher control, there are grounds for fearing that the venerable basilica has been despoiled of its ancient ornaments and religious objects.

The archiepiscopal seminary for philosophy at Gniezno has been requisitioned by the army. A German general has established his headquarters in the archbishop's palace. The houses of the expelled canons and those of the lower cathedral clergy have been occupied by the Germans. The State administration has requisitioned the retreat-house for aged priests. The fathers in religious orders have been expelled from their convent and parish which have been used as a place of detention for the Jews. The main parish church, that of the Most Holy Trinity, has been desecrated, the presbytery has been broken into and its inhabitants expelled.

(2) The German authorities, especially the Gestapo, are behaving with ferocity towards the Catholic clergy which is living under a nightmare of terror and under continual provocation without any means of legitimate defence.

[Here follows a list of ten priests manhandled by the Germans and of five others who died in prison or at forced labour, from ill-treatment or bombardment.]

Several priests have been imprisoned and are suffering humiliation, ill-treatment, etc. A certain number have been deported to Germany and nothing more has been heard of them. Others have been sent to concentration camps. Meanwhile they have begun expelling priests to Central Poland—and return from there is impossible and forbidden. The number of these is increasing. A group of priests has gone into hiding among ordinary civilians so as to carry on a minimum of pastoral work in those districts completely deprived of their clergy. Arrests and imprisonments have occurred in such a way that priests have had no opportunity of consuming or otherwise safeguarding the sacred species from sacrilege. The priests detained in the Kazmierz Biskupi camp are obliged to do forced labour if they lack the four złotys needed for their daily provisions. In the Gorna Grupa camp they are often ill-treated. It is no rare sight to see a priest in the labour squads mending roads and bridges, loading coal-trucks, working in the sugar factories, or even pulling down synagogues. Some of them have been seized at night in pyjamas, brutally beaten and submitted to other tortures. Here are three examples.

At Bydgoszcz in September some 5,000 men were so crammed in a building that there was not even room to sit down on the floor. A corner of the building was assigned to the needs of nature. Canon Casimir Stepczynski, the rural dean and parish priest of the place, was forced, accompanied by a Jew, to carry away the human excrement with his own hands, a disgusting task in view of the large number of prisoners. When the chaplain, Adam Musial, asked to take the place of that venerable priest, he was brutally flogged with a whip.

Fr. Anthony Dobrzynski, curate at Znin, was arrested in the street when, wearing his cotta and stole, he was carrying the viaticum to a dying person. His sacred vestments were torn off him, the sacrament was profaned, and the priest was taken to prison.

At Gniezno in November some 300 families were dragged from their homes without warning and transferred to a factory. A number of people were arrested in the street on their way back from church. They included several priests [names here given]. Fr. Lawrence Wnuk was seized without warning while he was undressing and locked up in prison wearing only his pyjamas. He was not allowed to send for his clothes till some days later. All these citizens, men and women, young and old, were thrown together promiscuously with the priests. . . . Finally they were all deported in sealed coaches to Central Poland.

(3) According to an authoritative source, 'between Bydgoszcz (Bromberg) and Gniezno all the churches, save for a few exceptions, have been closed'. In particular the priests have been removed

    —from all the 15 parishes in the deanery of Gniewkowo
    —from all the 12 parishes in the deanery of Lobsenica
    —from all the 16 parishes in the deanery of Naklo

—from all the 21 parishes in the deanery of Znin
—from 6 parishes of the rural deanery of Bydgoszcz
—from 16 parishes in the deanery of Inowroclaw
—from 9 parishes in the deanery of Kcybia
—from 7 parishes in the deanery of Powidz
—from 7 parishes in the deanery of Trzemeszno
—from 5 parishes in the deanery of Września

In the remaining eleven deaneries there is no possibility of calculating the parishes deprived of their priests. A considerable number of these are merely viewed by the German authorities as *aufgehoben* (removed or abolished). This situation (with at least half a total of 271 parishes without a priest) is very serious especially if we bear in mind that the Polish population is being forcibly driven away from the land of their fathers and their place is being taken by Germans brought in from various parts of Europe. Few of these latter are Catholics.

In churches where the priests are tacitly allowed to carry on their ministry, opening is barely allowed even on Sundays and only from 9 till 11 in the morning at that. At Bydgoszcz alone is there wider freedom. Sermons must be preached exclusively in German but this, at least so far, serves as a mere pretext for imprisoning the priests who transgress the order. Hymns in Polish are also forbidden. The people's devotion under such trials is very edifying. No sooner are the churches open than they rush to have their children baptized, go to confession, and receive Holy Communion—so much so that the priest has little time left to end Holy Mass before the fated hour of 11 o'clock. Marriages are not celebrated inasmuch as it is severely punished to bless a marriage that has not first been contracted before an official of the civil government. And, in principle, the latter does not admit of marriages between Poles. In several places the priests are under house arrest and are unable to take the last sacraments to the dying.

Crucifixes have been removed from the schools, and no religious instruction may be given. Church collections for charitable purposes are forbidden. The priests are obliged to recite a public prayer for Hitler at the end of Sunday Mass.

Given such conditions the religious confraternities are unable to function. Catholic Action, so flourishing six months ago, has been forbidden, and its better known apostles have been persecuted. Catholic charitable organizations, such as the Ladies of Charity and the St. Vincent de Paul conferences, have been dissolved and their funds confiscated.

Since the German troops entered these regions, numbers of

crucifixes and statues of Our Lord, the Blessed Virgin and the saints, adorning the streets, have been pulled down. The statues of the Holy Patrons, standing in the city squares, and even sacred pictures and monuments belonging to private houses or estates have been similarly dealt with. At Bydgoszcz the monument to the Sacred Heart of Jesus has been profaned and destroyed.

The Church, after ten centuries of apostolate, and after a glorious affirmation of religious life in these last twenty years, has been forced to take to the catacombs. Priests are beginning to say Mass and administer the sacraments secretly in private houses. Their zeal is truly amazing. Piety is stronger than ever and devotion to the Church truly heroic.

(4) The repressive measures against religious houses and their apostolate aim at abolishing them entirely. As we have already said, the members of religious orders in Gniezno have been imprisoned or deported. A fine new house and a magnificent church only just built by the Lazarist fathers in Bydgoszcz have been confiscated. The police have installed themselves in the house, while in the church—which has been closed for religious ceremonies—the German soldiers are carrying on licentious orgies. The Friars Minor have been driven out of their big new convent at Yarocin, and the same fate has befallen the Holy Ghost Fathers at Bydgoszcz, the novitiate of the missionary congregation of the Holy Family at Garka Klasztorna, the novitiate of the Pallotine Fathers at Suchary, the novitiate of the Oblates of the Immaculate Conception at Markowice, and the mother house as well as the novitiate of the Society of Christ for emigrants at Potulice.

Worse losses still have been suffered by the religious institutes for women. The Sisters of Charity of St. Vincent de Paul have lost fourteen houses including hospitals, orphanages and rest homes. The Congregation of the Sacred Heart has had its new High School occupied as well as the college and training school at Polska Wies. The Sisters of St. Elizabeth (Grey Sisters) have been expelled from 19 houses. The Daughters of Mary Immaculate, whose mother house is at Pleszew, have been forced to close the house for aspirants to the congregation, the novitiate, and 17 other houses. Two houses have been taken from the Dominican Third Order and from the Daughters of the Mother of the Saviour.

A horrible scene took place with the Franciscan Sisters of Perpetual Adoration in Bydgoszcz. The Gestapo entered the convent and forced all the Sisters to gather in the chapel where the Blessed Sacrament was exposed. A member of the police leapt into the pulpit and shouted at the Sisters that the time for prayer was over because 'God doesn't exist; for if God did exist, we wouldn't be here'. The Sisters, with the exception of the Mother Superior who was seriously ill, were removed from the convent and shut up for 24 hours in the rooms of the Passtelle (passport office). While the Gestapo was sacking the convent one of the police seized the pyx from the tabernacle, took it to the Mother Superior who was bed-ridden in her cell and ordered her to consume the consecrated hosts, shouting '*Auffressen*!' (eat them!). The Sister obeyed the order but at a given moment begged for water which she was re-fused. With an effort she managed to consume all the sacred species and so saved them from profanation.

(5) The Church is also in the hands of the Gestapo as regards its possessions. The funds of the archdiocesan curia have been requisitioned. The farms at Braciszewo, the property of the archiepiscopal seminary, are under watchful administration. The Archbishop's palace has been taken over as his headquarters by a general commanding a division, while the Gestapo has taken over the curia, the basilica, the diocesan archives, the ancient and famous archives, and the Chapter library. Parish registers have been removed. In the parishes whence the priests have been expelled, the German authorities see themselves as masters of the church, the cemetery, the presbytery, and all ecclesiastical and private property. Moreover, the administration of the lands constituting Church benefices and funds has been handed over to German government henchmen who give nothing to the church or the parish priest. Even in the parishes tacitly provided with priests, these have been expelled from their presbyteries to be replaced by faithful followers of Poland's new masters. The funds for church maintenance have begun to run out and the priests live exclusively on the charity of the faithful. Should this state of affairs continue much longer the Church will be completely despoiled, and the large means of maintenance collected over long centuries at the cost of enormous efforts of generosity for the service of God will be lost.

2. *Archdiocese of Poznań*

(6) The Vicar General Mgr. Valentine Dymek, an able, pious, generous and very active prelate, has been kept interned in his own house since 1 October.

The curia and the metropolitan courts of first and second instance for Cracow, Lwów and Włocławek are closed and under the control of the Gestapo who are sacking the registers. The Archbishop's palace was invaded by soldiers who remained there for weeks ruining the furnishings. The registers of the Primate's chancellery have been examined at leisure by the Gestapo, and they are still at it. They have also laid hands on important archiepiscopal archives.

The canons of the metropolitan chapter, Rucinski, Zborowski and Szreybrowsky have been imprisoned. Mgr. Pradzynski, who is seriously ill, is confined to his house under armed guard.

The cathedral of Poznań, the parish church for fourteen thousand souls, has been closed by the police on the pretext that it is unsuitable for use. The keys are in the hands of the Gestapo. The collegiate church of St. Mary Magdalen, one of the most beautiful in Poznań and parish church for twenty-three thousand souls, has also been closed and behind its closed doors the Germans seem to be carrying out work that arouses doubt and suspicion. The rural vicar and the parish priests of the city, save for a few in the suburbs, are in prison. A considerable number of coadjutors have been deported so that only about 25 per cent of the parish clergy for twenty-one parishes have remained at their posts.

The theological seminary which had 120 students in its four courses was closed by the German authorities in October and the buildings have been turned into a police school. Approximately 1,700 hectares of land belonging to the seminary has been entrusted to agents to work it.

(7) The clergy have undergone the same treatment as in the archdiocese of Gniezno: they have been manhandled, arrested, thrown into prison or concentration camps, deported to Germany or expelled to Central Poland. At the present moment some fifty priests are in prison or concentration camps.

Generally speaking the clergy live in a state of constant uncertainty, every day, every hour, under threat of arrest or violence. Yet here and there areas have remained calm, the wave of persecution having not yet reached them.

[Here follow the names of four priests who were shot, with the additional remark that they would be unlikely to have been the only ones, but the others were not shot in public.]

Generally speaking the illegal removal of clergy from their parishes has not reached the proportions noted in the archdiocese of Gniezno; but now colonization is being organized from the Baltic territories of Germany, i.e. in a north-south direction, and this is normally preceded by removing the clergy and closing the churches.

The churches still open are allowed to be used for services only on Sundays from 9 till 11. Priests have begun saying Mass on weekdays early in the morning and behind closed doors. No marriages can take place. There are no sermons or music. Crucifixes and holy pictures have been removed from schoolrooms and there is no religious instruction.

(8) The Polish episcopate had turned Poznan into the national centre for organizing and directing religious activities and especially Catholic Action for the whole Republic. Unfortunately all these centres of exceptional activity, charitable works, publications, etc., have been destroyed by the German authorities.

In particular:

(a) The national centres of the pontifical work for the propagation of the faith and of St. Peter the Apostle have been suppressed, and their funds amounting to some 250,000 złoty have been confiscated.

(b) The National Institute for Catholic Action has been suppressed. This was the headquarters of all Catholic activity in Poland. Its funds, some 70,000 złoty, its publications valued at at least 100,000 złoty, and its office furnishings and fittings have been requisitioned. The national president of Catholic Action, the lawyer Dziembowski, and the employees in his office, are in prison. The director of the National Institute, Fr. Francis Marlewski, was first imprisoned and then sent to Central Poland.

(c) The offices of the national centres of the Catholic Women's Association have been suppressed or put to other uses; and the same fate has befallen the offices of the Catholic Youth organizations for men and girls. The national president of the association for Catholic Youth, Edward Potworowski, an aristocrat from Gola and a private chamberlain of His Holiness, was publicly struck in Gostyn Square. The president of the association for Catholic girls, Maria Suchocka, also from a noble family, was deprived—together with her mother and brother—of their pharmacy at Pleszev; all her personal belongings were taken from her and she was sent to Central Poland.

(d) The school for Catholic social studies has been closed. It is a school of university standing and is perhaps unique in the Catholic world. It was started for a three-year course for specialists in writing, speaking, etc., on behalf of Catholic Action and in particular for Catholic social movements.

(e) The same fate has befallen the Catholic Institute of pedagogy. It was an officially recognized school aimed at training competent and qualified teachers, and women assistants, for the Catholic schools and hospitals. Many nuns attended it.

(f) The Catholic illustrated weekly, *Przewodnik Katolički*, a popular periodical, has ceased to exist after a brilliant career of forty-three years. It was technically on a level with the best papers in the world and its weekly circulation ran to 220,000.

(g) The Catholic paper of high standing, *Kultura*, has also been suppressed. It was a literary, cultural, social and artistic review for the fairly cultivated classes.

(h) *Tecza*, an illustrated Catholic literary paper of more than average standing, no longer appears.

(i) *Ruch Katolički* a monthly publication and official organ of Catholic Action has been suppressed.

(k) The same applies to *Przewodnik Spoleczny*, a Catholic monthly devoted to modern social questions.

(l) Also suppressed are *Zjednoczenie*, organ of the National Association of Catholic Women, *Przyjaciel Młodzieży* and *Mloda Polka*, organs of Catholic boys and girls respectively.

(m) *Teologia Praktyczna*, the monthly pastoral review for the Polish clergy, has been suppressed.

(n) The monthly review, *Ruch Charitatywny*, organ of Christian charity in Poland, has been suppressed.

Besides these national organizations and publications, all organizations and publications belonging to the Archdioceses of Gniezno and Poznan have been suppressed. In particular:

(a) The archdiocesan Institute of Catholic Action.

(b) The diocesan centres of Catholic associations for men, workers, women, boys and girls.

(c) The archdiocesan Institute for higher religious education.

(d) The archdiocesan *Caritas* organization.

(e) The Council of the Ladies of Charity and of the St. Vincent de Paul conferences.

(f) The headquarters of the Church Choristers' Union.

(g) The charitable association for aged priests.

The funds and capital of all these associations, institutions and publications have been confiscated.

The most serious loss of all for the Polish Church, and especially for the archdiocese of Gniezno and Poznań, has been the confiscation of the printing house and publishing office of St. Adalbert in Poznan. It was the most important publishing house in the whole Republic. It manufactured its own paper and provided the country with an abundant and well-selected Catholic literature as well as scientific works and others of practical importance. As it was a diocesan institution, it provided roughly half a million złoty a year for the fund for Catholic activities in the archdiocese. The buildings and machinery installations were all of the most up-to-date type, and these, together with its books and other material were valued at six million złoty.

(9) The losses suffered by religious institutions are of equal importance [here follows a long list of religious institutions for men and women affected by the confiscations].

(10) The Church's economic situation in the archdiocese of Poznan is similar to that of the archdiocese of Gniezno. . . .

After a short reference to the 'ruin of 631 churches, 454 chapels and oratories, and 253 religious houses,' the report ends with an impressive description of mass deportations of Poles to Germany— if able-bodied men—and to the General Governorship in the case of elderly women, children, old men and the sick.

DOCUMENT B

There is another document by the same author which we shall call Document B. It dates from a few months later than the previous Document, i.e. April 1940. It illustrates, by the same method, the situation in the other dioceses[7] in the areas annexed to the Reich. And in a few words it brings up to date the situation in the two dioceses dealt with in the first report. As regards Poznań, for instance, it says among other things that the city had been declared *Klosterfrei*—free from monasteries (i.e. Polish ones: only German communities could have any), and it gives the following terrifying summing-up:

5 priests shot.

27 priests confined in concentration camps at Stuthof and elsewhere in the *Altreich*.

190 priests in prison or in Polish concentration camps at Bruczków, Chludowo, Goruszki, Kaźmierz Biskupi, Lad, Lubin and Puszczykowo.

35 priests expelled to the General Governorship.

11 priests died in prison and burnt in the crematoria.

11 priests seriously ill as a result of ill-treatment.

122 parishes totally without priests.

To this first analytical part which it would be tedious to quote in its entirety, the author adds the following 'Concluding Observations':

(1) Hitlerism aims at the total and systematic destruction of the Catholic Church in the rich and fertile areas of Poland which have been incorporated into the Reich, in total disregard of all rights and justice—because of the metallurgical and textile industries of these

areas, the abundance of high quality coal, the fertility of the soil and the beauty of the forests.

Save for the diocese of Katowice where the invaders have kept within bounds so as not to provoke the Catholic workers in the metallurgical industries and the coalmines, almost everywhere the ecclesiastical administration of the dioceses has been virtually destroyed. Even the bishops who have been allowed to remain in their sees can carry out their pastoral offices only within very narrow limits. One of them has been deposed, together with his coadjutor. Two auxiliaries are in concentration camps.[8] No parish priest can pay visits in his own parish, even clandestinely, despite the fact that after so many disasters and persecutions his visits are more necessary than ever. The curias and their archives are in the hands of the police and hence unable to operate as they should.

The cathedrals have been closed and their keys taken by the occupying authorities—one of them has been turned into a garage. Five bishops' palaces have been occupied, one of which has been turned into a hotel, the bishop's chapel serving as a ballroom. The police have made a dog kennel out of the Primate's chapel in Poznań. All the students of the seminaries have been dispersed and the seminaries occupied by Nazi authorities.

The ordinary clergy have been persecuted even more harshly. It is reported that thirty-five priests have certainly been killed, but the real number of victims unquestionably amounts to over a hundred. More than twenty have died in prison; some hundred have been tortured and ill-treated; another hundred are in concentration camps; and yet another hundred have been moved to the Central Governorship; while those who have been allowed to remain are subject to all kinds of humiliations—they are entirely at the Gestapo's mercy with no possibility of appeal.

In some districts the life of the Church has been totally eliminated, given that the clergy has been driven out; the churches and the graveyards are in the hands of the invaders. Catholic rites are no longer practised, the word of God is no longer preached, and the sacraments are denied even to the dying. In some places it is forbidden to go to confession. In others, churches can be opened only on Sundays and for a very short time at that. Marriages between Poles have been forbidden for seven months. Catholic Action has been completely suppressed, and the Catholic press wiped out. . . . Societies and charitable works have been similarly abolished.

Monasteries and convents have been systematically suppressed together with their thriving educational establishments, their publications, their social and charitable works and their care of the sick. . . . Monks and friars have been imprisoned and a considerable number of nuns dispersed. Very soon not a trace will be left of the hundreds of pre-existing religious communities, and thus will be achieved the annihilation of the immense contribution they have made to the religious, moral and intellectual character of the population.

The invaders have taken possession of the Church's patrimony both on their own account and that of their masters. . . . They rob for themselves and for the State, and send to Germany everything that can be transported, leaving the rest for the new German colonists. The moral level of their behaviour is illustrated (to take one example among many) by the fact that at Wloclawek the furnishings and belongings of Mgr. Kozal have been given by the police to prostitutes.

Everything has been deliberately planned so as to destroy the Church and its vitality in one of the most religious areas of the whole world. The terrible process recorded earlier has been carried out with the same implacability and brutality in the last seven months. After century upon century spent in the service of the Church, Poland is witnessing the establishment at her very heart of a paganism so forgetful of God, so immoral, atrocious and inhuman that it could only be accepted by mentally sick people who have lost every vestige of human dignity and are blinded by hatred for the cross of Christ.

It seems like an apocalyptic vision of the *Fides depopulata.*
(2) The religious persecution in these deeply Catholic dioceses goes hand in hand with the *extermination of the Polish population.* From information derived from reliable Nazi sources it has now been proved beyond dispute that the invaders have decided to leave only a reduced number of Poles in these territories to serve as *Sklavenvolk* for the Germans who are to be established there in mass as masters or *Herrenvolk.*[9]

No words can express the cold-blooded calculated cruelty of the evil being inflicted on the Polish people so as to reduce them to slavery and promote the prosperity of the 'superior race'. The atrocities committed with premeditation on a vast scale are a diabolical plan to achieve the concept of German 'living space' or, in other words, to carry out a massive programme of monstrous and oppressive imperialism. They will constitute one of the darkest pages in the history of mankind.

Executions are carried out without trial or judgment, mercilessly and ruthlessly, in all cities and villages. Neither secular nor regular clergy are spared, neither the aristocracy nor the middle classes nor the peasants nor the students, nor women, boys and girls. And they press on relentlessly; only now their executions are performed in secret so that there is no means of knowing they have happened nor the names of the victims. The horrors of the packed prisons and concentration camps with their ever-renewed streams of victims surpass—in refinement of sadism—the crimes committed by the Reds in Russia. The lives of Poles are protected by no law nor by any human feeling on the part of the invader.

The *Polish population is being expropriated* without pity or any form of compensation. Dr. Paul Freibe of the German Ministry of Agriculture has written in the *Berliner Boersenzeitung* that in the province of Poznań, and the other parts of the district now called *Warthegau*, 3,000 large farms have been confiscated and at least 200,000 holdings. The Poles have now lost all right to possess land, house, garden, or any building of any kind, or even a cow. Those not yet dispossessed know that they will be so tomorrow. The inherited fortunes of the aristocracy and the peasantry, the houses of the urban middle class together with factories and industries, are all, without exception, the object of German rape. The Poles are becoming a proletariat of slaves. This is the inevitable conclusion of six months' experience during which the Poles have been driven from an area which was the cradle of their nation, of the Polish State, and of their ecclesiastical organization.

These *expulsions* are being carried out deliberately in the most inhuman way so as to achieve the death of the greatest possible number of Poles for whom the invaders have no use in territories incorporated into the Reich. Landowners have been dragged away from their ancient castles and peasants from their cottages. The traditionally established middle classes are faring likewise in the cities which, moreover, are being denuded of all their intellectuals, lawyers, doctors, engineers and even people in the civil service. In this way the nation is being stripped of its ruling class. All alike are being sent into exile once they have been robbed of their possessions. They reach the General Governorship with only ten marks in their pockets and there they increase the hunger of that already overpopulated region reserved for the Poles.

The tragedy of this inhuman banishment of millions of Poles lies in the horror of the refinements of cruelty practised by the invaders. Every imaginable resource is deployed to increase the sufferings of exile, and exile has been turned into an instrument of death. All those families snatched from their homes at night regardless of old people, children, the sick, the pregnant, will re-

main an everlasting and shameful testimony to the degradation of
mankind. One thinks of those long weeks of anguish waiting in
cold, dirt and hunger in the camps, followed by the endless death
trains in which the victims travel, at 15 to 30 degrees below zero,
for two, three, even five days, shut up in cattle trucks with no seats,
no blankets, no food and no water—in a word, with no alternative
to a wretched death from cold and fatigue. We need only remember
the frozen children thrown out by the police along the railway
lines; the dozens of people who have been found to have died of
cold in pretty well every train on reaching its funereal destination
between December and March; the hecatombs of victims of in-
flammation of the lungs; the countless people whose health has
been utterly destroyed. . . . The repulsive picture of Nazi cruelty
will never be forgotten by generations of Poles and will remain the
most terrible experience of their history.

The *Poles left behind* are not regarded as citizens but as barely-
tolerated outlaws. They can only buy food when they present
ration cards and after the Germans have been served—by which
time the shops may well be depleted. In the trams the Poles are not
allowed to be with the Germans but have to occupy places reserved for them. On the trains they have to travel in the worst
coaches which are never heated in winter. They have to make way
for the invaders everywhere, and undergo humiliations, insults and
interrogations. They live in a climate of unremitting terror and are
exposed at all times to the arbitrary actions of the Gestapo with
no possibility of appeal to any legal protection. They are arrested
without knowing why. They are seized by the police on the streets
and in the churches and taken off to work in all sorts of places—in
the camps or in some factory no matter how far away. . . . Many
have been deported to Germany. Women, girls, young men just
disappear, and cannot be found any more.

Polish families are brutally separated. The Poles are forbidden
to contract marriage. Bastard children are destined to be treated
as slaves inasmuch as they are the fruit of the violation of young
Polish girls by depraved Nazis. This business goes on in open
cynicism as a right owed to conquerors.

Simultaneously, in the dioceses incorporated into the Reich,
every monument or relic, every document or centre of Polish
culture, is being destroyed. And the same has happened to Polish
works of art in the museums, a large number of which have been
destroyed. The Polish archives have been transferred to Berlin.
The libraries have been sacked. With a view to obliterating all
Polish books, every Polish publication found in bookshops,

palaces or private houses is marked out for destruction and sent to the incinerator. . . .

Not a single Polish school is still in existence. Polish boys and girls are not admitted to the high schools. A Nazi atheist said recently that it is a good thing to give slaves the advantages of ignorance.

(3) Exterminated as a nation, oppressed in their Christian faith, separated from their families, destined to slavery and want, situated at the heart of a matchless tragedy, the Poles of the dioceses incorporated into the Reich are bitterly aware of being cut off from the civilized world, and of their plight remaining unknown to the rest of mankind, by a propaganda machine that has recourse to the most shameless lies. German propaganda is making every effort to cover up the Hitlerite crimes in Poland with a veil of silence. It denies the perfidy of the regime, calumniates the martyred nation, and threatens the neutral countries that could dare to publish the truth. The propaganda aims at spreading the belief, even in deluded Germany, that all is normal in Poland and that the Poles have never had it so good as now when they have the good fortune to be under Nazi domination.

In all this frightful desolation the Poles remain heroically faithful to their Catholic faith and to Christian principles. But they beg that they shall not be forgotten; they beg that the conscience of all the peoples of the world shall not let them be sacrificed to Hitlerite barbarity; they beg world opinion not to abandon them to the mercy of their oppressors. . . .

As for the territories of the General Governorship, we shall quote almost in its entirety[10] another Document (Document C), written by another author and put together rather later than the two previous ones; i.e. towards the end of 1940. Though it is more concise and summarized, it is effective enough.

DOCUMENT C

. . .[11]

. . . Contrary to the repeated statements of official German propaganda and to Governor-General Frank's declarations—i.e. that the religious convictions and traditions of the Polish nation are being respected—the facts of daily life prove exactly the opposite. The fight against religion becomes harsher every day. The persecution of the Catholic clergy persists without hope of abatement.

. . .[12]

. . . In one of Poland's most ancient and venerable sanctuaries, Wawell Cathedral in Cracow where the Polish Kings were crowned and lie buried, only one priest is allowed to say Mass, on Sundays and Wednesdays, behind closed doors and in the presence of a Gestapo agent. The keys of the Cathedral and its treasure are in the hands of the German authorities.

In many places, and even in the archdiocese of Warsaw, it is forbidden to celebrate marriages in church, and in Pomerania those celebrated since 1918 between Poles and Germans have been declared invalid. Recently sermons have been forbidden in a certain number of localities in the diocese of Siedlce.

In the dioceses of Częstochowa, Kielce, Sandomierz, and in various centres in the archdiocese of Warsaw, the clergy have been forbidden to teach religion in the schools. Dengel, the presiding commissioner for Warsaw, has removed priests from the hospitals despite the fact that they are usually Catholic foundations which were even recognized by the former Russian government. When Archbishop Gall intervened on this point, all he got from the occupying authorities was a boorish reply. The theological faculties and the seminaries have mostly been closed on the orders of the selfsame authorities and the buildings handed over to new occupants. The Warsaw seminary which was damaged during the bombardments still formally exists but the rector and the teachers cannot carry out their duties as they have been in prison since last October. They include Father Motylewski who returned to Poland a fortnight before the outbreak of war after seven years spent in studies in Rome.

Polish public opinion has been deeply shaken by the news of the confiscation of works of art from the churches—liturgical vessels, paintings and vestments. This is no less than pure theft of Polish ecclesiastical property. Despite explicit agreements in international law and the Hague Convention, the German authorities are seizing objects used for Catholic services, sending them abroad and using the money so gained for their war aims. Until now only Soviet Russia has done things like this.

Warsaw Cathedral has been robbed of, among other things, a sixteenth-century and a seventeenth-century chalice, one of which was the personal work of King Sigismond III—it was he who gave it to the cathedral. At Cracow the German authorities have seized not only the reredos engraved and embossed by Wit Stwosz but nine valuable paintings by Kulmbach—all from the church of St. Mary. The soldiers arrived during the 'forty hours' devotions and all appeals and protests by the parish priest, Fr. Kulinowski, who asked them to wait until the end of the service, were in vain. . . .

The martyrology of the Polish clergy is written in letters of blood. . . .

At Mszczonow, near Warsaw, the Gestapo killed the rector, Fr. Paciorkowski, without accusation or trial. In the second half of February this year Fr. Nowakowski, vicar of the parish of the Redeemer in Warsaw, was condemned to death merely for being found in his church praying for the independence of Poland. It is not yet known whether the sentence has been carried out, for the Gestapo refuses to divulge information when a priest or a layman has been condemned to death or to a concentration camp. When an execution takes place, the Gestapo does not hand over the body but buries it in some secret place at night. No news is known of many of the priests arrested in recent months, and there is no means of finding out whether they are still alive and, if so, where they are.

In the territory of the General Governorship a most cruel persecution has struck the clergy of the Lublin diocese although there were very few Germans there and hence no grounds for friction or motive for persecution. The reason for this cruelty is that the head of the Gestapo at Lublin is none other than the man who distinguished himself in Vienna for his outrageous behaviour to Cardinal Innitzer.

It was in mid-October of last year, on the anniversary of Bishop Fulman's consecration, when the local clergy were gathered in the episcopal residence to present their good wishes to the bishop, that Gestapo agents broke into the palace and arrested the bishop, his auxiliary, Mgr. Goral, and the whole assembled clergy. The bishop was accused of being in possession of a machine-gun which had been found in his garden near the city walls. Now the garden is at the very edge of the city near fields and open country from which it is very easy to throw anything over the walls.

And even honest Germans in the present Lublin administration make no secret of their conviction that the gun was planted there on the chief of police's own orders, as he is a specialist at persecuting the clergy. Moreover, if it was only Bishop Fulman who was accused of being in possession of a gun, why were his auxiliary and the other clerics condemned to death and subsequently to life-imprisonment as well as he? And then isn't it highly absurd to imagine that an old man of seventy-five, seriously ill and known for his kindness, could threaten the power of the German army with a machine-gun—a thing he had never touched in his life and wouldn't know how to use? The whole treatment meted out to Bishop Fulman, his auxiliary, and the priests who went with him to the Oranienburg concentration camp near Berlin, covers the twentieth century with shame. In November, after a few weeks' imprisonment at Lublin, the bishop and his companions were faced with court-martial (*Sondergericht*), secretly tried without defending counsel, and condemned to death. The Governor-General used his power of amnesty to mitigate the death sentence to life-imprisonment. . . .

One of the aims of the German police occupation in Poland is the annihilation of the intellectual classes which includes not only doctors, lawyers, teachers and so on, but also the clergy. Hence the large number of priests who have been imprisoned without accusation, trial or judgment. The occupying authorities maintain that these priests are merely interned. But on what principle? Why are they being ill-treated in prison like common criminals—for instance in Rzeszow, Tarnobrzeg and other cities—in the same cells as thieves and prostitutes? Since October of last year some 150 priests from the diocese of Lublin have been imprisoned—i.e. more than half the total clergy—and many others have to live in hiding, like Fr. Surdecki, the diocese administrator. There are thirty priests in prison in Warsaw, eighteen of whom belong to the archdiocese. . . . In the diocese of Cracow priests have been arrested for teaching religion and moved to the Wisnicz prison where there are also twenty-six Jesuits from Cracow.

Besides Bishops Fulman, Goral and Wetmanski, Bishop Tomczak's auxiliary was arrested at Łódż, beaten with rods on the arms until they bled, then forced to do street-cleaning. Fr. Stanislas Nowicki, the local director of Catholic action, was so brutally beaten on the head by the Gestapo during his interrogation that his skull had to be trepanned.

Four priests were so cruelly beaten up in Radom that their teeth were broken and their jaws dislocated. Among other questions that they were asked (as I can personally testify) was: 'Do you believe in God? If you do you're an idiot, and if you don't you're an imposter.' When the man questioned pointed out that the question was an insult, they spat in his face. Another question was, 'Who is the greatest statesman, Hitler or Mussolini?' The intellectual level of the questions, and the method used by the Gestapo in these interrogations, speaks for itself.

. . . Since the German occupation of Poland we have witnessed the appalling extermination and destruction of the Polish nation on a scale unprecedented in history. Every day numbers of people are killed. Organized loot of private property, museums, libraries, scientific laboratories, hospitals and churches is the order of the day. Almost every morning in the parishes of the Warsaw suburbs one sees a number of dead bodies (the average is about twenty), their heads riddled with Gestapo bullets—that is the method they have adopted for disposing of their victims. As the bodies have no documents on them, the clergy, whose duty it is to record the death certificate, have no means of knowing the names of the dead.

During the past month there has been a propaganda campaign to persuade the Polish population to emigrate to the Reich in search of work. But as the number of volunteers was small, every commune was forced to provide a given number. But this ruling was equally unsuccessful, so that men and women have been seized and deported to inner Germany. On the basis of present calculations, this method should recruit more than a million people. Fischer, the Governor of Warsaw, has recently stated that few of those who go will ever return. Once they have reached Germany, the victims of this slave raid are deprived of all religious or cultural support and are entirely at the disposal of their recruiting sergeants and the Hitlerite organizations.

One of the worst crimes of the present regime in Poland is the deportation of Poles far from their homes and the region where their ancestors have lived for more than a thousand years. . . . The 'liquidation' of the whole of a family's possessions can happen in less than half an hour. Nothing is allowed to be taken away except what can be carried in a handbag or suitcase. Recently I was able to visit Ostrowiec, near Radom, where the inhabitants of the parish of St. Martin in Poznań had been despatched together with their parish priest, Fr. Taczac. Three thousand people had been transported in cattle trucks to that small centre of 15,000 inhabitants. Their journey of more than 500 kilometres had taken four days. The trucks were unheated and had no lavatories. Men, women, children, the old and the sick, were thrown together indiscriminately in a temperature that reached 30 degrees below zero. On reaching Ostrowiec they were assembled in the school-building where they slept on straw on the ground. The place is very poor and absolutely insufficient to guarantee the maintenance of such a large number of deportees, so an attempt was made to collect provisions in neighbouring villages. But these, too, had been stripped of provisions by incessant German requisitioning. As a result the want soon became so terrible that infectious diseases, including typhus, broke out. I have come across similar situations in other places. . . . There are now hundreds of thousands of these deportees.

While I was staying in Poznań and Torun in January, parents came lamenting to me because their children had been taken off to Hitler Youth camps, or sterilized with X-rays—or because they had no news of them. Other laments concerned girls who had been taken off to German army brothels on the western front.

I have recently received a detailed report from doctors and nursing sisters in the present 'Governorship' of Lublin and the areas annexed to the Reich concerning the *frightful massacre of mentally defective children* in the sanatoriums of Chelm in the province of Lublin, of Lubliniec in Upper Silesia, and of Koscian in Poznania. Poland had set up model hospitals for these retarded children and provided them with every medical attention—often with encouraging results. After the occupation, the Germans declared that there was no point in preserving the lives of such children, and they were killed. At Chelm alone, 428 sick people have been liquidated, including many children. This massacre of the innocents has filled the whole country with horror.

The brutality of the German authorities to the sick and to children is confirmed by the continual requisitioning of hospitals nominally for the needs of the army—though often they are left completely empty. At Zakopane there is a large preventive sanatorium for children threatened with tuberculosis. It was built on the initiative of Archbishop Sapieha. In January the children were taken away and the sanatorium was requisitioned. To this day it has remained completely empty, and the same thing applies to other sanatoriums. . . .

Chapter 2

THE RELATIONS OF THE HOLY SEE
WITH OCCUPIED POLAND

So then, how much did the Vatican know of what was going on in Poland after the Nazi-Soviet invasion of that country?

To answer this question we must first answer another. What were the relations between the Holy See and Poland during the German occupation?

Before the war there were no difficulties about Rome's relations with the Polish government and the Polish episcopate. 'The bishops, the clergy and the faithful'—so went Article 11, paragraph 1, of the 1925 Concordat—'will have full and direct communication with the Holy See.' And this of course also applied the other way round. The same Concordat, 'with the object of maintaining friendly relations between the Holy See and the Republic of Poland', provided for an exchange of diplomatic representatives on both sides; 'an apostolic nuncio shall reside in Poland,' it said, 'and an ambassador shall be kept at the Holy See.' And it added: 'The power of the apostolic nuncio in Poland shall extend to the territory of the free City of Danzig.'[13]

1. The end of the nunciature in Warsaw

And that in fact happened. After the Concordat Poland had three papal nuncios of whom two, Lorenzo Lauri[14] and Francesco Marmaggi[15] were raised to the purple at the end of their missions, which suggested that they had held first-grade posts. Their prestige in the country that could boast of having had Achille Ratti, later Pope Pius XI, as its first nuncio (before the Concordat), was demonstrated by Marmaggi's triumphal departure from Warsaw to Rome in 1936.[16] On Christmas Eve of the same year Poland heard the name

132

of the man who was to be her last nuncio—at least up till the present: Filippo Cortesi,[17] an able Sicilian diplomat of sixty who had already brilliantly represented the Holy See in Venezuela (1921–26) and in the Argentine (1926–36; and in 1928 he also became the representative to Paraguay). On 4 June 1936 he had been appointed to the important nunciature of Madrid, but the military rising and the Spanish civil war prevented him from taking up his post, and that was why he was sent to Warsaw.

At the outbreak of Hitler's war, Mgr. Cortesi had already been in Poland for about two and a half years and, among other achievements, had reached the agreement on ecclesiastical possessions taken from Russia which was stipulated on 20 June 1938 and ratified in Rome on 16 March 1939.[18] He seems to have met with sympathy from both bishops and people, and the Poles unquestionably suffered great disillusionment when he abandoned not only Warsaw but the country itself immediately after the outbreak of war. Everyone remembered how, in the August of 1920, nuncio Ratti had remained at his post even when the Russian advance guard had reached within 15 kilometres of the capital and against all pressure from the diplomatic corps (which itself left the city almost to a man) and from the clergy.

As the author of a secret report dated 9 January 1942 put it:
A real misfortune for Poland lay in the departure, in September 1939, of the nuncio Cortesi, an intelligent man and on Poland's side. The old [*sic*!] man's nerves could not stand up to the bombardments, and he abandoned Poland despite the efforts of the clergy to prevent him leaving. His departure was not seen favourably in Rome.[19]

Whether out of fear, prudence, or the illusion that the Polish army might eventually recover, the fact is that Mgr. Cortesi joined up with the diplomatic corps as early as the morning of 5 September[20] and left for Nobezkow near Lublin, crossing the Rumanian frontier ten days later together with his counsellor, Mgr. Alfredo Pacini. It seems highly probable that his decision did no more than anticipate the fate of the Warsaw nunciature, but there is no doubt whatever that it made the task of the Wilhelmstrasse easier, for the latter had no obligation to find a motive for his dismissal. It is also certain that by his departure from Poland he made it quite impossible to engineer a return for as long as the German occupation lasted. True, it was urgent to get into safety all that could be salvaged of the nunciature's possessions and archives—already nearly destroyed by the bombardments; but this task came within the purview of the counsellor Pacini. However, he was not allowed to perform it. Authorization was given towards the middle of October 1939 when Mgr. Carlo Colli, counsellor at the Berlin nunciature, was allowed to visit Poland, though only for three days.

The Nazis wanted at all costs to prevent a papal representative from witnessing or obtaining information about what was happening in Poland—he might even re-organize the Polish Church to which they were disposed to permit at most a lethargic survival. And so, when in January 1940 there was question of transferring the archives, or what remained of them, Mgr. Colli obtained permission to visit Poland again, but for the last time and only briefly and only to the capital.

It was only natural that the Holy See should try every means to give the Berlin nunciature control over the two Polish areas dominated by the Reich, pretending to consider them both, but especially the first, as obvious extensions of the territories of the old Reich, to which latter its representative, Mgr. Cesare Orsenigo, was accredited. But all efforts, whether direct or indirect, were vain. In September and October 1939, for instance, the Reich government rejected the request made by the Berlin nuncio to communicate to Rome the lists of Polish prisoners so that their relations could be informed by radio. At the end of November that same year it similarly rejected the demand for an inquiry as to whether the SS were really responsible for the acts of violence against the civil population in occupied territories of which they were accused. While at the end of 1939 and the beginning of 1940 it laid down conditions on transmitting parcels through Rome such as to make this impracticable. And so on.[21]

In view of German intransigence, the Vatican considered the expedient of falling back on despatching an apostolic visitor to Poland, that is, a representative without diplomatic privileges, which might have seemed less alarming to the Reich government. The proposal was made personally by Cardinal Maglione, the Pope's Secretary of State, to the German Foreign Minister, von Ribbentrop, who was received in audience by Pius XII on 10 March 1940. Von Ribbentrop appears to have presented the Cardinal Secretary of State with an official German publication on the atrocities committed by the Poles against the Germans, and begged him to present it to the Pope.

The Secretary of State replied that the Holy See's only desire was to be accurately informed. For this reason it had on a number of occasions insisted on obtaining Berlin's agreement to sending a trustworthy ecclesiastic to Poland, namely Mgr. Colli . . . and had received no reply. Meanwhile plenty of news was circulating on the situation in Poland, some of which could not be questioned and was extremely distressing. Various bishops had been driven from their sees; and some, like the Bishop of Lublin, was in prison together with a number of priests; a considerable number of monks and friars were under arrest, while countless churches had been closed. . . .

Ribbentrop: 'But in Poland the ecclesiastics have been, and still are, mainly political; and they're hostile to the Germans.'

Maglione: 'Polish priests can be advised to stay quiet and devote themselves to their ministry as pastors, but they cannot be asked to stop loving their country. The Holy See cannot accept, without reservations, the news provided by the German embassy here regarding the occupied territories, still less make such news publicly known, without having its own means of investigation. Hence the Holy See must be able to send an Apostolic Visitor to Polish territory. His presence would serve to eliminate misunderstandings, and to strengthen priests in their exclusive dedication to their ministry as pastors.'

Ribbentrop: 'But Poland is under a military government: there can be no consuls or diplomats there.'

Maglione: 'The Holy See's envoy would have a religious, not a diplomatic, mission. While keeping in contact with the occupying authorities, he could give instructions and good advice and help the bishops to bring the religious situation gradually back to normal.'

Ribbentrop: 'But how in an occupied territory governed by the army can you have a . . .'.

Maglione: 'Representative of the Holy See? Your Excellency will recall that during the occupation of the Ruhr and the Saar the Holy See was glad to have an envoy in those places, and was invited to send one by the German government. Then the French government agreed to the presence of an apostolic visitor, whose work Germany certainly had no reason to complain of, if I remember rightly; indeed Germany showed its satisfaction more than France . . .'.[22]

The Cardinal then handed von Ribbentrop a note. This is what it said:

> The current religious situation in Polish territory, and especially the manifold restrictions on the freedom of the episcopate and the clergy, the obstacles to the practice of religion, the seizure of religious institutes, are all a source of grave concern to the Holy See. The conditions in the archdioceses of Gnesen and Poznań and the dioceses of Wladislav and Lublin are particularly pitiful.
>
> It is a matter of urgency to send an Apostolic Visitor to Poland. Our desire is to appoint the present counsellor at the Apostolic Nunciature in Berlin to that office.
>
> The task of the Visitor will be to provide for the normalization of the religious situation while remaining, insofar as it is necessary, in suitable contact with the civil and military authorities. . . .

Another of its point was:

> The Holy See has repeatedly made known that it intends, in its own name, to send and distribute help for the poor and needy Polish people.
>
> The Apostolic Visitor would also have the task of distributing this help.[23]

Ribbentrop's verbal reply to Maglione's pressure was in the nature of, 'Very well, I'll think about it'; but no Apostolic Visitor was ever allowed into Poland even for a temporary visit.[24] Hence the Holy See insisted all the more on having recourse to the nuncio in Berlin—though he was unable to take action as he lacked sufficient powers. This, for example, is how Woermann, head of the political department of the German Ministry for Foreign Affairs, recorded a meeting requested of him by Orsenigo and granted on 29 November 1939:

> Today the nuncio put the following questions to me, making it plain from the outset that he was speaking on his own initiative.
>
> From various sources . . . information had reached him regarding the treatment of Poles, especially in the district of Posen (Poznan) but also in other regions. . . . He was aware that he had no right, as nuncio, to raise the matter here; but felt obliged to do so as a human being. Recently things have happened that Germany should not permit even in her own interest. He did not want to argue about whether the execution of important landowners was justified; he was speaking only for the common people. Women, children and old people were being dragged from their beds and sent far away without being given a new house. The nuncio asked

me if I could tell him to whom he could turn about such matters.

I answered that I was unable to suggest any high-level authority to whom he could turn, as probably no one would have listened to him with the same calm as the present writer, but would have immediately pointed out to him that as nuncio he had no right to talk on subjects of this nature. Moreover I told him that I thought he was the victim of false rumours. The nuncio denied this and said he had used great prudence in weighing up such news. And he asked me to enable him to have at least one interview with the Secretary of State (von Weizsäcker) to see whether something could be done.[25]

This brief account gives a typical picture of the difficult situation with which the Berlin nuncio had to contend. It is confirmed by the nuncio's meetings with the Secretary of State, von Weizsäcker (on 15 March 1940, and 20 September and 11 December of the same year). Further evidence of the Holy See's efforts to intervene with the Reich through the nuncio in Germany is provided by a hitherto unknown letter from Cardinal Maglione to his colleague, Bertram, Archbishop of Breslau, dated 18 November 1942.

As early as October 1940, as the result of an appeal by a German bishop, the Apostolic See ordered the Apostolic Nuncio in Berlin to approach the German government so that the large number of Polish priests interned in concentration camps should be enabled to leave the country and go to neutral countries in Europe and America. Unfortunately this request was not received favourably. The German government rejected the request and all it promised to do was to make their fate somewhat easier, as the German bishops also wished, by putting them all together in one camp (Dachau) and allowing some of them to celebrate Mass and others to be present at it.

And in fact, though many priests were still detained elsewhere, the living conditions of those at Dachau were made more supportable, at least for a while.[26]

Yet though the Wilhelmstrasse did everything to discourage Mgr. Orsenigo's initiatives as regards Poland, it did allow him to make them—at least until the first half of 1942. This is confirmed by the book *Pius XII a Polska* (Pius XII and Poland) written by Casimir Papée, ambassador to the Holy See of the Polish government in exile.

[August to December 1941] was a period of large-scale diplomatic activity for the Apostolic Nunciature in Berlin on behalf of the priests and faithful of Poland. In 1941 the persecutions had gained momentum, news from the *lager* became increasingly tragic and there was an ever-increasing number of victims. In accordance with instructions from the Holy Father's Secretariat of State, the Berlin Nunciatures approached the *Auswaertiges Amt* during the second half of 1941—and particularly on 14 August, 29 September, 4 December, 5 December (personal interventions on the part of the Nuncio), and 12 December.[27]

But there was a drastic change after the Vatican note of 18 January 1942 in which the Holy See informed the Reich that it was unable to recognize the new juridical situation of certain countries due to current military operations. On 26 June von Weizsäcker informed Mgr. Orsenigo that the German government would no longer consent to activities or requests on the part of the Holy See concerning territories not belonging to the *Altreich*.[28] A few days earlier von Weizsäcker had explained to von Bergen, German ambassador to the Holy See, what this provision involved.

The Führer has taken the following decision about relations between Germany and the Catholic Church:

1. The Führer does not wish relations with the Catholic Church to be set up on an identical basis for the whole Reich.

2. Germany maintains relations with the Vatican solely for the old Reich (*Altreich*), that is to say for the part of the Reich for which the Concordat of 1933 was signed.

3. Though on various points the Concordat is out of date, the Führer regards it as still officially operative.

4. As the Vatican has informed the German government that, for the duration of the war, it cannot recognize any territorial change, it has automatically excluded the possibility of establishing official relations with territories annexed or occupied after September 1939. The Führer insists that these conditions be applied to what was formerly Austria as to all the territories annexed before 1939.

5. The representatives of Germany shall be the official representatives of the Reich in these territories (. . .); the Church shall be represented by local delegates, cardinals, bishops and so on.

Hence in matters regarding these territories diplomatic or political relations with the Vatican will not be authorized. It follows that the Ministry for Foreign Affairs is the sole source of appeal maintaining relations with the Vatican.[29]

No wonder, then, if after the communication of 26 April, Mgr. Orsenigo's attitude became more hesitant and resigned. This was Woermann's impression (15 October) and Weizsäcker's (6 November).[30] On 5 August 1943 Steengracht noted in his diary:

The nuncio called on me today and transmitted a statement to me, immediately adding that he knew the matter in question was outside the limits of his compétence and that he would be in entire agreement if nothing was done about it.[31]

If we reconstructed the personality of Mgr. Orsenigo from the large amount of evidence that has come to light in recent years, he would seem to us not so much a tired man who had lost confidence, but a cynic—if we did not know the more simple truth that he was a man unequal to his important and crucial task (his nunciature was the most important in the world in those years); and when we reflect on his end, on those last months of his life spent in Rome in an oblivion that was half imposed and half sought, and on his last private visit to Germany which he undertook so as to forget that he had not been elevated to the purple like various colleagues,[32] and during which he died, we cannot doubt that the man who was most hostile to him was perhaps Pius XII himself, his sovereign.[33] But it is nevertheless questionable whether a more gifted diplomat would have been any more successful in such a difficult situation and above all in treating with men so hostile to the Church as the Nazi leaders.

2. The German bishops as intermediaries

As reinforcement to the nuncio's activities, the Vatican unquestionably relied on the German bishops, at least on those whom it considered most influential with the authorities on the showing of their political past. The most weighty amongst them was Cardina Bertram who had been Archbishop of Breslau since the beginning of the First World War. In those days his behaviour must have been particularly pleasing to Benedict XV, for he made him cardinal *in petto* in 1916 and hurriedly gave him the hat in 1919 (two years before his compatriots Faulhaber and Schulte). The following year, however, Bertram's patriotic behaviour about the plebiscite in Upper Silesia gained him world-wide notice (as well as undeniable loathing from the Poles). As head of the German Episcopal Conference, he caused Hitler some preoccupation at one time owing to the stand taken at Fulda,[34] though he had given him generous support at the time of the Spanish Civil War. And the Nazis seem to have known nothing about the part he played in drawing up the encyclical *Mit Brennender Sorge*.[35] On the outbreak of the Second World War Bertram was exactly eighty, but still active and energetic. Hence no one was in a better position than he to intervene in the name of the Holy See—especially on behalf of the Poles.

We have already quoted a short passage from Cardinal Maglione's letter to him of 18 November 1942,[36] which testifies to the efforts he made on their behalf. We shall now quote the letter in its entirety, only omitting the passage already referred to.

<table>
<tr><td>Secretariat of State</td><td>From the Vatican,</td></tr>
<tr><td>of His Holiness.</td><td>18 November 1942</td></tr>
</table>

Your Eminence, and most revered Cardinal,

You have already concerned yourself with praiseworthy zeal on behalf of the Polish Catholics, both those who live in their native land and especially in the regions bordering on your diocese, and those who for motives of work or other reasons are living in the old Reich (*Altreich*).

I would particularly like to draw your attention to the orders of the *Reichministerium* for religion, communicated to you by letter on 11 September of this year.

There is no need to express the sorrow these orders have caused the Apostolic See. Indeed, owing to these provisions, many Catholics have been deprived of the comforts of religion and have difficulty in benefiting from the sacraments of the Church. In addition, the civil authority now arrogates to itself even the right to give orders about the administration of the sacraments, and this constitutes a threat to their validity; and on occasion it forbids the bestowal of sacraments, such as matrimony.

As these matters are so important and so harmful, I beg you to do all in your power, as indeed you have been doing, to see that Polish Catholic workers, whatever their occupations in the territory of the old Reich, are given religious and confessional freedom and are enabled to receive the holy sacraments without obstacles, as is their right (and this also applies to their children).

The second point deals with Polish priests imprisoned in concentration camps . . . [here comes the extract we have already quoted on p. 137. The letter continues:] ... The Holy See has been informed that in the concentration camps we have alluded to other priests are held prisoner besides Polish priests, even Germans. Hence the Holy See is doing everything it possibly can with the maximum of energy to try to alleviate their suffering. Recently news has been received that the number of German priests who are dying in these camps has returned to normal—at first the number surpassed normal limits and was certainly excessive. But the mortality of the Poles, even of young men, is unfortunately continually on the increase. The Apostolic Nuncio in Berlin is finding it more and more difficult to help the Catholic Poles, so that many of them suffer and die without even knowing the care which the Holy Father is bestowing on them.

It is for this reason that I appeal to your zeal and active piety, and I am sure that my request for your collaboration will not be in vain. You are certainly aware that his Excellency Monsignor Kozal, titular bishop of Lappa and suffragan of the Bishop of Włocłowek, is interned in Dachau, and in all probability his Excellency Wladislaw Goral, titular bishop of Melow in Isauria and auxiliary of the Bishop of Lublin, is in Oranienburg-Sachsenhausen. Should you have any chance, do all you can to help them and comfort them with special fraternal love.

Please realize that the Holy Father will welcome with gratitude all you can do to lighten the fate of the unfortunates of whom I have spoken. He is in anguish for them and for the sufferings of all the unfortunate, whose burden he shares.

Please accept, etc.   LUIGI CARD. MAGLIONE.

The primary importance of this document derives from the fact that it is an official step (made by the Secretariat of State) that suggests that there was constant contact and shows how the Holy See made use of Cardinal Bertram both to protect Polish bishops and priests in confinement in German territory and to guarantee religious assistance to all Poles who had willingly or forcibly emigrated to the *Altreich*.[37]

In addition it is almost certain that Pius XII, either in person or through the Secretariat of State, must have turned to other German prelates, to Bishop von Preysing or even the Fulda conference. Among those to whom the Vatican turned, a special place must be given to Mgr. Splett, Bishop of Danzig, whom Rome appointed Apostolic Administrator of the Polish diocese of Chełmno.

3. The isolation of the bishops

That all relations between the Holy See and the Polish bishops were severed, first by the war and then by the occupation, can be deduced beyond all question by Pius XII's lament to von Ribbentrop on 10 March 1940 that he had 'begged the Berlin government on a number of occasions to allow works of assistance to be carried out in the occupied territories and to permit contact with the bishops on spiritual matters—but in vain'.[38]

Above all we must not forget that not only had the Holy See lost its diplomatic representative in Poland, but the bishops had lost their leader, August Hlond, primate and Archbishop of Gniezno and Poznań[39]—and this only a few months after the death of Cardinal Alexander Kakowski, Archbishop of Warsaw, who had died aged seventy-seven on 30 December 1938.[40] But the primate, Hlond, was not dead. Like the nuncio, Cortesi, he had abandoned his country immediately after the invasion, and sought safety beyond the frontier with all the members of the government; indeed his flight was so hurried that by 18 September he was in Rome.

Three years earlier the *Osservatore Romano* (2–3 November 1936) had described how, during a festival of tribute to him in Poznań on 25 October, General Knoll-Kowaski had presented Hlond with a gift from the officers of the citizens' army with the words: 'We who boast that we carry on the glorious, warlike and Christian traditions of Poland, to You, a true warrior of Christ.'

But the 'true warrior of Christ' had been a bitter disappointment to the Polish people, and his inopportune arrival in Rome surprised Pius XII—who lacked the character of his predecessor and did not despatch him *ipso facto* back to his see, or ask for his cardinal's hat to be returned. True, some years later, he was tougher with another fugitive—Cardinal Tien-Ken-Sin, Archbishop of Pekin—and buried him in exile for years in the United States; but on this first occasion the delicacy of the war situation must have persuaded him to accept the *fait accompli*.[41] At first it was thought that the purpose of the Polish Primate's arrival was a request for mediation with Germany, then he was allowed to speak apocalyptically on Vatican Radio (28 September), which allowed him to burn his boats definitively. So it was hardly surprising that when the Holy See made moves for his return to Poland, Berlin refused to agree.[42]

According to the admissions made by Mgr. Kaczmarek, Bishop of Kielce, during his trial in September 1953,[43] Hlond was sent away from Rome in the spring of 1940 as his presence annoyed the Germanophile section of the Curia. However this may be, it hardly takes much imagination to see that his presence at the Vatican after his talks on the radio and at Castel Gandolfo, and after the publication of his 'reports', was bound to seem offensive and polemical to the Germans and worsen relations between Berlin and the Holy See. Hence Hlond was advised to go to France where he would also be nearer the Polish government in exile, established at Angers. Then when France was overrun by the Germans in her turn, he had no choice but to go into isolation at Lourdes, and later to the Haute-combe convent in Haute Savoie. Arrested by the Germans in 1944,[44] he was liberated by the American army on 8 April 1945.

In his book of documentation, *Pius XII a Polska*, the ambassador Papée published six letters[45] from Pius XII to Cardinal Hlond, all in answer to good wishes sent by the Cardinal for the New Year, his feast-day, or other anniversaries. They are cordial in tone, the more so as they were intended for publication. But the reconciliation only really took place when Hlond flew to Rome after he was set free and was received by the Pope on 13 April 1945. He not only received authorization to return home to Poland, but was given exceptional powers as a *legatus natus*.

Left without a leader, not to mention without a cardinal—for Kakowski's successor in Warsaw, Mgr. Gall, the vicar of the chapter, was a mere archbishop—the Polish bishops looked mainly to the Archbishop of Cracow, Adam Stephen of the princes of Sapieha,[46] both because of the prestige of his birth and the activity he deployed in his diocese, and because Cracow, an ancient bishopric and Metro-politan See, had been made the seat of the German administration of the General Governorship and Frank's residence. Though Sapieha was a modest man, he was also a symbol of patriotism. He had been personally chosen as bishop by Pius X in 1911, and in 1921 had been one of the three Polish bishops who went to Rome in the name of all their brethren to ask Benedict XV to withdraw nuncio Ratti, whom they viewed as Germanophile.

According to Fr. Martini, during the years of occupation he represented 'the figure of a pastor with an intrepid spirit. Defying all dangers and difficulties, he kept in contact with Rome in devious ways.' His palace stood opposite the central office of the Gestapo—the Gestapo which disturbed even Frank's sleep. This in part explains his caution save for what Pius XII called, in a letter of 28 October 1942, 'his secret line of communication with the Apostolic See'.[47]

In Papée's book quoted above there are only four letters from Pius XII to Sapieha, and none of them very interesting. But in Fr. Martini's article there are references to six others of much greater interest; four from the Archbishop of Cracow, i.e. Sapieha (one to Pius XII, two to Cardinal Maglione, and one to the Secretariat of State) and two to him (one from Maglione and one from the Secretariat of State).

We should add in another six letters (all for the jubilees of the recipients) sent by Pius XII to Archbishop Gall, Bishops Fulman, Szelazek and Lukomski, and the Metropolitans of Wilno and Lwów,[48] published by Papée; three exchanged between the Pope and the Metropolitan Szeptyckyi, and two from Maglione to Radonski, with answers. And there we have all the known correspondence between the Holy See and the Polish episcopate during the German occupation.

This correspondence is both scanty in quantity and disappointing in quality. Almost all the letters published by Papée contain praises and good wishes; of the others of a more concrete nature, and turning on matters of religious and political interest, Martini has so far revealed only a few rather lean extracts. Judging by the notes added by the two editors (if such we can call Martini, who only quotes passages bearing on his thesis), we gather that some of these letters reached their destination weeks late, and others when the addressee was absent and the sender had no idea what had happened to him in the meantime.[49]

So we are up against the problem of how intensive these exchanges of letters really were, or, to be more accurate, what channels existed to guarantee communications between the Polish bishops and Rome.

Did these channels exist? What did they consist in? Were they stable or temporary? Were they safe or dangerous? Before we can answer these questions we must distinguish between two periods in the Polish occupation: first, from September 1939 up till the outbreak of war between Germany and Russia (June 1941), and second, during the whole period of the eastern campaign up till Germany's military capitulation (i.e. from June 1941 to the winter of 1944–45). During the first period Poland was practically isolated; whereas during the second it formed the rear hinterland of the huge anti-Soviet front, the territory through which German and German-allied troops passed and had their clearing-stations: among these allies was the Italian expeditionary force, ARMIR.

Even in the first period there was an initial phase of adjustment lasting a few months, which enabled many Poles to flee from the two zones of occupation, and couriers to cross the frontiers. It was during this period that Cardinal Hlond, then in Rome, drew up two reports which he not only submitted to the Pope, but publicized[50] in Italy and a number of other countries during 1940. The text of the first of these reports is our Document A (see above, p. 112 ff.), dated from Rome, 6 January 1940. But it was followed by five other documents (not included here), dated, in the order of their printing, 29 November, 30 December, 31 December, 26 December and 10 December, 1939. Hlond's second report, too, is none other than our Document B (see above, p. 121 ff.), dated from Rome, 30 April 1940. It was entitled *The Religious Situation in the Polish dioceses of Chelm, Katowice, etc., incorporated into the Reich* and was followed by nine short documents, as appendices, written between 11 February and 8 April 1940. As the reader is aware, Hlond's two reports are as sober and unrhetorical as possible, though anything but approximative or uncritical about information obtained.

Document C, whose salient points we have also quoted, is more synthetic and is here and there an account of what the author saw himself, rather than a summary of reports obtained from others; and it goes into far more detail. It came slightly later than the second Hlond report and was rapidly publicized in Rome (entitled *La Situazione della Chiesa cattolica nella Polonia occupata dai tedeschi*) —The Position of the Catholic Church in German-occupied Poland)

and subsequently translated into various languages. Its author was Mgr. Sigismondo Kaczynski, head of the Polish Catholic press office in Warsaw, who left Poland a few months after the end of the war and became chaplain to the President of the Polish Republic in exile.[51]

The Persecution of the Catholic Church in German-occupied Poland, published in London in 1941 with an introduction by Cardinal Hinsley, contains the Hlond and Kaczynski documents, followed by seven other short reports dating from October 1939 to March 1941. These deal with the following subject matter: the events of Czestochowa—Fr. F. M., October 1939; the murder of Fr. Roman Pawlowski of Chocz, November 1939; the hunt for the leaders of Catholic Action in Poznania, 10 November 1939; the persecution of the clergy and people of Bydgoszcz, November 1939; the massacre at Chelm, Fr. D.R., 3 February 1940; the ill-treatment of the clergy in the concentration camps of Radogoszcz (near Łódż) and Opava (Troppau), March 1940; and the sufferings of the Polish clergy, March 1941.

These reports not only give an idea of the plentiful material reaching Rome—either the Secretariat of State (and part of it had been handed over to Vatican Radio for its broadcasts) or Cardinal Hlond and the Polish circles led by him—but also of the network of informants and couriers that was set up from the first moment of the German aggression against Poland so as to keep the Holy See informed about the Church's position in that country.

But by mid-1940 the situation had become much more forbidding. In the early stages Rumania had harboured tens of thousands of Polish refugees, and allowed their passage across the frontier, but now a major corrective came from the Reich in this regard, bringing Rumania to heel at once.[52] Meanwhile the Germans were intensifying the mass transfer of Poles into Germany, and of Germans into the newly-annexed areas, and this somewhat favoured contacts with the Berlin nunciature. In the course of his trial in 1953, Mgr. Kaczmarek admitted that the normal channel for relations between the Polish bishops and the Holy See, after 1940, was number 21 Rauchstrasse in Berlin, i.e. the nunciature. Moreover, as he said, in 1943 Mgr. Orsenigo had been appointed (but not officially, of course) pro-nuncio for the annexed zone and the General Governorship. Relations between the Polish episcopate and the Berlin nuncio were kept going (still according to the valuable revelations made by Mgr. Kaczmarek) by several priests of the Katowice diocese who often received permits to visit Germany—given that the administrator of the diocese was the Archbishop of Breslau (at least this is our view). But apart from this, the Polish Catholic hierarchy had also organized its own direct means of communication with Rome in 1940, and Rome had made use of its own more powerful means for guaranteeing the same thing.

However this may be, it is beyond question that it was the opening-up of the eastern front that restored to the Poles the feeling of being in communication with the world. As is well known, various German-allied countries despatched expeditionary forces against the Soviet Union; not only Italy, but Hungary, Slovakia, Spain, Croatia and so on. The most decisive factor in relations between Poland and the Holy See was the despatch in the summer of 1941 of the Italian expeditionary force. At first it was no more than a large army corps intended to be incorporated into the XIth German army. But after the failure to enter Moscow it rose, in July 1942, to 220,000 men.[53]

To transport the first of these armies to the 'disembarkation point', 225 trains and twenty-five days were required; to transport the second, 900 trains and three months. And if the first didn't touch Poland, but only Hungary and Rumania, the second involved the setting-up of a whole series of provisional headquarters at various points right across Poland. According to the Italian war-correspondent, Alceo Valcini, 'The Italian army passed through Poland so as to take over the Donetz section and reach Poltawa and Stalino. Various halting points were set up on the way, at Cracow, Lwów, Warsaw and Siedlce. The army's equipment, with its cannon, tanks, vehicles, hospital services and munitions passed along a line stretching from Warsaw, through Siedlce and Brest-Litovsk, towards Poltawa. The forces themselves were despatched from Cracow, through Przemys and Lwów to Poltawa'.[54]

Many of these military convoys passed near concentration camps and even the famous death camps. Moreover, when they halted, officers and men were able to make disconcerting discoveries. But the best-informed were those in charge of the halting-points. Valcini, who was correspondent of the *Corriere della Sera*, recounts in his book on war-time Poland how he went to the halting-point in Siedlce in the spring of 1942 to meet the Italian soldiers passing through. But once there, he discovered much more than he expected: for a Neapolitan lieutenant, Roberto Massari, attached to those head-quarters, showed him the city ghetto where he was able to witness the return of Jewish women and children condemned to forced labour. He was also taken to a camp for about 80,000 Russian prisoners four kilometres outside the town. It was forbidden to see the living, but not the dead; or, better, the huge mounds of earth covering the thousands of bodies mown down by hunger or execution squads.

> Europe was unaware that the Soviet prisoners-of-war at Siedlce were shot and thrown naked under the earth by the hundred. . . . The sickening smell from these mounds spread over a radius of two kilometres. Ravens and crows circled around this macabre cemetery. . . .[55]

A chaplain to the hospital trains of the Sovereign Order of Malta wrote:

> . . . in our periodical journeys by Auschwitz, only a few yards separated us from that infamous enclosure. At night we could see the search-lights from the watch-towers slowly turning in a point-less quest for impossible escapers, while the acrid smell from the crematoria reached us in nauseating whiffs. We were hopeless in our impotence and in that of the whole world, and we felt an over-powering need to rebel.[56]

It was all too natural for the Holy See and the Polish bishops to turn their thoughts to exploiting the situation to their advantage—above all by making use of the military chaplains and officers or other ranks in the Italian Expeditionary Force. But usually these were unable to give more than sporadic help. What was needed above all were people who could act as regular intermediaries be-tween Poland and Italy. So far as we can see, the men chosen were the chaplains on army trains, and preferably those on the trains of the Sovereign Order of Malta, for these men were less exposed to discipline and control and had more time at their disposal for special services.

In the recent controversies aroused by Hochhuth's *The Repre-*

sentative, two of these chaplains have come into the open in defence of Pius XII, disclosing their identities and their activities as the Holy See's clandestine 'couriers'. The first was Mgr. Quirino Paganuzzi, originating from the diocese of Piacenza, ex-employee of the Information Office, attached to the Papal Maestro di Camera's office in 1946, and appointed its first secretary in 1950, a post he retains to this day. According to his evidence, he began his secret missions in 1941, meeting, among others, the dean of the Warsaw Chapter, and the Archbishop of Cracow, Sapieha. This is how he describes his meeting with Sapieha (the sense of humour is not entirely felicitous):

A prelate in high authority who, I believe, was in the Secretariat of State concerned with the very delicate sector of Catholic life in martyred Poland (and he performed his task with deeply moving anxiety for the people involved) asked me whether I felt able to deliver some letters and packets to Mgr. Sapieha, containing what we could euphemistically call . . . propaganda. I gladly proffered my service to that cause. . . .

[Here follows a prolix and extravagant account of the help given by a German chaplain, Father Joseph Kaul, in conveying the material to the Archbishop's house in a small army truck, behind a screen of bottles.]

As always, Mgr. Sapieha's welcome was most affectionate, and he was particularly witty about the bottles. However he didn't waste much time in conventionalities. He opened the packets, read them, and commented on them in his pleasant voice. Then he opened the door of the large stove against the wall, started a fire, and threw the papers on to it. All the rest of the material shared the same fate.

On seeing my astonished face, he said in explanation: 'I'm most grateful to the Holy Father . . . no one is more grateful than we Poles for the Pope's interest in us . . . but we have no need of any outward show of the Pope's loving concern for our misfortunes, when it only serves to augment them. . . . But he doesn't know that if I give publicity to these things, and if they are found in my house, the head of every Pole wouldn't be enough for the reprisals Gauleiter Frank will order. . . . It's not just Jews. . . . Here they're killing us all . . . what would be the use of our saying something that everyone knows (that is, that the Pope stands with the Poles)?'

I began talking about the apocolyptic spectacle I had seen: the removal of the Jews from the Cracow ghetto.

'So you can see, Monsignor, how low they've brought us!' the Archbishop said, and went on: 'But the most painful thing of all is that those unfortunates should be left without help, cut off from the whole world. They are dying people deprived of even a comforting word. We can't, we mustn't, say it, for fear of shortening their lives. We're living through the tragedy of those unfortunate people, and none of us is in a position to help them any more. . . . There's no difference between Jews and Poles. They've taken away our bread and our freedom . . . but at least we still have our lives, and with life there's the hope of seeing the end of our calvary'.[57]

The second chaplain was a more typical figure of the Roman world, more humbly and genuinely religious. When he died on 9 September 1964 at the age of eighty, he was surrounded by the scarlet of cardinals, the violet robes of bishops, military uniforms and uniforms of knightly orders, but his real triumph lay in the distress of the common people. Pirro Scavizzi was the priest of the poor and the sick and the confessor of prisoners; but he was also, and above all, the people's 'missionary', indeed the 'imperial missionary', for that adjective implied nothing pompous or worldly but referred to an ancient Roman sodality of parish preachers. It was a title that meant more to him than the fact that he had preached the spiritual exercises to Pope John and his court in the Vatican in 1961.

Setting aside his deep sense of the apostolate, he had outstanding human attractions owing to his instinctive goodness and his astonishing versatility at improvising verses, composing songs, and even making technical inventions that were patented.[58] In the First World War he had been an army chaplain at the front, but at that time he was only thirty. When the Second World War broke out he was nearing sixty, yet managed to get himself put on the list of chaplains for hospital trains nonetheless. He reached the height of happiness when summoned to the Secretariat of State to be entrusted with an exceptionally delicate task.

Like Mgr. Paganuzzi, he began being a 'courier' in 1941, in his capacity 'as chaplain for a big hospital train destined for the Russian front, not only for both the Italian armies, but also for the Nazi army whether at the front or behind the lines.' As regards this activity, it is interesting to see how he expressed himself in May 1964:

When I volunteered as a chaplain at the age of nearly sixty, I obviously had other private aims concerning the Church and its work of salvation. I was enabled to see at close quarters the appalling cruelties of the Hitlerite organizations, especially of the SS, and so to inform the Holy Father. I was enabled to deliver important papal documents in Austria, Germany, Poland and the Ukraine, as well as secret and practical arrangements to defend and help the persecuted, and especially the Jews; for the work of exterminating them was taking its tragic course. My hospital train came to Rome twice to 'unload the hopelessly wounded' and I went to see Pius XII secretly to tell him everything without any preliminary formalities. Before my eyes he wept like a child and prayed like a saint. The second time the hospital train came to Rome I asked his permission to tell him something that would cause him even sharper pain. He agreed with that humble, and edifying, attitude of his.

'Holy Father, I have been talking to Cardinal Innitzer, Archbishop of Vienna, and have witnessed the acts of devastation, the attempts at arson, the defilement of holy images, the window from which the Nazis tried to throw the Archbishop; I've talked with the Archbishop of Cracow, Sapieha, and with other prelates and members of religious orders and people in various positions in the territories occupied by Hitler, and I heard the most tragic words: "We are completely isolated. Mgr. Orsenigo is the only remaining nuncio in all the states occupied by Hitler, but he is unable to get into touch with any of us; a constant watch is kept on him and he feels like a prisoner; no news from Rome reaches us, nor from the Holy Father, even by radio; the slaughter of the Jews and of minorities is still going on, etc." '

The next day he had some millions of highly valuable money handed over to me—he had to scrape the bottom of the barrel, for contributions were no longer coming in, as before—to distribute secretly to the Polish bishops so as to provide for the starving. . . .[59]

It would obviously be unwise to generalize from a few facts and accept such revelations as pure gold. The fact, for instance, that Father Pirro found access to the Pope so easy was largely due to the intimacy established in the past between this good priest and Pius XII and, indeed, the whole of the Pacelli family. Moreover the fact that the hospital train did not invariably go to Rome does not exclude the possibility that, when it stopped in North Italy, Hungary or Germany, he, like other chaplains in similar circumstances, had ways of exchanging material he had received with material to be taken on; this he would do with other couriers or simply with people (nuncios, bishops and so on) who were carrying on liaison work between the various couriers to and from Rome.

In his article on Pius XII and Poland, Fr. Martini quotes the instance of a military chaplain, who may well have been neither Paganuzzi nor Scavizzi, who in December 1942 presented the Secretariat of State with 'a memorandum on all the things he had seen in Poland, and on his *frequent* meetings with Archbishop Sapieha when in Cracow'. And he also refers to an 'Italian layman who was in close touch with the Polish bishops and especially with Monsignor Sapieha', and who in March 1943 appears to have forwarded another 'precise and accurate' memorandum obviously on his own account.[60]

We know from the evidence of F.L., a Polish student then in Rome, that he was asked to deliver to members of the Polish Embassy in the Vatican documents originating in his own country that were handed over to him by Italian officers on leave from the second expeditionary force. On receiving these documents, F.L. would go by arrangement to St. Peter's and stay there before an agreed altar in more or less spontaneous prayer (to avoid the attention of the spies who pullulated there), until such time as he would be approached by one of the would-be recipients, whereupon he would deliver the documents on the spot or be taken to the Secretariat of State so as to hand them over personally (once he was introduced to Cardinal Maglione himself).

It may be that the mysterious lay character mentioned by Fr. Martini was a member of the Royal Italian Mission set up in Cracow in the early winter of 1942 to take the place of the Italian Embassy in Warsaw which was closed in September 1939.[61] Between these two dates there were only temporary missions carried on by Fossombrone, the man who was later put in charge of the Royal Mission at Cracow. Of course the main aim of this Mission was to safeguard the rights of Italian citizens living in the General Governorship; but soon other aims developed, such as the protection of Poles and especially of people persecuted on political or racial grounds.

> The crisis [recounts Luciana Frassati] came to a head when the Reich government established a dateline by which time Jews married to Italians had to leave and go to Italy or else be subjected to the laws applying to all Jews.

The Mission's work was to use this channel to save other persecuted people and to react against the obstructionism of the political police. . . . It was a work without rest, and if we add to this the interventions made on behalf of the clergy and religious organizations, and the help extended to Jews even in the concentration camps, we can get some idea of what the activity involved.

Fossombrone said that neither Frank nor Bühler ever refused their support. I never got a clear idea of what this support consisted in, whereas I was very clear about the work he pointed out to me of an Italian called Cravez in Cracow, and another called Violo in Lwow, who managed to make friends among the Gestapo agents, and thus to take messages, money and food into the Jewish concentration camps. . . .[62]

But as regards this book, the most exciting revelations made by Luciana Frassati concerning Fossombrone deal with (1) his relations with Archbishop Sapieha, (2) his relations with Governor-General Frank, and (3) his activity as an informant.

The first visit made by Fossombrone in Cracow was to the Archbishop of Cracow, Mgr. Sapieha. There is no need to mention the uproar it caused, and the protests from extremist Nazi circles reached as far as the General Governorship. The Italian Mission merely answered by inaugurating the custom of Sunday Mass in the lovely church of Saint Anne.[63]

Still according to Luciana Frassati, Frank had been the main instigator of the setting-up of the Italian Mission, and Fossombrone's great supporter against Ribbentrop's opposition. He had his own reasons:

He planned to visit Rome with the hope of meeting the Holy Father and, under cover of facilitating a *détente* in relations between the Holy See and the Reich, to become promoter for a peace initiative, which he hoped might be announced to the peoples by Easter or, at the latest, by Christmas 1943. Frank thought that the Italian Mission in Cracow would make his connections with Italy notably easier, especially if entrusted to a man in his confidence. That was why he stressed the need for the Mission and the personality of Fossombrone, and as he was then at the beginning of his 'reign' and concessions had to be made to him, Ribbentrop this time had willy nilly to bow his head.[64]

However surprising such plans may seem at first sight, we now know for certain that similar initiatives were being cherished by a moderate number of Nazi and Fascist leaders, especially as they grew more and more preoccupied about the final outcome of the war. As regards Frank, this is what happened:

Meanwhile we were working at full pressure to prepare Frank's journey to Italy. Fossombrone, whom I saw in Rome in December 1942, told me that Frank was full of enthusiasm. He was convinced that if he could manage to talk to the Pope, he would be able to report to Berlin a concrete hope for peace.

With Collalto of the Ministry of National Education, a formula was found to provde a pretext for bringing Frank to Italy: a visit to the University of Modena, of which he was a doctor *honoris causa*, and to the University of Ferrara. In the spring of 1943, in April to be exact, all was ready for the journey: the saloon coach, which was to be attached to the 8 p.m. train for Vienna, was already waiting at Cracow station when, a few hours before the departure, Fossombrone was summoned to the Burg and Frank told him that he had received a communication from Ribbentrop in Berlin suspending the Governor-General's journey to Italy 'for reasons inherent in the general situation'.[65]

As for Fossombrone's activities as informant, Luciana Frassati puts the matter laconically:

Moreover Fossombrone was held guilty [by the Gestapo whose main accusation was of connivance with Frank in protecting the Jews despite Hitler's precise orders] of despatching to Rome alarmist accounts about the internal situation in Poland and what went on behind the front.[66]

It would not be all that surprising if, besides the official accounts for the Italian Foreign Office, Fossombrone sent other confidential accounts to the Vatican, with which he must have been in contact through Luciana Frassati at least, to prepare the way for Frank's visit; nor if the Italian Mission in Poland was sending through suitable channels to the Holy See news, appeals and memoranda on behalf of Mgr. Sapieha, among others. Anyway, such channels, if they existed, had a relatively short life and only lasted for a year and a half. On 9 September, 1943, that is the day after the Italian armistice, Fossombrone 'was publicly arrested by an SS colonel at Cracow station on his way back from an official visit to Lwów'.[67] And with his arrest the Italian Mission to the General Governorship came to an end.

In the last few pages we have made plentiful use of Luciana Frassati's evidence. But Signora Luciana Frassati Gowronski was more than a witness of events in Poland; she played a substantial part in the fortunes of her adopted country. She was the daughter of the senator, Alfredo Frassati (founder and owner of *La Stampa*, the Turin daily, as well as Giolitti's ambassador in Berlin from 1920 to 1922, and a staunch anti-Fascist).[68] She married the Polish diplomat, Gowronski, and lived first in Warsaw, then, from 1933 to 1938, in Vienna, where her husband was ambassador. The German aggression against Poland found her in Italy. But she was anxious to get back to Warsaw to join her children, and was able to do so on 14 November, 1939, and stayed there till the end of December. She subsequently managed to pay a number of visits to Poland: in 1940 (May and the autumn), 1941 (summer, after the outbreak of the Russian campaign) and 1942 (January, February, August and September).

All these journeys involved political meetings and missions: particularly those in 1940, during the first of which she met General Sikorski in Paris; he was the head of the Polish government in exile and managed to persuade her to take a suitcase full of złotys to Poland, to be distributed in various centres of the resistance before the registration date of 1 February laid down by the Germans with the aim of preventing an influx back into the country of large reserves transferred abroad by the emigré government. The second of the 1940 trips was determined by the arrival in Italy of Watys (the pseudonym used by Stanislaw Stoczewski) who was sent by the Sikorski government to try to bring together the various Polish parties, and organize the 'clandestine State' to which we shall refer later. Signora Frassati deputized for him in part.

In the course of her subsequent visits to Poland, she was able to protect various people whose lives were in danger and get them to safety; Piasecki, for instance, who was later to become the controversial leader of Polish Catholic progressivism and founder of the Pax association; later, through Mussolini's direct intervention, he was saved from the death penalty to which he had been sentenced by the Germans; and General Sikorski's wife, whom she took to Italy as her children's nurse. But we must confine ourselves to her activities 'pro Papa', as she called them in Chapter 19 of her book.

On the day I first left for Poland, 14 November 1939, Cardinal Hlond's secretary met me at the station with letters from his master addressed to various other prelates who had stayed behind in Poland.[69]

When she later returned to Rome she didn't see Cardinal Hlond, for he had already left for France, but she used to call on Fr. Ledochowski, the General of the Jesuits, who was a Polish aristocrat.[71] In one of her talks with him she found that he agreed with her that Frank was not so ferocious as he was said to be. 'Once he himself warned two Jesuits, who had just arrived in Cracow, that they were on the point of being arrested, and put a car at their disposal so that they could get back to the frontier at once'.[72]

But even before she called on Fr. Ledochowski, Signora Frassati used to drop in at the Secretariat of State to report to Mgr. Montini. She began doing this after having made the acquaintance of Fr. Biagio Marabotto, a member of the Don Orione religious order, who was sent to Poland in 1925, only five years after his ordination, and had remained there ever since.

> I learnt from him a great deal about the hardships and fate of the Catholic clergy in Poland, and he begged me to tell this to Mgr. Montini so that the Vatican should be informed and should make all possible provision. Hence, every time I returned I hurried to report to the Secretariat of State all the young priest had told me: owing to his wealth of faith and enthusiasm he was becoming more and more a legendary figure in Warsaw. Mgr. Montini, on his side, now began entrusting me with messages and letters for Poland, and begged me to undertake to find out the answers and opinions of the Polish clergy.[73]

Mgr. Montini was not the only person Signora Frassati met at the Secretariat of State. John XXIII's future Secretary of State, Mgr. Tardini, entrusted her with a task pretty unusual for a woman: which was, 'to take the investiture with *omnes facultates episcopi residentialis* to the bishop acting for Archbishop Gall of Warsaw after his death'.

> I left armed with a note specifying my task as a spokeswoman so that I would not cause confusion on my arrival in Warsaw. Thus the 79-year-old Bishop Szlagowski was able to take over the functions of the late Gall as vice-vicar of the chapter, and he carried out his work with outstanding energy and dignity.[74]

But, as we shall see, it was Mgr. Montini who arranged a private audience with Pius XII for Signora Frassati.

In the course of her various journeyings across Germany and Poland, Signora Frassati met the nuncio Orsenigo at least once, and she met Archbishop Sapieha frequently, as well as Archbishop Gall of Warsaw, his successor Szlagowski, and numerous other prelates and priests.

Amongst the latter we must also include Mgr. Gawlina, the army bishop who was wounded in September 1939, but managed to join the Polish army in France and then in England. Later, in the summer of 1941, still in an army bishop's uniform, he reached the Russo-Chinese frontier where the Polish army was grouping, and accompanied it to the Middle East and thence to Italy. Signora Frassati found herself travelling with him on the very train to which General Sikorski had assigned her with her famous suitcase of złotys. Mgr. Gawlina had a similar cargo, but he was unable to deliver it personally in his country.[75]

So Signora Frassati figures in our inquiry as an exceptional case, though certainly not the only one, of someone whose services could be used repeatedly by the Holy See and the Polish bishops (and not only them) so as to keep in contact. Her position as an Italian married to a Pole, the high social rank of her family and its network of aristocratic and political connections (these included von Papen) enabled her to travel without let or hindrance. Of course there was a risk, but there was also a margin of safety. She was ready, indeed eager, to take up delicate and complex assignments, and there can be no challenging her standard as a witness.

Finally, we must not forget the equally eloquent evidence of the refugees from Poland who managed to reach Italy and Rome. Mgr. Walerian Meystowicz, consultant canonist during the war for the Polish embassy to the Holy See, and now president of the Roman Institute for Polish historical studies, has recently stated that during the German occupation of Rome—that is, between 8 September 1943 and 4 June 1944—'a few Jews, escaped from concentration camps in Poland, reached the Vatican and came to tell me their terrifying news. Generally speaking, they were sole survivors from whole families who had been murdered'.[76] But this sort of thing had certainly also happened in the preceding years, perhaps more often and perhaps not only Jews.

4. The Holy See's relations with the Polish Government in Exile

As is well known, when the Germans occupied Poland they failed to capture the government or the army high command. The government, i.e. the President of the Republic, Moscicki, the Prime Minister, Slavoj Skladkowski, the Foreign Minister, Beck, and the rest of the cabinet, crossed the Rumanian frontier at Kuty on 17 September. They were followed next day by Marshal Smigly-Rydz. But as the government would be incapable of any political act once outside the national territory, President Moscicki made a special order appointing his successor, Wladislaw Raczkiewicz, before leaving the country. In spite of this he did not resign until September 30, the day the Polish ambassador in Paris announced that Raczkiewicz was the new president and that he had just witnessed him taking the oath as such, in the presence of the new commander-in-chief, General Sikorski, and others. The first act of the new president was to decree the retirement of the members of the Skladkowski cabinet and to appoint a ministry of national union and defence under the presidency of Sikorski.

The new government fixed its headquarters at Angers (north-west France) and immediately began organizing the army abroad and resistance at home. A few months later, owing to the collapse of France, it had to move to London.

One of the early decisions of the Angers government was to confirm Dr. Casimir Papée as Polish ambassador to the Holy See [76 bis]— he had first presented his credentials to Pius XII on 14 July 1939. Papée was an outstanding Polish diplomat with a brilliant career behind him at, amongst other places, the Hague, Berlin, Copenhagen and, finally, Prague. Eight months later, when Italy entered the war, he took refuge in the Vatican. He remained there until the liberation of Rome in June 1944.

Meanwhile the Holy See seemed to be in no hurry to renew the credentials of the former nuncio in Warsaw, Mgr. Cortesi, to the new government—he stayed on in Rumania helping Polish refugees.[77] But, as the Polish government kept up its insistence, on 15 January 1940 the Holy See appointed Mgr. Pacini, an attaché at the Vichy nunciature,[78] as interim chargé d'affaires at Angers. When the Polish government moved to London, Mgr. Pacini stayed on in Vichy, and the task of 'keeping in contact' with the Polish government was entrusted to the Apostolic Delegate to Great Britain, Mgr. Godfrey. It was only after yet further pressure from the Polish government, and only in the spring of 1943, that the Holy See appointed Mgr. Godfrey as chargé d'affaires. He had no successor.[79]

Hence active relations between the Holy See and the Polish government depended on the ambassador in Rome, Casimir Papée. It was probably because it had such a trusted man in Rome that the Vatican side-stepped appointing a representative in London—in any case such a representative would have had little to do. In *Pius XII a Polska*, Papée published ten documents or texts of letters between Pius XII and President Raczkiewicz. Unfortunately more than half of them date from the last year of the war and are now of secondary interest. Moreover one suspects that communications dealing with the first war years were only published in part.[80]

Once established in Angers, the Polish Foreign Ministry announced that it would publish a White Book and a Black Book on 20 February 1940. The White Book merely dealt with documents on German war guilt. The Black Book was divided into two parts, the first dealing with German atrocities during the *Blitzkrieg*, the second with those committed subsequently. Originally the Polish government intended to publish only one book, but the accumulation of statements and documentation, the importance of the facts, and the world-wide indignation aroused by the news from various fronts, persuaded it to denounce what 'was unprecedented in any war'. It would be no easy task to keep track of all the books published by the Polish government in exile from 20 February onwards.[81]

Of course the Germans were not behindhand in forestalling, or reacting to, this propaganda. We have already seen how von Ribbentrop presented Cardinal Maglione with a book for the Pope dealing with Polish crimes. This was almost certainly the book published by the Nazis on the preceding 14 February, dealing with Polish terrorism against German aliens in the Posen 'corridor' and Upper Eastern Silesia immediately after the First World War; it also recalled how in 1931 the Warsaw Central Institute of Statistics had stated that since 1919 a million Germans had left Poland.

This method of producing official 'books' was not only neutralized by counter-propaganda: it was also too slow. The system of presenting memoranda through diplomatic channels was more flexible and timely and they could always be brought up to date. They drew attention to sensational news and also presented more considered, over-all statements.

To indicate how Papée approached the Vatican Secretariat of State, we may quote a note of acknowledgment drawn up by Cardinal Maglione on 9 December 1941:

I have received your note of 21 November together with the enclosure—the new memorandum on the situation in occupied Poland based on information you have received. I have read this document with deep interest and am grateful to you for sending it. As you well know—as I have often told you in the course of this year—the Holy See has done all it possibly can in both the material and spiritual fields to help the bishops in Poland and, through them, the Poles in their distress. The Holy See intends to carry on this good work with all the means at its disposal.[82]

The note clearly refers to other memoranda provided by Papée, and to many *viva voce* conversations between Papée and the Cardinal Secretary of State about the situation in Poland. In the following year, as we shall see, the Polish ambassador took similar steps on an even more intensive scale.

Yet the relations between the Polish government in exile and the Holy See were not always idyllic. More than once they passed through periods of tension. These must be ascribed in part to the discontent of the Poles with Pius XII's 'silence', and in part to certain provisions made by the Holy See for the Polish Church which the Polish government viewed as unendurable acts of appeasement to the occupying authorities, and blatant violations of the 1925 Concordat.

A period of tension occurred after the appointment of Fr. Hilarius Breitinger, a Franciscan, as Apostolic Administrator for the German people in the parts of Eastern Poland incorporated into the Reich. The reader of Cardinal Hlond's two documents, which we have called A and B, has been able to see that in the annexed Polish provinces the process of Germanization involved (a) the gradual elimination of Poles whose place was taken by German populations moved in from elsewhere—the Baltic states, South Tyrol, etc.; and (b), as regards religious administration, the substitution of Polish ecclesiastical structures by those of the new occupants. With this second end in view the German authorities—having no illusions that they would find it easy to induce the Holy See to back their plans—decided to confront Rome with a *fait accompli,* i.e. the paralysis of the Polish framework, the elimination of bishops who could not be brought to heel, and the retention of those who were more flexible—though with limited powers.

The Holy See protested and stuck to its guns, trying, meanwhile, to take cover. It handed over the administration of the diocese of Chełmno to the Bishop of Danzig, and that of Katowice to the Archbishop of Breslau. Had such appointments failed to provoke protests from the Polish government it would have been amazing; but on this point we lack appropriate documents. Yet these appointments were obviously provisional, as the men involved were ordinaries of other sees.[83] In the case of Fr. Breitinger, whose only function lay in carrying out the tasks to which he had been freshly and controversially appointed, there was a new factor which, even worse, introduced an official division, and, so to speak, a dichotomy in the Church in Polish territory. It set a German Church side by side with a Polish Church and, in the circumstances, they could hardly co-exist in friendship.

The Polish government[84] first ordered its ambassador to ask for the situation to be clarified. When it obtained no satisfactory result, it ordered him to make a formal protest. Here we have two accounts on his activities given by Papée to his Minister for Foreign Affairs, and the text of his note of protest to Cardinal Maglione:[85]

Embassy of the Polish Republic
to the Holy See
N. 122/SA/237   SECRET
The Vatican, 12 October 1942

> To his Excellency the Minister for Foreign
> Affairs of the Polish Republic, London.

On the 9th of this month, immediately after the Cardinal Secretary of State's return from his holiday, I had a conversation with him about the appointment of Fr. Breitinger as Apostolic Administrator for the German population in the Warthegau area.
I told Cardinal Maglione that I had called to ask for guaranteed

information on these appointments which, at first sight, seem opposed to the principle of Church unity and to the already-established hierarchy, not to mention that they are difficult to justify in view of the Concordat between the Holy See and Poland. According to my instructions, it seems that the government of the Polish Republic feels bitter astonishment at this appointment; it is difficult to understand and difficult not to fear that it may create a precedent for the future.

The Cardinal Secretary of State began by declaring that, in this case, the Church has suffered more harm than the Polish government. The decisions made by the German authorities which oblige religious associations to register themselves, and bring into being two separate associations, one German and the other Polish, are a severe blow to the interests of the Catholic Church. It was only to save what still remained of religious life that the Holy See decided—after much debate—to conform with this provision. For it subverts the previously-established diocesan divisions and deals a blow to the inner unity of the Church. However, there was no escaping from this situation. The *salus animarum* demanded this last sacrifice, and the *summa necessitas* justifies and explains it. The decision to appoint Father Breitinger is only a matter of fact for the Holy See and in no way alters the juridical state of affairs. As before, the division of the Warthegau into dioceses is in agreement with the stipulations of the Concordat, and where there are episcopal ordinaries they have full jurisdiction. Where there are no ordinaries, Bishop Dymek[86] has received special powers. As the decision has been taken under duress, it has no juridical value for the Holy See; Bishop Dymek has the right, within the limits of his jurisdiction, to concern himself with the German Catholics, though this right is a secret. I insist on emphasizing—the Cardinal went on—that the decision taken under duress in no way invalidates the stipulation of the Concordat which the Holy See views as still existing and binding. Moreover, should the present situation continue, religious life in the Warthegau areas would have to go into the catacombs.

I answered that I was aware of the difficult situation of the Church in Western Poland and that I doubted whether the decision the Cardinal was speaking of could be fruitful. The more so as the decision seemed to be contrary to the Concordat. In addition it involved throwing over the principles that the Holy See had always kept to in similar situations. The power of the Ordinary is normally transferred by himself to the Vicar-General or eventually to other persons. In this way dioceses manage their own business and carry on in spite of external persecution so as to re-emerge automatically even after many years, as happened in the case of the Kamieniec diocese. I was very doubtful whether the present compromise would be of any use in helping the Polish Church and I feared that it might set a precedent. Surely it would have been better to say *Non possumus*?

At this point Cardinal Maglione answered with great emphasis:

'What we did, we did at the request of the local Polish clergy. Believe me, there was no other way to save what remained of religious life in Warthegau. Juridically speaking, we regard the Concordat as unbroken. Inform your government that we are as much the victims of German persecution as it is.'

I took note of the declaration concerning the validity of the Concordat. Nevertheless, in view of the vast extent of the persecution of the Church in Poland, could not the Holy Father speak out in defence of the country?

Cardinal Maglione answered with great liveliness and emphasis as follows:

'We have done our whole duty and whatever was necessary. The Holy Father has all the documentation. For the moment we must wait and not raise this question again just now.'

From this I was given to understand that the Secretary of State has done everything possible and that the matter is now in the hands of the Pope. My inclination is to interpret his statement in that way, especially in view of other information I have received. This seems to indicate that both within the Secretariat of State and outside it there are forces at work to get the Pope to take a stand. Apart from that, here we are unquestionably dealing with a 'raw nerve' deriving from the Pope's psychology.

(C. Papée's signature follows).

Embassy of the Polish Republic
to the Holy See
The Vatican, 18 Nov. '42   SECRET
N. 122/SA/262
1 enclosure N. 122/SA/262

To the Minister for Foreign Affairs
of the Republic of Poland, London.

Following orders received through other channels on the 12th instant, I have handed to the Cardinal Secretary of State the note of protest herewith appended.

I have already informed you of the long *entretien* I had with

Cardinal Maglione on 9 October (report N. 122/SA/237 of 12 October) concerning the appointment of Father Breitinger and the double ecclesiastical administration in the Warthegau region. We both remained in our respective positions. The fact that the Polish government has protested has made a deep impression on the Cardinal. He told me with some embarrassment that he would study the note and would give me an answer. He added that the Holy See in no way ceases to recognize the validity of the Concordat, but that the two appointments, of Bishop Dymek and Fr. Breitinger, were necessary 'for the good of souls'.

I answered that I was unable to share his opinion and that I reserved the right to raise the question again when the Cardinal had studied the note.

My meeting with Mgr. Montini enabled me to observe that the fact of the protest has caused perplexity at the Vatican. However, our note was absolutely necessary: the importance and the arguments of the note go beyond its concrete limits and the note constitutes *de facto* a criticism of the whole 'Polish' policy of the Vatican and of its pliability and weakness towards the German occupiers.

(Papée's signature follows).

Enclosure to the letter to the Minister
for Foreign Affairs
of 10 December 1942
translated from French
N. 122/SA/262

Most Reverend Eminence,

My government instructs me to inform Your Eminence that it is in possession of information showing that the administration of the ecclesiastical affairs of the German Catholics living in a part of Poland—to be exact, the territory which the occupiers call the Warthegau—has been entrusted to Fr. Breitinger, while Polish ecclesiastical affairs—in this same territory—have been entrusted by the Holy See to the Vicar-General of his Eminence Cardinal Hlond, of the Archdiocese of Poznań, namely his Excellency Mgr. Bishop Dymek, who is deprived of freedom and lives in isolation in his own house. These arrangements of the Holy See are transforming the Catholic hierarchy in the territory of the Archdiocese of Gniezno and Poznań, and in part of the neighbouring dioceses, into a new and provisional ecclesiastical organization. My government cannot view these changes as being in accord with article 9 of the Concordat between the Vatican and Poland.

The fact that latest decisions of the Holy See subordinate certain churches of the Archdiocese of Gniezno and Poznań and of other dioceses to the jurisdiction of Fr. Breitinger, in his new office, is contrary to article 23 of the same Concordat.

The Polish government is aware that the occupying authorities in Western Poland have ordered the creation of 'religious associations', on which they have conferred a juridical personality denied to the juridical ecclesiastical personalities recognized by the Concordat and Polish law. The same authorities have forbidden Poles to enter churches reserved to Germans.

The situation arising from these ordinances, by which the religious affairs of Poles have been entrusted to his Excellency Bishop Dymek, and the religious affairs of Germans to Fr. Breitinger, causes people to believe that the Apostolic See accepts, or at least takes tacit cognizance of, these illegal decisions. This obliges the Polish government to place a formal protest in the hands of Your most Reverend Eminence.

My government sorrowfully declares that such acceptance is arousing a strong reaction among Poles both abroad and in the country itself, which latter have no possibility of speaking freely, and are suffering because their churches have been taken away from them and given to foreign Catholics for unknown reasons.

My government sees it as a duty to state that this new form of religious organization accepted by the Holy See is wounding to the feelings of loyalty towards ancient forms, sometimes a thousand years old.

At the same time, the fact of separating Poles from other Catholics in the churches can only constitute a threat to increase certain centrifugal tendencies; these tendencies might be based on exaggerated nationalism and so make a return to the principles of Catholic unity more difficult.

My government holds the view that acceptance of the occupation forces' illegal decisions will in no way alter German behaviour towards the Church in Poland; in consequence it should be judged as a useless abandonment of the existing principles. My government is convinced that only a public and formal protest could strengthen these principles and preserve the sentiments that the Poles have always cherished towards the Apostolic See.

My government wishes to emphasize that it has been led to draw up the foregoing solely with the aim of preserving intact the loyalty of the nation it represents to the Church's cause; furthermore it wishes to put up effective opposition to those tendencies aimed at preventing a harmonious collaboration between Church and State after the war.

Please accept, etc., etc.

What should be our opinion about these two opposing points of view? Who was right? Was the Concordat really violated? The articles quoted by Papée say:

Article IX. No part of the Republic of Poland shall be under the jurisdiction of a bishop whose see lies outside the frontiers of the Polish State. . . .

The Holy See will not undertake any modification of the hierarchy as here set out, nor of the boundaries of the [ecclesiastical] provinces or dioceses, without previous agreement with the Polish government, save for minor rectifications of boundaries required for the good of souls.

Article XXIII. No change in the language used in dioceses of Latin language, either in preaching, prayers, supplementary prayers and courses [of religious instruction], except for those of the sacred sciences in the seminaries, shall be made without special authorization granted by the Bishops' Conference of Latin rite.[87]

Apart from this last article, whose tacit violation can hardly be denied, all the violations of the preceding article are debatable under one aspect or another. For instance, Archbishop Bertram obviously had his see outside Polish territory, but his jurisdiction over the diocese of Katowice was not that of an 'ordinary'. Similarly, in themselves, the provisions made by the Holy See entailed no change in the Polish Catholic hierarchy of Latin rite, and it would be excessive to hold them responsible for concrete upheavals to the detriment of the country's ecclesiastical boundaries. Fr. Breitinger's jurisdiction fell under the established Polish order without disturbing it as it was in some sense supra-territorial and purely personal.

When, in September 1945, the first post-war Communist Polish government denounced the Concordat and in substance appealed to the very arguments Papée had put forward, the *Osservatore Romano* replied as follows:

(a) In the two cases referred to, and in view of the extreme spiritual needs of the faithful, the Holy See, despite its concern not to contravene the Concordat, made provisions with the appointment of Apostolic Administrators *ad nutum Sanctae Sedis* rather than bishops and archbishops, leaving the dioceses in the hands of their respective bishops, even if, owing to exceptional circumstances, they were far from their residences or prevented from carrying out their ministry.

(b) The aforesaid provision 'in no way violates any principle or regulation of the Concordat because, with the precise intention of providing for exceptional circumstances, the Holy See does not admit that Concordats—and hence the one with Poland—may fix rules and limits in the appointment of Apostolic Administrators'.

(c) This matter deals with provisions outside the rules of Concordats, and in the system of Concordats 'acceptance' or 'recognition' is never asked for save through official channels. . . .[88]

Yet is is obvious that some anomaly had arisen in the Polish Church transcending any convincing juridical justification. But the facts were less serious in themselves than as an indication of the power over the Church achieved by the German *fait accompli*; not to mention that her subjection to Nazi impositions involved the sacrifice not only of her own rights (for all the nobility of the cause: the good of souls) but, much more, the rights of the Polish nation. And it was precisely this point that Papée noted, with a lucidity and harshness very unlike, alas, the tone of 'servile eulogy' he adopted later in *Pius XII a Polska*.

It only remains for us to note the dates of this diplomatic episode —immediately after the various steps taken during 1942, whether by the Polish or other governments, to urge the Holy See to make an open and solemn protest—to convince ourselves that, in a certain sense, it links up with the previous ones, and reveals itself as a small revenge for the pertinacious No of the Vatican.

5. The Holy See's relations with the clandestine Polish Government (the 'Delegatura')

As we have already seen, the Polish government in London had an opposite number in Poland itself, so it is permissible to ask whether the Holy See was also in some contact with the latter.

It took some time for this opposite number to come into being.[89] It was originally set up even before the fall of Warsaw by order of the Minister of Defence, Marshal Smigly-Rydz, when the SZP (*Sluzba Zwyciestwu Polski*—the Service for the Victory of Poland) was set up to dominate the many secret military organizations. The aim of the

SZP was to bring together the military and political forces, and it would have succeeded in this had not Sikorski unexpectedly set up from France in November 1939 the ZWZ (*Zwiazek Walki Zbrojnej—* Union for armed struggle) whose aims were purely military.

The rivalry between the two organizations would have been fatal, and to obviate it Colonel Stefan Rovecki put forward a plan to unite all the clandestine forces.[90] There were many disagreements, but in the end concord prevailed and the new leader of the clandestine movement, Cyril Ratajski, was chosen. He died a natural death in 1943.

A secret army was organized and shortly afterwards, in the following May, came the foundation of the *Gwardia Ludowa* (the People's Guard), a left-wing military organization which, in April 1943, emerged as the *Armia Ludowa* or A.L.—the People's Army. In 1944, on St. Sylvester's night, this latter proclaimed itself to be immediately and henceforward the sole legislative body representing the national struggle.

But these events have no bearing on our investigation. For the Holy See would never have entered into relations with what later became the Lublin Committee—decisively left wing and under the protection of Moscow. The only relations the Vatican could establish were with the representatives of the emigré government in London, i.e. the 'Delegatura'. And not, of course, official relations at that, these being already in operation with the emigré government. But was the Delegatura favourable to the Church? The following account by Luciana Frassati leaves us in doubt:

A conversation I had with a distinguished Polish prelate enabled me to see how there was a movement in full development in the country in opposition to the Vatican City's work of help by means of trainloads of provisions sent through Italy and Hungary: a movement political in character and sponsored by the Delegatura which, through its ministers and especially the Minister of Education, was exercising anti-papal action on the masses.

The close association between the Delegatura and the ZWZ put the Catholic Church in difficulties in the struggle, especially owing to the lack of a single programme and a single tactical plan, and principally owing to an almost total lack of means.

The majority of the serious Catholic organizations, after a certain period of independent activity, had fallen to pieces owing to financial difficulties, and were obliged to join up with the larger network of the ZWZ. On the other hand it was impossible to blame those brave people who had set out on the path of resistance to the oppressor and of ruthless struggle, and who didn't want to withdraw and be condemned to inaction.

Hence the movements that were basically Catholic and directly under the control of men loyal to the Church were constantly decreasing to the profit of less orthodox movements. 'It's no good,' said the prelate; 'in the struggle for one's life and one's country, people inevitably abandon those who have no money for those who have.'

Polish opinion hostile to the work of the Vatican was always on the increase, and people remembered with annoyance and reproach the sums spent to the profit of the Germans in the days of the plebiscite in Upper Silesia. So the unfavourable reaction increased with the loss of sympathy for the Holy Father who, in Polish eyes, should have sent money to support the active propaganda of the priests and the Catholic youth movements. Many of these young people had set up political organizations, some were even supported by armed bands, and were showing a will to equate their vision of a new Poland with the Christian ideology. These groups should have been helped in a full and continuous way until a common front could have been set up able to oppose the disintegrating and anti-Catholic pressure on the masses by the Delegatura and the ZWZ. For the latter had set up a Catholic branch known as *Front Odrodzenia Polski* [Front for the Rebirth of Poland] whose members, in good or bad faith, lacked any serious dogmatic foundation. Their leaflets, entirely financed by the ZWZ, were crammed with false ideological propositions whose frank heresies made them really dangerous.

My interlocutor quoted a few extracts which justified distrust of the whole movement. . . . The priest was very depressed and told me he had started an intense battle against these statements. But though his campaign seemed simple and just in appearance, in practice it was very hard-going by reason of the strange opposition, indirect though it was, brought by various Catholic authorities, including bishops and archbishops, as well as superiors of religious orders and communities. An active priest who was known for his pro-papal zeal and his tenacious and unbending opposition to these half-heresies, was transferred without explanation from Warsaw into the country. . . . Yet he did not give up: profiting by the peace and solitude of the country, he had written a violent pamphlet defending the Holy Father. And as he intended to print

10,000 copies of it, he was desperately looking around for the necessary money.

The distinguished prelate ended the conversation by begging me to inform Rome of these matters. He emphasized that the situation was worse in the country than in the towns, for in the towns the Catholics preserved many of their former attitudes. 'The country must be saved,' he said, 'because the peasants are specially subject to anti-Catholic influences, above all Communist ones.'[92]

Signora Frassati's interlocutor was in all likelihood an intransigent churchman with the typical clerical mentality of those who smell out dangers and heresies in everything lacking the seal of ecclesiastical leadership. Indeed he was so radical that he was not afraid to accuse even archbishops and bishops of treachery or laxness. This is why his evidence is interesting, for it shows that friction existed in the Catholic front even in such grave moments for Poland.

But, to go back to the Delegatura, it is obvious that among its members secular ideas were flourishing and opinions of every kind were to be found. Above all it is obvious that it reflected the general resentment—shared by the London government—concerning the Pope's evasive behaviour. But to say this is a far cry from maintaining that it was hostile to the Church and the Holy See. In its organizations Catholics and even priests (as we shall see) worked side by side with non-clericals of every shade of opinion, serving their country in the most coherent loyalty to their own ideology.

However this may be, the important fact is that at a given moment the Delegatura had no hesitation in providing the Holy See with all the religious news concerning the situation in occupied Poland gathered by its Office of Information and Political Propaganda, set up initially by the High Army Command and then Passing to its dependencies.

From November 1940 until the end of the war the director of this Office was Colonel Jan Rzepecki, now a member of the Department of History in the Polish Academy of Sciences. He remained loyal to his political convictions to the end, fighting against the Communists and backing the opposition movement to the new regime, until finally he was condemned to death. Set free as a result of an internal initiative for pacification, he continued to remain faithful to his ideals. His work in the Department of History is to examine wartime documents and sift the false or falsified material from the authentic, and help in interpreting and evaluating it.

It was from him personally[93] that we learnt what we have just said about the relations between the Delegatura and the Vatican, which were hitherto unknown. From him, too, we collected all the information on the activities of his Office that we are now going to deal with. When he first agreed to his appointment as director it only had two sections: political information and political studies (concerning the situation in occupied Poland, needless to say). Subsequently he enlarged it to include many other matters: organization, control, propaganda, the press, distribution of literature, and destructive propaganda in German. The teams composing it were very highly qualified: the Office for studies, for instance, made use of 90 per cent of the professors of history from Polish universities.

As this was the only office in a position to keep the London government informed, he was concerned with almost everything that happened in Poland or served the aims of the resistance: hence the enormous variety and range of his reports. Obviously his primary concern was military reports. These he despatched to London by radio (there were a hundred transmitters scattered over the country with this end in view). The others were microfilmed and entrusted to special messengers who got to London through Turkey or Sweden with halts in other neutral countries.

Every week his organization provided a report on espionage—in code—and every month a longer report on the same subject covering some thousand-odd pages of microfilm. The reports on the clandestine press were first fortnightly, then weekly. There was also a fortnightly report on 'German terrorism'. As can be imagined, this last always devoted some space to the persecution of the clergy and of the Church in general. Moreover, communiqués would sometimes reach London consisting of whole texts of certain documents regarded as particularly important (for instance, the decree on the requisition of church bells) or hard to come by (such as the speeches of Mgr. von Galen, Bishop of Munster, against the Nazi persecution of the Church and against euthanasia).

It was towards the end of 1941 or the beginning of 1942 that Rzepecki received orders to prepare special reports on the situation of the Church in Poland to be got through to the Vatican. Initially they were sent to the chaplain-in-chief of the ZWZ (and later to *Armia Krajowa*) whose task it was to forward them to Rome *per via propria*. The editor directly responsible for these reports was always the same man. The reports were drawn up every fortnight or, at the most, every month. They were always carefully drafted in regular form until the Warsaw insurrection.

As it lay outside his province, Rzepecki was unaware of the so-called 'channel of the clergy' or 'of the bishops' in the direction of Rome. Only those of the clergy who were ultimately responsible could say whether the contents of the reports handed over to the chaplain-in-chief of the A.K. arrived at the Vatican in their original state. At all events it is permissible to doubt whether all the material on religious affairs gathered or put together by the experts in Rzepecki's office arrived in Rome. The political behaviour of the clergy and the episcopate was continually being sounded and studied in the office. Now it is doubtless possible that some of these soundings, for special and rather obvious reasons, were sent to Rome, but the greater number of them must have been held exclusively at the disposal of the government and the Delegatura. As for the reports on the clandestine press, which frequently discussed the Vatican's attitude to Poland, we are unable to express an opinion as to whether they arrived in Rome unless we could delve into the Archives of the Secretariat of State. It was obviously urgent to the Delegatura and the Polish government in London that they should arrive, but can we say the same of the bishops?

A final doubt arises over the illustrations of German atrocities. The Office had a considerable number of cells devoted to photographing Nazi terrorism: one of them, for instance, was set up by the famous scenario-writer Andre Pronaszko and his wife. But it also happened that Polish photographers, to whom the Germans brought their films to be developed, would convey some of this material to the Office (it was in this way, for instance, that the hair-raising pictures of several episodes of cannibalism through hunger in concentration camps emerged—some sadistic German soldier or officer had thought it amusing to take photographs). It might seem natural to suppose that some of this material also reached the Vatican; but whether it did or not, and though it has its value, it is essentially accessory material and less persuasive, for it can easily be faked with clever trickery and touching-up.

Some part, infinitesimal though it may be, of the material collected and studied by this Office can now be found and consulted at the Archives of the Historical Section of the Party (*Wydzial Historii Partii, Archiwum*) at 18–20 Gomoslawska Street, Warsaw. This material comes partly from the Delegatura and partly from private collaborators. During the occupation it was hidden and then, but only in part, came to light after the end of the war from highly improbable hiding-places. It is divided into two groups:

1. Documents of the Delegatura of the Government of the Republic of Poland [*Delegatura Rzadu R.P. na Kraj*: abbreviation D.R.R.P.] from and for the government in London: microfilmed telegrams and reports. Of these there are 357 folders contained in ten yards of shelving.

2. Documents of the Headquarters of the National Army [*Armia Krajowa—Komanda Glowba*: abbreviation A.K.K.G.], dealing only in reports for the Information and Propaganda Office. About 300 folders in some seven yards of shelving.

Naturally, what concerns the Church and religious persecution is only a small part. And not always easy to interpret. For besides the material being almost always in code (consult the photographs), the information provided is sometimes dependent on a key. In the document on the bishops, for instance, which we reproduce further on, the key consists in the number allocated to each bishop—which avoided mentioning his name.

Here are a few examples of telegrams to and from London:

1636 A. No. 49/42[94]   17.2.1942

On the 10th and 11th of the present month representatives of the Gestapo called on Archbishop Gall (of Warsaw). They declared that the Polish clergy is involved in politics. And they warned him that if this continues they will not fail to take severe action. Finally they asked him to arrange things so that the clergy will henceforward cease opposing the Germans.

When the bishops asked them to name the priests opposing the Germans they refused to do so. So far their visit has had no grievous results.   **Fr.**

No. 45[95]

With reference to your message n. 3 I inform you that the representatives of the clergy declare that, at present, they have no request to formulate to the Polish government. They declare that they are in direct contact with Cardinal Hlond. I am informed from Wilno that Archbishop Jalbrzykowski and the Curia Chancellor Sawkicki have been moved to the Mariampol convent. The teachers and pupils of Vilna Seminary have been arrested.

18.3.1942.

No. 72, 25.8.1942[96]

It is reported in a newspaper that the Franciscan, Fr. Hilarius Breitinger of Poznań, has been appointed apostolic administrator for the archdiocese of Gniezno and Poznań. Send us information about this personage. . . . Received 1.9.1942.

No. 76, 12.9.1942[97]

According to information received from the Vatican, the German bishops have sent a letter to the Pope asking him to make a peace initiative. The letter is said to have been inspired by German official circles. The Vatican has denied this information.

Received 18.10.1942.

No. 91, 15.10.42[98]

Send me at the first possible moment information about the present persecution of the Jews in Poland. STEM.

Received 20.10.42.

No. 92, 17.10.42[99]

Your report on the reign of terror contains information about expulsions, burnings and destructions of whole villages. This can be used for propaganda purposes, hence we need the names of some of these villages and the maximum possible detail about these acts of barbarism. ESPE.   Received 20.10.42.

No. 134[100]

STEM. Your n. 72. The Franciscan Fr. Hilarius Breitinger is the Vicar-General of the archdiocese of Gniezno and Poznań, not its administrator; this changes everything essentially. He will exercise his jurisdiction at Łódź and Włocławek. It appears that he has no right to concern himself with Polish confessional questions. In the Warthegau 'the German Catholic Church' has been organized with its own juridical personnel and its own churches, which Poles have been forbidden to enter.   14.10.42.

No. 118, 1.6.1944[101]

I am sending a despatch from the Council of Priests for Thaddeus Orkan ('Hurricane').

The military court forwarded full powers to you and the League four months ago. I beg you to send me if possible the annual registers for the dioceses of Warmia, Gdansk, Włocławek. We have set up a commission of aid to the Church in Poland. Relations with the Holy See are excellent. Baziak[102] has been appointed coadjutor. But we have serious difficulties with Gawlina who has joined the Sanacja clique. First he fought Sikorski, not the present government. Relations with Radonski[103] are excellent. The government is working in full harmony and making every effort to guarantee a united and independent Poland. Greetings to our colleagues.

L . . . kzinski.[104]   Received 12.6.

As can be seen, there was an active interchange of information from both sides, as well as demands for further detail, corrections, and so on. Moreover private organizations were in touch, such as the undefined 'Council of Priests' in London, which was plainly on the government side. Later we shall be quoting despatches from government personalities, including Sikorski himself.

But now it is time to turn to extracts from reports sent to the government[105] to provide an organic illustration of the situation of the Church in Poland. The first is plainly retrospective—from 1 September 1939 to 30 May 1940—and is only concerned with the Western zones: the second, which is subdivided into two parts, from 1 February to 10 March 1941, and from 10 March to 30 April 1941, gives a picture of the religious situation in the country generally. We shall deal with the third later.

The first consists of thirty ordinary typescript pages and is rather ambitious in construction. It has a general introduction (a reference to the motives of the 'German revenge'), a distinction between the two halves of the period in the behaviour of the occupying forces (an illustration of each, with dates and incidents), and lastly a picture of the situation at the end of the period (May 1940). This is by far the most important section so we shall limit ourselves to quoting from that.

The Problem of Confessions

Last February, and despite the influx of German priests, the clergy in Pomerania were so few in number that, to satisfy the religious needs of the population, priests had to go from parish to parish and say two or three Masses a day. Besides this, confessions constituted a problem. In this respect the attitude of Bishop Splett of Danzig, administrator of the diocese of Chełmno, is of interest. In accord with general rulings of canon law, the itinerant priests told the people that in very exceptional circumstances when it was impossible for all who wanted to go to confession to do so . . . there could be collective confessions and general absolution. To this Mgr. Splett's reaction was violent. He forbade such procedure and denounced it as Protestant. Then, after a while, he substantially changed his attitude and gave his permission—but for reasons insufficient in canon law: reasons of nationality. On 25 May 1940 he published a decree forbidding confessions in Polish. There are grounds for thinking that this order emanated from the German authorities and the Gestapo, and he did no more than countersign it. Mgr. Splett's decree . . . involves both priest and penitent and sanctions are threatened if it be disobeyed. The decree can be summarized as follows:

1. A priest has no right to hear the confession of a penitent who enters the confessional and begins to list his sins in Polish. The priest is obliged to interrupt him, to forbid him to confess in Polish, and to order him to confess in German. Should the penitent fail to do so, the priest must refuse to listen.

2. No Catholic has a right to go to confession in Polish even if he knows no other language.

3. Anyone who knows German is bound in conscience to go to confession in German.

4. Those who do not know German must approach the confessional and express their repentance in gestures (striking their breasts for the *mea culpa*) and the priest can give them absolution without adding any penance.

5. General confession and absolution may also take place. [This is contrary to Catholic doctrine which only allows general absolution when individual confession is materially impossible, as when there are too few priests to hear penitents separately. But this does not arise when individual confession *is* possible and reasons of nationality form the only obstacle. Such reasons are unknown to canon law.]

6. It is forbidden to use the Polish language even when there is danger of death and even when the penitent knows no language other than Polish. In that case, in accord with canon law [as interpreted by Mgr. Splett] general absolution may be given.

7. Beside every confessional the words must be clearly written up: *Es wird nur deutschgebeichtet.* (Confessions only in German.)

8. Priests are obliged to inform the faithful of the terms of the decree.

In accordance with the decree, Mgr. Splett refuses to employ priests who show recalcitrance.

The reaction of the faithful has been varied. Some have entirely stopped going to confession as they are unwilling to confess in German even when they know that language. Those are the majority. Others refrain because they do not know German and are unwilling to recognize what they call 'German confession'. Finally, there's a section of the population that submits to the decree, given the ease of such confessions, despite the risk of leaning towards Protestantism.

The martyrology of the Catholic Church has been enriched by the names of two priests who died because they were guilty of hearing confessions in Polish.

1. Fr. Polomski was arrested on 14 June last year for hearing confessions in Polish. He was sent to Stuthof camp on 5 August and we have heard news of his death from the camp.

2. Fr. Kupczynski, parish priest of Tczew, was arrested for hearing confessions in Polish, but on the intervention of several German priests who were his friends he was set free but ordered to leave Polish territory immediately. His former vicar, Mgr. Stein, of German nationality and at present living in Berlin, put him up at his house. But that angered both ecclesiastical and civil authorities. Mgr. Stein was forced to leave his own parish and go and live elsewhere and was unable to take Fr. Kupczynski with him. The latter had to leave immediately and was completely without any means of livelihood. He found and rented a tiny lodging. Someone lent him a hand-cart and, though he was worn out, he set off with his belongings: but while he was pulling the cart he felt unwell, rested against a nearby fence, and fell down dead. . . .

Other priests have suffered and are still suffering for hearing confessions in Polish. One day the Gestapo picked up five priests: Frs. Bieszek of Rajkowy, Kuehn of Skorcz, Bystron of Swarozyna, Litwin of Zblewo and Kupczynski of Tczew. At Tczew the Gestapo ran into soldiers who had established themselves in the church. According to witnesses the Gestapo felt confused and went off, saying they would come back another time. And so they did, with the outcome that we know. Fr. Bystron was away and so escaped arrest, but he had to leave the parish. Fr. Bieszek and Fr.

Kuehn are Poles: whereas Fr. Litwin is a German who was sent here by his ecclesiastical superiors because he knows Polish. All three were arrested together. Richter, head of the Gestapo, hurried off in the car to take them to prison. They admitted that they had heard confessions in Polish from people in danger of death. They were finally allowed to go free on condition they left Polish territory. The ecclesiastical authorities in Germany are not allowed to employ them. But here we come to a new chapter.

The Behaviour of the German Ecclesiastical Authorities towards the Poles

Fr. Litwin is still unemployed and his parents are subjected to unremitting persecution. He has been the round of almost all the German dioceses and has been rejected for any employment whatsoever. The reason given was roughly this: '*Sie haben sich versündigt an die deutsch Volksgemeinschaft, und deshalb haben Sie das Vertrauen veloren. Für Sie haben wir keine Stelle.*'[106]

In February a certain number of Polish-speaking German priests reached Pomerania. Most of them were recalled shortly afterwards and some of them had blackened their reputations in German eyes —e.g. Fr. Litwin and Fr. Dziedzelewski who were favourable to the Poles (*gegenüber die Polen freundlich eingestellt*).

Others have taken their place. Their mission is: '*Für Vertreung der Volksdeutschen in Ostgebiet.*' The latter included priests such as the traitor Dertz (a Pole who formerly called himself Marszalkowski) and others who are not worth much, such as Frs. Preuss and Knob. This last lives at Wejherowo and is a member of the SS. When the faithful went to him, saying '*Gelobt sei Jesus Christus*', ('Praised be Jesus Christ'), he replied, '*Der deutsche Grüss ist Heil Hitler. Bitte, verlassen sie das Zimmer und kommen noch einmal zurück*'.[107] (The German greeting is Heil Hitler. Please leave the room and come back again.')

These priests lord it over the Poles, which is wounding to Polish feelings. The Polish population goes less and less to churches where these priests and their like are the ministers, and they say they are not priests but *Trauhenders*. In some areas such as Wabrzezno and Choinice, Mass is only said for *Volksdeutschen.*[108] Poles have to stand outside the door, whatever the weather, and can only go in when the *Volksdeutschen* have left. They join in very little as hymns and sermons in Polish are not allowed.

Such is the behaviour of the German priests sent from Germany to develop 'pastoral' activity. Moreover there is very little difference between them and some of their masters, e.g. Bishop Berning of Osnabrück. In 1933 this bishop was an open supporter of Hitler, a member of the Council of State, and was appointed protector of German Catholic emigrants. He was well known for the various privileges he asked for the Germans in Poland and for not having kept a single promise he made to the Poles. Now this bishop has forbidden German priests who have been called-up to act as 'pastors' to the Poles, because this 'would sully the dignity of the German soldier'. This piece of information comes from various priests who, finding themselves in Poland as soldiers, went to the churches to say Mass, but, in accordance with their instructions, refused to give Communion to the Poles.

Added to all this, the prayers of the German chaplain-bishop are well known: he implored God to give a just victory to the German cause. This is Bishop Rutkowski, and his name seems an indication that he is a traitor.

As regards the second report, we shall provide the full text of the first part of it, only omitting a few lines which we shall be quoting later:

Information concerning Religion in Poland from 1 February to 15 March 1941

In the religious field there is nothing outstanding to record. The general tendency to persecute the Church and religion continues in various places. It is extremely violent in the areas annexed to the Reich. Elsewhere it is no worse and no better.

The following activities may be noted:

Early in March a brief meeting of bishops took place in Warsaw. Present were five Ordinaries, i.e. the local Apostolic Administrator, Archbishop Gall; the Metropolitan of Cracow; and the Bishops of Kielce, Częstochowa and Sandomierz.

Before Easter a small number of gatherings were organized in the towns and in parts of the country—needless to say, in the General Governorship. The occupying authorities raised no objection—at least for the time being. The greatest difficulty comes from the 8 o'clock curfew which prevents the organization of teaching in the evenings and at night.

As to the seminaries, we still have the *status quo*. Up to date, the bishops' questions have remained unanswered. Except for Cracow and Sandomierz, clandestine courses are being organized but not for all the seminarians. Now and again Gestapo agents come for information, but they do so *molli manu*, without coming to any serious decision. We have noted a similar absence of decisive action in all that regards the studies organized by the various religious orders. Now and again they hold out threats of punishing all students—they carry out searches, as in the case of the Franciscans and Jesuits in Cracow, or they deny the right to go out, as with the Lazarites—but then they take no trouble to see that their orders are obeyed. Thanks to this state of affairs, studies can still be carried on in the religious orders somehow, and the Pallotine Fathers at Oltarzew near Warsaw have managed to recruit several dozen students from the Western dioceses as well as displaced persons from other religious orders, who can thus carry on their studies and be prepared for ordination. The auxiliary Bishop of Pinsk, Mgr. Niemica, who is now in Warsaw, is going to Oltarzew to ordain them.

This apart, we now and again have acts of violence, especially when anyone is accused of pursuing patriotic activities, whether real or imaginary. Thus a well-known Franciscan arrested in Cracow—Fr. Bonaventura Podchodecki—who appears to have been shot at Niepokalanow near Warsaw, though the information is not reliable. According to news coming from the prison at Pawiak,[109] other Franciscans have been arrested and subjected to physical violence; at Lowicz four priests (though two were later released) were arrested; and at Radom both the Gralewski priests appear to have been shot. There seem to have been many similar cases in other dioceses, but it is often hard to get news as the German police operate in secrecy.

In Warsaw there has been friction with the German authorities over the Catholic churches in the Jewish quarter. In the area marked out as the ghetto, there are three parish churches with several thousand parishioners. The German authorities wanted to prevent the priests having free access and wanted to close the churches. But despite this the churches have stayed open and the problem has remained unresolved.

Though at present we are unable to record a recrudescence of the reign of terror (apart from the facts already noted) we must point out that the big recrudescence of political terrorism inevitably influences religious life. There is no other way of putting it: what is happening is the hateful and systematic destruction of the whole nation. For there are endless arrests; a large number of executions; the destruction of property; expulsions from cities and villages; decrees whose only aim is to ill-treat the population; discrimination against the Poles over food-rationing; the impossibility of teaching the youth properly; the transfer of workers to Germany, etc.—it is a gruesome picture of persecution and terror never before seen in Poland. The very latest news is that sixty hostages have been taken for one German who was killed—and a man of doubtful origins at that—and they threaten to kill them all if the guilty party is not found. Result: they did not find the guilty party, they killed some of the hostages and put up a poster with the news in the streets. The terror and persecutions which cry to heaven for vengeance increase hatred endlessly and have undesirable repercussions on religion. Here and there people doubt the existence of Providence, there are reports of suicides and the Church is taken to task for its failure to condemn all this openly and publicly. There is friction and misunderstanding. Such feelings are not affecting the large majority of the people who are unheard, who cry to heaven for vengeance, and behave with a national spirit; but it must be admitted that the sight of such infamies constitutes a veritable ordeal for people's consciences. There is nothing but a constant and brutal destruction of works of art, of work centres, a grievous bringing of the country to its knees, with irreparable loss both on the national and family level. Apart from those killed in action or dead from wounds, the number of those shot and tortured, deprived of their freedom in prisons or concentration camps, or ruined by inhuman expulsion, amounts to over 500,000— especially in the male population but also including women. As for the young people and children who have yet to die from disease and under-nourishment, only the survivors will be able to tell the tale.

In the Western regions incorporated into the Reich, the nationalist terror has almost completed its work of devastation, and the annihilation of surviving religious institutions is almost complete. Recently the Germans have come to grips even with the princes of the Church. In early February the Bishop of Katowice [Mgr. Stanislas Adamski] and his auxiliary, Bieniek, were brutally carried off and, after a car journey, deposited in front of the Archbishop's palace in Cracow. The unworthy manœuvres of Bishop Adamski, which were an outrage to the Polish cause and, indirectly, to Catholicism, seem in no way to have served him. Later, in early March, there was an attack on the two bishops of Plock who had for long been under house arrest far from their diocese in the parish of Slupno. At two in the morning they were forced from their beds and taken to Plock by cart. There they were put on a bus crammed to bursting point and transferred a few hours' journey away to Dzialdowo, where there is a concentration camp for the segregation of prisoners. Nothing more has been heard of them. There is every sort of anxiety about Archbishop Nowowiejski, who is eighty-three and has a weak heart. The auxiliary bishop, Wetmanski, seems to have been beaten up. A week before the arrest of these two bishops, four aged priests had been taken from Plock of whom one, Mgr. Modzelewski, died as a result of a heart attack.

But it is not only people who are being persecuted: they are still savagely destroying religious objects, and sometimes we are even confronted with sacrilege. Thus, in the Jesuit house at Leczyca, from which the fathers were expelled on 15 October last, they decided in early March to 'tidy up' the liturgical objects. Sending for Jewish workers, they ordered them to bring all the objects out and pile them on carts: chalices, reliquaries, liturgical books and vestments, including seventeenth-century copes, linen and so on: the church had been closed, but one could see the sacred vessels placed on the steps of the high altar: two pyxes, one belonging to the church, the other to the chapel, had been placed there by Jewish hands.[110] N.B. When the Jesuits had been expelled, they had been forbidden to consume the hosts, and the holy objects had stayed there neglected for five months. Many stories of the same kind could be told. What remains of the religious orders continues to be eliminated, and now only scattered individuals remain; sometimes nuns are subjected to crushing housework, for instance the Ursulines.

In parts of the areas incorporated into the Reich a decree is in vigour forbidding young people to embrace any religion so that they can only make their choice when they reach fifteen.[111]

As for the Polish territories occupied by the Bolsheviks. . . .

Note. We have just had news that in the dioceses of the General Governorship permission has been granted to open seminaries. . . .

The second part of the document is especially important owing to the explanation it gives for the weakening of the persecution in the General Governorship and for its criticism of the nuncio, Mgr. Orsenigo, and one of the bishops, regarded as traitors.

Problems of the Church in Poland (from the second half of March to April 1941)

During this period certain gains may be noted.

First and foremost, the occupying authorities in the General Governorship have provisionally allowed seminaries, hitherto closed, to be reopened: and in addition they have allowed the activities of religious theological institutes to be reorganized which hitherto had been in grave difficulties. As a result young novices can henceforth undertake almost regular studies, and candidates for the priesthood can be consecrated.[112]

Moreover the German authorities have exempted ecclesiastics and those in religious orders from physical labour, which had been obligatory for many men under fifty.

Finally, for some time opposition to church collections during the 'forty hours'[113] has ceased, and we have to note fewer arrests of priests.

As for an explanation of this behaviour, all we can suggest is the following:

(1) Our persecutors may have become convinced that the regime of ruthless religious persecution is leading to no positive result and is, moreover, upsetting public opinion abroad.

(2) They have no desire to drive the population to despair in view of the war against Russia.

(3) They are obviously afraid that the Holy See will deplore the situation of Polish Catholicism. It is for this reason that some religious houses have been allowed to resume theological studies. For at the same time they said: tell Rome at once that you have obtained freedom to teach again.

Nevertheless, if the behaviour of the occupying authorities towards the Church has slightly improved, we are still far from what Governor Frank recently said in Cracow, i.e. that the Church enjoys full freedom in the General Governorship. This statement, like Frank's earlier utterances—according to which the nuncio Orsenigo had rejoiced at the wonderful development of Polish Catholicism under his regime—are the very opposite of the truth. Despite some easing-up in a few sectors, pressure continues, the activity of the societies is forbidden, religious literature is almost non-existent, large numbers of priests and members of religious orders are in prison or concentration camp, seminary buildings (e.g. in Cracow, Siedlce and to some extent Sandomierz) are requisitioned, religious houses, presbyteries and other buildings are occupied, churches have often been turned into store-houses for munitions and war material (at Siedlce only one church has been left free), processions and religious demonstrations have been prohibited, hundreds of dying people and people condemned to death in concentration camps have no religious consolation, Christian charity meets with obstacles on all sides, etc. From all this there obviously results a tendency to undermine the Church and its influence: especially as the Germans give their support to all that compromises social or religious activity, and do all they can to estrange the Poles from the Holy Father. . . . If we add to this the demoralization of the Polish population by cheap alcohol and gaming houses, if we consider the systematic destruction of our national life, above all through the young people who are unable to attend school (schools are closed) and have no normal work, if we note the social and economic pressure, it is not hard to reach the conclusion that the German authorities are openly trying to destroy our spirit and, first and foremost, weaken the Catholic faith.

Hence we must take *cum grano salis* the evidence of the henchman of the occupying authorities who deals with religious matters, Fr. Odilon, a Franciscan, who has just sent a letter in German to bishops and provincials of religious orders assuring them of the 'deepest sympathetic attitude and the completest understanding of the German authorities for the vital needs of Catholic life in Poland,'[114] and using such phrases as, for instance, the following (quoted by the *Deutsche Allgemeine Zeitung* on 13 April): 'The German administration has not set up the slightest obstacle in the way of the Church's life, as we were assured recently in an interview with the Bishop of Sandomierz.'[115]

And it is here that we must point out a very painful and disturbing problem for the more enlightened and ardent Polish Catholics. There is a ceaseless flow of news—some surely false, some surely true—that the *nuncio Orsenigo* is totally unconcerned about the fate of the Church in Poland and is even persuaded that the German authorities are behaving pretty decently towards it, and that the complaints of the Poles derive from the fact that they have improperly confused the religious cause with the national cause.

Such opinions held by a representative of the Holy See are extremely painful and are leading many to distrust the Holy See itself. If Poland was unjustly attacked, and if the invaders continue to persecute the innocent population in an inhuman way, the representative of the Church must view this evil as unjustified and must show compassion without cold distinctions between religious and national matters. Especially as with us the national cause and religion are closely interlocked, perhaps more than elsewhere; and with us, as, e.g. in Alsace, persecution of the nation is also a blow at religion.

And there is a related question that we feel bound to raise though we do so with regret.

For some time *the bishop of Katowice, Adamski*, removed from his diocese by the Germans, has taken up residence in Warsaw. We have referred in a previous report to the distressing blows inflicted by this pastor on the Catholics of Silesia. These blows have had their echo in the minds of all Polish Catholics. Now this prelate, whose earlier activities were always inspired by a desire to sail before the wind, with a view to obtaining a more important position, is trying to present his activities in Silesia as though they were solely dictated by the good of the Church, as though he was sacrificing the national cause to the higher good of the Church. In his false presentation of the facts, he is quoting the name of the nuncio Orsenigo and saying that he has always been in direct touch with the nunciature. Worse, he maintains that he still keeps up this contact and that the nuncio has assured him that his reports are the only reliable ones. Now we declare before God that Bishop Adamski's contacts with the nuncio in Poland, so notoriously hostile to our country, cannot do otherwise than yield bitter fruit both for the Church and the nation.

It is worth adding that the men close to him in Warsaw are whispering around that he will become Archbishop of Warsaw and a cardinal. Probably these rumours are based on the fact that his best friend and supporter is Kaczynski, the canon of Warsaw[116] who, though he has a bad reputation in serious circles in the city, insofar as he is an ill-behaved intriguer, has managed to get the post of chaplain to President Rackiewicz and is obviously a man of influence. We should emphasize again that in responsible Catholic and ecclesiastical circles in Warsaw, Bishop Adamski has had a cold and very unfavourable reception.

As for the general behaviour of the people we should say the following:

The large majority of the people are behaving well both from a religious and a national point of view. Despite the ever-growing difficulties in getting food, despite the arrests, despite the sending of men to Germany, and despite impositions of every kind, this majority remains unimpressed and looks to God. At Easter the churches were filled to overflowing, and many, even of those who had been keeping away from confession for years, went to Communion. We must emphasize that many of the national and political organizations, whether already existing or now being formed, have a positive Catholic basis. They are organizations making propaganda for genuine asceticism and aiming to create in the country a real religious and moral *élite*. In those sectors that act as *liaison* between these organizations and the Polish government there are reliable and enlightened priests.

But there are some shadows.

One source of deep apprehension is the percentage (from 30 to 40 per cent) of young people of both sexes who attended the higher forms in the high schools and are now no longer studying but do nothing but hang about the streets: smoking cigarettes, trying to earn money in dishonest ways and indulging in dangerous amusements. It is hard to come to terms with these young people given all the obstacles the Germans put up.

A certain percentage of the intellectuals, much smaller than the above, is no longer working, lives in poverty, has decreasing morale, and here and there is losing all hope. Their hopelessness is increased owing to the expulsions from home, the arrests, the despatch of near relatives to Germany, news of the death of fathers, sons or brothers assassinated or subject to torture in the concentration camps and prisons. Another kind of despair is experienced by other intellectuals, as well as by the inhabitants of the suburbs and above all by the people. These have acquired the habit of speculating in foreign currency or food and spend the money they get in drinking vodka and in the gambling *boîtes* which are very numerous in the city. One sees Polish girls picking up the German soldiers who pullulate everywhere in the country. This kind of moral deterioration deriving from inertia and despair is even affecting the most upright families.

Finally we must note with sadness the ill-feeling against the Holy Father. . . .

All we have said applies exclusively to the General Governorship. In the areas incorporated into the Reich religious and national persecution has reached a peak. In practice there is hardly any Catholic life left; many of the churches are closed, nearly all the religious orders have been scattered, church property has been requisitioned, and the remaining priests arrested. Only to give two instances of this martyrdom, we quote: the existence at Bojanowo, in the Poznań region, of a special concentration camp for nuns (around 200), and the treatment meted out to the two bishops of Plock.

We shall take just one extract—dealing with the western territories—from another report in the series: *The Problems of the Church in Poland*, dealing with the period from October to 15 November 1941.

On 6 October it was decreed that all the priests in the Warthegau territory should be interned. A mere handful remain. In the dioceses of Gniezno and Poznań, a mere 40. In some communes there is not a single one. The bishops or vicar-generals in the Warthegau have no right to transfer priests from one parish to another. This is done by the Gestapo without informing the ecclesiastical authorities. The priests just ask for ecclesiastical authorization after the transfer has taken place. All banners have been requisitioned in the last month. During the last round up of priests, chalices and monstrances were stolen from some of the churches. At Liuban near Poznań the tabernacle was opened, the sacred species thrown away and the pyxes seized. In some churches vestments and linen have been stolen. Missals and prayer-books have been burnt. Some priests have to do the work to which they are directed by the *Arbeitsamt* (office work, gardening, stable work and so on). The arrested priests have been transferred elsewhere: some to unknown destinations, some to the prison in Poznań, some to the concentration camp near Łódź. The Polish population is left without the consolation of religion and the sick are dying without the sacraments.[117]

An interesting detail about these reports is that they were put together by priests—as is shown by their style and treatment. We even know, if not the real name, at least the pseudonym of the author of the second report (sub-divided into two sections): it is T. Swinica, possibly a priest of the Warsaw clergy or anyway living in Warsaw. This shows how, over religious affairs, the Delegatura preferred, not without reason, to make use of the clergy (whether secular or in religious orders). In a pencilled note at the bottom of the first part of the second document we read:

7/6/41. This report should be regarded as initial material for the section on ecclesiastical affairs that is now being drafted. R.S.

And in another pencilled note at the beginning of the second part:

One part of this report has recently been sent off. The report stems from ecclesiastical circles, and personal problems are treated in a subjective way. General material for the section on ecclesiastical affairs which is now being set up with the BI [Office of Information?]—R.S.

To throw still further light on the general religious situation in Poland, in the light of these reports, we shall now translate part of an account[118] somewhat later than the previous ones. It is dated 19 September 1943 and signed 'Rev. . . .' (signature illegible) and concerns the second half of that year.

During recent months the Church in Poland has had to face serious losses.

Archdiocese of Cracow—Five Cistercians arrested at Mogila in

July. At Lubien, the parish priest and the curate. At Czulice, the parish priest.

Diocese of Kielce—A priest was imprisoned on grounds that he supported the Communist partisans, another was sent to a concentration camp, and six fled when threatened with arrest. Three dead in concentration camps and two from natural causes.

Diocese of Tarnov—On 29 July the German police killed Fr. Roman Ulatowski of Tuchow.

Diocese of Łódź—In the district attached to the General Governorship, at Piotrkow, the Vicar-General, Krzyszkowski, and a young curate of the parish were arrested for baptizing a Jew and carrying out a marriage ceremony. Both were taken to the local prison.

Diocese of Sandomierz—Three Oratorian fathers were arrested at Studziana and sent to Oswiecim towards the middle of August,

In the areas annexed to the Reich:

Archdiocese of Gniezno and Poznań—Mgr. Kazimierz Pajerowicz, president of missionary activities in Poland, died, not under arrest but in pathetic material circumstances.

Diocese of Chełmno—Six young priests arrested, two at Grudziaz.

Diocese of Lonza—Frs. Schmid and Peza shot, at Lomza and Rajgrod respectively.

[Archdiocese of Wilno, diocese of Pinsk and Luck. . . .]

Restrictions concerning pastoral activity and the education of new priests remain unchanged. Despite their promise to settle the problem of the first year of seminary studies, the German authorities have not cancelled the decision they made three years ago forbidding seminaries to admit candidates. Hence the seminaries are emptying. There are many vacancies for the first three years, and the same applies to novices in religious orders.

Atrocities involving the civil population continue and are even on the increase. Mass executions of the civil population are still carried out, especially in the districts of Bialystok and Polesia. The police are murdering whole families, including the children and the aged. Last July many Catholic gypsies were murdered in the Tarnow district (forty at Zabno and ninety-five at Szczurowa).

The Apostolic Administrator of the diocese, Mgr. Kruszynski, has protested against the inhuman behaviour of the authorities in the diocese of Lublin and has sent an *aide-mémoire* to the new governor of the Lublin district, Dr Wendler. [*Here follows a long résumé ending up with the closure of 41 Catholic churches in the Kielce region, 27 of them being parish churches—not including the*

*25 parish churches given to the Orthodox Ukranians by the German
authorities.*]

One of the great tragedies of the Polish Church is the situation
in the diocese of Padlachia [Siedlce]. The situation is unhealthy
and the blame does not, alas, fall solely on that part of the clergy
that lacks discipline and pastoral virtues; it must also be laid at the
door of the Apostolic Administrator, who, to put it mildly, is
devoid of tact. Unfortunately the present absence of relations with
Rome prevents a proper solution to the unhappy business.
19/IX/43. Father L . . .

As we have already said, some of the reports from the Office of
Information and Political Studies were particularly concerned with
the attitude of the clergy and the bishops. An interesting example is
provided by paragraph (h) of the *Report on the Situation from 15
August to 15 November 1941*[119] and the second part of a *Review of the
Problems of the Church in Poland* based on 'a meeting with X' on 9
January 1942[120].

(h) *The behaviour of the clergy.*

In view of the persecution of the clergy, the attitude to the
Germans is becoming increasingly hostile above all among the
lower clergy and young priests. The massive arrests in the areas
annexed to the Reich have reduced the number of Polish priests
in these regions down to an average of one-third. What makes
things worse is the arrival of German priests in parishes approved
by the papal nunciature in Berlin. The remaining Polish priests are
so terrorized that they are incapable of action. As for the priests
in the areas occupied by the Soviets. . . .

Generally speaking, the clergy in the General Governorship are
behaving with dignity and are only formally submitting to the
orders of the occupying authorities—with the exception of the
bishops of Sandomierz (Lorek) and Kielce (Kaczmarek), who have
for long had a reputation for opportunism. Recently the Bishop
of Siedlce has ceased to behave with dignity, inviting his clergy not
to oppose the requisition of church bells, and even asking them to
inform him of any instances of resistance.

The other administrators, and above all Archbishop Sapieha
and Archbishop Gall, are using passive resistance. They pass on
German orders without comment. Moreover they have refused—
unlike the Bishop of Kielce—to publish an official monthly review.
The attitude towards the Vatican varies. The higher clergy and
members of religious orders defend the Pope; the young priests

criticize him. The German Jesuits (in Berlin) are in contact with the Polish Jesuits (in Lublin) to co-ordinate the missionary activity of the Catholic Church in the East. In recent times the clergy have been playing an active part in works of charity which is particularly apparent in the matter of the RGO.[121]

Independently of all this, a large number of parishes are developing, under the screen of 'Caritas',[122] a movement for helping the poorest.

The clergy in no way interferes directly in political life, but influences it through its lay leadership. In some ecclesiastical circles attached to the National Party they are beginning to criticize General Sikorski's government because of its pro-Jewish and left-wing tendencies (good wishes for the Jewish new year, posthumous decoration of Libermann, etc.). But the majority of the priests are moderate and centre in tendency and the young ones sympathize with popular movements. Anti-Semitic tendencies among the clergy are fairly strong.

The attitude of the clergy is very varied and this is one of the greatest ills of the Church in Poland. The cause of this ill can be found in the very low level of the episcopate, and this in turn derives from the misguided policy of our government which systematically opposed the appointment of brave men. As a result, in 1939 several dioceses had no bishop and the majority of the bishops were incapable of behaving properly. Sapieha, the Metropolitan Archbishop, and the only one capable of showing proper independence, did not have sufficient moral and intellectual authority to impose a uniform policy on the other dioceses. Hence the dioceses were left to their own devices; and as the bishops displayed complete inertia, the clergy lacked all political directives. The result of this was a wide differentiation in the behaviour of the clergy towards the occupying authorities and in the struggle for independence. We can safely say that there have been no traitors among the clergy, save for a certain notoriously pro-German group. There is also a certain group that has gone astray, especially among those expelled from the western territories, and who, *via facti*, have secularized themselves and are now shouting at the tops of their voices for the abolition of celibacy and the creation of a 'national' Church. But in times of persecution such matters are pure routine, and, from the point of view of the Church, even desirable. The remainder—that is, the clergy in general—do their duty, but in a great variety of different ways: from active participation in illegal activities, through imprudent demonstrations of patriotism, to cowardly and selfish inactivity. Obviously there are no cases of fraternization with the Germans. Two years ago, the declarations made by Bishops Lorek and Kaczmarek caused a great stir. Today both are sincerely regretting their thoughtless gestures and nothing of the kind, we can be sure, will ever happen again. The Bishop of Siedlce's order to hand over church bells is more a manifestation of timidity than of 'collaboration' with the Germans. The government's last clandestine appeal to the clergy met with favour on points enumerating the duties of every priest and every patriot. But some difficulties may occur in carrying out orders to sell ex-votos and other church goods for patriotic or charitable ends. Canon law lays down that in every case of the sale of ex-votos a permit from the Holy See is necessary. Whereas in the case of bequests the agreement of the donator is enough. Anyway churches possessing an excess of valuable liturgical material (i.e. of gold or silver and not only gold plate) are few and far between. By and large the clergy are loyal to the London government. They are much more united in feeling than the laity: those upholding the Falanga[123] could be counted on the fingers of one hand. . . .

In the eastern regions the Church's activities are hampered by the lack of bishops in the more important dioceses, such as those of Luck and Pinsk, and also by the lack of priests—for many of them are dead or have been sent to Siberia. (The Soviet massacres of 1941 mainly affected the Uniate clergy in Galicia, as they were Ukrainians.) The Germans create obstacles to missionary activity by not allowing the clergy to move around. Yet there is a wonderful field for pastoral and Polish activity, above all in the former Soviet territories. . . .

But the most complex commentary on the attitude of the clergy is to be found in the 'pencilled notes' received in December 1942 and sent to L. (London?) on 6 January 1943. They were entitled:

Attitudes and Opinions of the Catholic Clergy in Poland[124]

If we are to describe the attitudes and political opinions of the Catholic clergy in Poland, we have to face the following interrelated problems: 1. the attitude of the episcopate; 2. the part played by religious orders; 3. the political activity of the clergy and the centres of activity; 4. the importance of the religious centre abroad; 5. general opinions.

1. *The attitude of the episcopate.*

Given the hierarchical system of the organization of the Catholic Church, the episcopate plays a preponderant part in the political life of the clergy. The lower clergy, above all in country places and thus far away from non-religious centres, normally follows the example and opinions that come from on high; so that, in the majority of cases, the political attitude of the bishops is decisive in the ideological and tactical behaviour of the priests in any given diocese.

This is illustrated by the favourable attitude taken by the priests in the dioceses of Sandomierz and Siedlce towards the activity of the occupying forces in the matter of sending workers to Germany (an attitude recently condemned by the press): such an attitude is analogous to that of Bishops 1 and 2.

At the moment the attitude of the episcopate is perfectly clear, and, if we judge from their attitude towards the occupying forces, it is easy to divide them into three distinct groups:

(a) The first group is formed by the bishops who represent a high ethical and patriotic level. As regards the forces of occupation, their attitude consists in *implacable* hostility. To this group belong bishops 3, 4, 5, 6, 7, 8 and 9.

These bishops are men of wide influence and great authority. They often play an active part in clandestine activities and are leaders in social and political action. No. 3 enjoys the greatest authority and his moral position is strengthened by the fact that, politically, he inclines to no party.

(b) The second group consists of those prelates whose activities could be called opportunist. These are bishops 10, 1 and 11. Unquestionably they are in good faith (which differentiates them from the third group) and are trying, in spite of the political situation, to save the Church. To reward them for the collaboration they provide and for their declarations of loyalty, the Germans allow them to publish pastoral letters and to have a diocesan printer (10)—a thing unthinkable for the first category of bishops. When Archbishop Gall was alive, and above all since his death, the Warsaw Metropolitan Curia has behaved in a more and more opportunist way. The cowardice and lack of patriotism of their excellencies[125] 12 and 13 were already apparent during the Archbishop's illness, when the Pope's letter written to him on his deathbed was concealed: the contents of the letter—said to be sensational—have been kept secret up to date. The appointment of his excellency 14 probably will not influence the Curia's attitude, given that he is an old man and also an invalid.

Situated between the second and third group is Bishop 15. His position is in general defined as 'opportunist but in good faith'. His main aim has been an effort to safeguard the national spirit and today, since the expulsion, though his attitude is judged unfavourably by Catholic opinion, this opinion considers him to be just. He was among the first to invite the Poles to become *Volks-deutsch*. And he profited by his relationships with the German episcopate to place the Silesian students in German seminaries.

(c) The third group, that of the traitors, is made up of the administrator of Siedlce, Bishop 20. Responsible ecclesiastical circles have already dealt with him. Not only does he infringe canon law and expel parish priests '*loco dati*', but he openly collaborates with the Germans. Recently there has been a good deal of talk about the reception he organized at Siedlce for the Gestapo when it came to make arrests. He is an opportunist in bad faith. He is badly seen by the clergy of the diocese, and lacks authority. With the exception of the few priests in his own circle, they all treat him with hostility. This is proved by the fact that the Siedlce clergy are approaching those responsible to have him removed. This same clergy provided proofs against Bishop 2.

2. *The part played by the religious orders.*

The religious orders are now setting up centres of action for independence and works of charity. The action for independence will be analysed in part when we come to the political activity of the clergy. Here we will only be speaking of it in general terms. There are three types of religious orders:

(a) The first type is that involved in political action, charitable action, and independence. It is the most positive type from the point of view of the State's interests. It includes the Pallotine Fathers, the Missionary Fathers and the Salesians.

(b) The second type consists of religious orders that carry out charitable activities. These include the Capuchins, the Benedictines and all the women's orders.

(c) The third type consists of the Jesuits. They represent the Vatican element in Polish political life. Their activity is preeminently political. It takes many forms, and they try to be discreet and to influence very different circles. This explains why their line of conduct seems rather incoherent (the role of Rev. 16 in the 'National Confederation' and of Fr. 17 in the National Party). The political head of the Jesuits is Rev. 17 which explains the measures taken by the Vatican (the appointment of Rev. 18 at Wilno and of Apostolic Administrators in the dioceses of Poznań and Pomerania) with a view to putting order into the religious life. Typical of Rev. 17 is his last action of propaganda, according to which the German clergy should not be indicted. In matters concerning the relations between Poland and the Vatican there are antagonisms between the Jesuits and the Pallotine Fathers, which latter represent the opinion of the government and the Polish State. The Jesuits (Rev. 17) are in close contact with the secret nuncio of the Vatican—an Italian priest hostile to the Poles. His attitude is illustrated by his phrase, 'the Poles are responsible for their fate.' It is very difficult to make an impartial judgment about the Jesuits given the lack of evidence. Our slight sketch here is based on what it has been possible to observe.

From the above it is apparent that the role of the religious orders has points in common with the political activity of the clergy and that the religious orders constitute the centre of that activity.

3. *The political activity of the Clergy.*

The clergy are divided into two principal political groups: one, known as the 'legalists', is active in the sector for independence; the other is an independent group for political action in home affairs.

The members of the 'legalist' group come first and foremost from the Missionary and Pallotine Fathers, and from secular priests. The most important personalities among them are the Rev. 20, the Rector 21, the Rev. 22, the Superior 23 and the Rev. 24. They are very active in the DR[126] (civil combat); they have drawn up a declaration addressed to the Catholic clergy and have dispatched to the government and to Bishop 25 a memorandum on the situation of the clergy. They have also drawn up an appeal to the clergy asking them to play a part in civil resistance (*inter alia* they have asked them to offer what objects of value they have for the sake of the struggle for independence and social aid).

Among the members of the independent group we must record that a certain role is maintained, or has been maintained, by the Revs. 26, 27, 16, 28 and 29, with Rev. 17 at the head. Rev. 26 (of the diocese of Sandomierz) tried to group the right-wing elements of the clergy within the National Party. Rev. 16 is active in the 'National Confederation'. Rev. 24 is co-founder of the 'F.O.P.' and 'Credo'; Rev. 27 is active in 'Credo', in 'F.O.P.' and is president of the 'Oriens' group; Rev. 28 is protector of the oriental rite in the 'Oriens' group (F.O.P.).

The 'official' Jesuits are defending Vatican policy, as we have already said. As for the current activity of the priests bound up with the former regime, we have no precise information (at first they emigrated, then some came back but remained inactive).

4. *The religious centre abroad.*

Despite the differences enumerated above, the attitude of the Catholic clergy towards priests who have emigrated to London is uniform. Bishops 30 and 31, living abroad, have no relationship with the views of the clergy in the country. It is said of them that they are not where they ought to be. The Catholic clergy in the country wants to have contact only with Bishop 25, regarded as their representative abroad.

All take a negative view of the Rev. 32, the president's chaplain and chief of the personnel section in the department of religion. This is why Bishops 3 and 7 refused to send their questions to London. It was said that the motive lay in the fact that the chaplain had signed the telegram (the Rev. 33, Superior of the Jesuits, has thrown definitive light on the situation in the country). In the memorandum sent by the 'legalists' to the government and to Bishop 25, there was a section hostile to the chaplain.

5. *General opinions.*

By and large, the Catholic clergy has lost its orientation. The presence in Poland of the Pope's secret nuncio—19 (with qualifications unknown), the lack of accurate information about the relations between the government and the Vatican, and about what concerns the policy of the Vatican, do nothing to clear up this situation. The Catholic clergy bewails the lack of directives over problems of major importance. The clergy think it at least desirable (if not necessary) that the Delegatura should keep them informed of the government's policy over religious questions.[127]

Only very lengthy research could provide a complete and reliable picture of the various groups of the Polish clergy in relation to the situation of the country occupied by the Nazis, and trace the history of the clergy's responsibilities during the tragic years of the Second World War. But this is not the object of our study. What we want to do is to examine the relations between the Holy See on the one side, and the London government and the Warsaw Delegatura on the other: relations through diplomatic means in the first case, and through the clandestine channels of the bishops in the second. Above all for this second case was it necessary to give a concrete idea of the news that could arrive directly in Rome or influence the attitude of the London government in its relations with the Vatican. The reports quoted above are sufficient for this purpose, and also for giving an idea of the complexity of the situation, and the confusion that it was bound to create at the Secretariat of State, called on to take a stand on the side of one or other of these currents in circumstances in themselves dramatic enough.

Now that we have completed this task, it remains for us to ask

ourselves whether the couriers at the disposal of the Polish episcopate—through the military command of the clandestine army—
were the only ones to go to and fro between Poland and Rome, or
whether, in due course and from time to time, the Delegatura made
use of its own personnel to drag from the Pope the condemnation of
Nazi atrocities it so ardently desired. Following on *Defeat in Victory*,
the memoirs of Jan Ciechanowski, former ambassador to Washington of the Polish government in London, Rolf Hochhuth has given
the example of Lieutenant Jan Karski, who was twice sent to
London and Washington 'as secret envoy of the clandestine Communist leaders in Poland, so as to transmit to the appropriate civil
and military authorities the reports and statements of eye-witnesses'.

Hochhuth tells us that Karski managed to be received by Roosevelt himself and thus had the opportunity of telling him about the
concentration camps where mass-murder was the order of the day.
He spoke of Oswiecim (Auschwitz), Majdanek, Dachau, Oranienburg, of the women's camp at Ravensbrück, and told the President
of his own hair-raising adventure when, disguised as a policeman, he
had paid a personal visit to the camps of Treblinka and Belzec where
Jews were being gassed in railway coaches.[128]

Surely an envoy such as Karski would have been an ideal man to
send on a mission to the Vatican and even perhaps to the Pope?
Hochhuth does not seem to have thought of this, but the fact is that
Karski, of whom he gives such a summary and unreliable account,
was in Rome, and was received in audience by Pius XII—and he left
with the Pope the same memorandum that he had already delivered in
London and Washington. Colonel Rzepecki was unable to guarantee
this as certain, while maintaining that it was far from impossible; but
confirmation of the fact coming to us through other sources (based
on hearsay) was finally and formally provided by a friend and
colleague of Karski's in clandestine activity. For special and
obviously grave reasons we cannot, alas, reveal this man's identity.
But Colonel Rzepecki, who knew Karski, has at least revealed *his*
real name: Jan Kozielewski.

Who was Karski-Kozielewski? By good fortune he himself provided us with information about himself, and that while the war was
still in progress. In the first half of 1944 he published with Houghton

Mifflin in Boston an autobiography dealing with the clandestine Polish State—*Story of a Secret State*. This book gives no impression that he was a Communist or, if so, he was a very odd one: first of all, he was a believer who went to confession and Communion; then, he was an employee of the Delegatura's secret services, not those of the Communist organizations; finally, he maintained and proclaimed with conviction the democratic ideals of the Free World. (And incidentally he remained in the Free World and is still alive.)

His only contacts with the Communists would appear to be those he had when taken prisoner by the Russians in September 1939; to which a successful escape soon put an end. By spring 1940 he had already reached Sikorski in France to take on his first mission. After a parenthesis of capture by the Gestapo and a fresh escape, he took up clandestine activities in his own country, passing secret information from one sector to the other, until in the autumn of 1942 he was given a mission as witness and spokesman to the Free World about what was really happening in Poland. Five weeks before leaving Warsaw for London (at the end of November) he met several Jewish leaders who persuaded him to visit the Warsaw ghetto.

He reached England through Spain and met the leaders of the emigré government, including two encounters with Sikorski, then began having similar meetings with British leaders, starting with Eden. In the United States, where he arrived early in 1943, he had contacts with political men (various members of the State Department, besides Roosevelt), and also had contacts with Jewish and Catholic circles. Among the latter he quotes Archbishop Mooney of Detroit and Stricht of Chicago, both future cardinals.

As he wrote his book while Rome was still under German occupation, Karski-Kozielewski was obviously unable to mention his mission to the Vatican. We have not been able to verify when this took place, whether before he went to London, or after the visit to Washington and perhaps at the suggestion of the two American prelates. But it is hard to think that such a step would not have been carefully prepared by the Delegatura. If his evidence was a great blow to the Allies, it must have caused an even greater shock in Curia circles and to the Pope himself.

Chapter 3

THE SILENCE OF PIUS XII

1. No one was better informed than the Pope about the situation in Poland

The conclusion that we draw from the previous chapter is inexorable. The Holy See was extremely well informed of the situation in Poland from the first day that country was invaded to the last day of the occupation. News flowed in through the Berlin nunciature and through the Polish embassy to the Vatican; through the 'route of the bishops' and through the activities of papal couriers both regular and extraordinary, With the help of all these channels the Holy See was able to know not only about the condition of the Church, but about that of every sector of the country's life—from the murder of the population (and especially the ruling class) to the depredations from the forced emigration of the people to the racial murder of the Jews, etc.

And it would be only too easy to discover traces of this total knowledge in certain rare but significant polemical writings in the *Osservatore Romano*[129] or in the very frequent communiqués issued from Vatican Radio. And equally easy to draw up a catalogue of further proof from the admissions made by other Roman prelates. For instance, it is well-known that in the summer of 1941 Cardinal Maglione said in confidence: 'If we were allowed to be carried away by the sense of grief and outrage that these horrors arouse, we would be so, and willingly indeed.'[130] But already in June 1940 Cardinal Tisserant had written in his famous letter to Cardinal Suhard: 'Germany and Italy will dedicate themselves to destroying the inhabitants of the regions they have occupied, just as they did in Poland.' And in early March 1942 Cardinal Tisserant was to say to the representative of the Ustaše government at the Vatican: '[In Poland] four million people have died either from cold or hunger.'

198

Moreover Tisserant knew that eruptive typhus had broken out in Poland and that the Germans were neglecting the civil population because they needed doctors for the Russian front.[131]

Moreover the position in Poland was well known to various other episcopates, in particular to the English and American bishops who not only made public declarations (as Cardinal Hinsley of Westminster did on the BBC)[132] and tried to keep the Vatican informed, but, as we shall see, protested—and even vigorously—to the Holy See for remaining silent.

But we have no need of circumstantial proof when there is an abundance of direct proof in the form of Pius XII's utterances, though admittedly the greater number of these were of a private nature. As the reader already knows, it was only after the end of the war—in his address of 2 June 1945—that Pius XII publicly revealed how much he knew; but in private he had never concealed that he was perfectly informed about what was going on in Poland. Here follows a list of texts in chronological order that prove the fact beyond dispute:

25.VI.'41: Letter to the President of the Republic of Poland:

Reading between the lines of Our expressions of deep sadness [i.e. in his Easter Message], You will have been able to realize, my very dear Son, that the present situation in Poland is well known to Us and that We are moved in a very special way by the difficult religious conditions in which the Polish bishops, clergy and faithful are placed. . . .[133]

11 January 1942: Letter to Cardinal Hlond:

. . . What You write to Us about the situation of the clergy in Poland We—to our great pain and infinite sadness—knew already from other sources of information and We were well aware of the many sufferings to which Polish priests are exposed in the situation of the world conflict and under threats.[134]

30 May '42: Letter to Cardinal Hlond:

. . . We know exactly and are enduring with great distress the repercussions of the present deplorable situation in Poland, struck by so many horrifying misfortunes and suffering unflinchingly every kind of blow and persecution. [135]

1 January 1943: Letter to Cardinal Hlond:

We are well aware of the grievous situation of our beloved Polish people and the distressing events to which it is exposed. . . .[136]

16 February 1943: Letter to the President of the Republic of Poland:

In the message that You have sent Us through Your Ambassador, You have expressed the wish to draw Our attention once again to the situation of Our dear sons in Poland as a result of the present circumstances; although on the other hand You are well aware that among the facts You put before Us and among the sorrowful feelings You experience there is not a single one that We do not know. In the general agonizing situation, an agonizing echo of all the evils afflicting humanity reaches Our ears every day. . . .[137]

30 April, 1943: Letter to Monsignor von Preysing, Bishop of Berlin:

We are thinking over the measures taken against the Church, of which You have informed Us in Your letter: the confiscation of ecclesiastical properties, the occupation of Your seminary at Hedwigschöhe, the restriction and prohibition of the apostolate to the Poles deported to Germany and of religious instruction to Polish children, the prohibition against carrying out marriages among Poles, etc. All this, now and always, is no more than a part of a vast plan aiming at stifling the life of the Church in the territory in which German authority is exercised. As You know, it is the Catholic Church of the Warthegau that has been struck most hard. We are suffering deeply from the unspeakable distress of the faithful of this region, the more so as all attempts to intervene with the government in their favour have met with brutal refusal. . . .[138]

2. But Pius said nothing

So Pius XII knew 'everything', 'exactly' and from 'various sources', 'there was not a single fact that he did not know', and it all caused him 'great distress'. Why, then, did he not rise in revolt? Why did he not denounce to the whole world the terrifying genocide of the Polish people?

In the pamphlet entitled *Information on Polish Losses due to the 1939–1945 War*, published in Warsaw in 1947 by the Office of War Reparations attached to the Presidium of the Council of Ministers of the Polish People's Republic (Russian edition), we find the following data:

Dead:

		per cent
in war operations (or as a result of them):		
army	123,000	2
civilians	521,000	8·7

by acts of violence of the occupying
forces, concentration camps, 'pacification', executions, liquidation of the
ghettoes .... 3,577,000 59·3
epidemics, ill-treatment in prison and
in the camps .... 1,286,000 21·3
died outside the camps but for the
same reason .... 521,000 8·7

Forms of Violence:
    concentration camps .... 863,000 3·2
    sent to Germany or elsewhere by force 2,460,000 9·1
    expelled from their homes .... 2,478,000 9·2

Destruction of Property:
    houses:
      in town 162,190
      in the country 353,876
    factories 14,000
    shops 199,751
    artisans' workshops 84,436
    flats 968,223
    cultural centres
      museums 25
      theatres 35
      cinemas 665
      cultural clubs 323
    Teaching:
      universities and high schools 17
      secondary schools 271
      technical schools 216
      primary schools 4,880
      other schools 768
    Health:
      hospitals 352
      sanatoriums 29
      hospitals for preventive medicine .. 24
      social institutions 47
      general hospitals and surgeries 778
      consulting rooms 1,450
    radio stations 13
    radio telegraph stations 7
    wireless sets 867,700
    Transport:
      engines 2,465

passenger trains	6,256	
goods trains	83,636	
passenger boats	25	
merchant ships	39	
railway lines	5,948	kilometres
Streets:		
second class	14,900	kilometres
bridges	15,500	kilometres
Telecommunications:		
telephones	243,250	
wires	350,700	kilometres
Timber	75,000,000	cu. metres

Losses among the Intelligentsia

historians of culture and art and archaeologists	62
artists (workers in museums, painters, sculptors)	235
composers and performers (major instrumentalists)	60
actors and directors	104
writers	56
journalists	122
judges and magistrates	1,100
lawyers	4,500
doctors	5,000
dentists	2,500
nurses	3,000
university and high school teachers	700
secondary school teachers	848
infant school teachers	34
primary school teachers	3,963
technical school teachers	340
teachers in other schools	411
librarians	54
archivists	91
experts in scientific institutes	32
Catholic priests	2,647
ministers of other religions	?
railway workers	6,124
postal workers	2,412
bank employees and financiers	3,958
employees in private companies	?
employees in State companies	1,183

| army officers | 9,000 |
| engineers and technicians | ? |

Even if we deduct a percentage of the toll, on the grounds that these statistics were compiled with a view to obtaining compensation in peace negotiations, the reality, especially in the loss of human lives, is not far from the truth. And there is no validity in the objection that figures such as these could only be obtained once the war was over. For five long years Pius XII was present as these tragic figures of people killed and property destroyed steadily if fitfully piled up. Yet he never spoke. Never.

His lips became sealed at the moment of the German aggression, and only became unsealed on rare occasions to make laments of a generalized kind, never to vibrate in a cry of protest. Of all the long list of his silences, echoing the piling-up of Nazi crimes, only the first silence is less mysterious and, at least from a subjective point of view, justifiable: the one that followed immediately after the outbreak of war. An American historian recently caused a scandal with a book on the German aggression against Poland by talking of '*Der erzwungene Krieg*',[139] but the fact is that twenty-five years ago Pius XII thought much the same thing. And if anyone had any remaining doubts about this, Saul Friedländer's book[140] has removed them.

For Pius XII considered that the intransigence of the Polish government, and especially of the foreign minister Colonel Beck,[141] concerning the 'corridor' and the free city of Danzig, was disproportionate, even downright absurd and morally blame-worthy, in face of the prospect of a Second World War. For this reason he did everything he could to persuade Warsaw to withdraw from its intransigent position, and even went so far at the last minute as to take direct action without consulting the Poles. Naturally Pius was fully aware of the series of aggressions that the Germans had perpetrated from the time of Hitler's rise to power onwards, but he was convinced that they had some right on their side in their aim to wipe out once and for all the injustices of the Treaty of Versailles and unite all Germans with their motherland. Only if he had gone beyond these claims of an obviously nationalistic nature would Hitler—in Pius's view—have appeared in the light of a gratuitous aggressor.

The cession of Danzig and the corridor would have put him to the test, though admittedly involving some sacrifices on the Polish side. For after that he could have no further pretext for upsetting the *status quo* of the European continent.

Against this background we have no reason to be astonished even by the assurance that Pius XII seems to have given von Bergen, Reich ambassador to the Holy See, towards the middle of August 1939: that he would not condemn Germany should she attack Poland.[142] Similarly we can understand that his resentment against the Polish government was not confined to the diplomatic plane but extended, at least partially, to the Polish people themselves, to whom he merely addressed a few cold words in his famous audience of 30 September.

It was only the tragic news coming from invaded Poland that little by little mitigated the original resentment and changed it into an increasingly sincere and genuinely-felt alarm. But by then his evaluation of the Polish drama became secondary in face of what he viewed as the much more serious problem caused by the cessation of the Soviet Union's isolation and hence the threat to the equilibrium of Europe caused by the Communist invasion. So that even though he was able to express remorse (to the Italian ambassador Alfieri, on 13 May 1940) 'for having been over-reserved about what had happened and was still happening in Poland',[143] his remorse never went so far as to entail reparation.

Moreover, it would be easy to show that the fate of the Polish Church was a worse blow to Pius XII than the fate of the Polish nation: he had before his eyes not so much the drama of the Polish people as the drama of the Polish bishops and priests. The numerous notes of appeal and protest transmitted by the Holy See to the Berlin government were concerned only with the religious freedom of Catholicism; they never, or only occasionally and indirectly, referred to the even more fundamental natural freedoms of life, honour, property, family and so on. And those notes never openly accused the Reich government of the horrifying genocide operating in Poland, especially that of the intelligentsia, or to the extermination of Jews, gypsies, prisoners of war, people considered incurably ill, backward children, and so on.

Even what Monsignor Tardini described as the 'terrible document' drawn up in the Secretariat of State between 14 May 1942 and March 1943[144] is no exception to this rule. Of course it said everything about the persecution of the Polish Church, but it was silent about many other and graver matters. Even if it had been published, it would have brought down blame on the heads of the Catholics, but it added very little to what was already known about Nazi hostility to Catholicism even in the Reich itself. Hence its echo would soon have been lost in the general indifference.

However this may be, the fact remains that the Holy See never had the faintest intention of publishing it. Labouring under the curious delusion that it might impress him, the Holy See was satisfied to have it reach the high places to which it was addressed—namely, foreign minister von Ribbentrop. And this was no easy matter, not because von Ribbentrop might fear the explosive contents of the document, but because, as it dealt with Poland, the Reich government had said it could not take into consideration notes concerning Polish affairs, for these were outside what concerned the relationship between Germany and the Holy See. The manœuvres to which the Secretariat of State and the Berlin nuncio had recourse to succeed in their enterprise are so grotesque that one hardly knows whether to react to them with laughter or disgust.

What happened was this. The memorandum was put into a double envelope and presented by the nuncio, Orsenigo, to the under-secretary of State, Weizsäcker, on 15 March 1943. Having read its contents, Weizsäcker summoned the nuncio two days later and handed him back the envelope, saying that if grave consequences were to be avoided it would be better to forget the whole matter. Weizsäcker wrote later to von Bergen:

> The nuncio was much upset by my explanations. He let me understand that taking the letter back involved a personal failure for himself, which Rome would take seriously into account.[145]

Anyway, the nuncio did take the document back and let Weizsäcker know that henceforth his days in Berlin were numbered. What he meant was that his career was finished, and that he could have no possible expectation of a cardinal's hat. But we have already explained why in practice he could not be removed. Maglione merely charged him yet again to deliver the document accompanying it with a firm note of protest which drew a harsh answer from von Ribbentrop on 5 May.

But Rome, too, claimed the victory. As Fr. Martini has written: 'In Rome it was noted that the Third Reich had not only received the Holy See's protest in favour of the Poles, but had put the reasons for its rejection in writing, whereas the previous year the Reich had not agreed to make anything more than verbal declarations'.[146] Such are the wonderful consolations of secret diplomacy. Rome could not boast of unmasking the crimes of the oppressor before the world, but she could boast of having approached him and whispered in his ear. The relief for the Polish victims can be left to the imagination.

But we must repeat that it would be a mistake to be surprised at the caution displayed in diplomatic notes which, if they are to be accepted, are subject to predetermined conditions, the first of which is their pertinence to the object. But is an exception ever permissible in a diplomatic dialogue? And above all is it inconceivable for the Pope and his Secretary of State to recall that they are first and foremost men of God and witnesses to the supreme laws of good and evil, and not just representatives and defenders of the material interests of their Church? Yet it was in this arid and rigid spirit that Pius XII and Maglione met von Ribbentrop on 10 March 1940. In the almost verbatim accounts published by Mgr. Giovannetti, we cannot find the faintest hint of even the most veiled kind to the innumerable wanton crimes already perpetrated in Poland by the Reich in the early months of the war.

To be sure, the encyclical *Summi Pontificatus* contained an open reference to Poland. And the Christmas message of 1939 referred to atrocities (by whatever side they were committed) and to the illicit use of means of destruction against 'non-combatants and refugees, against the old, women and children', but we know what mediocre reactions such vague and cautious words aroused among the Nazi authorities.[147] The *Osservatore Romano* could try as it might to defend the Pope's caution and maintain that 'in recent times the masses had become accustomed to a language of such vigour and even violence that a different manner of speaking seemed weak and involved by comparison';[148] but the fact remained that such guarded procedure played into the hands of Poland's murderers, certainly not into those of their victims.

The web of pontifical allusion was such that only the Pope himself and his Secretary of State could understand what he was saying. And it was always they, and not always with satisfactory results, who had to elucidate his words to others. Here, for instance, is what Pius XII wrote to the President of the Republic of Poland concerning his 1941 Easter message:

> You must have directed Your attention to the words, dictated to Us by Our duty as pastor, dealing with the obligations of the authorities in occupied countries. In appealing to the honour and conscience of all civilized nations, We were asking them not to forget the innate feelings of humanity towards the prisoners and the people of all occupied countries, and We were doing so in the name of God, who is able to bring comfort to the oppressed and will not fail to bless and reward moderation and mercy.[149]

And on 19 June 1942 the ambassador Papée noted in a report to his government:

> The Cardinal Secretary of State has told me that the Holy Father cannot always be explicit, but that all his public utterances referring to persecutions whose victims are the people, Catholics and families, are to be applied to Poland. And that everyone in fact knows that the Holy Father is always referring to Poland.[150]

Maglione would have been more accurate had he said that the Holy Father could never be explicit. If all the Pope's utterances about persecution were to be applied to Poland, then this would do less than justice to the other peoples—the Finns, Lithuanians, French, Belgians, Dutch, Serbs and so on, whom the Germans and Russians were grinding down. But we are willing to wager that Papée (*et pour cause*) left out his own comment on what Maglione had said. However this may be, the most symptomatic episode in the supposedly mediumistic interpretation of the papal texts in question occurred with the Christmas radio message for 1942, the one Mussolini described as 'worthy of the parish priest of Predappio', but which was nevertheless unquestionably the most courageous denunciation of all the acts of violence against civilians that Pius XII dared to pronounce during the whole war.

As is known, between Christmas Day and the end of the year, it is the custom for the Pope to receive all the diplomats accredited to the Holy See so as to present his New Year wishes. On this occasion not only he, but also his Secretary of State, made it their business to emphasize to the representatives of the anti-Axis countries the meaning of the allusions in the Christmas message. As regards the British minister, we have the witness of Angelo Donati:

> In August 1943 Sir [Francis D'Arcy] Osborne told me that after the publication of the papal encyclical [*sic*!] of Christmas 1942 which condemned in a general way all the atrocities committed throughout the war, the Cardinal Secretary of State said to the British Minister: 'You see that the Holy Father took account of your government's recommendations.' Sir [D'Arcy] Osborne replied that a condemnation which could equally well apply to the bombardment of German cities in no way corresponded to what the British government req lested.[151]

We have the text of a telegram sent on 5 January 1943 to Cordell Hull from President Roosevelt's personal representative to the Holy See, Harold Tittman, in which he describes an audience with the Pope of a few days previously:

> As regards the Christmas message, the Pope gave me the impression of sincerely believing that he had expressed himself with enough clarity to satisfy all those who in the past had pressed him to pronounce words of condemnation against the Nazi atrocities. And he seemed surprised when I told him that not everyone thought the same.
>
> He said that, in his opinion, it was obvious in the eyes of all that when he spoke of hundreds of thousands of innocent people killed or tortured, and at times solely because of their racial or national origins, he had in mind the Poles, the Jews and the hostages.
>
> He told me that, in speaking of atrocities, he could not have mentioned the Nazis without also mentioning the Bolsheviks, and this would surely not have pleased the Allies.
>
> He also said that he feared that Allied information on atrocities was, alas, only too true, though he gave me to understand from his attitude that, as he saw things, they contained a small element of exaggeration for the sake of propaganda. Taken as a whole, he believes that his message should be well received by the American people and I said that I agreed with him.[152]

And here we have Papée's report to the government in London (dated 30 December 1942):

> On 30 December I and our embassy staff were received in

audience by the Pope for the New Year good wishes. In the course of the audience the Pope particularly stressed that Poland is among the countries nearest to his heart; he has prayed God to give every grace and grandeur to Poland; and he gave his blessing to the Prime Minister, the government and the whole Polish nation, as well as to all Poles living in America. He made special reference to his Christmas message and explained that it makes clear reference to certain theories, certain ways of behaviour and certain states.

In conversation with the other ambassadors, the Holy Father declared that his Christmas speech is the condemnation that we asked for in our common appeal.[153]

And in a subsequent report on 24 January 1943 Papée wrote:

The Cardinal Secretary of State has made the following comment on the Holy Father's recent Christmas message: this time the Pope has said everything in his power. The Pope's message has been understood on all sides as it needed to be understood, and the best proof of this is the letter the cardinal received this morning from the Metropolitan Archbishop, Sapieha. In this the Archbishop thanks the Holy Father for his speech and says that it has been appreciated in Poland and has made a very deep impression.[154]

Considering the optimism of the phrase 'on all sides', Maglione's enthusiasm has all the characteristics of enthusiasm lacking the warmth of sincerity. But the curious thing is that, where Poland is concerned, he only quoted Sapieha and not the Polish government. The latter, in fact, can hardly have shared Sapieha's view, for not until 10 February did Edward Raczynski, secretary to the Foreign Minister in exile (and not the Minister himself), communicate the following to Papée:

The Polish government has invited its diplomatic representative to keep the papal message constantly in mind. Poland has received favourably the condemnation, indirectly contained [this qualifying adverb is surely no chance matter] in the Holy Father's last Christmas message, of the illegal and brutal actions by which the Polish nation is currently being victimized at the hands of the occupying forces. Poland expresses her gratitude to the Pope for his solemn words and for all the Holy Father is doing to alleviate the fate of the stricken Polish nation.[155]

Here we are obviously dealing with the text of an official press communiqué resulting from a meeting of ministers. It is propagandist in flavour, and it is significant that in his laudatory book on Pius XII and Poland Papée makes use of this text as showing the repercussions of the Christmas radio message rather than of earlier and more direct documents. The truth is, as we shall see, that the communiqué concealed an extremely delicate and bold approach taken towards the Pope—directly after the Christmas message and without mentioning it—by the President of the Polish Republic himself. As for Sapieha and the fervour of his gratitude, the least that can be said is that his words appear in contradiction to other attitudes he adopted and about which we shall soon be speaking. For there is no explaining why a text that 'has made a very deep impression' and 'been appreciated' in Poland did not provoke those tragic consequences which the Archbishop feared so much.

There can obviously be only one answer. For all its eloquence and clarity the Christmas radio message of 1942 was in no way understood by the Nazis against whom the Pope intended to aim it. Indeed Saul Friedländer bears witness that none of the documents in the Wilhelmstrasse dealing with the analysis of the papal message takes up this point.[156]

For all this, and as we saw in Tittman's account of his audience, Pius XII perhaps really was under the delusion that he had lifted a great weight off his conscience when he spoke as he did. On 30 April 1943 in a letter to von Preysing, Bishop of Berlin, he referred once again to his message:

> In Our Christmas message We said a word about what is at present being perpetrated against non-Aryans in areas under German authority. It was a very short passage but it was well understood. It is superfluous to say that Our love and paternal solicitude for non-Aryan or semi-Aryan Catholics, who are sons of the Church like others, should be greater now that their external existence is being annihilated and they are experiencing moral prostration. We are unable to bring them any other effective help than that of Our prayers. Nevertheless We have decided, as circumstances demand it or permit it, to raise Our voice once again in their favour.[157]

A year earlier, Montini had told Tittman that the moment might come when, despite the very serious consequences, the Pope might feel compelled to speak out clearly. But this moment never came for the Jews, even when they were Catholics, while the only way it came for the Poles was on 2 June 1943 when Pius XII expressed hope for the country's resurrection after the war. Naturally, it was a hope that could annoy no one, for it was obvious that when hostilities were over the Polish question would be solved in some way or another. Indeed the German ambassador to the Holy See, von Weizsäcker, had no hesitation in denying (to Prince Erwin Lobkowicz, representative of Ustaši Croatia at the Vatican) that the speech was aimed against the Germans. Not only that, but even a cardinal, the former nuncio to Vienna, Enrico Sibilia, also told Lobkowicz that, far from being aimed against the Reich, 'the whole speech was aimed against America, which is helping the Soviets—the greatest danger for Poland in existence'.[157 bis]. The truth is that the speech, though stronger than usual and even referring to 'repressive exterminations' on grounds of the innocent victims' nationality or race, was no more explicit than the others in indicating at whom it was aimed. Yet it helped to win back Polish sympathy for Pius XII, as we shall see. And at the Vatican it was considered so impressive that the Secretariat of State which, in agreement with Archbishop Sapieha, had just finished drafting a letter to the Polish episcopate in a tone which, if not explosive, was at least firmer than in the past, gave up the project, regarding it as now out of date.

In telling the story of the silences and reserved public revelations of the Pope, we must not forget the story of the Vatican press and radio, both of which started out fairly vigorously and became weaker as time passed. At an early stage the *Osservatore Romano* made a certain number of comments in favour of Poland that were incisive enough: there was the editorial of 18 September which denied that one could speak of a *finis Poloniae* (but we must remember that it was inspired by the news that on the morning of the 17th the Russians had crossed the Polish frontier to occupy the Eastern provinces), and the note of 12 December already quoted. Subsequently the language employed by the *Osservatore Romano* became increasingly cautious; so much so that in the article commemorating the death of Fr. Kolbe (14 August 1942) there was no mention of the circumstances in which it had occurred—namely at Auschwitz in the starvation Bunker where that friar had taken the place of one of his companions so as to save his life. The radio was incomparably bolder in the first weeks, even in the first months. Then it, too, became increasingly cautious, either because of the fears of the Polish bishops or because of the frequent protests of the German authorities. On 24 March 1941, von Bergen communicated to Berlin:

> When I protested about a transmission sent out by the Vatican radio station, I was impressed by a remark proceeding from that organization, according to which much more serious news had arrived at the Vatican but had not been used either by the Vatican press or radio out of regard for Germany.[158]

It is true that on 22 June von Bergen again complained about the Pope, but by now his zeal was quite superfluous. That very day Germany had attacked Russia and henceforward every allusion unfavourable to the Reich disappeared from the transmissions of Vatican radio out of homage to the anti-Communist crusade.[159] Silence as to the fate of the Poles thus became the price paid for the victory of the armies liberating Russia.

Perhaps, however, we should say something even more serious, namely that Pius XII's silence about Poland was not only a silence as to words, but also as to deeds. For example, the Polish Church would have felt stronger and more united, and, in consequence, the occupying forces would have had more difficulty in harming it, if it had had a leader, even *ad interim*, for the duration of the war and until the primate's return. This at least was the view of a number of Poles, including Archbishop Sapieha's secretary who, speaking to Luciana Frassati, 'gave illustrations of the tragic reality of the country—persecuted, oppressed, lacking a religious leader recognized by Rome—and begged *her* to describe the situation to the competent authority so that exceptional laws might be promulgated for the practice of religion, as it was very difficult for priests to comply with the usual regulations.'

> As soon as I got back to Rome [relates Signora Frassati] I called on Mgr. Montini and gave a detailed account of all that I had learnt, and handed over the documents and letters entrusted to my care.
>
> The Assistant Secretary of State showed himself deeply distressed by what I told him and urged me to ask for an audience with the Holy Father, so that I could tell him in detail the gravity of the information I had collected.
>
> Only three days later, on Tuesday, 30 September, at 11, I was received by Pius XII in private audience. His extreme kindness and the heart-felt way in which he slowly informed himself of the whole

Polish situation, over the three-quarters-of-an-hour of our con-versation, . . . urged me . . . to insist on the necessity of giving at least moral comfort to the Polish people who were all asking that the very noble figure of the resistance, Archbishop Sapieha, should be elevated to the cardinalate. His mere appointment would ring out as an act of protest on the part of the Catholic Church against German methods. . . .[160]

It seems probable that Pius XII took the view that the Polish Church would be better protected if it presented a scattered rather than a unified target—not to mention that it is even possible (though nothing so far gives any grounds for suspecting it) that he appointed a secret head of the Polish episcopate whose name he made known only to his colleagues. But the fact remains that it is easier for an enemy to strike at an army that is divided and knows that it lacks a leader than at an army gathered closely around its chief. In any case, Pius XII behaved quite otherwise with Poland when it was subject to the Communist regime. In 1953 he appointed Mgr. Wyszynski cardinal, and did likewise the same year with Stepinac in Yugoslavia —despite the fact that very bitter reactions could be foreseen to this second appointment.[161]

Chapter 4

APPEALS MADE TO PIUS XII TO SPEAK UP FOR POLAND

Pius XII's silence about Poland was not an easy one. In order to maintain it he had to resist all sorts of pressures both from the Poles and from other countries.

There is a whole story to be put together, for which the material (if it has been preserved) can only be provided by the Vatican archives, for the Holy See was the sole recipient of despatches from countless senders who may not have been interested to keep copies of their messages, or would have though it unwise, or had no safe places in which to hide them. Of course some of the appeals sent to Rome never reached their destination. A good part of them—from private people or small societies and movements—may well have been blocked at the point of departure by the bishops, the Berlin nuncio or the Delegatura, either because the initiative was not considered opportune at that moment, or because the tone was unsuitable, or simply because the couriers had more important things to carry. Moreover not all the couriers reached their destination intact with their cargo, for sometimes they had to get rid of it on the way in the interests of safety, and sometimes they were discovered and captured.

Yet, according to Colonel Rzepecki, there were continual appeals sent by the Delegatura to ask for the Holy See's intervention. A number of these were official, but the greater part would have come from widely different circles in Poland. The leaders of the Delegatura —we are still quoting Rzepecki—were for the most part deeply irritated by Pius XII's behaviour and were often tempted to take decisive steps: if they did not do so it was through a reluctance to arouse the papal fanaticism of part of the population and the conservative clergy, and anyway it was really the task of the London

214

government to take up an official position. But all were convinced of the great effect that a papal condemnation of Nazi atrocities would have, even if they were thinking less of its influence over the Germans than of its benefits to Polish morale. As Poland was an overwhelmingly Catholic country which by tradition looked on the Church and the Papacy as the backbone of the nation, nothing would be more certain to give the people faith and courage than a statement by the Pope. The possibility that a papal intervention might induce the Germans to make harsh reprisals was a secondary consideration, for 'Nothing could be worse than what was already happening'.[162]

As regards appeals from the clergy, we must confine ourselves to indicating the bishops' conflicting attitudes. Pius XII's official apologists have made much of a phrase contained in a letter of 28 October 1942 sent him by Archbishop Sapieha: 'We regret very much that we cannot communicate Your Holiness's letter to our faithful, but it would give rise to fresh persecutions.'[163] We do not believe that there is much to be said as to the significance of this phrase;[164] yet we are perplexed to discover that a few months later (23 March 1943) Sapieha, when asked by the Secretariat of State whether he thought it opportune to publish the Pope's letters to him during the war years, replied, 'I have given the matter lengthy consideration and have cautiously explored the opinions of others,' and went on to suggest that there should be a new letter from the Pope *ad episcopos Poloniae* along the lines of the one sent in August 1942 but with additional comment on the Holy Father's activity 'on behalf of our fellow-countrymen'. When we read the Pope's letters to Sapieha in Papée's book we see at once how harmless they were: their invitations to acceptance and resignation were anything but calculated to arouse German resentment. If there was to be reaction, this would surely have come from the Poles, exasperated by the Pope's scandalous acquiescence. Is this why the Archbishop suggested a new document? It is not impossible. But then why did he want it to be along the lines of the one he had rejected earlier? Was it because the situation had changed, and the Germans had become more cautious with the turn that the war had taken in their disfavour?[165]

Sapieha's attitude was a prudent and perhaps even an enlightened one. But it was not unanimous. Mgr. Radonski thought otherwise, but as he was living abroad his opinion cannot carry equal weight. Mgr. Szeptyckyi, Ruthenian Archbishop of Lwów, was living in Poland. He, too, thought it inadvisable to publish Pius XII's letter of August 1942—but for quite a different reason: 'So as not to expose something written by the Vicar of Christ to public confiscation.' And as for the persecutions, he thought they were insufficient: he stood for nothing less than mass martyrdom:

> If the persecution takes the form of massacres for the cause of religion, it may well be the salvation of this country. There is an enormous need for blood voluntarily offered up, to expiate the bloodshed caused by atrocities.[166]

We are far from knowing everything about the pressure put on the Pope by the Polish government in exile, though what is known is enough to prove that this pressure was almost ceaseless and often took the most solemn and urgent form. The memoirs of various ambassadors to the Holy See and other political figures are enough to confirm the discontent felt in Polish diplomatic and political circles about the Pope's conduct. We shall quote a report made by Prince Lobkowicz on 10 June (it will be remembered that we mentioned him when dealing with the Pope's speech on 2 June 1943):

> It has become known that political circles at the Vatican, like those abroad, were very upset by the Pope's reserve and silence about Poland. There have even been formal protests.[167]

And we hardly need recall the steps taken by Papée to prove the truth of this.[168] Moreover Papée was urged to action by the Polish government in exile, as is shown by these two telegrams, one from Sikorski, sent to the Warsaw Delegatura:

> Following n. 54 of the 2.VII.42.
>
> I am doing all I can so that the voice of Roosevelt, symbol of the ever more gigantic power of the United States, may impress the occupying forces and alleviate your fate.
>
> A similar appeal, accompanied by a strong diplomatic move, is to be sent to the Pope on behalf of the governments of the occupied countries. This will probably persuade the Vatican to take up a clearer position and condemn the war crimes. . . . Sikorski. Received 15.VIII.1942.[169]

> End of n. 19A, part III (received 18.VIII.42).
>
> The Polish ambassador is approaching the Holy See to urge it to take a stand on the persecutions in Poland. It is possible that a Vatican chargé d'affaires may be appointed to the Polish govern-

ment in London. Meetings which should decide the person to be appointed are taking place ... STEM. Received again 30.IX.42.[170]

As for the government in exile, it was being urged to take action in its turn—by the Polish people: witness this extract from the account of the situation in Poland (n. 6/42) secretly communicated by Stanislav Mikolajczyk, Minister of the Interior of the Polish government in London, to various government functionaries in a letter dated 23.XII.42:

> This propaganda [against the Pope] which is taking on ever-increasing proportions, is being facilitated by the government's failure to take official steps in the religious field. The Polish people are impatiently waiting for news about the government's attitude towards the Holy See, about the juridical status of the Bishop of Wilno, the Bishop of Gdansk, and the exarchs of the oriental rite, etc. The people would be relieved by official news about the protest of the Holy See and the Polish government, given the flagrant and never-hitherto-experienced persecution of the Church in Poland.

In fact the President of the Republic of Poland in London can be said to have intervened systematically with his messages to the Pope. We are not in possession of his message of 6 April 1941 but from the Pope's reply of 25 June we have no difficulty in deducing the nature of the eminent statesman's invitation to the Pope, asking him to come out openly in defence of his martyred country. Here is the beginning of the Pope's reply:

> At the moment when Your heart, afflicted by the fate of beloved Poland, was speaking trustfully to Our heart in the letter of 6 April, We were trying to find words of comfort, for We feel Your suffering deeply, and that of the other war victims. Our Easter message was intended to bring this comfort to You and to all Our sons who are suffering with You. . . .[171]

Happily, however, we have the text of what was perhaps the most explicit and vigorous appeal sent to Pius XII by the Polish President during the whole war: the one dated 2 January 1943, that is, some ten days after the famous broadcast in which the Pope deluded himself into thinking he had spoken out strongly and clearly.

The importance of this appeal extends beyond its literary and emotive content. It derives first and foremost from the outspoken passages in which the President says that the Polish people have less

need of material and diplomatic help than of a decisive and unequivocal condemnation of the evil and of those responsible for it; and
perhaps even more important are the passages maintaining that
what the Poles need is to be confirmed in their certainty that 'divine
law knows no compromise'. Here is the text in its entirety:[172]

Holy Father,

The laws of God trampled under foot, human dignity debased,
hundreds of thousands of men murdered without justice, families
separated, churches profaned and closed, religion in the catacombs—that is the picture of Poland as it appears from the reports
we are receiving from our country.

In this tragic moment my people are struggling not only for their
existence, but for all that they held holy. They do not want revenge,
but justice, they are not asking for material and diplomatic help—
for they know such help could only reach them in very small
measure—but they beg for a voice that points to the evil clearly and
strongly and condemns those who are at the service of this evil.

I am convinced that if it is confirmed with certainty that divine
law knows no compromise but stands above and beyond human
considerations of the moment, the Polish people will find the
strength to hold out. A confirmation of this kind will allow them
to preserve the spirit of supernatural courage that enabled the
Catholics of Warsaw to protest in the name of Christian principles
against the murder of the Jews despite the fact that every word of
their appeal could have drawn down on them even worse repressions.

In the past, in Poland's difficult times but never so full of blood
and tears as now, Your Holiness's great predecessors turned towards the Poles with fatherly words. Today, when in the greater
part of our territory it is impossible to preach or pray in Polish,
this silence should be broken by the voice of the Apostolic See,
and those who are dying without the comforts of religion, in
defence of their faith and their traditions, should be able to count
on the blessing of Christ's successor.

This, then, is the prayer of my suffering nation, that I place at
the feet of Your Holiness, in full awareness of my responsibilities
as Head of State.

London, 2 January 1943.   Wladislaw Raczkiewicz.

It is obvious that every word of this document is an indirect but
total criticism of Pius XII's reticent and tortuous behaviour. This
criticism, and the eloquent silence concerning the 1942 Christmas

broadcast, explain the Pope's evasive answer of the following 16 February and his efforts to defend himself from the accusations by saying, as usual, that everything possible has been done both by himself and by the organs of the Holy See.

In fact the Allied governments and the Polish government were not alone in being unfavourably impressed by the Pope's reserve. The impression was shared by the mass of Catholics and, here and there, if in a guarded manner, by various episcopates. The recently-published Wilhelmstrasse documents have brought to light a disagreement between the Secretariat of State and Mgr. Spellman during the first half of 1941. Naturally we must take account of the German informant's pleasure in stressing the importance of the episode, but what happened at a high level between Maglione and Spellman remains a fact that cannot be underestimated.

Here follow two reports, of 24 May and 18 July 1941 respectively:[173]

I

There is serious uneasiness in Vatican political circles about an exchange of letters between the Holy See and the Archbishop of New York, who, temporarily, has obtained permission to keep up contacts between the Vatican and the American government in view of action in favour of peace. The Archbishop demands from the Vatican that the belligerents should be invited to recognize ethnic principles as a basis for tracing new frontiers, in the event of an intervention in favour of peace. This would also appear to be the condition laid down by the American government as a basis for common action; like the Archbishop, the Polish delegation to the Vatican [that is, the embassy of the London government] has declared in no uncertain terms that only an extremely clear stand taken by the Vatican on this point can maintain the Pope's authority over American and Polish Catholics and dissipate certain doubts as to the Holy See's political independence. These doubts arise from the Pope's ambiguous statements about the events of the war. In the Vatican they are keeping complete secrecy about the exchange of letters with the Archbishop of New York.

II

The Vatican is still maintaining complete secrecy about the unpleasant polemics that have developed between the Archbishop of New York and Cardinal Maglione. . . . In one of his letters to the

Vatican, the Archbishop stated explicitly that the Pope's prestige was on the decline in America as a result of the ambiguity of his declarations on the responsibilities of the two belligerent sides, and that American Catholics no longer trusted the Pope in view of his Italian origins. There was the suspicion, not entirely unfounded, that the Pope sympathized, in spite of everything, with the imperialist ambitions of Italy and hence could no longer maintain his spiritual authority over the mass of United States Catholics. The Secretary of State appears to have answered that he could not even show the Pope such an offensive letter; and that the Archbishop had the duty not only to believe in the holiness of the Pope's intentions but also to defend his authority with American Catholics. . . . The Pope, he said, had adopted a perfectly clear attitude in the conflict . . . he condemned Germany's aggressions and her anti-Catholic policy, but at the same time did not look favourably on the fact that rich countries such as England and France were not disposed to hand over a part of their colonial empires to young peoples such as Germany and Italy. . . .

The deterioration of the relations between the Vatican and American Catholics cannot be concealed.

Chapter 5

POLISH REACTIONS TO PIUS XII's SILENCE

It could certainly be said that the Pope's silence was rendered, if not more inexplicable, certainly more serious, by the fact that it caused not only distress and bewilderment but genuine rebellion among part of the Polish clergy and Polish people. This was the case from the very beginning of the war and through a seesaw of oscillations that became increasingly critical after the famous speech at Castel Gandolfo on 30 September 1939.

We can bear witness to this both directly and indirectly through hitherto-unpublished documentary evidence extending over the most critical period of the war, from the second half of 1941 to the second half of 1943. The indirect documentary evidence is provided by accounts on which we have already abundantly drawn; the direct evidence is provided by a wide selection, made almost at random, from the clandestine press of the same period, whether right or left.

Here we have some extracts from reports collected from the Office of Political Information of the National Army and the Delegatura:

Report of 1 February–15 March 1941:[174]
In order to defend the Holy Father from the unworthy attacks and calumnies of German, Communist and masonic circles, an illegal publishing house has produced a good brochure entitled *Pius XII, the War and Poland*. A large number of copies of this brochure have been printed and are being distributed with every available means by Catholic associations and the faithful. . . . A further brochure is under preparation: a very worthy person has paid the publishers a large sum for the purpose. . . .

. . . There are undesirable repercussions on religion: here and there people are doubting Providence; even suicides have occurred; the Church is reproached because it has not condemned all this openly and publicly. . . .

221

Report of 15 March–15 April 1941:[175]

... the Germans are supporting everything that can compromise the social or religious activity of the Church; and, as if this were not enough, they are doing all in their power to alienate the hearts of Poles from the Holy Father. To achieve this aim, they are not only jamming Vatican Radio, but, here and there, are distributing pictures of the Pope (in cleverly faked photos) giving his blessing to Hitler and Mussolini; or else they are trying to convince our people that the Holy Father has given his personal approval to Hitler's plan for re-organizing the world—i.e. plans based on the assumption that an independent Poland shall never rise again. Apart from making use of the daily press, they employ loud speakers to disseminate certain parts of the Christmas allocution, or the phrase from the *Osservatore Romano* of 12 March which said that 'in him (i.e. Pius XII) the *novus ordo* has an irrefutable defender'.[176]

Finally we have to note with sadness that the agitation against the Holy Father as promoted by German and Communist circles has had disastrous and wide-spread results. In certain regions the country people are very sensitive about all that regards Rome (sometimes they walk out of church when the priest begins defending the Pope in his sermon); a large section of the intellectuals is adopting a hostile attitude to the Holy See and, here and there, there is talk of breaking off from Rome and founding a national Church, etc. It sometimes happens that even priests are rising up in protest against the father of Christianity.

Report of 15 August–15 November 1941:[177]

The critical attitude of the population towards the Vatican persists: reinforced by German propaganda talking of the Pope's sympathy for the Axis powers (for example the blessing sent to the defenders at Gondar). This in no way means that the Church and religion are being criticized, far from it: there is an increase in the number of church-goers. Nevertheless Vatican policy and the behaviour of a certain number of priests have strengthened criticism of the clergy. The people are watching the individual behaviour of representatives of the clergy more closely. For the moment, however, given the persecutions suffered by the Church and the priests, and the increased participation of the clergy in acts of charity, it is noticeable that the people are in some way drawing nearer to the clergy. One thing that influences public opinion favourably is the clergy's non-interference in politics.

The clergy's attitude towards the Vatican varies. The higher

clergy and the members of the religious orders are defending the
Pope; the young priests criticize him. . . .

Report of 9 January 1942:[178]
A more decisive stand is not being helped by the attitude of the
Vatican. It is said that the Pope has been knocked off his balance
by the situation: he would not dare to make a public declaration
against the Germans, although his feelings are on the other side.
In his last allocution he said he could no longer remain silent in
view of the terror and persecution in a country, but he did not
mention the Germans by name. The clergy have received no
political directive from the Vatican since the beginning of the war.
Communication is difficult. Correspondence is not formally prohibited, but it is impossible to speak of the difficulties in official and
censored letters. Of course illegal correspondence exists, but some
of the letters never reach their destinations and in any case they do
not give a complete picture of the situation.

Report of 15 November 1941–1 June 1942:[179]
. . . Vatican policy is being widely criticized among priests. They
maintain that the Pope is ill-informed as to what is happening in
Poland and they draw attention to the anti-Polish behaviour of the
Berlin nunciature. . . .

Report of September 1943:[180]
Anti-papal activities have considerably diminished thanks to the
people's understanding and the efficient counter-action carried out
in the name of the Church's interests and those of the whole
Nation. At this point we should draw attention to a small, but
well written, brochure, *Pius XII and the War*. There are, alas,
certain elements that take every opportunity to attack the Pope and
present an entirely mistaken version of his behaviour towards the
belligerents and Poland in particular. Thus, for instance, the
Wiadomosci Codzienne (Daily News) of August 1943 included
among its unjust accusations against the Pope . . . the statement,
though with no supporting proof, that 'Throughout three and a
half years of war, the Vatican has quite simply forgotten the existence of Poland'. Thank God, such declarations are much less
frequent than they used to be.

Report of 9 October 1943:[181]
. . . At the beginning of September the Germans began a strong

propaganda campaign against the Pope, whom they now accuse of having encouraged Italy's capitulation. In a Katowice theatre they are showing a play written *ad hoc* and called *Gregorio and Enrico*, in which the key idea is that Canossa only happened once. All schools are obliged to send their pupils.

The following are the main data drawn from the extracts we have quoted:

(a) the reality of a crisis of confidence among the Polish people regarding the Holy See in general and the Pope in particular;

(b) the extension of this crisis to a notable, if not predominant, section of the clergy (especially the young), of the intellectuals, and even of the people, not excluding the peasants;

(c) the determining causes of this crisis could be enumerated in the following order:

— first and foremost German propaganda, fully described as to its methods and means;

— secondly, Communist and masonic propaganda, only vaguely reported, however;

— the behaviour of the Vatican, held to be altogether unclear and inexplicit in its attitude, as well as failing to provide directives, especially for the clergy;

— finally, the attitude of a certain number of priests.

(d) regarding the need to resist this state of affairs, those who drew up the reports indicate first and foremost the usefulness of counter-propaganda by means of the press.

But here is direct proof of the distrust and alienation felt by many Poles towards the Church, and especially the Holy See and the Pope, taken from the Polish clandestine press of every colour. Our sources are not the clandestine press as such[182] but, as we have already said, the special services attached to the Office of Information for drawing up reports on the clandestine press for the use of either the Delegatura or the London government. Happily these services were not content to summarize the articles, but reproduced their thought in long extracts. Hence we can provide a small but significant anthology:

The Polish Press, 1–15 December 1941[183]

10. Poland and the Vatican

Chlopski boj (The Peasants' Struggle),[184] n. 35, 30 November 1941: *Does Independent Poland need Union with the Vatican?*

. . . For centuries one of the Church's most important duties has been the moral education of mankind. Christ's ethical teaching had a revolutionary value, given the moral laws and customs of the time. . . .

Today this ethic is the exact opposite of reality as it was then. . . .

As for Catholicism, it seems to have failed completely when confronted with the judgment of history. A great Catholic country—Italy—is on the Axis side, among the butchers of mankind. Another great Catholic country, and the eldest daughter of the Church—France—has provided the largest number of traitors. With the exception of Poland, which is saving the reputation of Catholicism, it is countries of other confessions (England, Holland, Norway, Greece, Yugoslavia) that have shown lively sentiments of honour and justice. . . .

It has been shown in our times that Catholicism has gone into shameful and dishonourable bankruptcy. In saying this we are thinking above all of moral bankruptcy. . . .

Today there are two dynamic ideologies: Communism and Fascism, or National-Socialism. They have turned the masses of mankind upside down and set them on a mistaken road.

The Church has had an exceptional—almost unique—opportunity of showing its own vitality as well as the actuality of the Christian ideal. . . .

Alas, it has not taken advantage of this opportunity, and hence the Catholic Church has suffered a defeat, and nothing, perhaps, can make it good.

The Pope's defenders are saying, as we have heard more than once, that he 'could not expose the possessions and organization of the Church' (to destruction). Thus we can see that the Christian ideal is dying. The Church today is a material and administrative power and a political force, but, alas, it has ceased to be a moral force.

In the person of the Pope we have found neither a great apostle nor a father. The evil goes deeper. . . . In measures taken by ecclesiastical authority the Christian ideal is relegated to the last place, politics and diplomacy coming first. Thus we wonder whether, when the Third Republic comes to birth, we shall need union with Rome and whether such a union will have any significance. And whether, by regaining our independence from the papal State, we shall experience political, ideological or moral loss. Perhaps this will not be the same as putting aside and breaking political and material links? And, finally, apart from the other important problems, we wonder whether the uninterrupted stream of our gold should continue to flow towards Rome to increase the wealth of the Sacred Palaces and the power of the man who was supposed to be the Vicar of Christ.

The Polish Press of 15–28 February 1942:[185]

c. The Peasants and the Catholic Church

Chlopski boj, 20 February, n. 43: *The Basic Elements of Popular Politics*

. . . As history clearly proves, the subordination of the Nation's and State's interests to the interests and necessities of religion, has always borne bad fruit. True, our venerable Skarga[186] used to say: 'Well, it doesn't matter if our temporal motherland perishes, so long as we can win the eternal motherland'—and this was of much comfort to many. But the last wars prove that only a strong Nation and a well-organized State can guarantee peace and the possibility of large-scale development to the people. The Church is an international institution. It is not intimately bound up with any single people and does not serve the individual aim of any one State. Yet a glance at our past is enough to show that the Church only takes the powerful into account, and only bends to their will. Hence, for social and international reasons, we should put the interests of the Polish Nation and Polish State before all else. All other problems, hence religious problems too, should not hide from us the dangers that constantly beset the Polish Nation.

The conclusion is simple: the Polish peasant, though not inimical to Catholicism, can no longer allow his political attitudes to be always and for ever dictated by those for whom the interests of Poland are subordinate to the interests of religion. The peasants must say this clearly, the more so as the Polish clergy have always been on the other side of the barricades.

The Polish Press of July 1942:[187]

14. Poland and the Vatican

Sprawa (The Cause),[188] n. 83, 18 July 1942: *Rome is Moving East*

The creation of the Byelo-Russian Church which, like the Greco-Catholic Church of the Ukraine, has every chance of becoming a national Church, is only one item in the vast action deployed by the Vatican in our Eastern territories. This action is too much opposed to Polish national interests to be passed over in silence, even if our public opinion, with stupefying obstinacy, persists in covering up the rage and contempt that Vatican policy arouses in us.

This action has given rise to a movement of popular protest because the preparation of a missionary base was equivalent, in last analysis, to Russification, and compromised relations in the East which were difficult enough already.

For opportunist reasons, our government has abandoned taking a stand and liquidating an enterprise as dangerous as it is useless.

The Vatican has set its sails to the wind of German imperialism, in the certainty that thus it can influence the situation in the East.

German political action goes hand in hand with Vatican religious action, and, by deepening it and completing it, becomes its instrument.

In union with Nazism, in which it has found a 'benevolent protector', the Vatican is putting the fate of Eastern union into the hands of new nationalisms and is subordinating the Lithuanian' Byelo-Russian and Ukrainian movements to its own reasons of State. We are not only dealing with a 'vote of confidence' in these movements, but with an active participation in their creation and consolidation; and this is done with the illusion that, thanks to the support given to their national and political tendencies, these movements will allow the Vatican to carry out an action of apostolic conquest under the form of one or other of these Churches.

One truth can be deduced from this friendly union between the Nazis and the Vatican. The Vatican's initiatives have thrown doubt on the vitality of our action; they suggest that we are a force with which there is no need to reckon. And the Vatican has concluded that it is better to uphold our enemies by gratifying them with its moral authority.

. . . If, in the end, we reach the conclusion that all that matters is our reason of State, and if we succeed in counter-attacking our enemies' plans, we shall have nothing to regret.[189]

Wies i miasto (Country and Town),[190] n. 5, July: *The Vatican's Betrayal of Poland*

A periodical entitled *Zryw* (Drive) writes: 'The Pole who by habit identifies Poland with the Church and the clergy, is receiving as guides in the sector of what remains of religious freedom, men who are known for their deep hatred of the Polish cause, both in the Western territories and the Wilno region.' This complicated sentence is no more than a repetition of news published by *WRN* and *Chlopski Boj*—namely that, contrary to the agreements with Poland, the Pope has appointed a Lithuanian bishop at Wilno and a Nazi bishop in Polish Pomerania. It is significant that the whole press is keeping silent so as not to incur the anger of the powerful clergy. Only the two publications mentioned above have timidly referred to the problem, but now *Zryw* is raising its voice in public protest and commiserating with those who put their trust in the Pope.

But *Zryw* is mistaken when it says that 'the Pole by habit identifies Poland with the Church and the clergy'. It is much worse than this. And this is why we note the Vatican's betrayal of Poland. We must keep a close watch to see that the Pope, who has shown himself to be a mere Italian bishop and a supporter of Mussolini's policy, has no further influence over Polish life. The only way lies in the separation of the State from the Church and the direct dependence of the clergy on their own faithful. Once the clergy have to do their accounts with their parishioners and public opinion, such a shameful betrayal—for that is the only word for this stab in the back by the Vatican—can never occur again.

Let us not forget this, and let us say it to all citizens. The Pope has disregarded Poland's existence, he has not appointed ambassadors (nuncios) to the Polish government, and contrary to the agreements (the Concordat) he is appointing on Polish territory bishops who are the enemies of Poland. Finally, with Peter's Pence, to which Poland also contributes, he is upholding Mussolini's government which is on the point of collapse. This means that there can be no return to the situation in which Poland was enslaved to the Vatican.

Glos Pracy (The Worker's Voice).[191] n. 28, 10 July 1942: *The Barque of Peter on a Stormy Sea*
. . . Where are those authoritative defenders who should have stopped this horrible martyrdom? Are there any authoritative voices left? Yes, there are. One of these authorities is supreme head of the Catholic Church, the Holy Father. But alas, the successor to St. Peter, the greatest leader of Christian souls, has shut himself up in the Vatican Palace and does not bother to defend his own faithful.

Great events provoke reforms, changes in regimes and systems, and they certainly do not omit the Church. In the eleventh century there was the separation of the Roman Church from the Byzantine Church; the separation that the Popes tried to nullify by the conquest of Russia. In the sixteenth century there was the Reformation, which brought into being Churches independent of the Pope. The present great upheaval may bring about important changes in the Catholic Church. Rome may find herself isolated, for the faithful of the Catholic Church have found in the Pope neither protection nor defence.

O supreme Shepherd! The so-called Christian nations are slaughtering defenceless Christians whom Chirst said they should love. Your predecessors hurled anathemas, which you disdain to hurl on the barbarians, just as you even refuse to command the Catholics of the whole world to withhold bread, water and warmth from the bandits. But if even an anathema had no result, You, Shepherd, should leave your noble castle in sign of protest, and the whole world would be moved. The Communists and schismatics are saying maliciously that, just as Leo XIII called on the Poles to pray for and admire the Tsars, so You are telling the Poles to persevere tenaciously in their martyrdom, to pray, and carry out faithfully what the brutal forces of occupation command us to do. . . .

Are You aware, O Shepherd, that the forces of occupation have transformed hundreds of churches into storehouses and whorehouses, that the cradle of Christianity in Poland, Gniezno cathedral, has been robbed and despoiled, and that thousands of priests have been hanged and are being tortured to death in the prisons? Come here and see with your own eyes, because it is certainly difficult to imagine all these horrors unless one is close to them. The Gestapo will do nothing to You, O Shepherd. You will not be so much as touched by the sacrilegious hand of a criminal, because You are protected by your Fisherman's ring and by your powerful authority. Pope Gregory VII overcame Emperor Henry IV by his authority alone, forced him to put on sackcloth and go to Canossa with a sword at his throat. Martin V forbade King Wladislaw Jagiellon[192] to join with the Czechs. Must You, Shepherd, stay mute and watch unmoved the horrors of this great cataclysm of history?

At least hurl an anathema at the Anti-Christ of the twentieth century and you will gain great merit in the eyes of mankind. This served in the case of King Boleslaw je Hardi[193] who used violence against just one man. Why then should this power fail to serve against tyrants who are bathing in the blood of innocent and peace-loving peoples?

O Shepherd, leave your golden palace, go out to meet your people, surround them with your care, as is your task by the will of Providence.

The Polish Press, August 1942[194]

Zywia i bronia (Food and Defence),[195] 13 August: *The Basis of Morality in the People's Poland*

It cannot be denied that religion is the most potent source of morality among the common people. This light could not disappear or be extinguished in the soul of the people.

The peasant movement has never aimed at upsetting this state of things. In its criticism, it has mainly stigmatized the priests who wanted to get rich at all costs, or has sought to defend the autonomy of peasant thought when this has been threatened by the militant clergy.

The Catholic clergy in Poland has always tried to suppress autonomous thought, because it regarded the governing of peasant opinion as its absolute privilege, not only in the religious field but also in that of politics. The peasant movement has had to defend itself and, in so doing, has sometimes adopted an anti-clerical tone, but no one has the right to identify this tone with a struggle against religion.

From this a conclusion may be drawn which ought to be embodied in the People's Poland. The 'reigning' Church could be an obstacle for Poland in her quest for freedom. We cannot forget Slowacki's words:[196] 'O Poland, in Rome lies your downfall.'

The Catholic clergy must not be allowed to smother the light, nor to act as an obstacle to progressive and cultural movements. The Concordat must not legalize the clergy's wealth, nor its illicit benefices, nor its independence with regard to the State. Side by side with capitalist ethics, the new moral principles of the workers' world are beginning to spread. According to these principles the source of all values and all goods lies in work . . . and work must never be a source of abuse, as has happened up till now. Here we have the new moral principles that demand the socialization of the national economy and the liberation of work from the profit of the minority.

The Polish Press, September 1942[197]

W.R.N. (Liberty, Equality, Independence), n. 99,[198] 19 November, 1942: *Sops from the Vatican*

After the brutal blows which Vatican policy has not spared Poland—breaking the Concordat and walking hand in hand with the Hitlerite and Lithuanian Fascists, appointing bishops at Wilno and in Pomerania without consulting the Polish government but in accord with Hitler's desires—here we have a few sops in the form of Vatican declarations whose aim it is to make people forget the effect of the facts just mentioned. The Pope has sent Cardinal Hlond a letter containing a few compliments directed to the Polish nation, and he has declared in the presence of a few Sisters of Nazareth that he loves Poland. Our clerical press has welcomed these incidents with enthusiasm and is publishing long articles to illustrate them. But this same press turned a deaf ear when the Pope showed his solidarity with Fascism and inflicted merciless blows on our country in such delicate matters as those of Wilno and Pomerania.

The Polish Press, October 1942[199]

6. Poland and the Vatican

Glos Pracy (The Worker's Voice), 30 October 1942, n. 44

In its article, *Which is more important, Poland's interests or the interests of the Church?* it mentions the appointment of German ecclesiastical administrators made by the Holy See in the so-called district of the Warthegau and in the Chełmno diocese. It says that 'obviously for the time being the interests of the Church are more important than those of Poland: this is proved not only by the appointments, but also by other facts . . . the support given to some Byelo-Russians and . . . to traitors and collaborationists. In the territories annexed to the Reich, the Church is slowly becoming the instrument of Germanization (confessions in German, prohibition of sermons in Polish, etc.)'.

The Polish Press, January 1943[200]

Nowa Polska (The New Poland),[201] 25 January 1943

. . . We believe that the Church is an indispensable and supernatural element in the life of the nation. We ought not to hold the Church responsible for our political defeats. We ask the Church to enable our clergy to return to the western and eastern territories, just as it has allowed the Germans to establish themselves there. We beg the Vatican to issue an effective condemnation of the German right of the strongest: this right is preventing us, after centuries, from praying in the language of our fathers. We beg the Vatican to condemn, no less effectively, Russian totalitarian absolutism.

Narod (The Nation),[202] January 1943

After a favourable analysis of the part played by the Church in Poland, past and present, it writes bitterly: 'Nothing can disguise the fact that almost all the Catholic countries of Europe are to be found on the side of Anti-Christ, and that Poland alone has saved the honour of Catholicism at the judgment-seat of history. In a moment such as this, the Vatican can no longer be a lay State protecting its own diplomatic neutrality. There is too much diplomacy in the Church of Christ. The justification of Vatican policy lies in the arguments of diplomats and not in the outcry of a Polish and Catholic conscience. It is not we who are pushing Poland towards a national Church: it is the Catholic diplomats. And it is only by tackling the evil there where it is, and not in a merely formal way, that the country can be saved from the danger of a national Church.'

Report on the weekly press of 14 March 1943[203]
     5. Poland and the Vatican
     W.R.N., 5 March 1943, *Is the Vatican Breaking the Concordat with Poland?* It quotes article 9 which stipulates: 'No part of the Republic of Poland shall be dependent on bishops living outside the national frontiers,' and it writes:
     'From the point of view of international law, the Vatican has seriously infringed the aforesaid stipulations, and if we add that, contrary to article 2 of the Concordat, the Vatican is not making direct contact with the clergy and the faithful, we see clearly that the Vatican regards the Concordat as void and is not abiding by it. . . . It is thus that the Vatican has broken the Concordat with Poland.'

Weekly report on the press, 28 March–4 April 1943[204]
     Wolnosc (Freedom)[205] *A Breathing-Space*
     Wolnosc describes the Vatican's behaviour towards the Polish Nation and State as perfidious. It maintains that this opinion 'reflects the opinion of the whole nation, which has had enough of the guile of the monsignori in the eternal city. Weak and few and far between have been the voices of those trying to save the situation and to draw a veil over the abyss created by Pius XII between the Polish people and the summit of ecclesiastical administration'.

Report on the press, 25 April–5 May 1943[206]
     6. Poland and the Vatican
     Wolnosc (Freedom), 6 April 1943, n. 23, in its article entitled *The Defenders of Vatican Policy have not been caught napping*, quarrels with the article in *Pravda* entitled *What the Catholic Church thinks of the War*. We read:
     'When the Polish cities were being destroyed by bombs the

Vatican, to which all eyes were turned, was silent, pretending not to know what was happening in Poland, Denmark, Belgium, Holland, France, Norway, Greece and Yugoslavia. ... The Vatican remained obstinately silent and the Italian bishops blessed the Fascist pennants and sent their blessings to the Nazi soldiers who visited the Vatican on their way to Africa. Only today, thanks to the death of innocent victims, thanks to the sacrifice of millions of men who have not submitted to Hitlerite power, thanks to the hard daily grind of the democracies of the world, and now that the inevitable defeat of Hitler and Nazi barbarism comes ever nearer, there, in the distant Vatican, are they beginning to change their minds and to see the world more clearly. ... The barbarians are the men who, having forgotten their mission of evangelization, not only put up no opposition to barbarism, but dare not even condemn it. We have never been supporters of a double standard of morality, and today we are less so than ever. Our custom is to practise our morality every day. Yet what we witness as regards the Vatican is absolutely contrary to the principles of the morality of Jesus Christ, based on justice and love of one's neighbour. It is a hard thing to say, but in the near future the Vatican will have to face the consequences of this specific kind of justice with which it judges human actions; neither Jesuitical cunning nor Machiavellianism will save it from these consequences. Once Hitler has been overthrown, the blood-drenched peoples of the world will not forget his allies, direct or indirect.'

Press Report, 4–11 July 1943[207]
  6. The Vatican and Poland
  Nurt (the Current),[208] May 1943, n. 2; in its article entitled *Europe*, writes:
  'We are a Catholic people with more ties with the Roman Church than any other people in Europe. The moral and cultural force of the Church has a fundamental importance for us, for it is one of the strands in the development of our national culture. In the struggle we are witnessing, in the struggle which has seen the Christian spirit of history ground to powder—not on the battlefields but in the *pogroms* on this side of the front lines—the voice of the Catholic Church is too weak and too cautious. The feeling of loneliness that accompanies our moral sufferings is perhaps a useful test of the strength of our national spirit: yet some things cannot be forgotten and they raise the question of what will be the Catholic basis of the forces uniting the peoples of Europe after the war. Will the only idea be never to see such butcheries again? But

if war leads to no clear result and does not permit the forces taking part in it to become crystallized, then nothing will enable Europe to lift herself out of her moral confusion.'

Report on the illegal Polish press, 1 July 1943[209]
5. The Vatican
The forecasts made by *Walka* (Struggle)[210] were all too accurate: public opinion has received very unfavourably the appointment of Archbishop Godfrey as nuncio [*sic*] to the Polish government; let it be said that 75 per cent of Polish opinion is vulnerable to German propaganda which represents the Vatican as being among the Axis allies. Even the intellectuals are not immune to this and, what is worse, they are somewhat violent in their attempts to prove, by means of this fact, that they are 'independent' from the religious point of view. Ill-will plays a very important part.

It would be timely to undertake a powerful counter-propaganda drive by publishing books, leaflets, cards, with the Pope's declarations on Poland, etc. Too little has been done (F.O.P.) or else a complete mistake has been made (the anonymous book on the charitable works of the Holy See on behalf of the Poles).[211]

Press Report, 26 July–1 August 1943[212]
6. Poland and the Vatican
In its article entitled *Changes in Vatican Policy*, *Wolnosc* (Freedom), in its issue of 25 June, writes:
'When enemy bombs were destroying our cities and burying the civilian population alive, the Vatican abstained from condemning the barbarians or comforting the stricken. On the contrary, the Holy Father Pius XII is the second Pope who, by his behaviour (incorporation of the archdiocese of Poznan into that of Königsberg, the appointment of a German bishop to Poznań), is seeking to legalize our slavery and ratify the new partition of Poland with international juridical documents.

'Yet when the Allied forces began bombing Italy, the Pope published a message deploring the bombing of Italian cities, thus showing he is merely an Italian bishop.

'Thus whenever we turn our eyes towards the Holy City, we do so with anger and resentment, and this is why the Polish people have lost faith in the Vicar of Christ; Poland and Vatican "politicians" have come to a parting of the ways and it is no longer possible that the atmosphere of collaboration and coexistence prior to 1939 should return.'

Report on the illegal Polish press, 15 August 1943[213]
International solidarity
Glos Pracy (The Worker's Voice), n. 31, 29 July 1943, comments on the Pope's famous letter after the bombing of Rome: 'In our opinion, Pius XII's message recalls, in its content, though not in its form, the directives of Goebbels's propaganda after the partial destruction of Cologne cathedral.

'It is clear to everyone that a single bombardment of Rome caused the fall of Mussolini and that one or two others would force Italy to capitulate. The Pope laments Poland's fate, but we have not had a single word from him condemning the behaviour of the invader. These ingenuous explanations have been invented by Vatican agents. The authentic behaviour of Pius XII, for many years nuncio in Berlin, ruthless politician and an Italian first and foremost, has been that of an ardent supporter of the Axis powers. Pius XII linked himself with Mussolini's Italy and hence with Nazism. For us Pius XII had false compassion, but blessings for the Teuton police (following the tradition of Grünwald). Pius XII's attitude during this war will influence future relations between Poland and the Vatican.

'There is no doubt but that the Pope will change his policy after the war, but he will find himself confronted with changes in Poland and the birth of a more independent attitude regarding the Vatican.'

Wolnosc—WRW, n. 35, 25 June 1943, expresses the view that 'Vatican policy constitutes a very great surprise for the Poles. By appointing bishops in the dioceses of Poznan and Pomerania, it has legalized the Occupation. We Poles, who are known for our loyalty to the Holy See, had a right to expect that Fascist barbarism would be condemned. But obviously the Pope is no more than an Italian bishop. The Polish people have lost faith in him and, as a result, Polish ways are no longer the ways of Vatican "politicians", and nothing can now be done to bring back the atmosphere of collaboration that existed before the war. Now the Pope has changed his attitude and has found a place for some warmer words about Poland. Papal propaganda is profiting by this and publishing books that attempt to create an atmosphere favourable to the Pope.'

To sum up, the reproaches made against the Pope and the Holy See and the judgments expressed on the Church by the clandestine Polish press (of not strictly Catholic observance) are substantially as follows:

1. The Pope showed that he was neither an apostle nor a father;

2. By his silence about the bombing of Polish cities and his plethora of appeals and telegrams about Italian cities, he showed himself to be no more than a bishop of a Mediterranean peninsula;

3. The vague expressions about Poland that he sometimes used in his allocutions were false compassion;

4. The Pope never dared to condemn Nazi barbarism, at best his voice was too weak and guarded;

5. The Vatican broke the Concordat and betrayed Poland by appointing foreign bishops in Polish areas, and hence it legalized the German occupation;

6. In western areas of Poland the Vatican became an instrument of Germanization, in eastern areas of Russification;

7. The Vatican tied itself up with the Nazis so as to conquer Russia for Catholicism, and to this end sacrificed Poland.

8. The Vatican was a mere lay State protecting its own neutrality;

9. In Rome there was too much diplomacy;

10. The Polish clergy always wanted to monopolize the minds of the people and prevent autonomy;

11. The Church failed infamously in its essential task: the moral education of mankind. Today it is a temporal, economic and political power—anything but a moral power;

12. The Church is an international power not subject to any nation, but in practice it is always hitched to the wagon of the strongest.

And the following lines of practical action are to be deduced from the above:

1. The Poland of tomorrow should adopt an entirely autonomous position with regard to Rome;

2. Poland should strengthen itself as a State by ceasing to view the interests of the Nation as secondary to those of the Church;

3. Poland should separate State from Church;

4. Poland should even be ready for a religious break by setting up a national Church, as happened in the eleventh and sixteenth centuries.

It is only natural to ask ourselves whether the Pope was aware of these complaints and reactions. Once again there can be no doubt as to the answer. Fr. Martini, to take one example, has quoted two episodes concerning 'the Poles' disquiet owing to the so-called silence of the Holy Father':

In December 1942 an Italian army chaplain produced a memorandum on what he had seen in Poland and on his frequent meetings with Mgr. Sapieha during his stay in Cracow. The Archbishop was unshakeable in his certainty of the Pope's love for Poland, but one day (27 June) there were present at the conversation another prelate and Count Roniker of Warsaw, president of the Committee for aid to the Poles (R.G.O.). From the Count's questions and reactions, the chaplain had realized the state of mind even among the devout.

In March 1943 an Italian layman, in close contact with the Polish bishops and particularly with Mgr. Sapieha, wrote a precise and detailed memorandum which, though recognizing among other things that there had been a diminution of expressions of resentment against the Pope, suggested 'a solemn demonstration on the part of the Pontiff on the occasion of the anniversary of one of the Polish saints whom the German authorities had forbidden to be invoked—so as to exalt Polish faith and loudly proclaim his belief in its resurrection.'[214]

We should add to these two episodes the two audiences we quoted in part earlier on, namely those given by Pius XII to Luciana Frassati and Mgr. Scavizzi. We deliberately omitted the following details:

His extreme kindness and cordiality prompted me, towards the end of the audience, to point out the peculiar position of His Holy Person and of the Catholic Church in Poland. I gave examples of the opposition towards him and the symptoms of rupture that were every day increasing. There were no direct attacks . . . but His image and His lofty work of charity were surrounded by general silence or, worse, by marked hostility.

The Holy Father showed distress at what I said, and commented on my words with, 'gratitude is not of this world'.[215]

Mgr. Scavizzi was far less explicit in his account of his audience, indeed he was deliberately reserved. But if we reflect on the discrepancy between his involved statements and Pius XII's dramatic answer, we can guess at what the old priest did not want to reveal (for he was dealing with the ordinary popular reader, not with historians); it cannot have been very different from Signora Frassati's disclosures. We have already quoted what he said: here are the words he attributed to the Pope:

The Pope, standing beside me, listened with deep emotion; then he raised his hands and said: 'Tell everyone, everyone you can, that the Pope is in anguish for them and with them! Say that many times he has thought of hurling excommunications at Nazism, of denouncing the bestiality of the extermination of the Jews to the civilized world. Serious threats of reprisal have come to our ears, not against our person, but against our unhappy sons who are now under Nazi domination. The liveliest recommendations have reached us through various channels that the Holy See should not take a drastic stand. After many tears and many prayers, I came to the conclusion that a protest from me wor 'd not only not help anyone, but would arouse the most ferocious anger against the Jews and multiply acts of cruelty because they are undefended. Perhaps my solemn protest would win me some praise from the civilized world, but would bring down on the poor Jews an even more implacable persecution than the one they are already enduring. . . .'[216]

Finally we may recall Pius XII's words addressed to a group of Polish nuns and quoted from a report received by the Delegatura on 28 August 1942:

'Write to your fellow sisters and tell them that the Vicar of Christ loves them all, and that the whole of Poland is present in his heart.' The Holy Father was deeply moved when he learnt that the nuns wanted to know about his state of health. He asked them if people in Poland really believed all that was being said against the Holy See. On being told that unfortunately some people were ill-informed, he repeated with emphasis: 'Write to them and tell them not to believe a word of it, because the Pope loves Poland deeply, and that is the truth.' He was very distressed to think that anyone could suspect him of lack of love for Poland.[217]

When we have all Pius XII's diplomatic and pastoral correspondence about Poland at our disposal, it will probably be easier to provide evidence by means of his own words as to his knowledge of Polish restlessness and rebellion. For the time being it is enough to quote this extract from one of his letters to the President of the Polish Republic dated June 1941—quite early on in the course of events in Poland:

. . . On the other hand We know that Our behaviour in the different periods of the present conflict has sometimes been misunderstood, and that ideas and words have been attributed to Us which are inexact or completely non-existent. Making use of the means at Our disposal, We have done everything possible to dispel these errors and misunderstandings. Neither obstacles nor mistaken judgements have made Us change Our attitude, nor have We on this account abandoned or restricted Our activity which now takes up a large part of Our pastoral and paternal office. . . .[218]

If, despite all the promptings to speak and the danger that his continuing silence caused to the unity and loyalty of the Polish people, he still did not speak, one of his motives—if a negative one—was doubtless that he knew he could count on the incredible and unlimited loyalty of Polish Catholics. This would hardly be the first time that the Holy See had put Poland to the test—Poland 'semper fidelis'. Moreover in whatever way the the Popes may have betrayed the Poles, the Poles have always been proof against abandoning the myth that Rome is their bulwark. Myths are created not because of their intrinsic basis in fact, but out of necessity. If a myth could be analysed rationally it would no longer be a myth. A myth lies beyond reason and links up with the ultimate roots of vital needs; it belongs to the realm of mother ideas.

Pius XII had no need to be reminded of all this. And should he have begun to doubt it, he was soon encouraged to believe it again by information coming from Poland. For even in the clandestine press itself we can detect an attenuation of criticism about his silence after the speech of 2 June 1943. All Pius XII had said was:

. . . We call your attention especially to the tragic fate of the Polish people, surrounded by powerful nations and subjected to the vicissitudes and ups and downs of a whirlwind drama of war. No one who knows the history of Christian Europe can neglect or forget the extent to which the Saints and Heroes of Poland, her learned men and her thinkers, have contributed to the spiritual patrimony of Europe and the world; nor how much the ordinary Polish people, by the silent heroism of their sufferings through the ages, have contributed to the development and preservation of a Christian Europe. And We implore the Heavenly Queen that for this people so sorely tried, and for the other peoples that have had to drink the bitter cup of this war, a future may be preserved in accord with the lawfulness of their aspirations and the greatness of their sacrifices, in a Europe rebuilt on Christian foundations, and in a comity of States free from the errors and deviations of the past.

The fact was that Poland had experienced much more than the

'vicissitudes' of a 'whirlwind drama of war'; she had lost her territorial integrity and her independence; yet this generalized reference was enough to spread the belief that the Pope was going to pursue a more courageous and decisive line of action, or a more clever and shrewd one. But this point of view had already been put forward, if tentatively, a few months earlier, as we see from *S*,[219] No. 13, 27 March, in its article, *The Vatican and Poland*.

Vatican policy is becoming increasingly sensitive to the developments of the diplomatic situation. True, the change in Vatican policy has not yet taken the form of a more explicit protest against the persecutions of the Church and of the Catholic population in the occupied areas, though the Vatican has received extremely detailed memoranda on the situation. But Vatican radio is beginning to talk of them more and more often, even if timidly.

Commenting on the letter in which the Holy Father thanks the Polish government for its good wishes on the anniversary of his coronation, *S* writes: 'These are very diplomatic words: but thanks all the same.'[220]

But *Walka* (The Struggle), No. 23, 16 June 1943, in an article called *The Inspiration of Poland*, declares emphatically (after publishing the papal speech of 2 June 1943):

Today, as ever, the Catholic Church is the inspiration of the Polish nation. We have never forgotten this. We recalled this truth to the struggling people when visible or concealed enemies were trying to undermine the Holy See's authority with a network of calumnies and half-truths. Today this campaign has been clamorously defeated. The rare attacks are no more than diversions. The Germans, our sworn enemies, have thrown off their mask and are showing their rancour when there is talk of the Pope.[221]

Even the Communist paper, *Glos Warszawy*[222] (The Voice of Warsaw), commented very favourably on the Whitsun speech and described it as 'decisively anti-Nazi and anti-Hitlerite'. Among the few that disagreed with this view was *Wolnosc* (Freedom) of 25 June 1943:

Having realized that democracy will be victorious in the end, Rome is making a rapid change in its political front, and the word 'Poland' has again appeared in the official language of the key figures in the Vatican. Even the Pope has said a few words about Poland which are warmer than usual.

And Rome's supporters in Poland have initiated action aimed at bringing about a change in the attitude of the Polish masses to the Vicar of Christ. They are trying to tell us of all the help the Pope has showered on us during the war. Reminding us of the figs and the marmalade. . . .

When we come to regularize our relations with the Vatican, we shall not forget the generous despatches of figs, and we shall try to organize things so that the Vatican treasury will have no need to go bankrupt by sending figs to Poland.[223]

Whereas Pius XII from that day onwards took not a single step forward in what he said about Poland, as if already he had gone too far. He was dissuaded on the one hand by the catastrophic news coming from Russia, and on the other by events in Italy—especially the occupation of Rome by the Nazis after the collapse of Fascism and the Italian armistice with the Allies. So prudence was more pressing than ever. And this the Poles were the first to understand and justify.

What was more serious was that Pius XII did not change his conduct when, exactly a year later on 14 June 1944, the Allies and General Anders's Polish troops reached Rome. For the Poles in Poland this event was a symbol of their own liberation. Then on 18 July came the first of many meetings between the Pope and the men who he thought represented the new Poland: over five hundred soldiers led by General Sosnkowski, commander-in-chief of the Polish armed forces, accompanied by General Anders, commander of the Polish expeditionary force fighting in Italy, and by other generals and higher officers, as well as the Apostolic Nuncio, Mgr. Cortesi, Papée, the army bishop, Mgr. Gawlina, and other military dignitaries and chaplains.

In his address Pius recalled, as was natural enough, the fatherly anxiety and care with which he had followed the tragic events that had lacerated and tormented the heroic country, and his constant and unshakeable faith in the future resurrection of Poland. And he added:

The truth is that, though your national soil is red with blood, your right is so certain that we have the firm hope that all nations will recognize their debt to Poland, the theatre and too often the stake of their conflicts, and that whoever holds a spark of truly human and Christian feeling in his heart will be prepared to claim for Poland the full position due to her, according to the principles of justice and true peace.

These words were more than enough to win back Polish hearts to the Pope. But once again there was no open condemnation of the crimes perpetrated in the martyred country against its inhabitants. No, the words that followed expressed anxiety for the fate of the butchers now in danger:

> He expressed his firm conviction that the Polish people would be able to rise above all purely human calculations and disdain the bitter satisfactions of reprisal and revenge, preferring the sublime mission of establishing their lawful claims, of rebuilding their country, of working together with all honest souls—plentiful in all nations—so as to re-establish brotherly relations among the members of God's great family. . . .[224]

A few days later, on 1 August, Warsaw rose against the Germans. Archbishop Gawlina wrote to Cardinal Maglione, and on the 13th the President of the Polish Republic sent an appeal to Pius XII that ended as follows:

> In this tragic moment for Poland, I turn to Your Holiness from the depths of my heart to ask You, Holy Father, to raise your voice in defence of the population, of the children and the women of the martyred capital.[225]

On 21 August, when the women of Poland broadcast the following message through Warsaw Radio:

> Holy Father, we Polish women who are fighting in Warsaw out of patriotism and our love for the religion and country of our fathers, are an object of mockery on the part of our enemies. We have nothing to eat and no medicine for the wounded. . . . Holy Father, successor of Our Lord, if you hear us, give the divine blessing to us mothers who are fighting for the Church and for freedom,[226]

Pius XII still had not answered. He answered on the 31st, but privately (as for the Polish women's appeal, he could not have heard it, for he did not answer either then or ever). Finally, when the *Osservatore Romano* had published two articles on the siege of Poland—two articles that for unknown reasons were anti-Soviet rather than anti-Nazi—the Pope made his answer generally known. Even so, he had yet again abstained from raising his voice. This notwithstanding, two days later, when receiving another 2,000 Polish soldiers, he dared to say:

We have done and shall continue to do everything that is in Our power, nor shall We cease to raise Our voice so as to inspire, on one side, sentiments of humanity against the unspeakable errors and atrocities of such a terrible war, and, on the other, thoughts of justice, that should respect your rights, and of brotherly charity, that should seek by all means possible to come to the help of the anguish in which innumerable unarmed and innocent people are agonizing no less than the combatants themselves.[227]

In other words, the *n*th text of the sibyl of Cumae. Or, better, an incredibly utopian attempt to reconcile the lamb with the lion— reeking but not yet utterly sated with its butchery (Warsaw surrendered on 2 October after sixty-three days of desperate fighting).

Nemesis or not, five months after the end of the war in Europe, the new Poland which had no intention of renewing diplomatic relations with the Vatican, tore up the Concordat. True, this Poland was not fully free to dispose of herself; but was it perhaps that the power to which Poland was subjected had pushed her to this polemical and vindictive action out of ingratitude? The Holy See had certainly avoided transforming the Nazis' war against the Soviets into a crusade. But was this scruple of caution quite enough to deceive people about the Vatican's underlying *Realpolitik*? And, moreover, who can say that, even if Poland had generously condoned and forgotten her bitter abandonment during the most tragic years of her existence, the memory of the long, tormenting and ever-frustrated wait—for words that came too late, and were only said when they were useless —would never occur to her again?

APPENDICES

We have chosen a few relevant documents as appendices. The first group (I: A, B and C) are essential and of obvious importance. They consist of two *notes verbales* (one to the Vatican Secretariat of State from the German Embassy to the Holy See; the other the Vatican's answer), and a report from the nuncio Orsenigo in Berlin to Cardinal Maglione. These documents show how the Holy See stood out against the appointment of German bishops in the regions occupied by the Nazi army—a thing for which the Reich government was constantly pressing. The second *note verbale* is the one which provoked the German government to refuse to treat with the Holy See on matters other than those concerned with the area of the old Reich. The remaining document casts light on the origin and consequences of what happened.

Amongst the documents that illustrate the situation (II: a, b and c) we transcribe: an example of the presentation of the material unearthed by the Office of Clandestine Information at Warsaw to the Prime Minister of the Polish government in London (a); an example of the presentation of information originating in Poland as made by the Polish Minister of the Interior in London to other members or functionaries of the emigré government (b); and finally two examples of despatches in code with the 'key' appended which were destined for transmission by the BBC. In the last we have included only the part dealing with religious news.[228]

APPENDIX I
A[229]

Note Verbale from the German Embassy to the Holy See to the Secretariat of State of His Holiness

29.VIII.1941

This note shows the nature of the German government's

claims on the appointment of local bishops. It is all the more important inasmuch as on 27.VII.1940 the German ambassador to the Holy See had declared in the course of an audience at the Secretariat of State that the sees of bishops of the Czech and Moravian Protectorate, as in Poland, should be entrusted to German priests or priests of German origin.

In view of the fact that the bishops appointed have to exercise their functions in territories depending upon the German authorities, the recent appointments of bishops by the Holy See oblige the Reich government to make the following statement:

In view of the importance of the appointments of office holders in high positions in the Catholic Church, the Reich government cannot renounce its sovereign rights which demand that it should be consulted every time there is a question of any such appointment. The Reich is obliged to attribute great importance to the possibility of presenting objections of a general or political character before the appointment of Archbishops, Bishops, Coadjutors with right of succession, Prelates *nullius*, throughout the whole territory of the Reich including Alsace, Lorraine, Luxembourg, the liberated territories of Lower Styria, of Carinthia and of the General Governorship.

The aforesaid government feels itself obliged to claim the same right in the case in which the posts listed above should be occupied for a longer or shorter period by an Apostolic Administrator, a Capitular Vicar or by any other ruler of a diocese.

With the aim of unifying the procedure over the whole of the Reich territory, the Reich government also holds that before the appointment of persons in charge of the above-mentioned posts on the territory of the Old Reich (Apostolic Administrators, Capitular Vicars and other diocesan administrators) a confidential contact with the government should be made so that the government may have the possibility of presenting eventual objections of a general or political character regarding the candidates envisaged.

Hence the Reich government begs the Holy See to inform it at an appropriate time before it proceeds with the above-mentioned appointments, so that in case of need it may have the possibility of presenting eventual objections of a general or political character.

B

Note Verbale from the Secretariat of State of His Holiness to the German Embassy to the Holy See

18.I.1942

This is the answer to the *note verbale* of the German Embassy of 29.VIII.1941.

It expounds the important legal and factual reasons which have obliged the Holy See to reject the claims listed by the Reich government concerning the appointment of bishops.

The Secretariat of State of His Holiness has the honour of acknowledging the receipt of the note of 29.VIII.1941.

In its note, the German Embassy informed the Secretariat of State [here follows an almost verbatim quotation from the German note].

The Secretariat of State takes this opportunity of assuring the German Embassy that the Holy See is deeply anxious about the true welfare of the German nation in the measure in which this depends on the Holy See. It does and continues to do everything possible within the limits of its rights and duties to improve the relations between Church and State in Germany.

This favourable disposition, not to mention other manifestations both frequent and significant, was solemnly expounded by the Holy Father, immediately after his ascent to the papal throne, in a signed letter sent to His Excellency the Führer and Chancellor of the Reich, on 6.III.1939.

In this letter His Holiness said among other things: 'Recalling with joy the long years during which, as Apostolic Nuncio in Germany, We had the pleasure of doing all in Our power to develop favourable relations between Church and State for the benefit of both parties, thanks to reciprocal good will and benevolent cooperation, We now consecrate to this cause all the desires that Our pastoral duty presents to Us and renders possible.'

Nevertheless, despite this deep desire of His Holiness, a desire shared by His Excellency the Führer and Chancellor of the Reich, as he affirms in his answer of 29 April of the same year, relations between Church and State in Germany are, alas, in no way what they ought to be.

This is attested by the multiplicity of arrests and other deeds carried out in the territory of the Reich itself and in the countries that have been occupied and incorporated; these arrests and other deeds are an extremely serious blow against the rights of the Church and are not only contrary to the existing Concordat and the principles of international law, as voted by the Hague Conference, but, which is even worse, they are often contrary to the principles of divine, natural and positive law.

In this regard it is sufficient to list, among other matters, the transformation of Catholic primary schools belonging to the State into non-religious schools; the closing down permanently or temporarily of various minor ecclesiastical seminaries, many major seminaries and some theological faculties; the abolition of almost all private Catholic schools and numbers of convents and teaching establishments; the unilateral renunciation of all financial obligations towards the Church both on the part of the State and the communes, etc.; the ever-increasing obstacles put in the way of religious congregations and associations in their pastoral, social and teaching activities; above all the suppression and confiscation of a large number of abbeys, convents and religious houses—which suggests an intention to make the very existence of religious congregations and associations absolutely impossible in Germany.

Similar acts, and even more serious, have been recorded, alas, in the occupied or incorporated territories, above all in the Polish territories of the Reichsgau Wartheland, where the Reich governor published on 13.IX of last year an 'order regarding religious associations and confessional groups' (*Verordnung über religiöse Vereinigungen und Religionsgesellschaften*), which is visibly against the fundamental principles of the constitution of the Church of God.

All this was and still is a motive of deep sorrow for the Holy See, and this sorrow finds an echo in the resentment felt by German Catholics and those of the whole world; but it has in no way weakened the will to see the restoration of a satisfactory situation for the Catholic religion in the Reich and in the territories dependent on the Reich, as the result of an improvement in the relations between the Holy See and the government.

As for the desire expressed by the Reich government concerning the appointment of persons charged with high positions in the Catholic Church, the Secretariat of State cannot but be in agreement with the government regarding the importance of these appointments to high positions.

In view of the very nature of his pastoral office, the person appointed to administer a diocese safeguards and fosters principles of order, discipline and social justice; that is to say the very principles that the State wishes to see practised by its citizens.

But the fact that the choice of a suitable candidate benefits the State, and can thus provide a motive for the government's interest, is not sufficient reason for allowing that government the right to influence the choice; in the same way as the appointment of an honest and just civil servant, someone unprejudiced and not hostile to the Church, has special importance in the eyes of ecclesiastical authorities, but this does not give them the right to interfere in the matter.

The Secretariat of State insists on bringing to the German Embassy's notice that the Church—which was founded by Jesus Christ and hence exists by divine law, with supernatural ends entrusted to her alone and for which she is provided, by divine constitution, with effective means—represents a perfect society and its organization is the best possible.

In a word the Church has her own unique and exclusive domain of activity in which she acts with complete independence.

It follows that in matters involving the Church in general and her inner structure in particular, and above all in the choice of persons who have to carry out functions of leadership, the State cannot arrogate to itself rights deriving from its sovereignty, which it possesses entirely in its own sphere, but this is inevitably restricted to civil and political activity.

The Church's special right to establish administrators of dioceses independently of any civil authority is reinforced by the fact that in countries where there are no special agreements between the Holy See and the governments, these governments—even though they keep up close and cordial diplomatic relations with the Holy See, as, for instance, in the cases of Brazil, Chile and Ireland—do not have any influence whatever on the appointment of bishops and are in no way forewarned about such appointments.

And if some governments—including that of the Reich—enjoy certain privileges in what regards the appointment of bishops, this does not stem from the fundamental rights of civil authorities, but depends, as is well known, from special agreements by which the Holy See, in view of its supreme power in the ecclesiastical domain (a power which is, moreover, recognized by the State when it contracts an international agreement of this sort), has made specific concessions, very closely defined. This privilege (which applies to Germany) is a concession on the part of the Holy See, as is proved by the fact that the Concordat with the Reich, like the Concordat with Bavaria, both of which were signed before this privilege was granted, recognized the Church's unshakeable right in the choice of Bishops.

Art. 14 of the Concordat with the Reich establishes the point: 'The Catholic Church has a maximum right of bestowing freely all ecclesiastical offices and benefices without the participation of the State or the Communes. . . . Before sending the Bulls appointing Archbishops, Bishops, Coadjutors *cum iure successionis* or Prelates *nullius*, the name of the person selected shall be communicated to the Governor of the Reich (*Reichsstatthalter*) in the State in question so as to ensure that there are no objections to him of a general political character.'

Art. 14 of the Concordat with Bavaria lays down: 'The appointment of Archbishops and Bishops belongs in full freedom to the Holy See. . . . Before the publication of the Bull the Holy See shall take semi-official steps to ensure that the Bavarian government has no objections to the candidate of a political order.'

Where the other Germanic countries enjoy a similar privilege it is always in virtue of concessions made by the Concordat.

On this point Art. 6, para. 1, of the Concordat with Prussia stipulates: 'The Holy See shall not appoint any Archbishop or Bishop until the electing Chapter has established with the Prussian government that there are no objections to him of a political character.' And in Art. 7: 'The Holy See shall not appoint any Prelate *nullius* or diocesan Bishop's Coadjutor with right of succession until it has ascertained from the Prussian government that there are no objections to the candidate of a political character.'

In Art. 3 of the Baden Concordat we read: '1. When the Archiepiscopal See is vacant, the Chapter will present to the Holy See a list of candidates canonically suitable. . . . 2. Before confirming the election, the Holy See shall ascertain with the Baden Ministry of State whether the government has objections to him of a general political character, excluding objections regarding his political party.' The final protocol in Art. 3 lays down: 'In the case of an appointment of a Coadjutor *cum iure successionis* to the Archbishop of Freiburg, the Holy See will act after it has been in contact with the Baden government.'

The German Embassy will be good enough to notice that in the stipulations laid down in the above-mentioned Concordats, just as in the Concordats with other countries, the privilege of raising objections of a political nature is no more than a concession and only involves Archbishops, Bishops, Coadjutors with the right of succession and Prelates *nullius*.

If we leave aside the choice of Vicars Capitular, made by the Chapters concerned without any interference from the Holy See, in accord with Canon Law, the Holy See has not adopted the habit or practice of conceding the privilege in question in the case of the appointment of Apostolic Administrators or other persons appointed to temporary administration of dioceses, as the Holy See intends to preserve full freedom regarding the appointment of persons to titular posts which, by their very nature, have only an exceptional and provisional character.

If the period during which these functions are exercised should happen to become prolonged, this is merely the consequence of special conditions for which the Holy See cannot in any way be held responsible.

The Secretariat of State considers that it is superfluous to bring to the notice of the German Embassy that to grant the Reich government the privilege of making objections of a general or political character to Apostolic Administrators or other persons who administrate certain ecclesiastical areas within Reich territory, could give rise to easily foreseeable claims on the part of other governments, just as concerned as is the Reich in such appointments and to which a concession of the kind has never been granted—even when they are governments with special merits owing to their good will towards the Church.

As regards the desire to dispose of the privilege expressing indictment of a general political nature in the territories listed in the abovementioned note but not forming part of the Alt-Reich, whether it is a question of Bishops, or of cases in which the administration of the ecclesiastical districts is temporarily bestowed 'for a prolonged period of time' to the Apostolic Administrator or the Vicar Capitular or, finally, to any other administrator, the Secretariat of State permits itself to point out that, from what has already been said, the concession of such a privilege would be in contradiction to the aforesaid traditional practice of the Holy See.

By behaving thus, the Holy See has adopted a stable, wise and discreet juridical norm, based on the highest moral and juridical principles, and on the basis of which no change whatsoever is made in the religious life of a country occupied or annexed as the result of a war; and this independently of the requests for agreements or privileges from the country itself, and until the moment when, after the end of hostilities, the new state of things has been formally recognized by the peace treaties or by competent international organizations, should such organizations exist.

The Holy See adopted the same practice during the last war. Thus, for example, though the bishops of German origin in Strasbourg and Metz offered to resign after the occupation of Alsace and Lorraine by French troops, the Holy See only accepted their resignations on the 10.VII.1919 and did not appoint French prelates until the 31.VII of the same year, after the peace treaty had come into operation.

The Holy See did the same when there was question of drawing boundaries to the Polish dioceses. Though the Polish government had requested it to do so, and despite the importance for religious interests of a solution to the problem, the Holy See renounced making final decisions until the problem of who would have right to Wilno was resolved by the international treaties.

It was only after the well-known decisions taken on the matter at the Ambassadors' Conference (of 14.III.1923) and at the League of Nations (3.XII.1923) that the Holy See, by Art. IX of the Concordat signed with Poland on 10.II.1925, decided to fix the new boundaries of the Polish dioceses.

The same procedure was adopted with other countries that made their appearance, or underwent changes, as a result of the treaties signed after the 1914–1918 war.

For the reasons here expounded, the Holy See, though always ready within the limits of its rights and duties to give attentive consideration to the just requests of the German government, has with deep regret to inform it that it cannot satisfy the desires expressed in the *note verbale* of 29.VIII of last year.

The Secretariat of State requests the Embassy to inform its government. . . .

C

Report of His Excellency Archbishop Cesare Orsenigo, Apostolic Nuncio in Germany, to His Eminence, His Holiness' Cardinal Secretary of State

27.VI.1942

His Excellency the Nuncio reports on the attitude of the Reich government as a result of the foregoing *note verbale* of the Secretariat of State.

Your Very Reverend Eminence had the courtesy to inform me by the telegram N.7214/41 of 21.IX of last year that the German government had decided to ask officially, by means of a *note verbale* sent to the Holy See through the German Embassy, that it be informed in advance—so as to have the possibility of raising objections of a general or political character—of the appointment of Archbishops, Bishops, Coadjutors *cum iure successionis*, Prelates *nullius*, Apostolic Administrators, Vicars Capitular (if they are to fill their posts for a fairly long time) or other diocesan administrators in areas including Alsace, Lorraine, Luxembourg, the liberated territories of Lower Styria, Carinthia and the General Governorship itself. And as for the territory of the Old Reich, it asked for the same procedure in the appointment of Apostolic Administrators, Vicars Capitular and other diocesan administrators.

In your telegram n. 610/42 of the 23.I of this year, Your Eminence has deigned to bring to my knowledge the *note verbale* that Your Eminence communicated in reply to the German Embassy to the Holy See on 18.I of this year.

Until yesterday the German government has made no reference to the *note verbale* received from the Holy See; but I have noted that all affairs regarding the new territories of the Reich are either being carried forward with unaccustomed delay or are lost in the bureaucratic channels through which they have to pass. Yesterday, at a meeting with His Excellency the Secretary of State at the Ministry of Foreign Affairs, Baron von Weizsäcker, I expressed a desire for news on the fate of the professors at the University of Lwów (Lublin), a question regarding which—as I have already communicated in my report n. 2034/47.693 of the 17th of this month—I had succeeded in interesting the government.

His Excellency the Secretary of State courteously explained to me that he was not yet in possession of the information I had asked for about the Lublin University professors, and added:

'However, as regards this matter and all others that have to do with the new Reich territories, that is the territories that do not belong to the Old Reich, it is opportune that I should inform you of something. It concerns'—he went on—'a decision taken by competent persons regarding the *note verbale* of 18 January with which His Eminence the Cardinal Secretary of State replied to our *note verbale* of 29.VIII. 1941 transmitted to His Eminence the Cardinal Secretary of State of His Holiness by our Embassy to the Holy See. Well, it has been decided to take no further note of the affairs or questions relative to the territories that do not belong to the Old Reich.'

I tried to understand exactly what he meant by these words, and asked if the provision applied to Austria, the Protectorate and the Sudeten Germans; to which his Excellency the Secretary answered yet again: 'All the territories that did not belong to the Old Reich.'

Then I tried to explain that the request of the German government amounted to introducing a disturbing innovation into what concerned the appointment of diocesan administrators and that the Holy See's reply was in conformity with traditional practice; furthermore I pointed out that the Holy See is following a traditional line which allows for no changes in territories occupied on account of war, and this applied until the end of hostilities.

His Excellency the Secretary of State answered: 'What can be done? It is a formal decision and our governments concerned have been notified of it.' So I asked him if he wanted the Holy See to be informed, and this was his answer: 'I leave it to Your Excellency's judgment.' I asked whether His Excellency Ambassador von Bergen had done so [informed the Holy See], and he replied: 'I do not think so, for he has received no precise instructions on the point.'

Then I brought my visit to an end, saying that I would think it over.

It can be foreseen that my future proposals concerning the Reich's new territories will either have no outcome or will be evaded.

I beg you to receive, etc.

APPENDIX II

(a)

Warsaw, 28.XII.1941

Wrzos

Mr. Prime Minister,

I send you herewith:

(1) The memorandum on the situation in Poland in October 1941.

(2) The Polish press during the occupation (November 1941).

(3) The memorandum on the situation in Poland in November and during the first half of December 1941.

(4) Information on the meeting between the ex-ambassador of Poland in Berlin and Governor Frank.

(5) A photostat of the interview given by the ex-prime minister, L. Kozlowski, to the representative of the Berlin press, published by the *Nowy Kurier Warszawski* (The New Warsaw Courier).

(6) Photographs of the *Dokumenty chwili*, n. 6 and *Rzeczy-pospolita* (Documents of the Moment), n.16, 17, 18.

As I have heard that the courier charged with delivering the report for the III quarter of 1941 never reached Budapest, I send you at the same time:

(1) The entire report for the III quarter of 1941 in which are to be found headings listed in my letter of 30 September 1941 (N. 1–17).

(2) The financial report for the III quarter of 1941.

(3) The letters of Messrs. Karwat, Vogt, Bargli and from the Central Committee of the Polish Socialists.

(4) The key to the code for the report of the III quarter and for the letters there enumerated.

(5) The plan for the President of the Republic's decree on the state of the war, with reasons.

At Rome's request[230] I send once more:

A. The report on the situation in Poland in June '41.

B. The memorandum on the situation of the Eastern territories of the Republic, of 12 August 1943.

C. The separate pages of the memorandum dealing with Poland's requests which, according to the Rome despatch, never reached their destination.

(b)

Ministry of the Interior	London, April 1942
N. K 1578/42	SECRET
Report n. 3/42	Exclusively for the needs of the service.

Sir,

I herewith enclose the report of the Government Delegate from 15.VIII to 15.IX.1941, as it contains matter indispensable for forming a complete idea of life in Poland—even though it has reached London with delay due to hitches.

The report is accompanied by many items of current information.

The Minister of the Interior
St(anislav) Mikolajczyk.

(c)

Telegram C-178 I of 16.III
Third radio-broadcast for the BBC

. . .

(3) The chapels and crosses in the areas incorporated into the Reich have been pulled down with such savagery, especially in the

region of Kutno, that the local *Landrat* has had to call a halt to the destruction as 'inadvertently even German works of art were being destroyed'.

'Kalina'

Addition to B-I-88

Addition to B-I-88. As regards your means of contact with Chateau-fort: I exclude the Paulius's because the Italian Minister for Foreign Affairs is involved, whence an eventual threat to the courier. I shall profit by Pauvrette, but make sure that this means is not based on contacts of the Paulius's. On 9.II the Centre communicates: 'We are in touch with Father K-R: so far he has nothing to tell us.'

'Kalina'

PART THREE

The Case of Croatia

Chapter 1

THE COLLAPSE OF YUGOSLAVIA IN 1941

The NDH (Nezavisna Država Hrvatska), or the 'Independent State of Croatia', was proclaimed on 10 April 1941, the day the German troops entered the capital of the former Banovina.

On the 6th Yugoslavia had been attacked from the north and east by German troops moving in from Austria, Hungary, Rumania and Bulgaria, and from the north-west by Italian troops fanning out from Istria towards Ljubljana and Dalmatia. By 17 April Yugoslavia had signed an armistice securing a cease-fire for midday on the following day.

A few days earlier the Hungarians, too, had moved in to recover the Bačka territories; and on the 19th the Bulgarians reoccupied the Macedonian region which they had lost after the First World War. Thus, mangled by four enemies, the State of Yugoslavia as set up by the Treaty of Versailles was no more than a historical memory.

The first warnings had occurred at the end of 1940 with various incidents at Bitola and in Montenegro. On 2 December, national independence day, Prince Regent Paul had said, 'We must overcome all difficulties with cool heads if we are to avoid war in our country'. But this aim, though more than legitimate, became daily more absurd and illusory in view of the protraction of the ill-fated Italo-Greek campaign. The fate of Yugoslavia was sealed when the Germans decided to intervene and help their Italian allies out of their impasse.

Moreover Yugoslavia was surrounded on all sides by Axis countries and Axis allies, and it was impossible to see how she could keep on friendly terms with them while preserving her neutrality. The Prime Minister, Cvetković, made a clever move when he asked the Soviet government to provide him with arms and at the same time to negotiate in favour of Yugoslavia in Berlin. There were plenty of promises but they never led anywhere.[1] Having no alternative, the

259

Yugoslavs finally set about sounding Germany directly. In December 1940 they had signed a pact of friendship with Hungary. Political relations with Italy had been satisfactory for some time and a commercial agreement was under weigh which was signed on 17 March. A month earlier, on 17 February 1941, Cvetković and his Foreign Minister Marković had been received by Hitler in his Alpine refuge at Berchtesgaden. The conclusion of this meeting was that Yugoslavia was to join the Tripartite Alliance.

But a minority in the Yugoslav government regarded this as a capitulation. In vain it was pointed out to them that the government had taken every precaution: that, for instance, the port of Salonika, offered by the Führer, had been refused, and that an additional clause had been insisted on whose aim was to guarantee Yugoslav territory from being crossed by Axis troops. At the political and military meeting held on 20 March at Belgrade, presided over by the Regent Paul, three ministers handed in their resignation.

This notwithstanding, Cvetković left for Vienna on the 25th and signed the pact by which his country joined the Tripartite Alliance. The crisis seemed to have been overcome by events; yet on his return to Belgrade the armed guard, which was supposed to do him honour, arrested him. What had happened was that during the night of 27 March a group of patriots, led by General Dušan Simović, Commander-in-Chief of aviation and including an officer of the High Command, Colonel Draža Mihajlović, had seized power, overthrown the Council of Regency, and offered the throne to the young king Peter who was not yet eighteen.

No one could fail to see what this *Putsch* meant, and all held their breath to await Hitler's reaction. Naturally no one could have known that the Führer was taken by surprise, fully employed as he was in preparing the attack on Russia planned for mid-May. Colonel Mihajlović made haste to assure him that, despite the overthrow of the government, Yugoslavia would remain faithful to the Tripartite Alliance as well as to every other national agreement. So he in his turn was offered the port of Salonika in return for help in an eventual attack on Greece. Naturally he refused, but he was beginning to persuade himself that the worst was over, at least for the time being, when the bombing of Belgrade made it plain that the invasion had begun.

In the dismemberment of Yugoslavia the harshest punishment fell on Serbia, which was subjected to German military occupation from August onwards under the screen of the puppet government led by the 'Quisling' General Milan Nedić. Whereas Croatia, which had been hostile to and victimized by Serbia during the twenty-three years of the federation set up at Versailles, attained independence. Early in 1939, when the protectorate of Bohemia and Moravia was set up, Mussolini, by means of an exchange of letters between Ciano and Ribbentrop, had obtained German non-involvement in Croatia should Yugoslavia be dissolved.

When the German troops entered Zagreb on 10 April 1941, they were also accompanied by a non-German general, Slavko Kvaternik, a former Austrian officer who had remained incurably Prussophile. He it was who proclaimed the independence of the new Croatian State, not in his own name but in that of Ante Pavelić,[2] the Balkan *Duce* who had been in Italy awaiting developments. In 1919 Kvaternik and Pavelić had founded an irredentist organization known as the 'Ustaše' (from the verb *'ustati'* which means 'to leap to one's feet', 'to rise up', etc.) whose aim was to use all means, peaceful or otherwise, from propaganda to sabotage and assassination, to oppose the new Yugoslav State. Probably their movement would have had a very uncertain future had not Pavelić succeeded in interesting Benito Mussolini in it. In 1929 he reached an agreement with the Italian dictator.[3]

This allowed Pavelić to set up a secret service for Fascist expansion in the Balkans, gave him the use of some training camps for his recruits in the Aeolian islands and at Bovino (Val di Toro), and put some Radio-Bari transmissions at his disposal. The activities carried on by the Ustaše formations were highly secret and limited to acts of violence either as demonstrations or to cause terror in Yugoslav territory. Only once, perhaps, did European and world opinion have an inkling of what was going on. This was on 6 October 1934 when a Macedonian terrorist belonging to the movement killed King Alexander, then dictator of Yugoslavia, and the French President, Barthou, just after the President had welcomed the King at Marseilles as a guest of his country.[4]

Chapter 2

CROATIA IN THE TWENTY YEARS OF YUGOSLAV RULE

But the Ustaše were not the only Croatian movement aiming at autonomy. The majority of the Croats, though bowing to *force majeure*, had never accepted coexistence in the Federation with the other States, and least of all with Serbia. But in Yugoslavia itself the Ustaše movement had been banned by law. Hence Croatia's rights had to be represented by an officially recognized party. This was the Croatian Peasant Party (HSS), founded by Radić (who died as a result of an act of terrorism in the Belgrade parliament on 28 June 1928,[5]) and subsequently led by Vlado Maček. The intransigent resistance put up by Maček was long and tenacious, and it yielded fruit in the end.

On 25 August 1939, just before the oubreak of war, the Regent Paul achieved the so-called Maček-Cvetković compromise by which Croatia obtained autonomy similar to that which she had enjoyed in the past within the framework of the Austro-Hungarian Empire. The 'Banovina of the Sava', set up in 1929, which associated Croatia and Slovenia, now gave way to the 'Banovina of Croatia', extending from the Danube to the Adriatic and taking in, besides Croatia and Slovenia, Dalmatia (including Ragusa but excluding the 'Bocche di Cattaro') i.e. the former 'maritime Banovina' and the Catholic areas of Western Bosnia and Southern Hercegovina. In all 66,000 square kilometres and $4\frac{1}{2}$ million inhabitants.

The autonomous administration of the new Banovina was wide and covered the following sectors: agriculture, industry and commerce, mines and forests, public works, social services, education, and home rule. The executive power was exercised by the King through the 'Bano' appointed by him. The Ban of Croatia was represented in the central government by a vice-president (Maček) and five ministers.

The compromise largely satisfied the political aspirations of the Croats, and was no less advantageous to their religious aspirations. An article in *Civiltà Cattolica* of 4 January 1941, unquestionably from the pen of a Croatian Jesuit,[6] expressed optimism as follows:

It is certainly comforting for every Catholic to see how relations between the Church and the civil authorities have improved since the establishment of the Banat of Croatia. The organ of the Archbishop of Sarajevo, *Katolički Tjednik* [Catholic Weekly] writes in its fourth number this year: 'In the Banat of Croatia the desires of the Church are being met and our Christian and Catholic traditions are being respected. All has not yet been achieved, but there is good will and a healthy atmosphere. There is no shadow of animosity and distrust and no talk of any anti-ecclesiastical or anti-Christian procedure. Relations with the Church are not only correct but friendly. Legislation regarding education and schools is slowly coming into line with the Christian idea. Holders of office in the national youth movement include well-known people from the Catholic side; ecclesiastical institutions meet with favour; the free development of Catholic schools is permitted; practising Catholics are given responsible posts without difficulty in State and political organizations. For instance we now have priests as headmasters of government schools without having had to ask for this; the emoluments of the pastoral clergy, both active and retired, have been increased; many Catholic institutions have received financial assistance. . . .'

The same article comments about masonry:

Masonry, in the subject countries of Yugoslavia, suspended of its own accord the work of the lodges, which were very strong—so strong that they always had some ministers in every Belgrade government. In the Banovina of Croatia we are now expecting the publication of the names of all the Brothers .·. who have done so much harm to the Croatian people both in the politico-national and religious fields.

The only alarm expressed by this anonymous correspondent was about Communism which in his view had gained impetus, among other things, from the commercial and navigational treaty signed between Russia and Yugoslavia on 11 May 1940. Communism was now marshalling its attack on Croatia from its bases in Serbia and Montenegro, concentrating for the most part on the coast and the larger towns.

But this writer placed great hopes on the celebration of the thirteenth centenary of Croatia's conversion to Catholicism which fell in 1941:

> This year the Croatian people will celebrate the thirteenth centenary of their first relations with Rome and the first baptisms of their ancestors. For this occasion the Holy Father has granted a special Jubilee to the people of Croatia; and all the dioceses are competing to renew the spirit of faith—with missions, spiritual exercises, solemn renewal of baptismal vows, and other pious practices. In June 1941 a national eucharistic congress will be held in Zagreb, the capital of Croatia, and earlier an exhibition of Catholic culture is to be inaugurated; while a large liturgical meeting is to be held at Salona, near Spalato. Meanwhile the Croatian Catholics will hold their fourth social studies week in Zagreb, at the same time as the annual reunion of the liturgical movement will take place . . . led by the zealous Bishop of Lesina (Hvar). . . .[7]

Though the autonomy already attained could hardly be all that Croatia desired, it nevertheless constituted a notable and comforting achievement. Moreover it was reasonable to suppose that the success of the Peasants' Party would hasten the decline of the Ustaše. But if peace favoured the Peasants' Party, war was calculated to favour their adversaries. True, Maček's followers, in foreign politics, looked kindly on the Axis countries and especially Italy; but while they merely looked kindly, the Ustaše were already fanatical Fascists and Nazis. Indeed the only thing that differentiated Fascism and Nazism from Pavelić and his followers was the latter's burning Catholicism. The amalgam of totalitarianism, racism and neo-Josephism characteristic of their ideology was, from an objective point of view, the most absurd thing that could be imagined; but precisely for this reason it was the most stirring and the best adapted to the Croats—humiliated for centuries in their national pride, ground down in slavery, eaten up by hatred for their rivals, the Serbs, who had subjugated them and, worse, had become the standard-bearers and propagators of heresy (i.e. Orthodoxy) in their land.

An essay entitled *The Catholic Formation of Croatia*[8] by the priest Ivo Guberina, at the time Reader in the University of Zagreb, gives compelling expression of this Croatian sense of vocation. We quote it in extract:

> Immediately after their baptism in the seventh century, the Croats made a special pact with the Pope unlike anything we find

with any other people. The contents of the pact were preserved by the Byzantine emperor, Constantine Porphirogenitus: he says, 'After their baptism, these Croats made pacts signed with their own hand, and firm and inviolable vows to St. Peter the Apostle, that they would never invade the lands of others to make war, but would live in peace with those who wanted peace; and the Pope himself would pray for them that, should other peoples invade the lands of the Croats and oblige them to make war, God would fight for the Croats and help them, and Peter, Christ's disciple, would procure them victory' (Racki: Doc. pp. 291/2).

We learn from Croatian history that *in thirteen centuries of life,* since this pact, the people of Croatia have never undertaken a war of invasion. . . . The Croats have shown that they are neither cowards nor fatalists who in all circumstances reject war and conflict; on the contrary, they accept conflict if it be imposed on them by an invasion of their territory. On such occasions the conflict has a religious character because 'God will come to their aid every time another people invades Croatian soil.'

Here Ivo Guberina recalls the contacts between the Croats and the Popes in the course of the centuries and up to the time of King Zvonimir and Pope Gregory VII:

The ever-increasing organic link between the Holy See and the Croats lies at the root of the special spiritual physiognomy of Croatia. Since their national life on the Adriatic began, the Croats have based their spiritual unity on Christian ideas and it is these ideas that have given their unity its direction and have so uplifted it that it is from this that the people of Croatia derive the peculiar characteristics of their national life. These characteristics are: *love of peace, deep consideration for the rights and property of others, together with an extremely proud and tenacious struggle to the bitter end when defending their own individuality, their own nationality and their own good name.* These marks are underlined by the whole history of the Croatian people and are distinctive spiritual and ethical indications . . . Catholicism has carved in the spirit of the people of Croatia such noble characteristics. . . .

Here Guberina gives a summary of successive centuries of heroic resistance to the Turks, and then goes on:

Croatia became the bulwark and stronghold of Catholicism and Christianity in its most critical moments.

He then goes on to make a distinction between Croatian nationalism in the nineteenth century and the secular nationalisms that derived from the French Revolution:

The principal characteristic of contemporary Croatian national-ism is its accentuated Western and religious tone.

And he gives as example the theorist and martyr, Milan Sufflay, who was murdered on 12 February 1931 by a Belgrade assassin and wrote:

Every cultivated Croat, even a philosopher, is perfectly aware that Croatian nationalism is far above the nationalism of any other people who are not frontier people. Croatian nationalism is one of the most important bulwarks of Western civilization. And as long as this civilization is in danger—as it is today—Croatian nationalism does not only mean love for the native soil . . . it does not only mean local patriotism, it means *loyal service given to the whole West and therefore absolutely positive.*

That this was not a minority view[9] but was whole-heartedly shared and even inculcated by the Holy See is proved by Pius XII's allocu-tion to the Croats on 14 November 1939 on the occasion of their national pilgrimage to Rome to beg for the canonization of their martyr, Nicola Tavelić, a Franciscan friar. When Pius answered the addresses of homage made by the Archbishop of Zagreb, Monsignor Stepinac, and by Dr. Maršić, a Zagreb deputy and Maček's special envoy, he greeted all present in the words once addressed to the Croats by Pope John VIII:

We open our arms to embrace you to our hearts. We welcome you with fatherly affection and wish to shower on you an ever-lasting apostolic benevolence.

He immediately went on to remind the Croats of their ancestors' loyalty to the Holy See which earned them Pope Leo X's definition of Croatia as the 'outpost of Christianity'. He then proceeded to point out the ways in which they should remain worthy of their tradition:

Use all your vital ecclesiastical organizations and especially Catholic Action so that the benefits of Christian faith radiate through the whole sphere of public life. We give you this en-couragement today with an increased trust because the hope of a better future seems to be smiling on you—a future in which the relations between Church and State in your country will be regu-lated in harmonious action to the advantage of both.[10]

We must now hark back to the twenty pre-war years when the Yugoslav State was in existence. During that period the Croats had seen their political dignity and their cultural and economic standard of life, both as citizens and as a people, humiliated by the Serbs; they had also witnessed the mortification of their faith and their religious feelings. In the declarations he made at the end of his trial in 1946 and shortly before his sentence, i.e. at a deeply dramatic and solemn moment of his life, Archbishop Stepinac voiced these feelings by declaring:

It would be wrong of me not to feel the heart of the Croatian people beating within me—the people formerly enslaved by Yugoslavia . . . Croats were not permitted to attain a high rank in the army or take up a diplomatic career unless they changed their religion and married a woman of another faith.

And Ivo Guberina, too, in the article from which we have already quoted, summarizes the wrongs suffered by the Croats as believers under their Serbo-Orthodox adversaries. If we neglected these earlier events, the excesses that occurred under the NDH would be incomprehensible.

In towns historically and actually entirely Catholic, *they built splendid Orthodox churches.* The foreign visitor coming from the West would be greeted by monumental churches in Byzantine style intended to indicate the confessional character of the State he was entering. But these churches were mere theatre, because there were very few Orthodox in those areas (Sušak, Ston, Vis, Ljubljana, Celje, etc).

The Government of Belgrade helped both morally and materially the foundation in Croatia of the sect of the so-called 'Old Catholics' which was intended as a means to make Catholics go into schism. . . .[11]

Going over to Orthodoxy was more or less openly favoured. We need only recall the apostasy of Catholic settlers in the diaspora of Kosovo and Bistrenci (Macedonia) and in scattered parts of Dalmatia. . . . In open contradiction to the laws obtaining, Ukrainian Catholics of Eastern rite living in northern Bosnia (Prnjavor, Lišnja, Hrvaćani, etc.) were forced into schism. Even their churches were taken from them. On the island of Lissa (Vis), always outstandingly Catholic, a magnificent Byzantine church was built. . . .

Mixed marriages at the expense of the Catholic Church were skilfully encouraged. Among the methods used to promote this aim, young Catholic teachers at girls' schools were sent to Orthodox areas while Orthodox officers were despatched to Catholic areas. Orthodox army officers were bound by a confidential circular to celebrate matrimony with a Catholic girl solely according to the Orthodox rite. Up to 1940 there were more than 30,000 of these mixed marriages. The effects of such a policy were not long in showing themselves. Competent and informed people have calculated that in Yugoslavia the Catholic Church lost around 200,000 Catholics through *apostasy* and *mixed marriages*. But these figures do not deal only with Croatian Catholics. . . .

In school text-books . . . it is not uncommon to find mystifications, falsifications and genuine insults regarding the Papacy and the Catholic Church. (In 1936 this was denounced in a pastoral letter by the Bishop of Veglia, Dr. Josip Srebrnić, who gives an impressive list of books guilty of this. . . .)

Catholic schools were hampered in every possible way. The opening of new confessional schools was not allowed, and efforts were made to abolish those already in existence—causing unending complaints and protests from the Catholic bishops.

During a certain period students in secondary schools were forbidden to join Marian sodalities, and some Catholic Action organizations were abolished.

Catholics were overlooked in the administrative posts of the State. For instance: in the Ministry for Home Affairs 113 out of the 127 officials were Orthodox Serbs; in the Ministry for Foreign Affairs there were 180 Orthodox out of a total of 219; in the Ministry of Justice there were 116 Orthodox out of 137; in the Ministry of the Royal Court there were 30 out of 31 Orthodox (Pezet-Simondet, *La Yougoslavie en péril?*, Paris, 1933, p. 107). 115 out of 117 army generals were Orthodox Serbs and only one was Catholic (though for some years there was not even one). . . .

Catholic areas were systematically colonized by the Orthodox. Thus, of the land comprised by the agrarian reform in Slovenia, 96 per cent was handed over to the Orthodox and 4 per cent to the Catholics (6,394 Orthodox families and 284 Catholic families).

The State budget allocated proportionately less part to the Catholic than to the Orthodox Church, not to mention the insignificant sect of 'Old Catholics', etc. Thus in 1921 the Orthodox Church was granted 141,236,436 crowns and the Catholic Church only 10,903,999 crowns. . . . This obvious disproportion improved as the years passed so that in 1934–1935 the Orthodox Church was granted 45,926,630 dinars, and the Catholic Church 32,567,385 dinars (cf. Rogošić, OFM: *The State of the Catholic Church in Yugoslavia*, p. 25).[12]

But what humiliated the Catholic Croats most of all was the fate of the Concordat. In 1930 all the Churches had regulated their relations with the State: whereas for the Roman Church, although an official project for an agreement had been prepared as early as 1925, the opposition of the Serb Orthodox Church made its fulfilment impossible. In 1934 the way to agreement seemed unexpectedly opened up and indeed on 25 July, 1935, the document was signed. But it then had to pass through Parliament, and this sealed its doom. It was presented to the lower chamber in November 1936 and approved the following July; but the death, within a few days, of the Orthodox Patriarch Varnaba, who had protested vehemently and even excommunicated its principal planners (almost all, members of Parliament), together with the riots that followed, caused the government to postpone presenting the text to the Senate and then to withdraw it definitively.

Chapter 3

HOW THE NDH WAS RECEIVED BY THE CATHOLICS

In claiming reparation for their honour which had been trampled underfoot, the Peasants' Party was certainly not luke-warm; yet neither was it red-hot. Though it respected the religion of the majority and was determined to recognize its undeniable rights, it was far from being a confessional party. For instance—as the Jesuit author of the text quoted above complained—its social organization did not explicitly echo the social doctrine of the Church. Whereas the Ustaše movement was a hyper-confessional national movement which in some way wanted to restore the ancient kingdom of the Croats as vassal of the Pope. Its leaders had constantly on their lips the names of God and religion, of the Pope and the Church. Soon they would invoke the Holy Spirit with the hymn *Veni Creator* to inspire their Sabor (parliament), to whose seats they had summoned various bishops. As for the Poglavnik (or leader) of the movement, not only did he constantly keep round him priest-advisers and have a priest as tutor to his children, but he also had his own confessor and was ostentatious about the presence of a chapel in his palace.

Moreover the statute given by the Ustaše movement to the new State speaks for itself: it

> emphasizes as one of its basic principles that . . . 'the centre of gravity of the moral force of the Croatian people lies in a well-ordered religious and family life'. And then: '. . . (it wishes and seeks to provide) that each member of the national community should be conscious that the faith and the family are the foundation of an ordered, healthy, contented and happy life.' And hence it considers 'decent and morally incorrupt men to be the only ones suitable for the work of construction'; these should fight against 'atheism, cursing and swearing, drunkenness, bad behaviour, discord, lies and calumnies' among the people; promote 'readiness for sacrifice for the common good without expectation of reward';

270

wage war against 'a soft and superficial life'; uphold 'the sanctity of marriage and the family . . . by uplifting the honour of women and mothers . . . and protecting and defending the honour of girls'. Furthermore the statute imposes 'careful watch over the purity of the national struggle . . . never soiling oneself either in fighting or working, never sinning against the innocent lives of others or their goods . . . by abusing one's own position to satisfy one's own whims for enjoyment or profit of any kind, and never sinning against justice by false or superficial denunciations. . . .'

This anachronistically puritan State was racist, true enough, but not, or only partly, on merely biological grounds; the main grounds were religious. Its aim was not to turn the Croats into a pure people by the elimination of any mixture of blood but by the elimination of elements extraneous to its faith. Hence, as we shall see, it quickly imposed on the mass of Serbs rooted in its territory (they numbered 2,200,000) a choice between abandoning the State or embracing the Catholic faith. Baptism was enough to make them perfect Croats and unexceptionable from the point of view of race.

It was owing to this unprecedented synchretist ideology, in which religion was contaminated by biology and social ethics by confessionalism, that the Ustaše movement had been able to make many converts well before the war—both among the clergy (even in the episcopate, for Monsignor Šarić, Bishop of Sarajevo since 1922, had joined the movement in 1934) and Catholic Action militants.[13] It was probably this equivocal ferment that gave Yugoslav Catholic Action, already before 1941, the astonishing vitality that delighted our much-quoted chronicler in *Civiltà Cattolica* when he wrote about its largest branch, the 'Crusaders':[14]

The Crusaders' organization has 540 local sections with a central office in Zagreb. It claims 30,000 members including students, young peasants and young workers; every year it holds over 3,000 meetings in church, monthly communions, hours of adoration and so on; it organizes some 20,000 study meetings and numbers of camps, especially for secondary school-children and university students, with numbers of lectures given by our excellent priests and professors. The feminine branch is the largest Catholic woman's organization among the Croats, with 460 parish sections led from Zagreb, and 20,000 members. At the moment the Crusaders' organ is the weekly *Nedjelja* (Sunday), with *Za Vjeru i Dom* (For Faith and Fatherland) for the women's branch.

It would be too bold to say that the founders and inspirers of the 'Crusaders' were crypto-Ustaše—the names mentioned in our chronicler's text do not figure among the names of priests who were outspoken in their support of Pavelić's government. But what is certain is that after the foundation of the NDH, various of the Crusaders' lay leaders revealed double personalities—rising as Ustaše leaders with incredible speed in the country's administration and police, and reaping as booty the position of prefect, chief of police, director of rationing, and so on. They even obtained substantial recognition for seniority in service: a year of seniority in administrative posts for every year that they had been members of the Catholic associations.

And there is a significant detail concerning the clergy. On 11 April 1941, i.e. the day the NDH came into existence, the Ustaše authorities issued a communiqué through Radio Zagreb to the effect that the country population should apply to the priests who would give them directives as to what to do and how to behave towards the occupying forces.

So we can hardly be surprised if even the bishops seemed unconditionally to welcome the new situation. We need only recall the behaviour of the Archbishop of Zagreb, Monsignor Stepinac, head of the Croatian episcopate[15] (the Croatian hierarchy consisted of sixteen diocesan Ordinaries out of twenty in former Yugoslavia). To judge by appearances, he could hardly have shown more explicitly the fervour with which he accepted the new state of affairs. In the course of the first twenty days of the new government, he went to pay his homage to General Kvaternik (the day after the proclamation of the new State); was present at the funeral of that General's brother, Petar, who had fallen while proclaiming independent Croatia in a Dalmatian city (he personally blessed the remains); called on Pavelić who had just reached Zagreb (16 April) and gave a dinner party in his residence in honour of the Ustaše who had been in exile with the dictator; gave his good wishes to the new Croatian State which had risen like Christ (according to his Easter Sunday sermon); and published a pastoral letter entreating both clergy and people to collaborate in the Poglavnik's work (28 April).[16] And this only applies to his public actions; for in private, as we shall see,

Stepinac was actively working during those days to get the NDH recognized *de facto* by the Holy See.

Was he really, in his inmost self, in harmony with these external attitudes? It is usually difficult to answer questions of this kind. But in Stepinac's case we know—if only in extract—his diary from 30 May 1934 up till 13 February 1945. Judging by the notes he made on 27 April 1941 the answer seems to be an unhesitating Yes. The extract referring to his first meeting with the Poglavnik (in the palace of the Ban on 16 April) is valuable also for its revelations regarding religious policy whose main lines the Poglavnik had already worked out:

> . . . The Archbishop gave him his blessing for his work. . . . When the Archbishop had finished, the Poglavnik answered that he wanted to give all his help to the Catholic Church. He also said that he would uproot the sect of Old Catholics which was nothing more than a society for divorce.[17] He went on to say that he would not show tolerance towards the Orthodox Serbian Church because, as he saw things, it was not a Church but a political organization.[18] All this left the Archbishop with the impression that the Poglavnik was a sincere Catholic and that the Church would have freedom of action, even if the Archbishop did not delude himself into thinking that all these things could happen easily.

In other words Stepinac was not preoccupied by the fact that a programme of this kind would end up by unleashing a religious war. Still less did he put forward any objection to the legitimacy of the measures that the Poglavnik outlined—such as obliterating the Old Catholics and persecuting the Orthodox Church (these were gifts too precious to be compromised by ethical and juridical objections). If he did not openly congratulate the Poglavnik on his plans and did not encourage him to carry them out (though this is not excluded), he deduced privately that the Catholicism of the Ustaše leader was unconditionally positive and sincere, as if genuine Catholicism required that a Catholic chief of State should restrict religious liberty to the Roman Church alone. His only reservation—in accord with his character which was inclined to doubt and pessimism—was about how the plan could be carried out in practice given the conditions both inside and outside the country.

The frontiers of New Croatia in fact still needed definition, but it was already known what the frequent diplomatic meetings between 20 April and 7 May with the Axis political leaders would lay down: that the NDH could count on the territories comprising Croatia strictly speaking, Slovenia, Bosnia, Herzegovina, and a great part of Dalmatia including the islands of Pag, Lošinj and Brač.[19] Within these boundaries, the new Croatia would have an extent of territory almost double that of the Banat of 1939 (102,724 square kilometres against rather more than 60,000), and its population would be increased by over a third (6,663,156 inhabitants in December 1941 as against 4,500,000 in 1939).

Unfortunately this spectacular increase in territory involved serious disadvantages. Out of 6,700,000 inhabitants, only 3,300,000 were Croats—and hence Catholics almost to a man. Orthodox Serbs numbered around 2,200,000, Moslems around 750,000, Protestants around 70,000 and Jews around 45,000—other minorities apart. Given such conditions, adapting the new State to the Ustaše racist doctrine involved almost insoluble problems. Insoluble for Stepinac; not for Pavelić and his henchmen who had been personally spurred on by Hitler to use radical methods. [19 bis]

According to the Ustaše leaders, the Jews presented no obstacle to the spiritual unity of the country, for a decree (of 30 April) set in motion their tacit elimination according to criteria identical to those operative in the Third Reich. As for the Protestants, they constituted in practice no more than an island of German-type culture having no influence on the surrounding nation. And, surprising as it may seem, neither were the 750,000 Moslems regarded by the Ustaše leaders as a body extraneous to the nation.

Theoretically, certainly, the presence of such a notable body of Moslems was an absurdity in an ideal Croatian kingdom which was not only Catholic but, so to speak, popish. In last analysis, however, they formed a kind of closed caste that was peaceful and disinclined to make converts. Moreover, just as during the twenty years in which the Yugoslav Federation existed the Moslem community had been claimed by both Serbs and Croats in the hope of having its help in their mutual rivalries, so now it was vital for the Ustaše not to come up against obstacles on the Moslem side when they were facing the far greater problem of the Orthodox.

Chapter 4

THE PERSECUTION OF THE ORTHODOX SERBS

The main and obvious victims were thus the Orthodox Serbs. From 25 April, when the Poglavnik issued an order prohibiting the use of Cyrillic script in private and public life (letters, printed books, newspapers, posters, etc.), decree followed decree against the Orthodox, each more hateful than the one before. We need only quote a few at random:

On 3 June 1941 all primary and infant schools depending on Serb (and Czech) confessional organizations were closed;

on 25 June the 10 per cent tax levied by the State on behalf of the Orthodox patriarchate was abolished;

on 19 July the use of the phrase 'Serbo-Orthodox religion' was forbidden and replaced by the phrase 'Greco-Oriental religion';

on 20 September it was decided to requisition all property involving ecclesiastical or cultural organizations of the Metropolitanate of Karlovac in the city of Sremski Karlovci.

These decrees were obviously aimed at undermining the organization of the Serbian-Orthodox Church by striking at its financial and cultural bases and so preparing the ground for a delousing operation on the part of the Catholic Church. But at this stage they did not yet imply the forcible conversion of the Orthodox to Catholicism. Indeed this was never laid down in any act of the legislature. Even the famous decree of May 1941 that was to prove the key law of the new State as regards its demographic and spiritual set-up made no reference to this. It merely said:

Para 1—Until the laws have been promulgated concerning the relations between the various confessions, all the legal norms already in existence regarding the manner in which people can change over from one religion to another are annulled. In order for such a change to be valid it is necessary for the person who changes his faith to present a written request to the competent

275

authority (of the region or urban area) to communicate ^is decision and obtain the appropriate receipt; moreover he must fulfil all the religious rules of that cult to which he asks to change over.

Para 2—This legal order comes into vigour on the day of publication, etc.[20]

Certainly State control imposed on an act in itself strictly religious was evident, as was the blackmail lying behind the suspension of all the preceding laws so that the phenomenon of conversion should henceforth be a one-way affair. However it was only two months later that the real aim of this measure was made authoritatively explicit—in a circular[21] emanating from the religious section of the Ministry of Justice and Religion on 14 July 1941 and sent to all the episcopal Ordinaries of the NDH. It said:

To the Bishops in Ordinary of the NDH

We beg the esteemed Ordinary to communicate confidentially to all parishes the rules relating to the reception of Orthodox persons into the Catholic Church.

In no circumstances may the Orthodox be allowed to go over to the Greco-Catholic Church.

The Croatian government does not intend to accept within the Catholic Church either priests or schoolmasters or, in a word, any of the intelligentsia—including rich Orthodox tradesmen and artisans—because specific ordinances in their regard will be promulgated later, and also so that they shall not impair the prestige of Catholicism. Nevertheless if any individual of this group is in some way tied up with the Catholic faith (as, for instance, if he has married someone of the Catholic faith and Croatian nationality) then he can be received, granting approval has been given by the Ministry of Justice and Religion, which will weigh up all the data in favour of receiving him. In such a case what is decisive is that the marriage should have been contracted in the Catholic Church and that the children should have received a Catholic education. All such personal cases must be previously declared to this Ministry with the necessary recommendations from the Catholic priests and the Croatian national organizations.

Reception of the common Orthodox people and the poor is allowed after instruction in the truths of Catholicism. If the other categories insist on being received then they must be suitably delayed as catechumens or dismissed in some other way.

Director of the Religious Section

A. R. Glavas, v.r.

But it would be a mistake to think that the religious policy of the government between 3 May and 14 July was unknown to the public and, still less, to the Catholic hierarchy. As regards the masses, the Party bosses, great and small, spoke for them; so did the press, and above all the radio. We have an example of how one of the regime's leaders, Mile Budak, then Minister of Education, drove home its intolerant programme. On 8 June he declared at Vukovar:

As for the Serbs living here, they are not Serbs but people brought here from the East by the Turks who used them as vassals and servants. They are united only because they belong to the Orthodox Church and we have not succeeded in assimilating them. Meanwhile it would be as well for them to know our motto: 'either submit or get out.'

And on 19 June this same man said to Catholic Action representatives:

The Orthodox came to these regions as visitors. And now is the time for them to leave this country once and for all. It is true that many of them do not want to go, but in that case they must accept our religion.

Finally, on 6 July, to the 'Crusaders':

The Serbs reached our regions in the wake of Turkish bands as the plunderers and refuse of the Balkans. We cannot allow two peoples to govern our national State. God is one, and the people that governs is also one: and this is the Croatian people. Those who came to our fatherland two or three hundred years ago ought to return to where they came from. . . . What must be known is that we are a State of two faiths: the Catholic faith and Islam.[22]

But more eloquent than words were deeds: the terrible episodes, passed from mouth to mouth, whose significance as religious discrimination (anti-Orthodox) was gaining ascendency over that of racial (anti-Serb) discrimination. Such episodes dated back to the earliest days of the NDH. On 28 April, for instance, some hundreds of Ustaše surrounded the Serb villages of Gudovac, Tuke, Brezovac, Klokočevac, and Bolč (in the Bjelovar district) in the middle of the night, picked out 250 men, mostly peasants, as well as the priest Bozin and the schoolmaster Stevan Ivanković, led them into the fields, forced them to dig a ditch, bound them with wire, and buried them alive. That same night near Vukovar on the banks of the Danube, another 180 Serbs had their throats cut and were then thrown into the river. A few days later another mass-arrest took place at Otočac, involving 331 Serbs plus the priest and former Serb deputy, Branko Dobrosavljević, with his son. After the usual system of digging ditches and binding the victims, the execution was carried out with axes. But the priest and his son were kept to the end. The boy was cut to pieces under the eyes of his father who was forced to recite the prayers for the dying. When the priest had carried out this task, he was submitted to slow torture: first his hair was torn off, then his beard, then his skin; when they had dug out his eyes the show was still far from completion.

But the most sacrilegious episode and horrifying symbol of the whole immense butchery carried out by Pavelić's Croats happened at Glina. On 14 May some hundreds of Serbs from the country and nearby villages were herded together on the pretext of attending a religious ceremony—a *Te Deum* of thanks was to be sung for the constitution of the NDH. Having been driven into the church they found everything laid out as if Mass was to be celebrated, so they imagined that the programme had been changed—they did not suspect the worst even when they heard a military truck stop outside the church. But all doubt was dispelled when they saw a horrible gang of police entering, brandishing knives and axes. The Ustaše officer asked who among those present had a certificate of conversion to Catholicism. There were only two, and they were immediately released. After that the doors were barred and the massacre began. The church was transformed into a human slaughter-house and re-sounded for hours with cries, wails and groans.[22 bis]

Of course things were carried out differently elsewhere, almost idyllically, with flowers and festivals. As in the Vedro region where the celebration of re-baptism, as it was called, had to be filmed for the NDH newsreel: 'Croatia in words and pictures.' But this usually happened after terror had been raging nearby, and people dared not face the same fate. In addition to the cinema, the press carried news of 'conversions', and to increase the propaganda Pavelić himself received a group of forced converts at least once.

Chapter 5

THE CROATIAN CATHOLIC EPISCOPATE BETWEEN INTRANSIGENCE OF PRINCIPLE AND ADAPTATION TO REALITY

Faced with this appalling mixture of massacres and festivals, of churches attacked and burnt down here, and festooned with lights there, the first reaction of the Catholic religious authorities was one of sheer perplexity. Their main impression must have been that such terrible events could not possibly be ascribed to the central authorities but were surely the result of the change in regime—which did not lack its adversaries. Private protests were made. Monsignor Stepinac, for instance, intervened by open letters of disagreement deploring the murder of some Serb hostages, the hanging of others, the Glina massacre, the deportation of the inhabitants of Kordun, and so on.

It was Stepinac, too, who made the clearest and firmest stand against the mass movement of Orthodox conversions carried out under direct or indirect terror. And if we bear in mind the importance of his See (he was Primate) we may be permitted to suppose that his example must have been followed in most, if not all, of the dioceses of Croatia. And it is interesting to note that Stepinac did not wait to define the Church's position until provoked to do so by the government circular of 14 July. The document quoted below appeared in *Katolički List* of the Zagreb Curia on 15 May 1941 (No. 19).[23]

Circular No. 4104/41

(following the ordinance of the head of State made on 3 May 1941)

In recent times many people are coming to our presbyteries and expressing their desire to join the Catholic Church, possibly also with the intention of validating marriages contracted outside the

279

Catholic Church either civilly or in some other confession . . . and hence not validly according to canon law.

With this in view we instruct our dearly beloved clergy as follows:

1. Only those persons who are certain and sincere in their desire, and are convinced of the truth of our holy faith and of its necessity for the salvation of souls, should be allowed to join it. Faith is a question of free conscience and thus dishonest motives must be excluded from any decision to embrace it.

2. All persons desiring to join the Catholic Church should receive instruction about the truths of the Catholic faith. Throughout their instruction they should take part in divine service and listen to the word of God in fasting and abstinence, etc., so as to be introduced into the practice of religious life in the Catholic Church.

3. Only persons disposed to live according to Catholic principles may enter the Catholic Church. Hence those who are living in a matrimonial state which is invalid in the eyes of the Catholic Church and which the Catholic Church cannot validate, may not be received.

4. Persons desiring to enter the Catholic Church who are tied in a marriage that cannot be validated by the Catholic Church, may only be received on condition that they baptize and educate all eventual children in the Catholic Church, and bring into the Catholic Church all children over whom they still have parental power.

5. [This clause lays down how the application should be made.]

6. The attention of parish priests is drawn to the fact that in these delicate questions of the human soul they must proceed strictly in accord with the principles of the Catholic Church, that they must safeguard its dignity and must reject *a limine* all those attempting to enter it without valid motives and merely so as to defend their interests.

On the other hand deep understanding is required, especially for those who, during the last twenty years and under the direct or indirect pressure of the authorities who in all points favoured non-Catholics and above all the Orthodox, went against their deepest religious convictions in a moment of weakness and for the sake of their careers or for other reasons of a personal nature abandoned Catholicism. Such people deserve especial care if it emerges that during their period of lapse they maintained a relationship with the Catholic Church and educated their children in the Catholic spirit as far as they were able. Schismatics of this kind and their families can unfortunately be numbered by the thousand and for them there is need of much love and of all possible effort to get them to return to the Catholic Church and so save themselves and their children.

The Archbishop's Chancellery.

And here is the letter that Stepinac sent to the Ministry of Justice and Religion immediately after its absurd circular:[24]

N. 9259/1941
Subject: Legal conversions of the Orthodox.
To the Ministry of Justice and Religion
In reply to your most esteemed letter of 14 July 1941, N. 42678-B-1941, on the subject of legal changes of religion, this archdiocese begs to answer as follows:

1. The concern shown by the NDH to safeguard itself from these elements who, by an eventual change of religion, would like to introduce themselves into the national organism of the Croats with the intention of destroying it, is understandable to everyone and more than justified.

2. Though this Archbishopric is forwarding the Ministry's circular to the parishes, it holds itself bound in duty to make various observations:

(a) It is a fact that very few people are joining the Greco-Catholic rite. Nevertheless and in all circumstances this Archbishopric maintains that to prohibit such action on principle is a violation of the Church's competence, for the Church views the Greco-Catholic rite and the Roman rite to be on the same level. Such a prohibition would also offend our Greco-Catholics who have faithfully preserved their Catholic credo and their Croatian consciousness and have always defended places sacred to Catholics and Croats. Hence we feel it necessary that there should be a change and an attenuation in the rules regarding changing over to the Greco-Catholic Church.

(b) As for conversion from Orthodoxy of priests, schoolmasters, tradesmen, artisans and rich peasants, there is an obvious need for caution about accepting their requests when made. At the same time it must be borne in mind that it would be against the spirit and duty of the Catholic Church to refuse to receive the whole intelligentsia on principle. Christ came into the world to save all men and bring them to the knowledge of the truth. This is also the task of his Church, indeed it is a difficult and sacred duty which the Church received from Christ when he said, 'Go ye and teach all nations.' God's mercy acts invisibly on the souls of his creatures and, in these difficult days, he could open the eyes of many and make the truth known. It is hardly opportune to close the road of truth to the whole of the Orthodox intelligentsia, as this would be in obvious contradiction to the divine mission of the Church of Christ. If in the past there were but few cases when the Orthodox intelligentsia accepted the Catholic Church with all their hearts, yet some there were, and they were people who in practice showed themselves more Catholic than the Catholics themselves. This is also possible now. No limits can be put to God's mercy.

For all these reasons may we be allowed to remark that the Church cannot give up her right and her divine duty to accept in her bosom a schismatic who produces certain proof of his sincere and honest intentions about entering the Catholic Church.

The Ministry's contention that it should receive an account of every conversion together with a recommendation from the parish and the Croatian national organizations gives ground for thinking that this would involve the already over-worked clergy in an excess of work. On the other hand we are in agreement about the receiving of poor people because in their case we can be more certain that no material interests are involved and thus that the intention is purer. But even in these cases the Church will always be very cautious because she does not want her deep sanctity to be profaned.

In conclusion, this Archbishopric will do all it can to realize to the maximum the intentions of the Croatian government, but with one reservation that can hardly be resented by this Ministry, namely, that the supreme law of Christ's gospel is never outraged.

Zagreb, 16 July 1941.   By order of the Archbishop
                                                        the Vicar-General
                                                        Dr. Josip Lach.

It is superfluous to point out that both these documents are in perfect agreement with the theological and canonical principles of Christian doctrine. The first, while welcoming with satisfaction a state of affairs promising to the Church, clearly distinguishes the Church's religious and pastoral expectations from the political expectations of the government, and is concerned not to share the latter's haste and superficiality in something so important as conversion to a new faith; the second ventures courageously beyond protest and claim, demanding no more nor less than a modification of the government's decrees. Unfortunately the strong protest concerning discrimination against the Orthodox intelligentsia completely leaves out the matter of discrimination against the Jews—as though they were not equally threatened in their natural and fundamental rights.[25]

A few days after this last document had been brought to the government's notice, the episcopal conference of new Croatia assembled in Zagreb. There are grounds for thinking that it wanted to assemble much earlier, and ought to have done so, to make contact with the rulers of the new State; but probably the intense political activity of the Poglavnik and his most important collaborators earlier on, the negotiations on foot between the NDH and the Holy See for setting up mutual relations, and the ever-delayed arrival of the Papal Legate appointed on 13 June, forced the episcopal conference to be repeatedly put off.

We do not know what the Croatian episcopate decided at its meeting of 26 July. But we do know that the first collective meeting of the bishops with the Poglavnik took place during the conference and that there was a cordial exchange of speeches. In all probability— especially if we remember that the bishops were still awaiting the arrival of the Pope's representative to confer with him and seek his advice—the conference merely took stock of the situation and cleared up certain points. But one thing is certain: Pavelić was not satisfied with the homage paid him. On 30 July, with a view to breaking down the bishops' resistance, a circular was sent from Zagreb to all the chapters of the country. It emanated from the Ministry of Justice and Religion, the Ministry of the Interior, the Ustaše Command, and the State Bureau for Economic Renewal.[26] Here it is:

NDH

N. 46468/1941   Zagreb, 30-VII-1941
Circular

Given that many Greco-Orthodox have recently been presenting requests to change over to Catholicism, the government lays down the following directives:

1. The Croatian government desires that persons of Greco-Oriental rite should not change over to the Greco-Catholic rite save in those Greco-Catholic parishes which already exist and have already received Greco-Orientals.

2. Greco-Orientals who present themselves at Catholic presby-

teries with the aim of being received should present a certificate of good conduct from the district or commune duly franked by the State for 30 *kuna*. The authorities of the commune or district will issue certificates of good conduct in agreement with the Ustaše authorities of the 'logor' and the 'tabor'. The communes and districts are under an obligation to inform the Ministry of Justice and Religion on the number of certificates granted and refused.

3. Special attention must be paid to schoolmasters, priests, tradesmen, artisans and rich peasants, and generally speaking to the Greco-Oriental intelligentsia to see that certificates are not granted save when their personal honesty can really be proved. It is a basic principle of the government that such certificates should not be granted to such persons.

4. As regards mixed marriages with Greco-Orthodox, the following rules apply:

(a) Only in exceptional circumstances is there an obstacle to receiving the non-Catholic partner in a mixed marriage contracted in the Catholic Church granting the children are baptized and brought up in the spirit of Catholicism. Where the children of such marriages are baptized and brought up in a non-Catholic way, the local and regional authorities, in agreement with the 'logor' and 'tabor' of the Ustaše, will examine every single case and decide whether the certificate should be granted either to the children or the parents.

(b) In the case of marriages contracted before an Orthodox priest, and if the children are baptized and brought up in a non-Catholic way, the above-mentioned authorities are under an obligation to examine each case and decide only after thorough investigation. In reports to the Ministry on the number of those who have passed over to Catholicism, besides the names of the persons, it is also necessary to add a note when dealing with cases of this nature.

(c) Orthodox couples married in the Orthodox Church and their children baptized and brought up in a non-Catholic way cannot be accepted without the approval of the Ministry of Justice and Religion.

5. Peasants, save in exceptional cases, may receive a certificate of good conduct without difficulty.

6. These rules are valid for all the 'velike Župe' [Ustaše regional areas] in the territory of the NDH except Gora, Krbava and Psat. In these 'Župe' the 'veliki zupani' [area directors], in agreement with the Ustaše 'logor' and 'tabor', may circulate rules suited to their territory according to the local situation.

7. Should Greco-Orientals or others go over to Protestantism and join the *Kulturbund* while not belonging by blood to the German minority, they shall not be allowed the rights enjoyed by minorities of German nationality.

8. Registers of the Greco-Orientals will be kept by local authorities who will record births and deaths until a regular parish has been formed. The local authorities will be responsible for this activity to their civil superiors.

As regards buildings and lands possessed by the Greco-Oriental Church, the decision rests with the Ministry of Peasant Administration together with the Ministry of Justice and Religion.

9. The government is aware that many Jews are presenting requests to pass over to Catholicism. This can have no influence on the situation of such persons in their relations with the State in view of the existence of the law on non-Aryans (of 30/IV/1941).

[Here follow the signatures of the officials of the various Ministries, etc.][27]

This circular, then, openly defied the episcopate—whose acts of protest it appeared to ignore and hold in contempt; and it tended to bring a disturbing form of pressure on the bishops by obliging them not to impede the government's activity which, with more and more circulars, was hastening the work of conversions. Among the most dangerous initiatives taken by the civil authorities in that same summer of 1941 was the recruitment of the clergy as 'missionaries' for the re-baptism campaigns carried out through the 'Ponova'—an organization created for the purpose, partly by the Ustaše Command to which many priests were subject as members of the Party, and partly by local authorities. This mobilization—added to the other mobilization of real and proper Ustaše chaplains[28]—not only denuded the parishes and rendered priests homeless, but in many cases contaminated these improvised 'missionaries' with a spirit of fanaticism or even violence, and transformed them into thoroughgoing butcher-leaders.

On the other hand the bishops soon became aware of the danger of the privilege that the government had bestowed on the Catholic Church by maintaining that the only permissible 'conversion' was to Catholicism. For the methods adopted changed the Orthodox not into Catholics but into pseudo-converts or martyrs; the Church was compromised by all the horrors committed in its name; and finally the other denominations became more and more hostile to it, not excluding the Moslems.

This last is a fact that we must stress, not least because the two documents from which we are about to quote are of unusual interest for highlighting the religious ambitions of the Ustaši as well as for providing documentation on the absurd and incredible dimensions of the persecution they unleashed. By an odd coincidence the documents either immediately precede, or are of the same date as, the text that immediately follows, which was issued by the second episcopal conference of that year—the first at which the Papal Legate was present. The first of our documents is a partial reproduction of the protest sent by the evangelical bishop, Philip Popp, on 19 November 1941, to the Presidency of the Croat government and all the ministers, as well as to the Ustaše Supreme Command and the State Department for Renewal.[29] Popp wrote:

> Almost every day, and from almost every part of our free Croatia, there come protests to this office against the behaviour of the State authorities, especially of the regional and local authorities, as well as against Ustaše henchmen who despise and insult the evangelical Church—treating it as a Church that does not enjoy equal rights with the Catholic Church and with the Moslem religious community.
>
> A large number of Orthodox wish to embrace the evangelical Church, but their conversion is hindered by State organizations which withhold the certificate of good conduct without which conversion from one faith to another is impossible. But if these same Orthodox express a desire to join the Catholic Church, then they obtain the necessary documents.
>
> This behaviour of State and Ustaši authorities confirms that Protestantism is despised in our State.
>
> Orthodox faithful who were received into the evangelical Church before a certificate of good conduct was required are persecuted as if they had not been converted, whereas those who have gone over to Catholicism are not.
>
> The authorities are spreading the idea—more or less openly, but usually through some secret channel—that the conversion of the Orthodox to the evangelical faith is no defence, and hence it is suggested that they should go over to the Roman Church. . . .
>
> Though so far the evangelical Church has not received the Orthodox in mass but only individually—perhaps 1,500 in the

whole State—this office nevertheless feels bound to appeal to the government against the methods employed by the State and Ustaše authorities.

Despite the fact that within our State Protestants number only some 70,000, we beg that it should not be forgotten that behind them stands world Protestantism with some 250,000,000 adherents, and that the most evolved countries are Protestant. . . .

The appeal went on to ask that the authorities should publish an official declaration showing that the evangelical Church in the NDH enjoyed the same legal rights as the Catholic Church and the Moslem religious community, and that an order should be issued granting equal validity to conversions to the evangelical Church. And it concluded:

At this very moment we have learnt that some Orthodox faithful of Slatina and its neighbourhood, having asked to join the evangelical Church, have been transferred to a concentration camp. [And it went on to quote similar cases.]

And here is part of the 'Resolution of the Moslem leaders of Banjaluka' sent to the Zagreb government on 13 November 1941:

The slaughter of priests and leaders without trial or judgment, the mass-shootings of people often entirely innocent, of women and children, the expulsion of entire families from their houses within the space of an hour or two at most, their deportation to an unknown destination, the appropriation of their possessions, and their forced conversion to the Catholic faith—these are events that have filled honest people with dismay and left the worst possible impression on us Moslems in the regions concerned. . . . For we doubt whether it would be possible to find in the history of any other people such things as are happening with us. . . . Religious toleration, which had attained such a high level in Bosnia and Herzegovina despite the multiplicity of beliefs, has been shattered. The offensive and provocative behaviour of our Catholics towards us is often of such dimensions that we are obliged to take it into serious consideration. Some of the Catholic clergy hold that their hour has come and they are exploiting it without scruple. Propaganda for Catholicism has become so intense that we are reminded of the Spanish Inquisition. With the agreement of the Church and the tolerance of the State organizations, many Christians have gone over in mass to Catholicism. In this way people who previously enjoyed no civil rights have obtained equality and have become Croats by nationality merely by embracing the Catholic Church. Islam's equality in power, which has often been recognized by the very highest authorities, is now in practice being called into question, and conversion to Islam, for which we have never made any propaganda, does not in practice give the same protection as conversion to the Catholic faith. Many intellectuals have paid for such an attempt with their lives, as in the town of Travnik. . . . Catholics are often heard singing songs offensive to the religious feeling of Moslems—and, worse, Moslems are told that their fate will be the same as that of the Orthodox. . . . We know of cases where the Ustaše have killed people while wearing the fez. This happened in the city of Bosanski Novi, where four trucks full of Ustaše wearing the fez and accompanied by Moslem criminals, made mass killings of Orthodox.[30]

It has been estimated that by the end of the summer of 1941 the victims of the Ustaše already numbered 350,000. So, as can be seen, the Catholic bishops could no longer delay taking an official and collective stand—the more so in' that the Papal Legate had reached Zagreb in early August. So it was in his presence that they gathered on 17 and 18 November with this massive agenda (about which we know from a congratulatory letter from Cardinal Maglione, Secretary of State, on 21 February 1942): more humane treatment for citizens of Jewish origin, help for evicted Slovenes and especially the clergy, the religious and moral requirements of Croatian workers in Germany, the strengthening of the Catholic press, and so on.

As regards the conversion of the Orthodox to Catholicism, the bishops attacked it with a document as strong and dignified as the one sent out by the Archdiocese of Zagreb on 15 July, but even more concrete. It was directed to the Poglavnik personally, and ran as follows:

Poglavnik! The Croatian Catholic bishops gathered in plenary annual conference on 17 and 18 November have reached the following conclusions regarding the conversion of Greco-Orientals to the Catholic faith:

1. They maintain as a principle of dogma that all investigation and decision about appeals regarding the conversion of Greco-Orientals to the Catholic faith fall exclusively within the competence of the hierarchy of the Catholic Church which alone, by God's will and by canon law, is authorized to promulgate directives and rules on this question, so that any intervention other than that of the ecclesiastical authority should be excluded.

2. It follows that no one outside the hierarchy of the Catholic

Church has the right to appoint 'missionaries' to promote the conversion of Greco-Orientals to the Catholic faith. Every missionary must receive his mission and the jurisdiction for his spiritual work from the local Ordinary. It follows that it is against dogma and against canon law for the authorities of the region or commune, or for Ustaše employees, or for the religious section of the State Directorate for Renewal, or for any other secular authority, to charge anyone with such a mission without the permission of the diocesan Ordinary.

3. In their spiritual work, missionaries must be subject solely to the local Ordinary either directly or indirectly through the parish priest.

4. The Catholic Church can only recognize as valid those conversions that take place in accordance with these dogmatic principles.

5. The secular authorities cannot 'annul' conversions that have taken place not only according to ecclesiastical rules but also according to civil rules.

6. With this in view, the Croatian Catholic episcopate is electing from its members a committee of three, comprising: the president of the Episcopal Conference, Archbishop Stepinac, the Bishop of Senj, Mgr. Viktor Burić, and the Apostolic Administrator of the diocese of Križevac, Doctor Janko Simrak. This Committee will discuss and resolve all questions arising from conversions of Greco-Orientals to the Catholic faith. The Committee will work in harmony with the Minister for Justice and Religion in promulgating regulations concerning conversions.

7. As members of the executive Committee for the conversion of Greco-Orientals to the Catholic faith, the Croat bishops have selected the following persons: Dr. Franjo Herman, professor in the theological faculty of Zagreb; Dr. Augustin Juretić, consultant for the Episcopal Conference; Dr. Janko Kalaj, professor of religion in secondary schools and of *glagoljica*[31] in the faculty of theology; Nikola Borić, director of the Chancellery of the Archbishopric of Zagreb; and Dr. Krunoslav Draganović, professor at the faculty of theology. This Committee will carry out all the work involved in requests for conversion to the Catholic faith on the part of Greco-Orientals, under the supervision of the bishops' Committee for conversions.

. . .

Poglavnik! These are the conclusions of the Croatian episcopate, prompted by great love and concern for the Croatian people, for the NDH and for the Catholic faith which is the faith of the majority of the Croatian people. Here we are dealing only with the errors on account of which the conversion of Greco-Orientals has not been able to develop as widely and successfully as would have been possible had they not been committed. We do not blame the government of the NDH for these errors. We do not desire to represent them as systematic but as the result of irresponsible elements unaware of their great responsibilities and of the consequences. We know that these elements are in reaction against the policies of the last twenty years and the misdeeds of the Četniks and the Communists who brought about much bloodshed among our quiet Croatian people. We thank Almighty God that through your work, Poglavnik, the situation is beginning to be more ordered, and thus the Catholic episcopate propounds the foregoing not in recrimination but so that in future the action of irresponsible elements may be prevented, and the reason for the failure of conversions may be discovered, and what should be done for the work to go in the right direction and not be lost in useless experiments.[31 bis]

This document is important, above all for the resolution with which it affirms the theological and juridical principles which had already been laid down (as we have seen) in the letter from the Archbishop of Zagreb's Chancellery to the Minister of Justice and Religion. It is also important for the skill with which it dissociates the bishops and even the government authorities from the methods so far adopted in re-baptisms. As regards the bishops, it closed what could be called the early period of chaos in which the forced conversions of Orthodox Serbs to Catholicism took place.

Up till then—and the document explicitly recognizes the fact—proselytizing activities among the Orthodox had been almost exclusively in the hands of the civil authorities. The ministerial organizations had provided the basic directives, and the religious section of the Ministry for Justice and Religion the directives for action, even though this was more a matter of *laisser faire* than of real planning. Naturally that section had its importance as it occupied the post of link between the government and the episcopate and in practice presided over the whole ecclesiastical policy of Croatia. But in a State that was still disorganized and at the mercy of the whim of small or would-be bosses who wanted to make themselves felt, it was only relatively effective.

But things did not change much after the bishop's conference and the consignment of its conclusions to the Poglavnik (in the second collective audience within a few months). The religious section, so it seems, continued to guarantee a preponderating role to the 'Ponova' (renewal) organization which was in charge of the technical preparation and full execution of the 'conversions'. Whether members of the Party or not, priests went on working as 'missionaries'. According to an admission made by Stepinac at his trial on 2 October 1946 the Committee of Three never met because 'it was not able to'; in other words it never even began to function and had no purpose at all. The Archbishop said that this was owing to *force majeure*. He did not want to explain himself further, and only added that in any case each bishop 'worked in his own territory'.

Another proof that the State continued to act independently can be found in its organization of new parishes or sub-parishes created to meet the number of new converts. The Ministry of Justice and Religion, for instance, ordered on 25 November 1941, N. CDXXV-2099-Z-1941 (the order was signed by the Poglavnik) that there should be a State subsidy of 1,000 *kune*[32] for parish priests. The provision was accompanied by an executive order from the Minister of Justice and Religion, Dr. Mirko Puk, on 9 January 1942, N. 224-Z-1942, stating that: parishes of the kind could only be established if the converts attained two thirds of the inhabitants and approval of the Ministry was obtained; parish priests would have to be living on the spot (or, in exceptional cases, in their former parishes); they would have to claim the subsidy of 1,000 *kune* which would be paid out to them through their diocesan Ordinaries; they could not accept money or any other compensation for parish work from the faithful; the Ministry would provide for all the needs of the Chancellery; etc., etc.

The only new fact to be noted, and over which the bishops naturally had still less influence, was the setting-up of the 'Croatian Orthdodox Church' ordained by the Poglavnik in the spring of 1942. Compared with the original intransigence, it involved some mitigation—temporary, at least in intention—and an admission that the State was powerless to resolve by force the problem of turning the Orthodox Serbs into Croats, especially in the cities. Probably it was a strategic retreat imposed on Pavelić by Allied propaganda which accused him of wanting to exterminate Orthodoxy and the Orthodox. In any case we know that the decision was taken rather unexpectedly. We need only recall that as late as 25 February, 1942, the Minister for Justice and Religion, Puk, had denied on principle that the Serbs could have their own independent religious life in Croatia. Hence, he added, they should break off from the Serb Orthodox Church and return to the Catholicism to which they had once belonged. 'Anyone who for any reason does not want to admit this historic state of affairs can leave the territory of the NDH.' Yet three days later Pavelić had no hesitation in flatly contradicting him: 'It is not true that Croatia is trying to convert the Orthodox to the Catholic Church. No one is touching the Orthodox, but in Croatia there is not room for a Serb Orthodox Church.'

The new 'Croatian Orthodox Church'—entrusted to a Russian emigré Metropolitan, Germogen—was little more than a facade, indeed a real parody of a Church. Its upper hierarchy and lower clergy were mainly refugees from the Serb Orthodox Church or members who had been expelled or punished by their official superiors. Moreover it was a trap, for the regime obviously aimed at using it to hold down the Serbs who had resisted re-baptism; so it is not surprising that it had little success and was in practice deserted.[33]

Hence, but also because the New Church had, and had to have, its main bases in the cities, pressure for the conversion of the Orthodox to Catholicism continued all over the national territory.

In view of the aims of this study, however, there is no need to proceed with detailed documentation as to later developments of the terrible Ustaše crusade. Especially as it underwent no particular changes. Suffice it to say that it continued throughout the whole of 1942 and possibly into early 1943 when it finally waned (though without ever ceasing entirely) and became assimilated into the struggle against the partisans. But this diminution was not deliberate; rather, it was imposed by the precarious position of the NDH—increasingly threatened in its own territory, and especially in the cities, by bands of Četniks[34] and above all by Tito's freedom movement. Yet even before this, Ustaše violence against the Orthodox had been slowed down in another way—by the Italian army of occupation which concerned itself with rescuing the Jews and had orders to prevent massacres on religious pretexts.

Despite these obstacles, the victims *in odium fidei* of the Ustaše reached a very high total. It is surely no exaggeration to put the figure around 700,000—that is, some 10 to 15 per cent of the population of Greater Croatia. This was the figure adopted by the London government in May 1943[34 bis] and was at that time certainly excessive. The *Encyclopedia Britannica* omits any quantitative estimate but maintains that the massacre of the Serbs was only surpassed in violence and savagery by the mass extermination of the Polish Jews.

As we lack official statistics from present-day Yugoslavia, we shall quote those supplied by Tito's Minister for Foreign Affairs, Edward Kardelj, in his speech to the Belgrade parliament in December 1952 regarding the rupture of diplomatic relations with the Vatican:

> In the territory of the so-called 'Free State of Croatia', the Ustaše bands destroyed and burnt 299 Greco-Orthodox churches, and killed 128 Greco-Orthodox priests and hundreds of thousands of faithful: men, women and children.

The losses among leading members of the Serb Orthodox Church seem in fact to have been much heavier than that: 300 priests were killed and five bishops. But such data tell us nothing about the cruelty with which the murders were carried out. Only to restrict ourselves to bishops: Mgr. Dositej, Orthodox Ordinary of Zagreb, was subjected to such tortures that he was driven out of his mind; the eighty-year-old Bishop Petar Simonić of Sarajevo had his throat cut; while Bishop Platov of Banjaluka, who was eighty-one, had his feet shod as if he were a horse and was forced to walk in public until he collapsed. They then tore off his beard and made a fire on his chest. These examples of sadism were no more than refinements on the methods used in 'normal' mass executions, namely throat-cutting, quartering (and it was not unusual for the bodies to be hung up in butchers' shops and labelled 'human meat'), burning victims crowded into houses and churches, etc. And we must not forget the children impaled at Vlasenica and Kladanj, and the tortures practised for fun during the Ustaše nightly orgies. . . .

So far as we can see, all this happened without the Croat Catholic episcopate feeling that it had a special duty to condemn these crimes perpetrated against the members of the sister Church. On the contrary, while his Orthodox colleague at Sarajevo, Bishop Simonić, was being killed in the way we have described, the Catholic Archbishop of the same city, Mgr. Ivan Šarić, not only wrote odes in honour of his 'beloved leader', the Poglavnik, but had the impertinence to exalt the use of revolutionary methods 'in the service of truth, justice and honour' in the Catholic weekly of his diocese. He even maintained that it was 'stupid and unworthy of Christ's disciples to think that the struggle against evil [*sic*] could be waged in a noble way and with gloves on'.

Of course background memories of the twenty years of Yugoslav rule may help to explain such silence, but they can never justify it. All the more as the history of Serbo-Croat relations did not begin in 1918 even on the strictly religious plane.

No one would dream of maintaining that the Catholic bishops of Greater Croatia desired those massacres. There can be no doubt but that they deprecated the useless bloodshed, if only in general terms and rather as they deprecated the State's financial speculations on conversions—in other words, because they thought it all constituted a serious obstacle to conversions. The uneasiness experienced by most responsible bishops when they saw how the NDH was gravely compromising the Church itself, was well expressed by the octogenarian Bishop of Mostar, Mgr. Louis Mišić, in a letter to Stepinac as president of the Episcopal Conference:

> By the grace of God there is today an opportunity such as has never before occurred to help the Croatian cause and to save a large number of souls, men of good will, and peace-loving peasants. . . . Alas a few intruders, uneducated and inexperienced young men, who make use of fire and violence instead of reason and intelligence, are arrogating to themselves the right to give orders. While the neo-converts are in church hearing holy Mass, they seize them, men and women, young and old, drive them out like beasts, and dispatch them to eternity wholesale. This can serve neither the holy Catholic cause nor the Croatian cause. Within a year or two everyone will condemn these senseless acts, and meanwhile we are losing a wonderfully favourable opportunity for the Croatian cause and the holy Catholic cause to change from being the minority that we are in Bosnia and Herzegovina to being a majority. . . .

The style is naïve though effective. Yet we cannot help suspecting that the old Franciscan bishop was not so much scandalized as irritated (obviously the acts he describes were a great deal more than 'senseless'). As for what he says in the concluding lines, this was a fixed idea of his as can be seen in another letter:

> The conversion of the Orthodox to Catholicism has completely failed. If Our Lord had granted greater reason and understanding to the competent authorities, and enabled them to carry out conversions to Catholicism with more tact, in this propitious period the number of Catholics would have increased by at least 500,000 or 600,000, and thus in Bosnia and Herzegovina we would have moved from the present number of 700,000 to 1,300,000.[35]

Such laments certainly show that not all the bishops had the same severe criteria as the Primate Stepinac for guaranteeing the integrity and disinterestedness of aspiring 'converts'.[36] That some of the bishops were Ustaše is beyond doubt, and proved by the flight of Bishop Šărić (already mentioned) and Bishop Parić of Banja Luka when the NDH collapsed; Bishop Simrak of the Byzantine rite of Križevci was not so lucky—he was arrested and condemned to death, while Bishop Karević disappeared mysteriously directly after the arrival of the national army of liberation. Yet we have no grounds for supposing that they personally stained their hands with blood—though the same, alas, cannot be said of a number of priests and members of religious orders. But whether Ustaše or not, there is no denying that they witnessed the demolition of the Orthodox Church with satisfaction and rushed to collect the spoils.

Monsignor Stepinac did not convincingly exculpate himself from this last accusation when, at his trial, he was reminded of his request to the Poglavnik to hand over the Orahovica Serb monastery to the Trappists whom Hitler had expelled from their monastery at Reichenburg.[37] The following document proves that similar advantages were reaped elsewhere—in this case at the expense of individual Jews—and that even the Papal Legate, Abbot Marcone, considered such profiteering inevitable.[38]

Prot. 1092/43
Bona immobilia Archidioecesi
serajensi oblata.
Excellentissime Domine,
    Dr. Joannes Saric archiepiscopus Serajensis quaesivit et tandem

a Gubernio croatico dono accepit bona quaedam immobilia, quae olim Judaei cujusdam origine hungarici erant.

Quidam ex clero et etiam ex civibus Archidioecesis Serajensis, hoc donum aegre ferentes, me certiorem reddiderunt et rogaverunt ut rem melius componerem.

Doctori Antonio Filpanović tunc temporis thesauri publici Ministro proposui, ut pro bonis immobilibus ad Judaeum quondam pertinentibus Archiepiscopo Saric vel pecuniae summam, vel alia bona immobilia tribuere dignaretur. Praedictus Doctor consilium meum benigne excepit, attamen paulo post gravi morbo correptus, munus suum deponere coaptus est.

Enixe Excellentiam Vestram rogo, ut si fieri potest praedictum negotium secundum votum meum perficiatur.

✠ Joseph Ramirus Marcone
S. Sedis Legatus

Excellentissimo Viro
Dri NICOLAO MANDIĆ
Ministrorum Praesidi
Zagreb

Obviously Abbot Marcone's behaviour went far beyond the cautious yet nevertheless surprising directives that had reached him from Rome, transmitted through Cardinal Maglione from the Holy Office. Here is the letter [38bis] that he sent Archbishop Stepinac as president of the Croatian Episcopal Conference:

Prot. 134/41   Zagabriae, die 9 Decembris
Ecclesiae et bona   1941
dissidentium qui convertuntur
Excellentissime Domine,

Quaestioni a me propositae: utrum Episcopis catholicis recipere liceat Ecclesias et bona immobilia ecclesiastica dissidentium qui convertuntur, Em.mus Card. Secretarius Status haec die 21 Nov. h.a. respondit:

'As soon as I received your esteemed account of 27 September (N. 29/41) in which your Reverence asked whether Catholic bishops may accept the offer of churches, houses and parish endowments formerly belonging to the schismatics, and use them to set up Catholic parishes, I submitted the matter to the supreme court of the Holy Office. I now hasten to convey to your Reverence that the most Eminent and Reverend Fathers of the aforesaid sacred court have laid down the following instructions as a rule for your Reverence:

'In places where the schismatics are converted and a Catholic church already exists, you should not take possession of the schismatic church but the converts should be invited to participate in religious instruction and functions in the already existing Catholic church.

'But where there is no Catholic church and all or nearly all the schismatics have been converted, the schismatic church already there may be employed for religious instruction and divine service. But first the schismatic church should be blessed with a simple rite. Solemn consecration should be excluded for the time being.

'But if the converts are a minority, it is improper to take over the schismatic church; some suitable hall should be adapted instead. New parishes should not be established, but parish priests in the Catholic areas where such conversions take place may be authorized to be present at the marriages of the catechumens, especially in urgent cases, and should follow the norms of canon and moral law, juxta probatos auctores. As regards property, it is not suitable to accept it unless there is certainty regarding the freedom and sincerity of the offer made by the lawful owners.'

Dum Tuis orationibus me enixe commendo, humiliter me confiteor.

Tibi addictissimum in Domino
✠ Jos. Ramirus Marcone, Abb. Ord.

A final sinister note in this chapter of the history of Croatian Catholicism concerns the part played by a group of priests and members of religious orders not only in stirring up, but even in carrying out, massacres. We have made a deliberate distinction between this situation and the responsibility of the bishops. The collusion of some of the bishops with the Ustaše does not imply, short of specific and unequivocal proof, that the cut-throats in cassocks and habits acted on the orders and in agreement with their diocesan Ordinaries.[39] The possibility is excluded by the mere fact that, as we have seen, the bishops and the government were in profound disagreement as to the methods to be adopted in the 'campaign for conversions'. Knowing that, if need arose, they could rely on the government against their respective superiors, many restless elements in the clergy offered themselves to the civil and military authorities as 'missionaries' or chaplains, and remained at their posts despite the fact that they were recalled by their bishops, and despite the punishments that very soon fell on the worst of them.

For some of these priests the bishops put forward a defence, denying that they were criminals; regarding others, they avoided making a statement which amounted to admitting the accusations against them.[40] From our point of view, individual cases are of only relative importance: what matters is that such things happened and on a scale to fill us with horror—even if only a few dozen people were implicated. Moreover we fully realize that cases like the Franciscan Miroslav Filipović, head of *lager* Jasenovac (the Croatian Auschwitz), where more than 200,000 people met their death and not a few of them thanks to his personal services as an accomplished cut-throat, savour more of pathology than criminology.

Allowing for exceptions here and there, the phenomenon just described is characteristic of Ustaši massacres—as opposed to exterminations in other countries during the Second World War—in that it is almost impossible to imagine a Ustaše punitive expedition without a priest at its head or spurring it on, and usually a Franciscan.[41] Quite a number of these new crusaders *in sacris* even went around armed. There was Fr. Augustus Cievola, of the Franciscan convent in Split, whose revolver was a notable part of his habit. There was the secular priest, Božidar Bralo, who went around with nothing less than a machine gun. And there were not a few who set an example to the faithful. Božidar Bralo, for instance, who was known to be a protector of the famous flying division 'Crna Legija' (Black Legion), was accused of having taken part in the massacre of 180 Serbs at Ali-pašin-Most, and of having danced a macabre dance round their bodies in his soutane with the Ustaše militiamen. Another priest, Nicolas Pilogrvić of Banjaluka, was responsible for other acts of butchery. And similarly the Jesuits Lipovac and Cvitan, and the Franciscans Joseph Vukelić, Zvonimir Brekalo, Justin Medić, and Nunko Prlić, chaplains all, killed prisoners, set fire to houses and sacked villages as they beat through the Bosnia countryside at the head of Ustaše bands.[42]

The scandal of such behaviour even filtered into the press of countries allied to Croatia, as we see by an inquiry conducted by

Corrado Zoli of the Italian Geographical Society, published in the *Resto del Carlino*, September 1941.

The situation is complicated by the terrifying aspects of a religious war. There have been, and probably still are, bands of murderers led and inflamed by Catholic priests and monks. The thing has been proved to the hilt: at Travnik, a hundred kilometres south of Banjaluka, in the early days, a friar who was caught urging on with his crucifix a band of which he was the leader, was sentenced and shot. So we have the Middle Ages, but made much worse by the use of machine guns, hand grenades, tins of petrol and charges of dynamite.

The article was entitled *The Birds of Graciac*, and with reason, as is shown by a further quotation:

The first Franciscan of Assisi called the birds his brothers and sisters, whereas these disciples and spiritual descendents of his, living in the NDH, are full of hate, killing innocent people, their brothers in the Father of Heaven, in language, in blood, and in homeland . . .; they kill, they bury alive, they throw the dead into rivers, into the sea, over precipices. . . .

On the Zagreb-Ogulin train, Corrado Zoli fell in with a Bavarian from Ingoldstadt, an artillery major, deeply disgusted by Ustaše violence, who said:

German officers and soldiers haven't hesitated, from the first, to make vigorous armed interventions against people who disturbed the peace, whether Ustaše, Catholics, Orthodox, Croats, Serbs, or even regular units of the new Croatian army.[43]

But the grimmest part was played not by the lunatic fringe who performed these acts, but by the instigators, the theoreticians and propagandists for the Ustaše crusade among their brothers in the clergy and in the ranks of militant laymen. Among many examples we quote Ivo Guberina, the author mentioned earlier in our study as an interpreter of the Croatian Catholic soul and an upholder of his people's peaceful ways. In the same year that saw the publication of his essay in *Croazia Sacra*, he published an article in the review *Hrvatska Smotra* (Croatian Review) (7 October 1943), from which we take this extract:

Certain people in Croatia who, during the Yugoslav regime, had the task of liquidating the Croatian nation and State . . . and of impeding it in the role entrusted to it by Providence (that of being a bulwark of Catholicism against the East) have, since the fall of

Yugoslavia, remained within the Croatian organism without changing one jot or tittle in their anti-Croatian aims. The Croatian State and Croatian people have a natural right to rid their organism of this poison. The Ustaše movement began the work, by using the means that every doctor uses to cure a person's body. Where necessary, it operates. The Ustaše movement would prefer these foreign and hostile elements to become freely assimilated, or for this poison to be removed from the body (and go back to the places from which it came). But if these elements do not want to do this, but intend to remain in Croatia as a fifth column so as to undermine her or, worse, take up arms then, according to all the principles of Catholic morality, they must be viewed as aggressors and the Croatian State has a right to annihilate them by the sword. . . . Defence by the sword is permissible against an enemy of this kind, and if necessary even by preventive action taken in advance. . . . These are principles on which natural law is founded and hence every Catholic is obliged in conscience to help in carrying them out. If the Ustaše movement in present circumstances has taken on the task of achieving this end in Croatia, to put difficulties in its way would imply ignorance of what the Catholic mission is. . . . This being so, it would be a sin against the Creator to stand aside from the final struggle, and to be on the other side of the barricades would be a betrayal of God's cause. It is the Catholic's duty to be an instrument of the complete expression of what is essential and positive in the Ustaše movement. . . . The Church will be all the more satisfied if her faithful . . . fight in the ranks of the Ustaše movement which, by its traditions and its leadership, and above all by its programme, is developing a social and political State in which the Church can achieve her supernatural mission without hindrance.

Chapter 6

THE VATICAN WAS AWARE OF USTAŠE CRIMES

We have now pointed out the causes, proportions and methods of one of the most absurd and revolting civilian massacres known to history. We have seen how the State of Croatia turned a racist-religious policy into one of its main hinges and based itself on the thousand-year-old tradition of intimate alliance with the Church of Rome. We have seen how the episcopate conscientiously laid down rules to guarantee the free choice and genuine character of the conversion of the schismatics, but failed to raise its voice against the suppression of the rights of other religious minorities, and closed its eyes on the destruction of a sister Church and the butchery of its leaders. We have seen how the clergy and the religious orders were compromised by the crimes of some of their members. We have seen how confessional organizations and their leaders were involved in an unprecedented way in the immoral activities of the Ustaše party. We have seen a Catholic press full of high praise for a leader and a government drenched with blood and providing theories for Ustaše doctrines. So the time has now come to ask how the Holy See reacted, and in particular Pius XII; to ask what the Vatican did to discourage the NDH government from its absurd plan for Croatian pan-Catholicism; what directives it gave to the Catholic hierarchy of the country; and, above all, what steps it took to prevent a racial and religious persecution accompanied by massacres, depredations, acts of violence, forced emigration, and so on.

The answer to these questions has to be made in stages, even if this seems monotonous to the reader. We have to find out whether the Vatican, and above all the Pope, were aware of the situation, and whether they had adequate means for bringing their influence to bear on the State and the episcopate. Finally, if the answer be Yes,

301

we have to discover if they really tried to control the homicidal mania of the Ustaše, or if they refrained from doing so.

The first question, that of knowledge of the facts, is—unlike the instance of Poland—the easiest to answer. It is not hard to see why. As Croatia was on the borders of Italy both by land and sea, it was one of the nearest countries to Rome and had the easiest communications. In addition, the close political relationship between the NDH and Italy in those years ended up in something like a personal union of the two kingdoms—in view of the kinship of their sovereigns (even if the king-designate of Croatia, Duke Aimone of Savoia-Aosta[44] delayed in accepting Zvonimir's crown). The occupation of the country by the Italian army (a third of it at first, then more later, but only for a while)[45] further increased knowledge of events in Croatia, not only in a general way, but also in a detailed and even an official way (making it even easier than usual for the Vatican to profit by news from army chaplains stationed in the country).[46]

In any case, even if the barrier between the Vatican and Italy had been more rigid than in fact it was, the Holy See had *de facto* relations with the NDH with a mutual exchange of representatives. This naturally does not mean that the Ustaše representatives at the Vatican were at pains to reveal to the Pope the bloody achievements of their comrades in Zagreb. But Marcone, the Papal Legate, who could come and go between Zagreb and Rome as and when he wanted, knew the situation in Croatia well, for he often travelled through the country, and was in a position to speak and, indeed, obliged to do so. True, the activities of the rebels (both Četniks and Communists) made travel from one end of Croatia to the other unsavory; but to make things easier the government put military planes at his disposal so that when the situation was fairly calm the papal representative could proceed from his place of destination to other nearby cities.[47]

Furthermore, in view of the privileged position granted to the Catholic Church by the regime—with some bishops and priests sitting in parliament—the Croatian bishops were entirely free to carry on their own activities within their individual dioceses and in addition had full freedom for relations with the Holy See. Their use of this freedom[48] is shown by the following extract from a report made on

10 June 1943 by the Ustaše representative at the Vatican, Prince Lobkowicz, to the Zagreb Foreign Ministry:

> The ecclesiastical counsellor of the Hungarian embassy, Monsignor Lutor, once met me in the Vatican and came up to me full of emotion, asking me why so many of our bishops had come to Rome. Obviously he was referring to the visits of the Archbishop of Zagreb and the Bishop of Mostar. In wartime there exists a dispensation for bishops from the rules of canon law whereby all alike are obliged to visit the Vatican to give accounts [on their respective dioceses]. The Hungarian bishops are taking advantage of the dispensation and none of them are coming. He added that the arrival of so many Croatian bishops was causing much comment in diplomatic circles. I answered that we believed close contact between the bishops and the Holy See to be a good and useful thing. . . .

This report dates from a period that was already less favourable to journeys between Croatia and Rome. Shortly afterwards, with the fall of Mussolini and the Italian armistice, they probably had to cease altogether. But the most interesting detail about these visits lies in the evident anxiety felt by the Ustaše representatives at the Vatican as to how the bishops had spoken of their government to the Pope and other members of the Curia[49]—which shows that the bishops were not specially chosen but acted on their own initiative. So whatever their views concerning the Ustaše, the Vatican could listen to them, make them speak, demand that they hold nothing back, etc.

But the Papal Legate, Marcone, and the various bishops had more than personal reports to take to Rome. They often had petitions and appeals from their clergy and their faithful, like the document sent by a group of Slovene priests to the Bishop of Belgrade, to be forwarded to the Pope, and dealing with events in Croatia. And even if for any reason the bishops by common consent withheld information from the Vatican, the Holy See would still have known what was happening in Croatia—whether through public attacks in the Allied press and radio on Pavelić's government and the presumed connivance of the bishops, or through the diligence of the Yugoslav minister to the Holy See who was resident at the Vatican.[50] On the BBC, for instance, it was anything but uncommon to hear remarks such as the following, made by Večeslav Vilder, a member of the Yugoslav government in exile in London, on 16 February 1942:

The worst atrocities are being committed in the environs of the Archbishop of Zagreb (Stepinac). The blood of brothers is flowing in streams. . . . The Orthodox are being forcibly converted to Catholicism and we do not hear the Archbishop's voice preaching revolt. Instead it is reported that he is taking part in Nazi and Fascist parades.

It was Pius XII himself who took care to make a revelation regarding the activity of the Yugoslav diplomat representing the government in exile in London. When, during Stepinac's trial in 1946, he realized that he was accused of having approved the 'forced conversions' of the Orthodox, he quoted (on 6 October of that year)[51] the following *pro memoria* (dated 25 January 1942) issued by his Secretariat of State in reply to the note from the royal Yugoslav legation to the Holy See (N. 1/42) dated 9 January 1942:

According to the principles of Catholic doctrine, conversion should not be the result of external coercion but of the soul's adherence to the truths taught by the Catholic Church.

It is for this reason that the Catholic Church does not admit to her heart adults who ask to enter the Church or return to her except on condition that they are fully conscious of the importance and the consequences of the action they intend to take.

Hence the unexpectedly large number of dissidents in Croatia asking to be received into the Catholic Church was bound to cause concern among the Croatian episcopate whose natural task it is to defend and protect Catholic interest in Croatia.

Far from merely observing this state of affairs, the episcopate, either explicitly or implicitly, felt bound to give formal reminder to those concerned that the return of dissidents must of necessity be carried out in full freedom; and it simultaneously claimed that the ecclesiastical authority was the only authority competent to issue orders and directives concerning conversions.

An episcopal committee was forthwith set up to deal with and resolve all the questions this matter entailed. This was done in conformity with the principles of Catholic doctrine with the aim of ensuring that conversions were the outcome of persuasion and not of coercion.

For its own part, the Holy See did not fail to recommend and inculcate exact observance of the canonical rules and directives given on this matter.[52]

Unfortunately Pius XII did not reveal the text of the Yugoslav Legation's note concerning conversions, but he stated that it recognized 'expressly that neither the Holy See nor the Catholic episcopate in Croatia had taken any part [in them]'. Obviously this was an allusion to the Ustaše standards of violence in carrying them out. The Secretary of State's *pro memoria* was unquestionably accurate in its reference to the official action taken by the bishops, except where it maintained that they had 'forthwith' set up a committee to deal with and resolve the matter (in fact they even instituted two).

As for the directives imparted by the Holy See (by the Secretary of State himself and the various departments concerned: the Consistorial Congregation, the Congregation for Eastern Churches, etc.), there is no doubt whatsoever that these were issued. But they must have been a necessary reaction to an emergency situation sufficiently well known to the Vatican departments. The first documents of this kind that we know of are mainly important for their dating, as they go back to the first months in the life of the State of Croatia—not, unfortunately, for the light they throw on the acts of violence accompanying the so-called 're-baptism' of the Orthodox.

The first known document comes from the Sacred Congregation for Eastern Churches and dates from 17 July 1941 (2.116/36)—a date, that is, when it was hardly possible that news of the communication issued by the religious section of the Ministry for Justice and Religion in the NDH three days earlier could have reached Rome. If this was so, though it is not absolutely certain, the intervention of the Roman department could have resulted from news sent to Rome by the Ordinary of the Križevci province,[53] a diocese which took in all the Catholics of Byzantine rite in Yugoslavia. The letter was sent to the president of the Croatian Episcopal Conference, Mgr. Stepinac, signed by the Secretary, Cardinal Tisserant, and countersigned by the assessor, Mgr. Antonio Arata, Bishop of Sardi. It said:

> The Sacred Congregation of Eastern Churches recalls Your Excellency's attention to the fact that the parish priests of Latin rite in Croatia should be warned by their bishops that in the case of the conversion of schismatics no obstacle should be put in the way of their natural return to the Eastern rite if it is a question of persons who previously belonged to the Church of Eastern rite and under the threats and pressures of the Orthodox eventually abandoned their Catholic faith. By bringing this duty to the notice of your colleagues in Croatia, Your Excellency will . . . reap the

benefits . . . given that there are great hopes for the conversion of schismatics. . . .[54]

The Congregation for Eastern Churches was the official protector of the surviving areas of Eastern rite in the Roman Catholic Church. So it intended in this way to defend the rights of its subjects who, in view of their inveterate enmity for anything that recalled the style of the schismatic Churches, could easily be annexed by the Croatian priests of Latin rite. The same department defined its directives even better on 18 August of the same year when it ordered:

> Wherever Greco-Catholic parishes are already in existence, schismatics desiring to be converted should be sent to them. Should these schismatics not wish or be able to adhere to their Eastern rite, they may be allowed to embrace the Latin rite.[55]

Of more notable importance, even if more recent, is the document written by Cardinal Maglione, the Secretary of State. Having received the resolutions made by the Episcopal Conference of November 1941 from the papal representative at Zagreb, he replied, on 21 February 1942 as follows:

> The criteria on which their Excellencies the Bishops have chosen the questions to be discussed, and the speed with which they have reached practical solutions, show a lively sense of the responsibilities weighing on them in such extremely delicate circumstances as exist at present.
>
> The care with which they are trying to guarantee the schismatics equal rights with other citizens, to obtain humane treatment for citizens of Jewish origin, to help the evicted Slovenes, especially the clergy, to tend to the needs and the religious and moral life of the Croatian workers in Germany, and to strengthen the valuable activities of the Catholic press, deserve praise; but the firmness with which their Excellencies the Bishops are requesting the government to restore to them the right to publish decrees and instructions about re-baptism deserves even greater praise; and so does their intention to defend the principle that these re-baptisms should spring from a personal conviction and not from external coercion.
>
> As for this last point, I am convinced that their interest in it will not fail, even in the future, and that they will intervene when necessary, so that this principle may always be strictly followed and so that everything that could impede or make more difficult a sincere return of the schismatics to the Church may be avoided with equal energy; and likewise, that anything that could coerce

consciences to speed up such a return may also be avoided. I must call the attention of Your Excellency to the fact that the title 'Orthodox' which, regardless of its meaning, is given to the schismatics, should be substituted by another, namely 'Schismatics'.

Having read the report, the Holy Father was pleased to express great satisfaction for the Croatian Bishops' demonstration of pastoral zeal. As proof of his satisfaction and of the paternal feelings with which he received the expression of filial devotion offered him in the name of his fellow bishops by Mgr. Stepinac, His Holiness bestows his apostolic blessing on them and on their faithful.[56]

These documents, despite the wide gap in dates between them, leave no doubt that Rome was acquainted with the developments in Croatia at a fairly early date. Especially as we have Pius XII's word as to the existence of other documents besides the few we ourselves have gleaned. And we can easily add further proofs, drawn from the memoirs of one of Pavelić's ambassadors extraordinary, Fr. Seguic, and from the reports of the Ustaše representative at the Vatican, Rusinović.[57]

Fr. Cherubino Seguic[58] reached Rome to carry out his secret mission during the September of 1941, that is to say only five months after the foundation of the NDH. He went from one surprise to the next:

> All that one hears about Croatia in Italy [he wrote in his diary][59] has a hint of calumny about it. Everything is either distorted or invented. We are made out to be a crowd of barbarians and cannibals.[60]

He failed to meet Maglione, who was just recovering from an attack of influenza, but was received by Mgr. Montini, deputy of the Secretariat of State, who confirmed the impression he had formed during talks with Mgr. Boehm of the *Osservatore Romano*:

> [Mgr. Montini] asked for full information on the events in Croatia. I was not short of words. He listened with great interest and attention. The calumnies have reached the Vatican and must be convincingly exposed.

Several months later the same refrain crops up again in the despatches of the first Ustaše representative to the Holy See. On 8 February 1942, for instance, he relates his visit to Mgr. Sigismondi, Secretary of Propaganda Fide:

On Saturday I visited Mgr. Sigismondi, head of the Office for Croatian affairs at the Vatican. . . . He tells me that enemy propaganda against us is pretty active. In our talk we touched on the question of converts. The Holy See is pleased about it, but he stressed that both the American and the English press are attacking us about this, saying that the conversions have been carried out under strong government pressure. He reminded me that occasionally the Italian papers carry news of mass conversions of the Orthodox to Catholicism. . . .

On the 26th of the same month Rusinović writes an account of his meeting with Cardinal Maglione during which they discussed:

the question of the converted, about whom the foreign press asserts that they have abandoned their faith under government pressure, and have adopted Catholicism in order to save their lives. It seems that this problem interests him most of all. . . .

A few days later, Mgr. Montini seemed to him to be downright aggressive:

Right at the beginning of the talk he asked me, 'What is going on in Croatia? Why has the world made such an uproar about your country? Is it possible that so many crimes have been committed? And is it true that prisoners are being ill-treated?'[61]

On the other hand Mgr. Tardini alluded more diplomatically to the 'mistakes' made by the young Ustaše State; pardonable—or at least understandable as are all youthful mistakes.[62] But Cardinal Tisserant, whom Rusinović visited on 5 March, was the most explicit of them all. The French Cardinal from Lorraine, who on the 28th of the following May was to reproach him with the figure of 350,000 Serbs suppressed with their clergy, said:

In Croatia everyone has more power than the Croats. That's how things are. And if you knew what the Italian authorities on the coast say about you, you would be horrified . . . killings, fires, acts of banditry and looting are the order of the day in those parts. I don't know whether all this is true, but I know for a fact that it is the Franciscans themselves, as for example Fr. Simić of Knin, who have taken part in attacks against the Orthodox populations so as to destroy the Orthodox Church. (In the same way you destroyed the Orthodox Church in Banja Luka). I know for sure that the Franciscans in Bosnia and Herzegovina have acted abominably, and this pains me. Such acts cannot be committed by educated, cultured, civilized people, let alone by priests.

And coming back to the same topic, further on:

I know the Italians are not kindly disposed towards you, and that therefore many tales will be told, but the case of Simić is well known to me, as well as the destruction of the Banja Luka Church, and the persecution of the Orthodox population. You must punish the authors of these crimes.[63]

Less than two weeks later Rusinović rushed to Maglione. He had received news that the Turkish newspaper, *La République*, had published a protest addressed to the Pope by no less a person than the Orthodox Patriarch of Constantinople about the killing of Serbs in Croatia, and he intended to defend the NDH from the accusations of that schismatic prelate. However he found the Cardinal completely in the dark about the matter, though he (the Cardinal) confirmed that 'information was arriving at the Vatican concerning the Ustaše NDH' dealing with the same subject.[64]

And in the offices and corridors of the Roman Congregations rumours of what was happening in their country pursued the Ustaši representatives. Here is an extract from a report, most probably by Fr. Wurster, dated 9 February, 1942:

> The following episode may effectively illustrate what people here knew about Croatia. A colleague, having gone to the Congregation of the Sacraments, was told by a certain Cardinal who is a person of importance there, that many priests have been driven out of Croatia, that the Germans are making use of terrorism in word and deed in all matters of religion. This same man has not the faintest idea of our geographical position nor of our history. Of the Poglavnik he only knows that he murdered King Alexander and nothing else whatever. . . .
>
> I heard a professor at the Gregorian University say that in our country there reigns disorder, butchery, tyranny, and an altogether impossible situation. The Ustaše are committing crimes almost unparalleled in history. Not only do we slaughter innocents by the thousand, but we use sadistic and brutal torture. The Church enjoys no freedom and the priests are condemned to death under the accusation of Communism. Lončar [a canon of Zagreb] is being proclaimed a martyr for Holy Faith. I was furious as I listened to all this. . . .

Chapter 7

THE CONTRADICTORY ATTITUDE OF THE VATICAN TOWARDS FORCED 'RE-BAPTISM' AND THE PERSECUTION OF THE ORTHODOX SERBS

To put it briefly, then, as early as the first weeks of 1942 the Vatican was perfectly aware of the Croatian situation. And not only as to the forced conversions of the Orthodox, but also—as is proved by Maglione's letter of 21 February—as to the situation of the Jews, etc. So how did the Holy See react to all this? It had numerous courses of action open to it: it could put pressure on the Ustaše government with the help of the Papal Legate Marcone, avail itself of the good offices of the Italian government, or act upon the episcopate. The fact that the Holy See did not neglect any one of these measures shows just how preoccupied it was by the situation in Croatia: but was it preoccupied about it in itself, or mainly in relation to the general situation? That is the question to be answered.

a. Vatican pressure on the Croatian episcopate

However insufficient the available documents are, in view of the discretion of the Vatican's secret archives, there is reason to assume that the Holy See adopted the same attitude towards the Croatian bishops as towards the bishops of other countries devastated by war —that is to say, the Holy See left them with full responsibility for choices and decisions in the political field as regards the Ustaše government. Of course all the bishops had to act within the spirit and the limits of their well-defined religious and ecclesiastical duties, i.e. within the spirit and rules of Canon Law. But the autonomy of individual bishops allowed the Holy See to avoid burning its fingers, above all when it came to the post-war situation, supposing that the bishops of a given country had taken the wrong path. A very clever tactic in theory, but one which in practice has not always been productive, and in Yugoslavia (as in Poland) less than elsewhere.

Indeed the Croatian bishops were bound to opt for the National State of Croatia. They could perhaps have discussed the different types of regime to adopt, but they could never have admitted the possibility of a choice between an autonomous State of Croatia and a federated Croatia. And given the typical nationalistic exaltation of the Croatians, which they shared to the full,[65] it was first for psychological reasons, then for historical ones—in view of their bitter experience of Yugoslavia—that they could not contemplate federation. The restricted autonomy of the Banavina of Croatia between 1939 and 1941 had had too short and superficial a duration, even if a promising one, to alter their aspirations and expectations.

Moreover, neither the bishops nor the country were asked to choose the regime of autonomy. They found it imposed upon them. If they were guilty of optimism in its regard, this was because of the equivocation about confessionalism which was characteristic of the NDH. However this may be, the majority of the bishops were able to maintain their own dignity. Stepinac, particularly, was never Ustaše in either spirit or ideals. Had he been so even moderately, Pavelić would never have gone so far as to put pressure on Rome to have him replaced.[66] But if he had no Ustaše sympathies, this was not through lack of nationalism and patriotism, but because of the racial errors and violent excesses that characterized the movement. Had he been able to rid the regime of these faults he would certainly have become its most uncompromising collaborator. The drama that tormented him during these years was that he saw all his attempts at improvement availing nothing.

The word drama is not empty rhetoric. For Stepinac knew that his defeat would threaten not only his own patriotism but the fate of Croatia herself, and, as he saw things, the fate of the Church in Croatia too. Thus despite everything he defended the State of Croatia everywhere, and above all in Rome. During his trial in 1946, the public prosecutor showed him a long written statement, accompanied by a series of documents, and asked him if he recognized it as the one he showed the Pope during his visit to Rome in May 1943;

and Stepinac did not deny it. Though this document is relevant, it is so long (sixteen type-written pages among the enclosures of volume IV of Stepinac's *Diary*) that we can only reproduce the beginning and end. We shall draw on the original provisional Italian version:

Holy Father!

The vast responsibility that I hold as Archbishop of the only Catholic State in the Balkans and as Metropolitan of Croatia and Slovenia, obliges me to report to You, with the full responsibility of a priest in distress, the infernal plot for the annihilation of Catholicism on the eastern coast of the Adriatic which the enemies of the Church are preparing in that area.

Let us not mention the horrible fate that would befall the Catholics in Croatia should the Bolshevik beast win through and even occupy those regions that come under its sphere of interest—the whole Balkan peninsula and the Danube basin of which the Independent State of Croatia is a part. In such a case the fate of the Catholics in Croatia would not differ in any respect from that of the Catholics in Poland or Rumania, and I do not here intend to speak of this eventuality from which may God's mercy preserve us.

. . .

Holy Father! Today the eyes of a world bleeding from a thousand wounds are turned towards You, who through the wonderful significance of Your name, bring to wretched mankind the peace of Heaven, which it so sorely needs. In bringing peace to the world, think, Holy Father, *of the Croatian nation, ever faithful to Christ and to You.* The new *State of Croatia,* born under more terrible and more difficult conditions than any other State for several centuries, and now fighting desperately for its existence, shows at every turn that it longs to remain faithful to its splendid Catholic traditions and to win for the Catholic Church in this corner of the world a better and brighter hope for the future. On the other hand, by its loss or even its fatal reduction (thousands of the most sincere Croatian faithful and priests would gladly and joyfully give their lives to prevent this terrible possibility) not only would the 240,000 converts from Serbian Orthodoxy be annihilated, but also the whole Catholic population of these territories, and with them all their churches and convents.

In the natural order of things, if God does not perform a great miracle, the progress of Catholicism, as well as its existence and salvation are closely linked to the progress of the State of Croatia.

Holy Father! As I believe deeply in Divine Mercy and God's Providence, of which You are the chosen instrument, I commit our Independent State of Croatia to Your paternal care and to

Your prayers, bearing in mind that in so doing I am committing in the best possible way the Holy Faith in my country and in the Balkans.

Always Your most devoted in the Sacred Heart of Jesus. . . .

The *Osservatore Romano* has hinted that there are doubts as to the authenticity of this document, but its contents reveal nothing politically scandalous[67] or contrary to Stepinac's way of thinking. Moreover it is difficult to see what motives the Belgrade authorities could have had to risk alleging a forgery (and had they 'fabricated' the document they would have included an anti-Communist, and not exclusively an anti-Četnik, slant). To explain Stepinac's radical nationalism and anti-Communism, there was a much more convincing public document dating from just before the end of the war: the famous collective letter[68] from the Croatian bishops of 25 March 1945. Here are a few extracts:

. . . False witnesses have risen up against the bishops, the priests and the faithful, accusing us of wanting to shed blood in our Croatia. . . .

. . . now from the bottom of our hearts, we utter a cry of protest before God and mankind, against the systematic killings and persecutions that the enemies of the Catholic Church, in their diabolical frenzy, are perpetrating against innocent priests and faithful.

The enemies of the Catholic Church are also the followers of materialistic Communism, which the whole State of Croatia rejects by common accord (whosoever dared to assert the contrary would be a brazen liar). By blood and fire have our enemies exterminated the most outstanding priests and faithful. . . .

And here is the final—surely absurd and masochistic—defence of the NDH:

History bears witness that the people of Croatia, after almost a thousand years, have never given up their right to make themselves into a nation. They wish the same freedom for all the other peoples of the world. In the course of this Second World War, the people of Croatia have achieved their ambition and their right, organizing their own independent State and recognizing the will of their people, and the bishops of Croatia have approved this, as was lawful. Therefore no one has the right to accuse any citizen of the State of Croatia, nor its bishops, because the bishops have ratified the determination of the people of Croatia in a matter within their jurisdiction, according to both divine and human law. . . .

Eight months previously, on 7 July 1944, Stepinac had spoken in the same vein:

> Croatia is going through a grave period and possibly something still more serious will befall her, but we must go on hoping, we must believe that Croatia will survive and that she cannot be destroyed. The people of Croatia who shed their blood for their State will preserve and save it. No one must lose heart because of the attacks on the people and the autonomy of Croatia. All must apply themselves with even greater effort to the defence and building-up of the State.[69]

Of course it can reasonably be objected that, given the circumstances, this could seem an ambiguous statement; but it is evident that the very delicacy of the situation prevented Stepinac from being more explicit if he were not himself to bring about the end of independent Croatia by undermining its only support, that of the Church. It would be fairer to accuse him of having on numbers of occasions been frankly contradictory in his relations with the Ustaše State. Rusinović's account of Stepinac's visit to the Vatican in 1942 is undoubtedly perplexing:

> As you must certainly know, the Archbishop has already returned to Zagreb after a twelve-day visit to Rome. On the basis of the agreements that we came to during my stay in Zagreb, I convinced him and advised him to undertake the journey. So when we met, he said, 'You see, I have not disobeyed you'. He was in a very good mood, and really belligerent about all the potential enemies of our country. He has presented a report, of nine type-written pages, to the Holy Father. He informed me of its essential contents and so I can assure you that it is absolutely positive in all that concerns us. In his attack on the Serbs, the Četniks and the Communists as the cause of all the evil that has befallen Croatia, he has produced arguments that not even I knew. I shall not enumerate to you the particular crimes he has recorded, but you must know that his is a really valid contribution to all that I have done up till now. He considers that the situation in the country is favourable, and he praises the work and effort of the government. In particular he is eloquent in his praise of the attempts made by the Poglavnik to restore order, and in the description of his religious attitude and his relationship with the Church. He also states that earlier on he had never been sure of the fate of the people and State of Croatia, but that now he has no doubts as both leaders and people have shown their determination to restore the ancient

traditions of life. Of course the attitude of certain individuals has irritated him, but he has finally convinced himself that these were only isolated cases, and that the leaders had nothing at all to do with them, indeed that they had only been harmed by them. He considers that it is necessary to prevent the evils, wherever they come from; that one cannot and must not allow anyone to attack the NDH; and that disorder is harmful for the people of Croatia, and that is why he came to Rome—with the intention of contradicting the lies that have been insinuated at the Holy See. Stepinac was received by the Holy Father—after he had presented him with his report—and had an audience with him for an hour; afterwards he visited Maglione, Montini, other cardinals and various dignitaries of the Vatican. He discussed numbers of problems, in particular that of the Orthodox, and the Italians in Dalmatia and on the coast, their attitude towards the Catholic Church, the people and the schismatics. He will report all this to the Poglavnik. We also talked about how he could meet you. I warmly recommended the idea to him, and I now suggest it to you, as it is good that he should hear a few words from our side too, and not only from those who support everybody save us. Hoping to put him in a good mood I was very kind and attentive to him. I put a car at his disposal and yesterday I had a dinner prepared at my new house. The other guests were some of our priests, the ex-nuncio Felici and Mgr. Prettner-Cippico of the Secretariat of State. The evening passed off in a very cordial atmosphere: I proposed his health and he replied with a toast. . . .[70]

Obviously at that time Stepinac must have suddenly been given firm hopes of changes in the NDH.[71] But his visit to the Vatican the following year seems to have been even more serious. Lobkowicz described it in a letter to Zagreb as follows:

The Archbishop of Zagreb stayed in Rome from 26 May to 3 June. I was continually in touch with him. Vatican circles were delighted by the Archbishop's arrival and he himself was pleased with their welcome. According to information from various sources and according to the Archbishop's own statement, he made a very positive report about Croatia. He revealed that he had kept quiet about some things with which he is not at all in agreement in order to be able to show Croatia in the best possible light. He mentioned our laws against abortion, a point very well received in the Vatican. Basing his arguments on these laws, the Archbishop justified in part the methods used against the Jews, who in our country are the greatest defenders of crimes of this kind and the most frequent perpetrators of them. The Archbishop declared that he had clearly noted the difference in the Vatican's present attitude towards the State of Croatia and that of a year ago. He noted an improvement in every sense.[72]

There is no need to stress the seriousness of the concealments referred to and the justifications put forward (especially as regards the Jews). But, only a few months later, we find Stepinac making one of his most violent speeches against the regime: that of 31 October.[73] Given on the feast of Christ the King, it was used directly for anti-Ustaše propaganda by Tito's radio and press.

How can such oscillations be explained? Doubtless they were partly caused by sudden changes in events. Stepinac was undoubtedly a man of God, upright and loyal: indeed an ascetic, with no human ambition. He is accused of never having lost a chance to take part in the regime's ceremonial occasions, side by side with Pavelić: and in fact hundreds of photographs do exist proving his official participation in such events; but better than any speech, these photographs show his detachment from what is going on around him. With his pale and emaciated face of a perpetually adolescent seminarian, in an attitude of disgust, and with eyes cast down, he certainly did not appear at ease, nor to be proud and confident at finding himself on show among the military and political leaders of his country and her allies. The conduct of someone like the Bishop of Sarajevo was very different on similar occasions.

A man like Stepinac, much more suited to convent life than to governing a diocese or presiding over the bishops of an entire nation, particularly in such a tragically stormy period, felt no attraction for the things of this world, and though this has a positive side for a man of religion, the bad side of it for him was that he felt lost in the world, incapable of judging men[74] and even more incapable of judging times and circumstances and of applying principles to existing situations. This explains his uncertain and contradictory procedure, now over-trusting, now over-suspicious, often impulsive and incurably impractical.

However, by all accounts, from the second half of 1943 his pessimism regarding the Ustaše State was always on the increase, making him uncompromising in his attitude towards its excesses, or more precisely towards all those excesses which in his eyes lacked patriotic or confessional justification. At that time, and not without the comfort of Pius XII's example and encouragement, he became more and more fanatically anti-Communist and, while this drove him to seek every support the Holy See and the Allies could offer to assure the survival of independent Croatia, it also made him adopt a more and more idealistic attitude toward the need for opposing the Soviet danger and for an anti-Communist crusade. This was within his rights and even, as a bishop, within his duties, so long as he did not go beyond the exigencies of the already-existing political reality (the establishment, in 1945, of the People's State), and deny *a priori* any possibility of co-existence between the Church and the new social order. However, the fact that he paid in person, with dignity and without any trace of rhetoric, the price of his rash opposition, makes him unquestionably worthy of our respect and of our qualified admiration.[75]

It does not seem fair to compare him—to his disadvantage, naturally—with the Serbian Orthodox Patriarch of Belgrade. Gavrilo was a figure of admirable uprightness and heroism. In the first place he took part in the *coup d'état* that overthrew Cvetković; then he refused to leave his residence to go into safety with the government in London; finally he defied the Germans by giving clear anti-Fascist instructions to the clergy and people, thereby provoking his capture and imprisonment in Mauthausen, where he finally triumphed over his gaolers by his death in 1943. Stepinac's situation was much more complex, and one that did not admit of a straightforward, open line of conduct.

As for the Holy See, or rather as for Pius XII, the only person responsible for the decisions made by the Vatican, it must not be forgotten that, as at first he left the Croatian bishops free to pursue their dangerous adventure with the NDH, so he then urged them to put up a resistance beyond all measure to the subsequent regime. We have already referred to the needless provocation of Stepinac's election to the cardinalate (for which naturally only Stepinac and the Catholics of Croatia had to bear the consequences). But we must not forget that from 1946 Tito's government tried to avoid the trial of the Archbishop of Zagreb, by asking the Vatican, in diplomatic secrecy, for his withdrawal.[76] Rome turned a deaf ear, with the result that the situation grew needlessly worse, as the regime, as was inevitable, eventually imposed itself and the Church adapted herself.[77]

b. Vatican pressure on the Italian occupation forces in Croatia

As regards the pressure exerted by the Holy See on Croatia's Allies, the information up till now has been sketchy and vague and only refers to dealings with Italy and not, for obvious reasons, with Germany.

Leon Poliakov has drawn attention to the friction between Italians and Germans in Croatia on the question of the Jews. According to a report of the German ambassador at Zagreb, Kasche, to the Wilhelmstrasse, dated 20 November 1942, the Italian military authorities in Croatia were opposed 'to any interference by the Croats, and even to their taking part in measures already planned and in the preparations for a census of the Jews'. Indeed it appears that the Italian diplomats and generals skilfully co-ordinated their directives so as to avoid a head-on collision with the Germans. Among other things they said it was necessary to set up a general inquiry into the situation making sure that, given the situation's complexity, the inquiry would never come to an end.

> The Italian army must avoid soiling its hands in this matter [wrote a member of the Italian staff in Croatia]. If the Croats really want to hand over the Jews, let them, but let them do it themselves, let them consign them directly into the hands of the Germans, without our having to play the part of intermediary or even worse. It is already distressing enough for the army of a great country to have to see and permit crimes of this kind.[78]

It seems certain that the Italian attitude in favour of the Jews was determined not only by their natural aversion to every kind of racial violence and their ingrained antagonism to the Germans, but also by precise pressure from the Holy See. If nothing else, this would be in accordance with what emerges from the Archives of the Secretariat of State,[79] namely, that Abbot Marcone 'as early as 1941 . . . had received express orders to come to the help of the Jews'. The 'innumerable dealings' carried out by the nuncio at the Quirinal, Mgr. Borgoncini Duca, and by the Jesuit Tacchi Venturi at the Italian

Foreign Office—which gave 'directives and support' to the Army—cannot have concerned only the behaviour of the Army in France, but also in Croatia. In fact, at a given moment, the Italian troops of the Second Army were deliberately moved from Zones I and II (as they were called)—that is to say outside their normal jurisdiction—precisely for that purpose and perhaps even as a result of that pressure.

The fact that General Mario Roatta, Commander of the Second Army, should not have mentioned any intervention outside the military field in his book *Cento milioni di baionette* (A Hundred Million Bayonets), obviously does not exclude such interventions. He writes:

> The Ustaše began to carry out a massive extermination of the Serbian Orthodox population (. . .) and of the Jews, for the most part very prosperous.
>
> Extermination . . ., since the campaign which we are discussing involved killing tens of thousands of people, including old men, women and children, while other tens of thousands, imprisoned in so-called concentration camps (barren land without any kind of shelter surrounded by barbed wire or cordoned off by sentries), were left to die of starvation and exhaustion.
>
> The Italian forces (the Second Army) could not watch such excesses unmoved, if only because of their extremely humane feelings. And so they straightway intervened, there where they happened to be (because at first they only occupied part of Croatian territory). And in September 1941, as soon as the Rome government had approved the proposal put to it by the Army Command, they proceeded to occupy the rest of the territory assigned to them and to assume civil powers.
>
> Thus the Army saved the lives and possessions of numbers of Serbian Orthodox (their authorities put the number at 600,000). It also took under its protection some thousands of Jews who had fled from Zagreb and the parts of Croatia under German occupation, as well as some hundreds of Poles who had taken refuge at that time in Yugoslavia and for whom the Germans were looking.

Further on General Roatta adds that the Ustaše

> made two vain attempts in '42 at armed penetration into areas held by our forces with the intention of committing more excesses against the population. The Italian Command blocked their way by deploying detachments of troops and artillery and warning that they would open fire if there was any attempt to get through.

And in the most serious case the Army Command immediately notified the Zagreb government (which secretly supported Ustaše undertakings) that it would take action by land and air against the city of Sarajevo, although this city lay on the far side of the Italo-German 'demarcation line' and although the Command of a German division was stationed there.[80]

This resolute attitude of the Italian Army resulted, among other things, according to Roatta, in arousing a strong feeling of resentment among the Ustaše against the Italian military authorities—all the more so as the latter were helping the Četniks by supplying them with arms. And this reaction, as we have seen, was fully shared by Mgr. Stepinac, although, alas, for other and completely unacceptable reasons. In his view, and in that of the other Croatian bishops, by allowing religious freedom to non-Catholics, and especially to the Orthodox, the Italians were guilty of a terrible crime. Stepinac complained to the Bishop of Mostar:

The Italians have returned and assumed civil and military authority. The schismatic Churches have immediately come to life again, and the Orthodox priests, in hiding up till now, have reappeared in freedom. The Italians seem to be favourably disposed towards the Serbs and severe towards the Catholics.[81]

And Stepinac wrote (in Italian) to the Minister for Italian Affairs at Zagreb, Raffaele Casertano:

It is obvious that such a state of affairs should have a religious as well as a political and national aspect. Besides it must be recalled that the Italians are basically Catholic, and are fortunate enough to have in their capital Christ's Vicar, the Head of the Catholic Church, a fact that renders more noteworthy any abuse committed by members of the noble Italian people against the rights of people living in occupied and annexed Croatian territory. It so happens that in the Croatian territory annexed to Italy a constant decline in religious life is to be observed, and a certain discernable shift from Catholicism to schism. If that most Catholic part of Croatia should cease in the future to be so, the blame and the responsibility before God and history will lie with Catholic Italy. This religious aspect of the problem I am discussing makes it my duty to speak in such plain and open terms, since I am responsible for the religious well-being of Croatia.[82]

The reports of the NDH representatives at the Holy See bear witness at nearly every stage to the increasing ill-humour of the

Ustaše. But the behaviour of those in charge at the Secretariat of State, and that of the Pope himself, is symptomatic: either they did not listen to their interlocutors' complaints or they promised to take the necessary steps, but above all they took advantage of the opportunity to advise them to rely on support from Catholic Italy rather than from Nazi Germany. This extract from a report by Rusinović on his audience with Mgr. Tardini is typical.

> Croatia [said Tardini] is a fundamentally Catholic State and for this reason should form strong and sincere ties with great Catholic countries like Italy, for no one knows what may happen after this great conflict.

And Rusinović adds:

> This last remark surprised me a little. It is hopeless: one is always made to realize that they are Italians.[85]

c. Vatican pressure on the Ustaše representatives in Rome and its own legate in Zagreb

If, all things considered, the Holy See could not (and would not) prevent the Croatian bishops from living out their patriotic adventure, it is equally obvious that pressure for Italian mediation and reconciliation was limited and, however optimistically viewed, could hardly be more than marginal. The most and best that the Vatican could do, therefore, was to make direct approaches to the government of the new Greater Croatia. But how was that possible at a time when the Holy See was committed to diplomatic relations with the royal government of Yugoslavia, and therefore could not enter into diplomatic relations with the NDH without showing a dangerous preference highly contrary to its traditions?

The simple answer lay in establishing *de facto* relations. And this is exactly what the Holy See did, and with an unusual determination, even if accompanied by all the safeguards and circumspection the situation demanded.

In the *Osservatore Romano* of 9–10 June 1941, in an informal note criticizing the ill-will of various people 'who set themselves up in the public eye as interpreters and commentators of his (the Pope's) various actions', there was the following passage:

> . . . Deep and rapid political and territorial changes are taking place in the Balkans? This has provided the newspapers—and also

the news agencies from which no one expects great political acumen—with an immediate opportunity for stating that the Holy See is working actively to establish new diplomatic representations. The Holy Father, in response to filial wishes that have been formally expressed to him, is giving audiences to Catholic personalities? It will be asserted and repeated that such audiences have a political purpose and significance.

There is a certain disingenuousness here. Even if we were prepared to concede, without actually admitting it, that Pavelić's visit to the Pope twenty days before had had a purely devotional purpose, there remains the fact that, at exactly that time, the Holy See was about to recognize *de facto* the Independent State of Croatia, and on the 13th of that same month appointed—still, of course, in secret, and therefore 'sine titulo'—the Benedictine abbot of Montevergine, Mgr. Ramiro Marcone, as Apostolic Legate to Zagreb.

The first move to obtain this recognition had been made by Pavelić and Stepinac, in complete agreement, a few days after the establishment of the NDH. Indeed in the Archbishop's *Diary* of 27 April 1941, the master of ceremonies, Cvetan, noted:

> The Auditor of the nunciature[84] has arrived in Zagreb from Belgrade on his way to Rome. He has visited the Archbishop who explained the situation to him and begged him to inform the Holy Father, as the mail was not operating. The Archbishop expressed strong hopes that the Holy See would grant *de facto* recognition to Independent Croatia as soon as possible. . . .
>
> After his conversation with the Auditor, the Archbishop called on the Poglavnik and intimated to him that he had taken the first steps to set up a point of contact between the Holy See and the NDH. The Poglavnik listened with great attention.

Pius XII's reply arrived two weeks later:

> The Auditor of the Belgrade nunciature has returned from Rome [states Stepinac's *Diary*] and has stopped here on his way to give the Archbishop an account of his audience with the Pope. It seems that the Holy Father listened very attentively, then charged the Auditor to tell the Archbishop to send a written report to Rome as soon as possible. At the same time the Holy Father said that on the question of diplomatic relations, the initiative should come from the government, and that up till now the Holy See had received no intimation.

Whereupon Stepinac had to pay another visit to the Poglavnik who, in the meantime, had already sent an official document to the

Holy See communicating the fact that the proclamation of the NDH had occurred. During their discussion they decided to send a new document to the Pope in Latin, asking for the new State to be recognized and for the Pope to send a personal representative. The document was cleverly worded.[85] After expressing his strong Catholic feelings and his absolute fidelity and filial devotion to the Pope, Pavelić claimed to see the coincidence of Croatian independence with the thirteenth centenary of the baptism of the nation as a symbol, indeed the 'hand of God', as well as the outcome 'of the powerful intercession of the Prince of the Apostles to whom the Croats have always remained faithful'. Then he went on:

> Holy Father! When God's gentle providence allowed me to stand at the helm of my people and my country, I resolved and hoped with all my strength that the people of Croatia, always faithful to their glorious past, would remain faithful in future to the Blessed Apostle Peter and his successors, and that our country, imbued with the law of the Gospel, would become the kingdom of God. In order to carry out this magnificent task I ardently appeal to Your Holiness for help. And my first hope in this regard is that Your Holiness shall recognize our State with Your supreme apostolic authority, then that You shall deign to send me Your representative as soon as possible, who will assist me with Your paternal advice. Finally I beg You bestow Your apostolic blessing on me and my people. Prostrate at the feet of Your Holiness, I kiss Your consecrated right hand and declare myself a devoted son of Your Holiness. . . .

As we have already seen in our general survey, and in the part of this book devoted to Poland, the Holy See wanted nothing better during the war than to have representatives in every country: properly accredited diplomats wherever possible, and at least Apostolic Visitors. Very cleverly, Pavelić had been vague about the type of representative the Pope might decide to send to Zagreb. Archbishop Stepinac must have explained to him that, while war lasted, the Holy See was not in the habit of making any *de jure* recognitions, that is to say of undertaking exchanges of diplomatic representatives with governments created by the events of war. This applied all the more in the case of Croatia, as the representative of the Royal Legation of Yugoslavia[86] was still accredited to the Holy See, and indeed was living as a guest at the Vatican. However it can-

not have been Pavelić himself who said that he would be satisfied
with a mere Apostolic Visitor. Indeed, when he learnt that the papal
representative appointed to the NDH would have that very title, he
protested: Croatia was not a missionary country, and could not be
considered by such standards. Whereupon the Holy See settled on the
compromise of an Apostolic Legate (a personal and temporary post,
whereas an Apostolic Delegate is institutional and permanent).

The appointment was made on 13 June (i.e. on Pavelić's name day,
as was later pointed out in Croatia). The Legate was a Benedictine
abbot: the famous legates Martin and Gebizon, sent to Croatia
respectively by Pope John VIII in the ninth century and Gregory VII
in the eleventh, had also been Benedictines—this, too, was pointed
out later. He was not a professional diplomat, but a sixty-year-old
monk[87] born on an estate of the Abbey of Monte Cassino, who had
had a promising career as lecturer in philosophy at the University of
his Order (i.e. of Sant' Anselmo in Rome)—so much so that he became a co-opted member of the Roman Pontifical Academy of St.
Thomas Aquinas—and who had for twenty years and more—that
is to say since 1918 when he had doffed the grey-green uniform of a
military chaplain—taken over the mitre and crozier as head of his
famous abbey.

The curious thing about Marcone's arrival in Zagreb on 3 August
1941 was its almost clandestine nature. The only mention of it is to
be found in Stepinac's *Diary:*

On 3 August at 3 o'clock the Pope's delegate, Mgr. Ramiro
Marcone, with his secretary, Giuseppe Masucci, arrived from
Rome. He went straight to the convent of the Holy Ghost Fathers.
No one knew anything of his arrival. As soon as the Archbishop
heard of it, he called on him and asked him to move into his
palace, since no other suitable accommodation could be found for
him. He moved into the palace on 6 August.

That Marcone's appointment should not have appeared in the
Osservatore Romano or the *Acta Apostolicae Sedis* is not surprising
in view of the private nature of his mission (the *Annuario Pontificio*
continued to mention him simply as the Abbot of Montevergine until
the end of 1945). One could perhaps have thought that it was the
Holy See that had asked the Ustaše government not to make any fuss
of its representative, at least for the time being. The truth of the

matter was, however, that Pavelić was offended by the choice of someone outside the diplomatic profession. Indeed he took his revenge almost certainly for that same reason, first by waiting some months before appointing his own representative (but Fr. Seguic—sent to Rome in September 1941—had to make yet another attempt to set up real official relations, besides putting pressure on the Vatican to persuade Aimone to accept the crown of Croatia), and, second, by appointing as his representative a mere doctor who until a short while before had been practising in a Roman hospital: Dr. Nikola Rusinović.[88] Later, in view of the Vatican's resistance, and as it came to appreciate the zeal of Abbot Marcone, the Ustaše government decided to change its attitude. It began to rejoice in the presence of the Pope's representative and promised as successor to Rusinović in Rome Prince Erwin Lobkowicz, the descendent of an illustrious family of Bohemian origin, who, in addition, had been a secret chamberlain *di spada e cappa* of His Holiness since the days of Pius XI.[89]

Finally, the recognition of the NDH by the Holy See is only of interest to our study in so far as we can find out whether the Vatican made use of its moral prestige and political weight to counsel and, when necessary, to impose the needed moderation in the struggle against the Serbs in which the Church herself was so seriously implicated.

Now the first thing to remember is that the recognition of the NDH was not brought about by Croatia's peculiar religious situation. The steps leading to recognition had already been taken before the explosion of the events recalled above; so that even if these events may have influenced the speed at which recognition was implemented (and there is no proof of this) the influence can only have been marginal. It follows that the Holy See was led to *de facto* recognition of the NDH for other no less serious reasons, whether religious or political, which can easily be guessed: first, because of the need to control the ecclesiastical situation in much of the area of former Yugoslavia so as to support and possibly strengthen its structure before the end of the war; next, because of the need to flank a State that sooner or later would enter the Tripartite Alliance, thus becoming one of the constituent elements of the new order that the Axis was to establish after its victory; and, finally, because of the opportunity to support a martially anti-Communist Catholic country situated at the very heart of the Balkans, where the Soviets did not lack sympathizers, and that at a time when Germany (and the Vatican knew this) was preparing to attack the Soviet Union.

Since these are the reasons that decided the Vatican to recognize the NDH, they must be regarded as basic and pre-eminent over any others that might crop up later. So that if it came to a conflict of ideas, the later—so to speak, accessory—reasons would be sacrificed, not the original ones. It is conceivable that as the drama of the persecution of the Orthodox and the Catholics of Byzantine rite developed, it too, despite its serious and potentially dangerous nature, ended up by taking second place to the original motives. In fact this seems undoubtedly true.

What we need to note, first of all, is the exceptional nature of the relations with Ustaše Croatia in the earliest stages, followed immediately afterwards by their sudden and apparently unjustified cessation;[90] then the constant care on the part of the Holy See, in its contacts with the representatives and the Zagreb government, to keep away from the question of forcing the Orthodox to adopt the Catholic faith—as if the Vatican viewed this last as a regrettable incident needlessly endangering the understanding between the two parties which had begun so well.

True, the relations between the Vatican and Croatia were always strictly unofficial; but this was inevitable in view of the existence (already mentioned) of the Yugoslav government in exile, and the untimeliness of an expression of sympathy with an Axis ally. On this last point, the report by Dr. Rusinović on his first meeting with Cardinal Maglione, Secretary of State, removes all doubt:

> Finally, on 4 February, I was received by Cardinal Maglione. It was conveyed to me that my mission was of an absolutely private nature, and that nevertheless the Holy See welcomed and greeted with pleasure the person sent by the Poglavnik.
>
> Cardinal Maglione was very cordial. I greeted him in the name of the Poglavnik, and emphasized the Catholicism of the Croatian people, stressing Croatia's relations with the Holy See from the foundation of the State to the present day. He thanked me for the greeting and asked me to return his greeting to the Poglavnik. He

added that the Holy See cannot recognize the NDH *de jure* since, for at least a century, they have adopted the procedure of not recognizing political situations created during a war. In this connection he reminded me that Abyssinia has not yet been recognized as an integral part of the Roman Empire [*sic*!]. However, the Holy See does not forget its sons who are undergoing difficult trials during the war, and does not mean to hurt them by giving them the faintest chance of thinking they are forgotten. The Holy See has Croatia constantly in mind, since Croat is synonymous with Catholic and the Holy See cannot imagine a Croat who is not a Catholic. The audience lasted twenty-five minutes, and at the end the Cardinal told me he was at my disposal three days a week; only I must inform him in advance by telephone of my intended visit. As I was leaving I asked him to obtain an audience for me with the Holy Father; he agreed at once, but again stressed that even such an audience would have to be strictly private, and take place a little later. I suppose that the Pope's special audiences are reported in the *Osservatore Romano* so that if I was received immediately after having been with the Secretary my audience would be considered official, and that would give our enemies the chance to protest to the Vatican, a thing the Vatican intends to avoid. Indeed, I have heard that my mission, although a private one and unknown to the public, has already caused protests.[91]

We need only read Rusinović's (and also some of Lobkowicz's) reports to realize that the 'privacy' of his position at the Holy See was such that quite a number of people whom he visited with a view to winning them over the the cause of the NDH were astonished to find that he was a Ustaše representative at all. Among these were even cardinals, such as the Prefect of Propaganda Fide, Fumasoni-Biondi, who was also protector of the Ecclesiastical College for Croats in the Holy City (San Girolamo degli Illirici—St. Jerome of the Illyrians).

The consistency and firmness of the Vatican in standing by its simple *de facto* recognition is all the more significant as the attempts of the Zagreb government and its representatives to persuade it to agree to official recognition never ceased. Indeed, when they realized that neither emissaries nor discourtesies had any effect, they changed their tactics. When the existence of the papal representative was finally revealed, at least seven months after his arrival, on the occasion of the opening of the first legislature of the Sabor in February 1942—on that occasion he appeared on the diplomatic rostrum dressed in white, with his round, puffy, mastiff-like face—the Ustaše governors were not content merely to emphasize the significance of his presence in Croatia over the radio and in the press. They treated him like a full member of the diplomatic corps, indeed as the doyen of the small group of diplomats accredited to the NDH. This was obvious at all official ceremonies, for he was unfailingly given precedence; and it promptly became recorded in political etiquette and even in the official list of diplomats issued by the Ustaše Foreign Office. Nor was that all: his name day and birthday were celebrated by clergy and civilians alike and there were special festivities for 26 March 1943, the twenty-fifth anniversary of his consecration as abbot.

Despite this crafty blackmail, Rome did not give in, although eventually, if not without protest, the second Ustaše representative, Prince Lobkowicz, was conceded a certain equality of treatment when he asked to be allowed to enjoy the benefits of supplies and petrol granted to other diplomats.[92]

However, despite these rigid restrictions (mostly imposed by the continued protests that reached the Vatican about its relations with Croatia) it is obvious—still from the same sources—that in the Secretariat of State and in Vatican circles proper they made every effort to make as many concessions as possible to the Ustaše representatives to make up for what, by force of circumstances, was not considered permissible. Thus, unable to be invited to the papal ceremonies in Saint Peter's where they would have found themselves shoulder to shoulder with the Yugoslav deputy-minister, it was proposed that they should be present at the Gregorian College in honour of the Pope where their rivals could not be present since they were confined to the Vatican, and where they would still be in good company among diplomats of the Axis and the neutral powers.[93] Once even Lobkowicz was given 'precedence over a waiting ambassador' at an audience with Mgr. Montini.[94]

Besides these acts of courtesy towards specific people, we must also mention the eager desire in the Vatican to satisfy every Ustaše request. This applies in particular to audiences with the Pope, sometimes requested at the last minute and not always for serious motives. Such things occurred on several occasions. For instance, in his report of 14 April 1943, Lobkowicz mentions the audience requested by the Mayor of Zagreb:

> The request for an audience with the Holy Father was put on the agenda only after the Mayor's arrival in Rome; the embassy to the Quirinal knew nothing about it until the last minute. It was very difficult to obtain an audience as so many other visits had to be taken into account. And in the Vatican they are not inclined to grant audiences with specific terms of reference without valid reason. Moreover the Pope had just resumed work after his illness and needed to make up for all the time lost. In spite of this we managed to obtain an audience on a Sunday, when the Pope usually does not receive. So on Sunday, 11 April, Wurster, the secretary of this office,[95] was able to accompany the Mayor of Zagreb and his suite to the Vatican. As they passed by, the sentry stood to attention, and the Swiss guard was lined up by the entrance to the Sala Clementina. Such honours are rare, and we did not expect them. Still less had we imagined that the Pope would hold the audience in the Throne Room, which is next door to his study. It is in that room that heads of state are received. . . .

On the occasion of the audience granted to the Ustaše minister, Simčić, leading man of confidence with the Staff of the Second Italian Army, something really exciting took place. In his case too the audience was requested and granted in record time, only no one was expecting the invitation to be addressed to him 'as to a Minister, with all the titles due to his position'.

> It is the first time [comments Lobkowicz] that the Vatican has acted in this way. Up till now all the important figures from Croatia have been received as private persons, with no formal recognition of their office. Even the invitation to the audience sent to the Mayor of Zagreb was merely headed 'Signor Ivan Werner'.[96]

Of course we must not make too much of such episodes. Indeed, they show how faithfully the Vatican stood by its own regulations. They were nothing more than compensations for what the Holy See did not want to concede, as being too dangerous. This applied to the audience Rusinović requested of the Pope. He probably did obtain it, just as he was about to leave Rome and give up his appointment, but there is no reference to it in his surviving reports. Certainly by the end of June 1942, the date of the last report from him that we possess, he had still not succeeded. The reason is obvious. He had no other claims to such an honour, and so granting an audience would have revealed his position at the Vatican.

They even tried to put Lobkowicz off. However, the Prince was determined to react: he said plainly to Mgr. Montini that 'in that case his mission was rendered superfluous', and he repeated his threats to have recourse to other important persons in the Vatican—with such effect that scarcely two weeks later, on 22 October 1942, he was granted an audience, on condition that he dressed as a private chamberlain and carried out his normal duties first. The strange thing was that on that day the private chamberlain was fetched from his own home by a Vatican car. Half capitulation and half victory.[97]

Another proof of Vatican intransigence so as to save appearances lies in the determined stand against any official recognition of the audience probably accorded to the Poglavnik which was announced just before that of Simčić. The Poglavnik had been received by the Pope once already, on 18 May 1941, a month after his rise to power; even then it had been 'a strictly private audience'. His suite was introduced as 'a group of Catholic Croats accompanied by His Excellency Mgr. Francesco Salis-Seewis, titular bishop of Corico, and auxiliary of Zagreb'.[98]

In May 1943, the Ustaše ambassador to the Quirinal and the Pleni-potentiary's Office at the Holy See were informed of Pavelic's probable arrival in Rome during the following month, and of his intention to profit by the occasion to visit the Pope. Prince Lob-kowicz openly mentioned such a possibility to Cardinal Maglione, then referred it to his Minister:

> . . . I stated that should the Poglavnik come to Rome he would be pleased to pay a visit to the Pope. But as he realizes that such a visit could cause difficulties, he suggests that the meeting with the Duce could take place somewhere else; in any case the matter rests entirely with the Italian government. Cardinal Maglione said he would discuss it with the Holy Father and that I could rest assured that there were no difficulties attached to the Poglavnik's visit to the Holy Father except that he could not be received as a sovereign. The Cardinal then added that he was sorry that he personally would not be able to see the Poglavnik on that occasion, as such an act could be interpreted as a departure from the policy of neutrality so scrupulously practised by the Vatican.[99]

This behaviour on the part of the Secretariat of State clearly shows a desire to gain time while keeping up the morale of the Ustaše representatives and the Zagreb government. Indeed concessions soon went to extremes such as were rarely reached with other countries in the same or analogous situations. Consider the appointment of two bishops, made during the April of 1942:

> . . . From the very moment I reached here [writes Rusinović] I busied myself among other things with the appointment of the new bishops, as I thought it might turn out to be a success for us. I learnt from the Spanish how hard they are struggling, though without success, to have bishops appointed to the vacant sees in Spain—so that today there are eleven unoccupied sees. The facts are these: when the Vatican wants to show its disapproval of certain events that are taking place in a country, it omits the appointment of bishops, and this serves as a kind of retaliation. I heard from Dr. Galvanek that, despite all the government's efforts, in former Czechoslovakia the Holy See would not appoint bishops for more than a year after the Republic had been proclaimed. And during the last few days I have been able to witness the truth of these assertions. When our friends learnt of the appointments, they congratulated me explaining the event as a successful move of ours *vis-à-vis* the Vatican. In the first place the whole colony of ecclesiastics in the city congratulated themselves, while among the diplomats the Slovak representatives at the Quirinal and the Vatican seemed to be particularly glad, interpreting it as a step forward in our relations with the Holy See.[100]

This quotation is important, not only for the comment on the very special relations between the Holy See and the NDH, but also because the fact of the appointment was rightly interpreted by Rusinović, and indirectly by the governors in Zagreb, as a declaration of innocence as regards their conduct; and by the governments of the Axis and of associated countries as a generous and unexpected absolution of Ustaše home policy.

In his report Dr. Rusinović went on to give his Minister a long lesson on ecclesiastical law, explaining, with many quotations from canon law, the procedure followed by the Holy See in the appointment of bishops and how it worked:

> In our case [he concluded] I was informed by the Vatican Secretariat of State that Abbot Marcone had been given fresh instructions to inform the government twenty-four hours in advance of the appointments of the Pope's intention to appoint those per-

sons as bishops of the two vacant sees in Croatia. I do not know how Marcone carried out these instructions. . . . However, I can tell you in all honesty that these appointments are viewed as a success for us. I have been put on my guard against the famous Yugoslav government, which might attempt, through London, to protest against the appointments.[101]

Rusinović had already discussed the matter with the Poglavnik and with the Zagreb Office for Foreign Affairs. Subsequently he had made a report on 27 April when he had learnt that the Holy See was about to make the appointments 'although we are not in diplomatic relations' with it; and to say that the Poglavnik would be told the names of the candidates by the legate Marcone. From this report it seems that he was also aware of the strange cases of Djakovo,[102] Ragusa, Mostar and Križevci. The see at Ragusa, he said, would remain unoccupied for some time longer. At Križevci Dr. Simrak would probably be installed. On the other hand there were several candidates for Djakovo: Gas, Gunčević and Šeper.[103] As for Mostar, 'the Vatican did not want a Franciscan as bishop,' although the Franciscans were making every effort to achieve this.[104] Indeed, the Vatican was consulting the government on the matter, 'so that people worthy of being bishops in both a national and a religious sense could be selected'.

In fact on 15 April the bishops of Mostar and Križevci[105] were appointed: Mgr. Petar Cule and Mgr. Janko Simrak respectively. The appointment of the incumbent of Ragusa was postponed, as was that of the bishop of Djakovo: Lobkowicz, Rusinović's successor, went on to say more about the most likely candidate there (Mgr. Josip Gunčević):

> I want to stress that, until recently, the Vatican considered that new bishops should not be appointed, except in cases of great need, until the end of the war, so that the candidates chosen would fit in with the post-war situation. Now it appears that the Vatican has changed its ground and is prepared both to make the appointments and to come to an advance agreement with the government of Croatia about the men under consideration.[106]

But Lobkowicz was mistaken. There were to be no more episcopal elections in Croatia, as the position of the Axis powers—and therefore of Croatia—was obviously worsening. When in 1942 the appointment of the bishops of Mostar and Križevci was achieved, it had been for exactly the opposite reason: namely, because of the cheerful future that seemed to be in store for the Tripartite Powers. The Holy See, that is, allowed itself to be influenced mainly, if not exclusively, by the events that had a bearing on the probable post-war future.

To illustrate this, we need only quote the imprudent promises made by the directors of Vatican policy about the establishment of official relations between Croatia and the Vatican. On 13 September 1941 Fr. Seguic met Mgr. Boehm, editor of the *Osservatore Romano*, in Rome, and of course they broached the subject of 'recognition'. This is what Boehm replied:

> The Holy See always acts in this way. It acted in the same way about Poland, when that country was constituted. It watches over the whole Catholic world, and cannot afford to seem partial. If one of the great neutral countries recognized you, the Pope would follow immediately. Brazil or Argentine could make the first move. It is up to you Croats to create favourable conditions in your regard.
> —Spain has recognized us, or will do so within a few days.
> —That is not enough, because Spain is not a neutral country. It is allied to the Axis. Switzerland has not recognized you. But the Holy See will give proof of its affection towards the Croats and their country when it is necessary.[107]

The monsignor-journalist's attitude is a facile one. But strangely enough when, on the following day, Don Seguic paid a second visit to Mgr. Tardini, he seemed to find confirmation of Boehm's opinion.

> He, too, gave me the impression that the Holy See would recognize the NDH *de jure* the minute some neutral American or Latin American leader did so.[108]

Perhaps this impression was over-optimistic. What is certain is that the explanations Rusinović gathered a few months later from various other prelates he consulted—Mgr. Arborio Mella, Mgr. Prettner-Cippico, etc.—were not very different from the prospects held out by Boehm. And there did seem to be real grounds for optimism. At the beginning of March 1942, Mgr. Montini let it be clearly understood that official relations could be viewed as much more than a hypothetical aim.

> Recommend gentleness to your government and government circles, and our relations will work themselves out. As long as you behave correctly the form of the relations will come of their own accord.[109]

Pius XII was still more explicit when he received Lobkowicz on 22 October of the same year:

> The Holy Father welcomed me in his usual extremely benevolent manner, emphasizing with a smile that he was receiving me as his private chamberlain, but that he hoped he would soon be receiving me in a different capacity.[110]

The continual improvement in the Vatican's attitude towards Croatia proves that this was an aim soon to be attained. As Dr. Rusinović wrote, the ice was melting more and more. In his reports we can easily follow the progress he personally was making, and hence the progress of the cause he was serving:

> 4/3/42: First I must tell you that the Vatican's interest in us and our affairs increases every day. As a result my work is becoming a little easier. . . .
>
> 27/4/42: Day by day the Vatican's attitude towards us improves. The attitude to the NDH is definitely positive.
>
> 28/5/42: Now things begin to go well for me too.[111] Indeed, I am visited daily by priests and friars, not only that, but Vatican people come too, as well as other diplomatic representatives of my acquaintance.

Lobkowicz, in his letter of 15 July 1943 to the head of the political sector in Zagreb, Dr. Vilo Bačić, says (shortly before the fall of Fascism):

> Throughout our activities we have often noted that the Vatican's attitude towards Croatia has undergone continual improvement, and that the Vatican has come to understand the importance and the role of Croatia as regards the Church in South-East Europe.

d. The behaviour of the heads of the Secretariat of State

If the long-awaited day never dawned, it was only because the fortunes of war turned against the Axis, and the Holy See finally decided it was useless to waste time on the Ustaše regime. But until the situation became clear, the civil servants and the heads of the Secretariat of State were careful not to compromise any relations that might bear fruit in the future. Indeed, with this end in view they made every possible effort to avoid giving too much weight to events in Croatia, or, when they did have to touch on them for the good of the NDH itself and of the Holy See, they always did so with the greatest circumspection.

The first striking illustration of this 'diplomatic control' was provided by Mgr. Sigismondi, the then head of the Office for Croatian Affairs in the Secretariat of State, when he broached with Rusinović 'the problem of conversions'.

> . . . The Holy See is pleased about it, but he stressed that both the American and English press are attacking us on this point, saying that the conversions have come about under governmental pressure. The Holy See does not believe a word of this; but recommends slow action to avoid reproaches, calumnies and difficulties for the Holy See itself. . . .[112]

Less unbiased, but equally *souple*, was the behaviour of the heads of Vatican policy: Montini, Tardini and Maglione. We already know of the initial attack of the first of these aimed at the inexperienced diplomat:

> What is going on in Croatia? Is it possible that so many crimes have been committed? Why has the world made such an uproar about your country? And is it true that prisoners are being ill-treated?

Unexpectedly the matter went no further, and Rusinović reports with complacency:

> I settled everything, revealing the enemy propaganda in its true light and, as for the concentration camps, I said that he would do better to obtain his information from the Apostolic Delegation at Zagreb. I also added that foreign journalists were invited to visit the concentration camps and that when they left they declared that the camps were perfectly suited to regular habitation and satisfied the requirements of hygiene. Liberated prisoners speak well of them and particularly praise the way they were treated. He claimed to be satisfied, and added that the Holy See received news (against Croatia) guardedly, and is happy to hear a Croatian Catholic speak openly of these matters.[113]

And the report continues:

> He was especially interested in the Slovenes living in Croatia. He is sorry for them and has given Marcone instructions to help them as much as he can even materially. The Holy See does not have large resources but will do everything in its power to help them. He told me that the Holy See was very grateful to the government of Croatia for having taken them in and is aware of the government's chivalrous behaviour. He used that very phrase. He also added that perhaps the Slovenes do not at the moment realize how well they have been treated by the Croats in such

difficult times, but the time will come when they do appreciate it properly. God will reward the Croats who, while struggling with so many difficulties, yet manage to show understanding to those who suffer.

Then we talked about Dalmatia, and he asked me how many Croatian dioceses had been annexed to Italy. When I told him that these included the dioceses of Krk, Šibenik and Split, he expressed great surprise and said, 'That must be very painful for the people of Croatia, but you must be patient!' He went on to assure me that the Holy Father is very devoted to the Croatian people and is ready to help them. 'I am most grateful to you for this visit; it has given me great pleasure to speak with a representative of the Catholic people of Croatia. So far your people have fulfilled their mission in history, and they will certainly continue to do so.' That was how he ended our talk, and immediately afterwards asked me how many Catholics there were in Croatia. When I told him that there were five million of us, he said that that was of great significance for the Catholic Church in the area. 'The Holy Father will help you, rest assured of that,' he said as I took my leave.

Simulated attack, patient listening, generous surrender: these were the three stages characteristic of every audience granted to the Ustaše representatives by the heads of the Secretariat of State. The following year Montini pursued the same tactics with Lobkowicz who visited him to present him with various publications:

> He is enthusiastic about the publication of *Ustaše Principles* and hopes that their realization will have as much success as the book. He has heard of the *Grey Book*. He is convinced that Croatia may be a bulwark (*ein Bollwerk*) against Bolshevism: he says that the Holy See realizes that it is in the interests of everyone that Croatia should keep her present Eastern frontiers. The Croats can never be amalgamated with the Serbs. However he said: 'You cannot imagine how many protests come in from Croatia about the reprisals carried out by the Ustaše authorities who make no distinction between the guilty and the innocent, just as you say with regard to the Italians; except that the Italians are in a country that is not their own, among peoples unknown to them, whereas you are unjust towards your own people.' Finally he added that the Holy Father was very pleased with the Poglavnik's telegram for the anniversary of his coronation.[114]

Once again an initial reference to Ustaše crimes comes from Montini; not only that, but the word he uses—'reprisals'—is a fairly strong one, and he adds that he has firm grounds for what he says. So why the last digression? Was not the Poglavnik the theorist and strategist in the struggle to exterminate the Serbs? So how could the Pope be grateful for any communication received from such a person?

Nor do we find Mgr. Tardini's attitude very different. He was the only one of the three heads of the Papal Secretariat with first-hand knowledge of Croatia—during one of his journeys he had crossed that country and probably made one or two halts, enabling him to say that he 'knows the Croats well' and had formed 'a very high opinion of them'. Such a high one, he cleverly adds, 'that he is astonished that all the things that cause their enemies to slander them could have happened'. But this is his final repartee upon his first meeting with Rusinović. Tardini, as Secretary for Extraordinary Ecclesiastical Affairs had begun with weaving this bitter-sweet rebuke at the school-boy standing before him who, after all, was not all that rebellious:

'Croatia is a young country [*sic*], younger still as a State, and the young often make mistakes—inevitably, because of their age. So it is hardly surprising that Croatia, too, is guilty of this. It is human, understandable, justifiable; your enemies, however, are not prepared to understand and justify, indeed they even find mistakes that have not been made. This is the cause of all the trouble about Croatia. But today Croatia has been in existence for about a year, and has a certain amount of experience. The bad elements must be jettisoned. The greatest virtue, whether in an individual or a society, a people or a State, is the ability to admit mistakes that have been made, as this is the only way that they can be corrected. Croatia is rich in fine traditions and these are a guarantee for a brilliant future, if those who guide the people of Croatia will accept the invitation addressed them by Providence and always keep in mind their historical mission in their own territory and in the general world situation. We are well aware of the difficulty of Croatia's position, but with intelligence, good will and God's help you will overcome all the difficulties.

'As for your internal policy, you have the problem of the Serbs. The Holy See is fully aware of all that the Croats suffered during the twenty years of United Monarchy'—these are the exact words he used to refer to Yugoslavia. 'We remember very well the instructions we gave our nuncio in Belgrade. But you can rest assured that he intervened on behalf of the Croats and in any case always tried to stand in the way of their oppressor. It was hard for you, you were treated unjustly, but as you are good Catholics and live Christian lives you know that the Christian should forgive his enemies, and so must you. Even putting aside that consideration, it is unwise politically speaking to make enemies of the people who live under the same roof as you. You must be patient and gentle and find a way to assimilate them with you: and this will take time. That is the only way of achieving lasting success. Croatia must also follow closely the general development of political events. She is a fundamentally Catholic State and for this reason should form strong and sincere ties with great Catholic countries like Italy, for no one knows what may happen after this great conflict. . . .'

Then we discussed Parliament. I must report that the meeting of Parliament has been politically very well received, not only in the Vatican but also by political circles over here. The work being done by Parliament is followed by people in the Vatican and is reported in the *Osservatore Romano*. However, I could not understand why they did not report that the whole Parliament and government, headed by the Poglavnik, went to Church for the 'Veni Creator', which ought really to have interested them most of all, and I blamed the editing. Tardini told me that it must have been a slip, as the news was sure to have been reported by Stefani or one of the other news agencies. The action has been greeted with great pleasure. . . .

Our talk finished in a cordial atmosphere and, as he was saying goodbye, Tardini expressed his best wishes for the people and the State of Croatia, and assured me that should I need anything he was at my disposal.[115]

One feels like saying, 'let those who have ears to hear, let them hear'. The text is clear. The hints are unambiguous. And if the rebuke sounds gentle, we must remember that this was the first meeting with the new representative. But does the tone really change later? It is difficult to find anything in Rusinović's report to support this. In a report from Lobkowicz a year later (14 April 1943), the main subject is the appointment of bishops and the uncertain future of Croatia. Tardini is pessimistic: 'All the indications go to show that we can expect a peace as unjust as that of Versailles, irrespective of who makes it'; the news grows worse day by day; '*L'avenir c'est noir*'. But at the outset Lobkowicz had given him a copy of *Ustaše Principles* translated into Latin, and had pointed out that they were imbued with Christian feeling; and suddenly, with a malicious smile, Tardini had aimed his dart, 'And you call this Christian feeling?' Then, the next minute, he was praising Pavelić's *Horror of Errors*, saying that he had heard very favourable criticism of it. In short: a dart, then the immediate application of a pain-killer to soothe the wound should there be one. However, neither Rusinović nor Lobkowicz ever felt seriously ill-at-ease before the two heads of the Secretariat of State, or, if they did, it was only for a moment. The fact that they were always allowed to get their own back meant that they left the audiences in a state of mild euphoria.[115 bis]

Despite appearances, this is also basically true of the meetings with the Cardinal Secretary of State, the person whom they would consult most easily (probably the reason was to give them official importance and, at the same time, to make up for the unavailability of the Pope). The sole difference was that, unlike his colleagues, the Secretary of State preferred listening to talking, and always avoided expressing opinions, so that it became a real puzzle to interpret his silences.[116] In the reports of the two Ustaše representatives, Maglione's character assumes a solemn austerity, always completely self-controlled, precise without pedantry, firm without eloquence, not very priestly and almost inhumanly cold, but unexceptionable in the performance of his duty and in the defence of his principles: it is obvious that the Secretary of State frightened and awed them.

His way of behaving is perfectly reproduced in Rusinović's report of 8 February 1942, four days after he had been granted his first audience (cf. p. 326). In a later report, of 4 March, the comparison between Maglione's behaviour and that of Montini and Tardini is significant:

> Conversation was easier and more relaxed with them than with Cardinal Maglione, who is a man of few words, and who left it to me to keep the conversation going both times. . . .

It never occurred to the inexperienced diplomat that this might be the tactic of a clever investigator and also a proof of distrust as well as prudence.

The fact is that, with Maglione, Rusinović was obliged to keep up long monologues (on one occasion lasting forty minutes)[116 bis] of a historical apologetical nature on the relations between Croats and Serbs from the far-distant past to the present time. Maglione always listened in silence without any interruption or comment; then he would thank him laconically for his 'accurate information' and still refrain from making any favourable remark.

> I expounded to him the facts of the situation in those areas. He made no comment, but was surprised.[117]

Surprised at what? Favourably surprised by the reasons put forward, or unfavourably surprised by the indiscretion (or good faith) of his informant? The silence—and the surprise—remain a mystery. Rusinović, we surmise, was perplexed by such behaviour, but, as he has no grounds for suspecting the worst, refrained from making any judgment. In early February, when he informed Zagreb that he had given Maglione a copy of the *Grey Book* on crimes committed by the Serbs, he remarks simply:

> [Maglione] was appalled by the horrors described, but passed no judgment.[118]

Even the few words that the Secretary of State occasionally allowed himself do not help us to solve the mystery. Rusinović wrote on 25 March 1942:

> [The cardinal] has confirmed that not very good news about us has reached them [i.e. the Secretariat of State].

And again:

> Finally Maglione tells me that Croatia must be urged to use gentleness which is more powerful than violence; also that the Holy See is very glad to hear of the conversions, from which Croatia can derive political advantage, but that it is necessary to avoid giving the enemy any excuse for slander.

If the euphemism in the first quotation—'not very good news'—is icily ironical, in the second quotation 'gentleness'[119] is completely inadequate in the context of the scorched earth policy as currently being adopted in Croatia. However this may be, should forced conversions be avoided for their own sake, owing to their inherent sacrilege and the revolting blood-thirstiness accompanying them, or should they be avoided to keep the enemy quiet? And is the enemy really guilty of slander if he reports an atrocious truth?

But with Maglione too, nearly every leave-taking brought capitulation. In a talk reported by Rusinović on 26 February 1942, the latter told Maglione about the Catholicism of the NDH leaders:

> ... the government of Croatia is eminently Catholic, led by some-

one who is Catholic in deeds as well as words, and who has a chapel in his own house; a sincere practising Catholic who could never have permitted the crimes his enemies attribute to him. We know that faith is not sincere if it does not spring from the soul and is not spontaneous.

At these words, spoken assuredly with fervour and conviction, Maglione seems to have been really moved:

> The cardinal answered: 'I am very grateful to you for these fine words, and I beg you to come to me when you have any good news to tell me.'

Yet Maglione not only gradually thawed,[120] but in his efforts to please the Ustaše representatives he behaved in such a way as to arouse real bewilderment—as, for instance, when he put pressure on Stepinac to be more flexible with the rulers in Zagreb. In May 1943 Lobkowicz reports (report No. 7/43):

> I touched on the Archbishop of Zagreb's attitude, which is not always felicitous, as I have deduced from my talks with the Poglav-nik and Mgr. Marcone. I could see from the cardinal's reaction and words that he had already been informed of this. He spoke very openly, saying that he considered it unfortunate that the Archbishop has been unable to find the right level in his relations with the State; he will take advantage of the Archbishop's forth-coming visit to suggest to him, very respectfully, a more suitable, sincere and friendly attitude. The cardinal considers that the Arch-bishop, in his function as shepherd of souls, can have a substantial effect in the matter of unpleasant occurrences, but that he must first manage to win the government's confidence.

And Mgr. Montini pursued the same course:

> I paid a visit to the second secretary of the Secretariat of State, Mgr. Montini, to discuss with him the topics I have already men-tioned. Mgr. Montini promised that he would see that the Arch-bishop adopts a more suitable attitude.

It is hardly surprising that the two diplomats *in spe*, seeing that their interlocutors always gave in, should have persuaded them-selves that, taken all in all, it was child's play to face the heads of the Vatican Secretariat—a little chat soon brought them to see reason.

The surprising thing about the behaviour of the three leaders of the Holy See's policy is that, in their dealings with Ustaše Croatia, they should have abandoned the rule in operation under Pius XII, at least during the lifetime of his first and only Cardinal Secretary of

State—what we might call the rule of the division of duties: fatherly affability on the part of the Pope, and, when it was necessary (as in the case of Ribbentrop's visit in March 1940), the use of frank uncompromising denunciation on the part of his colleagues. Their silence, hardly diminished by the occasional vague hint, is all the more astonishing in that the position of the two Ustaše representatives was thankless because of its intrinsic precariousness, and was certainly not improved—at least in Rusinović's case—by their personalities. He was not only young and inexperienced as a diplomat, but, above all, new to the Vatican atmosphere—to such an extent that Fr. Wurster writes that his knowledge of the Holy See was drawn from a biography of Pius XII and the *Annuario Pontificio*. Even at the end of his mission he frankly admitted to his friend, Mladen Lorković, 'I'm perched in the air, like a building that's neither in the sky nor on the ground'. The heads of the Secretariat of State hardly needed to summon up their courage to speak firmly, on their own ground, to an embarrassed youth.

As can be seen in the *Appendix*, in curial circles the Ustaše found nothing but ignorance and dislike of their regime: the NDH could count its friends or sympathizers on the fingers of one hand. If the directors of Vatican policy preferred to remain silent, it was obviously because they wanted to avoid pointless friction with a Catholic State, which, if subdued and faithful, could always be useful to the Holy See.

Of course we can also presume that the heads of the Secretariat of State held the representatives of the NDH at the Holy See to be of little account, and put all their trust in the legate chosen to represent them in Zagreb. But was the man entrusted with such a delicate task really able to carry out the duties he had been ordered to perform? Once again we cannot give a definite answer since, apart from the documents already quoted, there is nothing to give an adequate picture of the legate Marcone's behaviour towards the Croatian episcopate or government. But the attitude of the government in Zagreb, and Rusinović's and Lobkowicz's faith in the abbot,[120 bis] tend to point to a negative answer.

By way of induction, we can even throw light on why he was chosen. As he was a fellow countryman and friend of Maglione's, it must obviously have been the Cardinal Secretary of State who chose him as ideal candidate for the post, especially as he was aware of his links with the House of Savoy, or at least with Crown Prince Umberto.[121] He was certainly not anti-Fascist in his political ideas, even if he was not so favourably disposed towards the regime as his secretary. It is in fact true that Fr. Giuseppe Masucci[122] was a particularly dear disciple of his, and this was why he selected him to accompany him on his mission.

Acording to Mgr. Prettner-Cippico, Abbot Marcone of Monte-vergine was delighted by his appointment as Papal Legate to Zagreb, and was very grateful to his friend and protector, Maglione. Marcone turned out to be one of the most zealous of the Holy See's representatives, if only because of the frequency and fullness of his reports (nearly always in long hand rather than typescript). On the other hand the Ustaše press provides proof beyond question of his assiduous participation[123] in the political and religious life of Croatia. Besides making regular tours of the country, there was no ceremony of any importance which he did not attend; and this obviously delighted the local authorities.

It was this that aroused the most serious doubts: indeed, the Ustaše leaders, who had already kept him quiet for seven months (because of a controversy with the Vatican—nothing to do with him personally), would hardly have hesitated to silence him again had they discovered him to be a critic or slanderer of the system. Then what are we to think of the numerous protests regarding Ustaše crimes which, according to Mgr. Cippico, the Holy See communicated to him? Did he pass them on too half-heartedly to those for whom they were intended? Or did the protests themselves exclude serious threats—such as a threat to remove the legate and break off relations with the NDH representatives in Rome? Why then (if the first explanation be the true one) did the Holy See not see to it that its representative was more efficient, all the more so in view of the impression of official omnipresence given by Marcone, both within and outside Croatia, and implicating the Holy See? Or, in the case of the second explanation, have we not fresh proof of the strangely slack and reticent attitude towards a regime which, when all is said and done, was hardly likely to inspire the Vatican with terror?

e. Pius XII's personal behaviour

By this time any conjecture as to the personal activity of Pius XII can be more or less discounted. Here too, of course, the only definitive and exhaustive answer could be found in the Vatican's secret archives. However the available documents permit us to formulate, very cautiously to be sure, several suppositions that show Pius XII as a more than benevolent supporter of Ustaše Croatia. Obviously, as he took great care never to give any public expression of his opinions, all we can do is read through the reports of his audiences. We may begin with the audience granted to Fr. Seguic in September 1941 (though the aim of Seguic's report does not guarantee the integrity of its contents):

> . . . I was received by Mgr. Prettner-Cippico, so that I might be instructed on the protocol with which the Head of the Church should be approached.
>
> The Holy Father showed interest in all that was happening in Croatia: in particular he asked me about the Poglavnik and all the other members of the government, about their religious feelings and religious education. He learnt with great delight that the Holy See can always count on Croatia as a Catholic State. He knows that the Croats are creditors in Europe as they have defended Christian, indeed Catholic, civilization. . . . He asked me whether the Croats were happy with Marcone. 'The person whom the Holy Father has sent us can only be for our happiness and well-being. . . .' The audience lasted for more than half an hour, to Mgr. Cippico's surprise, since even the audiences granted to Archbishops only last from ten to fifteen minutes.[124]

Of the two Ustaše representatives in Rome, we only know of papal audiences granted to Lobkowicz: the first, so to speak, para-official, i.e. for the Prince alone; the second for his family too. However, of the two the second is the more revealing. Here they both are:

> 22 October 1942: The Holy Father received me in his usual extremely benevolent manner, emphasizing with an understanding smile that he was receiving me as his private chamberlain, but that he hoped he would soon be doing so in a different capacity. I informed the Holy Father of the situation in Croatia—he showed great interest and understanding. I took the opportunity of telling the Holy Father of the impossible behaviour of the Italian govern-

ment in the occupied and annexed regions. The Holy Father listened to this too, but without making any comment. In any case I could not use this first meeting as an opportunity for going into details.[125]

31 January 1943: The Pope was very amiable, and expressed his pleasure at the personal letter he had received from our Poglavnik. . . .

The Holy Father showed especial interest in the activity of Ustaše youth, having heard about it from my eldest daughter.

I told him of the terrible sufferings endured by our men in various concentration camps in Italy, and the Holy Father promised that he would take a personal interest in the matter. I should add here that I have heard in the Vatican that the Vatican will grant a sum of money to help our prisoners.

As regards the situation in general, the Pope said that nothing could be seen on the horizon capable of suggesting the possibility of an immediate peace. Despite this, the Holy Father has been in a very good humour these last two weeks: the members of his suite have noticed it. His Maestro di Camera, Mgr. Arborio Mella di Sant' Elia, told me that one can guess from the Holy Father's mood that perhaps a more favourable development may be expected in events concerning peace, which is the Pope's greatest concern.

During the rest of the conversation the Holy Father told me he was disappointed that, in spite of everything, no one wants to acknowledge the one, real and principal enemy of Europe; no true, communal military crusade against Bolshevism has been initiated.

This declaration may cause some surprise in the light of the Pope's customary reticence on this subject.[126]

Was this a moment's unguardedness on the part of the highly self-controlled Pope Pacelli, a moment favoured by the 'family atmosphere' of the meeting? Or was it his exceptional state of euphoria that made him so optimistic and inclined to confidences? And how should we judge his satisfaction with the activities of the Ustaše youth?

A few months later Lobkowicz reported to Zagreb an even more significant episode:

Given my position as 'unrecognized' diplomatic representative, it is not possible for me to take part with other diplomats in the various celebrations. To make up for this in some way, and to avoid the impression of isolating Croatia's representative, I am invited to play the part of private chamberlain at the celebrations attended by the diplomatic corps. I was in uniform among the Pope's retinue for the celebration of the anniversary of his coronation on 12 March, and also on the occasion of the Pope's entry into the basilica of St. Peter's during Lent, Sunday, 11 April. At the end of this second ceremony, as he took leave of his retinue, and against all the rules of protocol, the Holy Father came up to me and said: 'I know the special significance of Your presence here: receive my special blessing.' Certainly this special declaration of the Pope's was intended as an honour for Croatia.[127]

Can one blame Lobkowicz for forming this conclusion? The tone of these audiences shows beyond all doubt that Pius XII, in his relations with the Ustaše representatives, was not content with his normal benevolence but willingly went beyond it. Of course this was mainly tact on his part, in view of their thankless position; but was it only that? And anyway, in the light of what was happening in Croatia, was not this tact, accompanied by such a generous display of benevolence towards the heads and institutions of that country, somewhat excessive? Although the general situation, or rather the situation of the Axis powers, was rather delicate during those first months of 1943, did Pius XII still count on the survival of the NDH?

We can only say Yes with reservations, as is proved by what took place during the audience granted to the Minister Simčić, and withheld from Lobkowicz in the official reports released to him. This was divulged by Simčić himself, on 2 June 1947, during a trial in Zagreb of several war criminals at which he was a witness. According to his evidence, the most authoritative of Croatia's leaders had realized during the early months of 1943 that the war had taken a turn for the worse as far as Fascism and they themselves were concerned: not only did they foresee a Russian invasion of the continent, but from one moment to the next they expected the Anglo-American forces to disembark on the Adriatic coast. Hence, out of self-preservation, they decided to support Maček's Peasant Party, on the pretext that when the moment came he would be arbiter of the situation.

Simčić came to Rome as spokesman and deputy for his colleagues (and also because of his duties as general man of confidence with the staff of the Italian Second Army), to sound the possibilities of support either in Fascist circles or the Vatican, and with this end in view he had meetings with Mgr. Arborio Mella, with Mgr. Madjerec, principal of the Croatian College, with the diplomat Galli, former Italian ambassador to Belgrade, with ambassador Guariglia, later minister in Badoglio's government, with Brosio who was also to become a member of that government, and with others. These people were in touch with Ciano, and Ciano with the Vatican, all hoping (according to Simčić) to save Fascism—if necessary, without Mussolini—by breaking away from Germany and going over to the Allied camp. Simčić's plan to save Ustaše Croatia was welcomed, as all were against the revival of Yugoslavia and prepared to re-open the question of Croatia's frontiers. The only difficulty lay in their sympathy for the Četniks.

When it came to arranging an audience with the Pope, the problem was how to mention the subject that needed to be discussed. But His Holiness's Maestro di Camera, Mgr. Arborio Mella, took charge of that side of things, and Pius XII opened the discussion in such a way as to allow Simčić to put forward his own ideas. In the Ustaše minister's own words:

> When we came to the world situation (having spoken of the situation in Croatia) . . . the Pope said to me: 'Italy will soon find a way of getting out of the war, and the Italians will help to bring about peace in the world. Italy is searching for, and will find, the way. I am working towards this end. So must the others. We must find in each nation the people who can actively work to this end.' The Pope was particularly interested in Maček and the Croatian Peasant Party, affirming that that party measured up to the new developments in Croatia. Then he spoke of the danger of Communism as a world-menace. Later he explained how the problem of Croatia and other States should be solved. Croatia should know how to play her part. In Italy all the politicians would collaborate; not just those in the opposition, but those in power (the Fascists) too, and as they saw the dangers of Communism, and Germany's fruitless struggle, they would find the way to salvation. 'I believe,' the Pope continued, 'that the German people will also act in this way, and it is important that the Balkan nations should adopt the same line. I am pleased about the recent visit from General Antonescu. While speaking to him, I realized that in the Balkans, as in the whole world, there exist the conditions and the determination to follow that path, and I am working towards that end.'[128]

If Simčić's retrospective account of these events be true, it is extremely interesting. But it cannot possibly be enough to absolve Pius XII from the charge of supporting the Ustaše regime. Critics in Tito's Yugoslavia used to make bitter attacks on the various audiences granted by Pius XII, between May 1941 and June 1943, to the NDH leaders and to groups of Ustaše police and young people. We already know about the private audiences. Those granted to groups were the following:

July '41: audience for a hundred constables of the Croatian police force, guests of the Italian *carabinieri*, and led by the head of the Zagreb police force, Eugen Kvaternik-Dido.

6 February '42: audience for Ustaše youth in Rome (206 people in all).

At the end of the same month: audience for the Croatian colony in Rome.

December '42: a second audience for Ustaše youth.

Not so very many after all, and in any case not so full of sinister intent as has been made out.[129] On 22 July 1941 the NDH and its police force had only been in existence for three months. In the meantime, admittedly, it had committed a number of crimes, but the Vatican could very well not have known about them, or have heard a version that excused them (the need for retaliation against attacks from the Serbs or enemies of the regime that certainly developed during the first weeks of Independent Croatia). Then, according to information in our possession, it seems that most of the young people at the audience of 6 February were Croatian theological students attending universities in Rome. Finally, Pius XII's parting remark to those attending the audience in December of that same year, 'Long live the Croats!', was certainly not a political cry, praising or sanctioning Croatia's claims to home rule, or, still less, recognizing the legitimacy of the Ustaše regime—though Lobkowicz was so pleasantly surprised by it:

> (He did not do this at the end of the audience for the Croatian colony in Rome in February this year. When we know that in the Vatican every single act and word is premeditated, then even in this incident we can note a small improvement.)[130]

A totally different problem is raised by the audiences granted to the Poglavnik—one granted, another only promised—and, even more, by the relations kept up with him for at least four years. It all seems to come down to the Pope's readiness to acknowledge every message of good will sent him by Pavelić, or every modest gift, such as the rosary mentioned by Rusinović in one of his reports. This was all perfectly permissible and would not have worried anybody had Pavelić not been the head of a government responsible, directly or indirectly, for the outrages we know.

True, no one has yet written an unbiased historical study of Pavelić. He has been charged with making statements that could hardly have come even from Hitler's mouth,[131] and the most hair-raising incidents have been attributed to him (like the tale of the basket full of human eyes that Curzio Malaparte claims to have seen on his work-table during an interview). But in rumours of this kind it is difficult to sift fact from fiction. His physical appearance in thousands of photographs (hundreds of which show him in the company of bishops, priests, nuns, novices, friars or seminarists) is always reserved and severe. We never see a smile, but there is nothing of Hitler's mad stare, or the demogogic bluster and vulgarity of Mussolini. Today anyone can visit the famous Villa Rebar, a few kilometres from Zagreb, which was his residence until it was threatened by the partisans: but no tales of orgies and depravity are attached to it.

Of course this has no bearing on his responsibility before history. We are judging Pavelić the public, not the private, man. Even had he been an ascetic in his private life, even if his words and his actions had been innocent of violence, the public Pavelić bears on his shoulders an unbelievable load of barbarity and slaughter. And if Pius XII, as a priest, could allow himself to take an interest in him as a private individual, he could not forget, as Pope, that he was dealing first and foremost with a Head of State. So the first disconcerting thing in the Pope's attitude towards the Ustaše dictator is his continuous display of enthusiasm for his 'sincere Catholicism'. That he should have gone that far with Seguic in September 1941 is understandable, but it is really too much to find the farce repeated in July 1943, and on the Pope's initiative. According to Simčić's account of his audience:

At the very end of the discussion the Pope said that Croatia was a country of good Catholics and that he was very glad to have had the chance of talking to the Poglavnik, whom everybody says is a practising Catholic—this comforts him and fills him with joy. I confirmed this fact, and added that the Poglavnik's arrival in Italy was expected and that I was sure that he would then want to ask for the Pope's blessing. The Pope replied: 'I shall willingly impart it, also on this occasion.'[132]

Of course there can be no objection to reasons of State counselling a private audience for Pavelić, but what is inconceivable is that Pope Pacelli should not have perceived the irony of the adjective '*practising* Catholic' as applied to the Poglavnik of Croatia.

Another cause for amazement is that every courtesy on Pavelić's part, however self-interested, seemed to delight Pius XII. For instance, in one of Lobkowicz's reports (but many others, even one of Rusinović's, repeat the same thing) we read:

The Pope expressed his pleasure at the personal letter he had received from our Poglavnik . . . with the Latin translation of *Ustaše Principles*. He was obviously delighted by this attention.[133]

But the most astonishing fact of all in Pius XII's behaviour—it is not only incomprehensible but quite unacceptable—is that he should have avoided even mentioning the constant massacres perpetrated in Croatia, either to the Poglavnik or to the various Ustaše representatives who managed to approach him. Judging by the Pope's words, Croatia was an exemplary, not to say idyllic, kingdom, with which the Holy See was impatient to establish long-lasting and official relations so as to weld modern developments on to the history of its glorious past: it was not the country where hundreds of thousands of Orthodox were being slaughtered for religious and racial reasons, where Jews and gypsies were bloodily pursued. New Croatia had leaders who were extremely Christian, it was about to give Catholicism recognition as the State religion, the bishops were honoured with the *lacticlavium*, it looked on its priests as civil authorities, it was dispersing what remained of the new as well as the old schismatic Churches, it was again becoming the *antemurale christianitatis* against the threat of Communism, and so on. All this is surely rather provocative. . . .

Are we then to assume that Pius XII was completely indifferent to the drama that was being acted out in the grim theatre of the

Balkans—the more so because there, at least, none of the victims were Catholics? Or because political reasons—the NDH's probable survival through the war, its contribution to anti-Communist resistance—forced him to adopt this attitude? And in this second case, was his conscience soothed by the despatches sent to Abbot Marcone on his instructions, proposing the use of 'gentleness' to the Ustaše and their leaders?

Unfortunately, in the present state of research, it is impossible to answer such questions. Not one letter of the correspondence that Pius XII must have carried on, even briefly, with the bishops of Croatia, and especially with their leader, Stepinac, during the NDH period, has come to light or been published: and a letter would have revealed his state of mind. For the moment one can only make a provisional judgment on his public and diplomatic activities and, all things considered, the judgment is a disconcerting one. Especially since, however tentative we try to be, we cannot forget that only once between 1941 and 1945 did Pope Pacelli mention the name Croatia in a public speech—and this was not while the Ustaše were surrounding the Serb villages, burning Orthodox churches crowded with faithful, or competing as to who was the best cut-throat in the NDH concentration camps, but when at the end of the struggle the role of the Catholic executioners seemed to have been taken over by the Communists: by a regime, that is, which had only been a few days in existence and which, in the circumstances, should have been granted, as in the case of the Ustaše regime, the benefit of a legitimate suspension of judgment. However, in this case, there were no extenuating circumstances:

Unfortunately [said Pius XII on 2 June 1945] in more than one region we have had to deplore the killing of priests, the deportation of civilians, the massacre of citizens without trial or for motives of private vengeance: no less sad than this is the news that has come to us from Slovenia and Croatia. . . .

Appendix

Important Figures in the Roman Curia and among those who frequented it with whom the Ustaše representatives to the Holy See came into contact

In the reports of the two Ustaše agents, Rusinović and Lobkowicz, frequently quoted in the foregoing pages, we meet a great range of important people, mainly ecclesiastics, but also laymen, living in, or attached to, the Vatican. Some of them figure continuously, others, the majority, appear once or twice, others still put in only a fleeting appearance. For this reason we shall not mention them all here. We shall exclude, with justified exceptions, all those whose relations with the Ustaše representatives had no bearing on their mission. But those mentioned here are free from any *a priori* accusation of collaborating or even sympathizing with the Ustaše. In any case in this *Appendix*, it is not our intention to indulge a taste for scandal by reproducing in detail what in the *Introduction* to this book we viewed as an extraordinary split in the Roman Curia and its regular visitors and guests. The following pages are aimed at filling out still more the documents already reproduced, by making use of material that could not be given full examination in a confined and concise treatise such as this. Finally, when the need arises, we shall make use of the reports of the Jesuit, Antun Wurster, secretary at the office of the 'plenipotentiary', Lobkowicz.

Mgr. Boehm and Count Della Torre of the 'Osservatore Romano'

It is not surprising that among the various peripheral Vatican fortresses, the two Ustaše representatives should have tried to win over the *Osservatore Romano*, the Holy See's daily newspaper. Judging by appearances, their contacts with the Italian Catholic press were slight. Only once does Rusinović quote as 'people who could be use-

352

ful to us' Mario Luzi[134] 'a great friend of Montini's', and Pio Bondioli[135] 'head of the Italian Catholic agency which provides news for all the Catholic newspapers'. What he found most surprising about both of these was their ignorance of Croatian affairs. He probably remained in touch with them (like his colleague Lendić of the Legation to the Quirinal), but we do not know what particular purpose they served. Father Wurster mentions Mgr. Pucci, 'director of *L'Avvenire*' of Rome—a prelate well-known for his high-level Fascist contacts—as a 'friend' of whom more use could be made.

As for the *Osservatore Romano*, their insistent attempts to gain an entry in that quarter are only too obvious. And yet in this they had been triumphantly preceded by Don Cherubino Seguic, at least according to Seguic himself. In his *Diary* the Poglavnik's enthusiastic friend makes special mention of his meeting with Mgr. Boehm, the newspaper's ecclesiastical reporter, a man who emerges (but it is difficult to say with what justification) as one of those people whose job seems infinitely below their capabilities and their worth, people who like to pretend that their job is a blind for their true and really valuable activities. Anyone who approaches such a person falls under his mysterious influence: he is an 'eminence grise' who holds the threads of true power in his hands. Usually they use the royal 'we', as they see themselves as representatives of the institution and as having those who really control it under their thumb. Their conversation is full of plans that will never come off in practice, but which while they are talking seem to be indisputable and successful realities, etc.

Seguic was anything but a psychologist or a writer, and yet, in his diary, the humble Milanese journalist of the *Osservatore* is portrayed in a typical way—Milanese despite the Teutonic boom of his name. So we shall quote most of the passage that concerns him:

. . . He is desirous of information. Everything one hears about Croatia in Italy smells of scandal. . . . We must discredit this idea. He would like me to establish myself in Rome, at least for some time, write for the paper (the *Osservatore*) and expose the scandal. He showed displeasure because the sea has been taken from us. Without the sea Croatia cannot live. He assured me that they, the Vatican organs, will try their utmost to get at least Split and Sebenico restored to us. Then he revealed to me some secret disagreements between Italy and Germany. . . . I was delighted to hear that the question of Croatia is considered by the Vatican as its own problem. . . . [And regarding the lack of recognition], Boehm says: 'The Holy See always behaves like that. . . . But when the time comes the Holy See will reveal its devotion to the Croats and Croatia.'

A man of action, if only in secret revenge for his disappointed ambitions (thus we continue to fill in the portrait, probably anything but exact, from what we can deduce from our sources), Mgr. Boehm is of course always in search of men of action and new settings for action. When he learns that a representative of the NDH at the Vatican is in Rome and 'in abscondito', he has to see him immediately,[136] and immediately stuffs him full of ideas and especially words. But here is the first clash with reality—bitterly disappointing. As Rusinović reports on 20 March 1942:

> At last I have managed to reach the editorial staff of the *Osservatore Romano*. I was received by Mgr. Boehm. He is very kind and courteous, but at the same time I realized that his attitude towards us is very hostile. We talked at length and when I pointed out very politely that the *Osservatore* carries very little news about Croatia, he showed me an entire library on the subject, and said that it was not his fault that that was how things were, since Mgr. Seguic, the correspondent, has not written for a long time—indeed it was only two or three days ago that a letter from him had arrived. He is prepared to write, but needs the material; then he will publish anything that does not conflict with the principles of Vatican policy.

Three months later the situation was still hopeless, as Fr. Wurster shows in his report of 12 June 1942:

> On the whole the *Osservatore* seems clearly hostile to us. While they print unpleasant articles about Croatia, they refuse any collaboration. Thus they returned an article of ours on the religious life of the Croatian colony in Rome. Once we noticed that they did not even open the newspaper *Za dom* (For the Fatherland) when they received it. Someone on the staff said that as he didn't know Croatian he would not get anything out of it. We have a friend in Vatican circles who has twice written some very friendly news about Croatia for an Italian publication. He is a young Jesuit. The Head of the Radio, also a Jesuit, does not look on us with favour.

Only a year later, on 14 April 1943, Lobkowicz could point with optimism to some improvement, and refer to his meeting with the editor of the *Osservatore*, Count Della Torre:[137]

One gets the impression that the Vatican paper is not favourably disposed towards us. . . . However, and we have already pointed this out, there has been an improvement recently thanks to the bulletins issued by our Embassy to the Quirinal. To clear up the matter once and for all, I called on the Editor of the newspaper, Count Della Torre. I presented him with *Ustaše Principles*, the *Grey Book* and *The Horror of Errors*. Della Torre showed interest in our situation, especially in the Poglavnik, and the problem of the King-designate. I explained to him our problems in general, and our relations with Italy in particular. He told me that twenty-three years ago he stopped understanding anything about Italian policy, whether domestic or foreign. Unquestionably he supports the Danube confederation. He promised to publish any politically controversial articles.

And in prompt fulfilment of his prognostications, he was writing on the following day:

An article has appeared in the *Osservatore Romano*, dated 14 April, about the visit here of the Mayor of the City of Zagreb, Signor Ivan Werner. It is fairly long and written with warmth, and it has attracted attention as it is not usual for the Vatican paper to record that kind of event.

The General of the Premonstratensians

Other fortresses on the fringe of the Vatican proper that had to be conquered by Rusinović and Lobkowicz were the generals and heads of the major religious orders. One or two offered no resistance, but these were among the least influential: a few others, of very different weight, were stormed with difficulty and conquered only in part. In the first category were the Premonstratensians; in the second, the Jesuits.

Rusinović recounts on 28 May 1942:

I have met by chance the general of the Premonstratensians. It is a very ancient Order whose custom it was to accept noblemen wishing to dedicate their lives to God. The general is a Flemish Belgian. His name is Noots. He is a man of great learning: he speaks English, Italian, German and French perfectly, and even a little Hungarian. We have had two meetings and spoke of everything involving Croatia and the Holy See. He is well aware of our position as he has visited Croatia several times, he knows about our struggle for independence and is wholeheartedly sympathetic towards us. I have had an invitation to his convent for dinner and there I shall meet people from the Vatican who have influence with the Holy Father. He is arranging this to facilitate my meeting them. He is very highly thought of in the Vatican and, as I learnt later, very close to the Holy Father. His kindness and cordiality surprised me greatly.

In the Jesuit Stronghold

On the subject of the Jesuits Rusinović states, at the beginning of his mission (26 February 1942):

... the Jesuits ... have no sympathy for us, indeed they are very hostile to us, as is shown by an article published in an important Swiss Catholic review, *Apologetische Rundschau* of Zürich, n. 2, entitled 'On the Persecutions of the Catholic Church in Slovenia'. I've been told that the author of this article is a Slovene, Father Prešeren, general assistant to the Polish General of the Jesuits, Ledochowski. In his article Father Prešeren says the following:

(1) ...

(2) Discussing the situation of brutal violence in Slovenia at the moment, he states that the same thing is happening in Croatia.

(3) ...

As you see, this is really good propaganda and perhaps you have already heard about it. The author of the article presents us as a blind instrument in the hands of the Germans. If these people can write in this way without any concern for us, if they can state things that are not true, and offer them to a public opinion already out of sympathy with us, you can imagine what they say about us to the Holy Father and to the other Vatican dignitaries.

In reality the situation was neither so simple nor so hopeless. And we can take Fr. Wurster's word for it, as he was referring to his own home ground. In his report of 12 June 1942 we read:

The Jesuit Curia faithfully reflects the Vatican. The General loves the Croats personally, and is pleased at their independence; but he is worried about their future. There are two Slovenes in the Curia: the assistant for Slav jurisdiction, Fr. Prešeren, and the Chief Censor of books, Fr. Zore. They are both too Slovene to be our friends. On Prešeren's instigation an article was published in a Swiss weekly discussing the situation in Slovenia and carrying three very unpleasant and slanderous statements about the Croats. I can prove that Prešeren is all for the resurrection of Yugoslavia.

Zore is in touch with Mgr. Moscatello. Fr. Sakac's presence is of great benefit to us, as he is heart and soul in favour of Ustaše Croatia. But, as he is at the Oriental Institute, his influence is rather weak. The Oriental Institute is in the hands of the French, the Belgians and the Czechs, who have no sympathy for us. Indeed much of the information that is damaging to our cause comes from there.

On the subject of the General of the Jesuits, Lobkowicz is in agreement with Wurster. After a visit to him, soon after taking up office as 'Plenipotentiary', he informed Zagreb:

He received me with great cordiality, assuring me repeatedly that he will help me in every way. It was easy to see that he feels great sympathy towards us.

But fate willed that Fr. Ledochowski should not fulfil his promise. Indeed on 20 December 1942 Lobkowicz was reporting:

Among the events of political and religious importance during recent times, the death of Wladimir Ledochowski, General of the Jesuits, must not be forgotten. He was certainly one of the finest Generals of this powerful and famous Order. As we have already said in an earlier report, he was sympathetic towards the Croats and did not share the opinion of official Vatican circles. Besides, his attitude differed from the official Vatican attitude in some other matters too—especially political ones—as I learnt from his own words in a private talk. In particular he did not share the Vatican opinion on Russia. With his death Croatia has lost a friend.

And, unfortunately for the NDH, an irreplaceable friend. Indeed, Lobkowicz went on:

After his death, his place as head of the Order was taken by the general assistant for Italy, Alessio Magni, who will direct the Society until the General Congregation can be convened.

After saying that this could not take place until the end of the war, and that thus Fr. Magni would be at the head of the Jesuits throughout the struggle, he makes more specific remarks about him:

With Magni's appointment, for the first time in 200 years an Italian is again at the head of the Jesuits. According to definite information, Magni is an Italian in his attitude to Fascism and is not kindly disposed towards the Croats.

In the spring of 1943 Lobkowicz went to visit him, and this is his report:

I visited the General of the Jesuits, Magni, who cannot even be

compared to Ledochowski's shadow. . . . He is a man of limited
outlook. I explained our position to him, and asked him to help
us, which he kindly promised to do.

However, a friendly General, were he even the 'Black Pope' himself, does not imply the friendship of the whole Order: and *vice versa*.
On the other hand, even individual members are capable of changing
their convictions in one or other direction. This, at least, seems to
have happened with Fr. Prešeren. Immediately after his account of
his visit to Fr. Magni, Lobkowicz added:

> I also visited Fr. Prešeren, the Jesuit in charge of the Slav
> regions. As a Slovene, he was at first our enemy and caused us
> quite a number of difficulties. The present situation of Slovenia
> has taught him a lesson, and now he is much more favourably dis-
> posed towards us. He told me that the Poles are dissatisfied be-
> cause the Holy See behaves with too much reserve towards them.
> They had expected more help. This is a common complaint. Every-
> body considers that the Holy See is abandoning them in these
> difficult times.

It would have been strange had the Ustaše representatives, and
especially a Vatican chamberlain like Lobkowicz, with his wider
contacts, allowed a Jesuit such as Fr. Leiber to slip between their
fingers. And in fact he figures twice in Lobkowicz's reports. For
instance on 9 February 1943:

> During my visit to the Gregoriana I met Fr. Leiber, Professor of
> Ecclesiastical History and (historical) Methodology, and reputedly
> a man of great influence at the Vatican. He was the present Pope's
> chief adviser when the latter was nuncio in Germany. When the
> present Pope became Cardinal Secretary of State, he called Fr.
> Leiber to Rome to continue to advise him. Today, despite the fact
> that he only works behind the scenes, Fr. Leiber is one of the Pope's
> closest collaborators. It is known that Leiber is the author of
> several addresses which the Pope has read out over Radio Vatican
> and which have caused great interest and widespread comment.

> I tried to explain our position to the priest, lamenting the
> Vatican's over-cautious and reticent behaviour towards Croatia.
> Fr. Leiber tried to persuade me of the justice of such reticence,
> saying that this must not and cannot be considered as indicating a
> lack of goodwill towards the Croats: the Vatican displays the same
> reticence towards all without distinction in these moments of un-
> certainty, and the Croats are not the only ones who see lack of
> good will in this attitude.

In the course of our conversation he said among other things that the ideal State in Europe today was Portugal, because on the one hand it puts its Catholic principles into practice, and on the other—unlike Dollfuss's Austria—it does not compromise the Church and its teaching.

I gave him a copy of the *Grey Book* and spoke to him of the part the Italians play in our difficulties, adding that the fact that the Vatican itself was largely composed of Italians perhaps accounted for its attitude towards the Croats. Leiber resolutely denied this, saying that the Pope, like the Secretary of State and their closest collaborators, were above any kind of national prejudice.

And on 14 April he added:

I again called on the Jesuit Fr. Leiber. . . . We must keep in touch with him, as he is one of the Holy Father's closest advisors. I gave him, as I have given all the others, a copy of *Ustaše Principles*, etc. I managed to arouse in him a great interest in our case and I think he will help us.

Fr. Paolo Dezza, Rector of the Gregoriana

With Fr. Dezza, another Jesuit, we enter a different sector, no less interesting or important for the two Croatian representatives than the previous ones: that of the universities and the pontifical ecclesiastical institutes. Indeed at that time Fr. Dezza was Rector of the Pontifical Gregorian University, and during Rusinović's mission he found himself having to face a revolt among the Croatian students who were angered by the fact that they had been classified as Yugoslavs in the university year-book.

Yesterday [Rusinović relates to his Minister on 8 February 1942] I received the priests from San Girolamo [the Ecclesiastical College for the 'Illyrians'] as well as several Ustaše Jesuits: they were all furious and stirred up against their 'Gregorianum' [*sic*] University, because it had classified them in its year-book as Yugoslavs, and had 'Yugoslavia' inscribed next to the pupils' names under the heading of 'Natio' (status politicus). They have already voiced their protests to the Rector, and will also do so in writing, despite the fact that the Rector maintains he is sorry for what has happened and was acting under orders from the Vatican. I learnt of this after the event. . . .

Rusinović comes back to this topic in his next report (26 February), enclosing the text of the protest, and adding:

Not everybody was prepared to sign it, for fear of the consequences. However, they did achieve some little success and satisfaction since they obtained a promise from the Rector that this
would never happen again; indeed he expressed his sincere regret
for the incident. . . .

Such ready compliance gives rise to some doubt, doubt increased
by this report from Lobkowicz a year later:

I visited the Rector of the Pontifical Gregorian University which
is attended by a great number of students from our country. The
Rector, Fr. Dezza, S.J., a Jesuit like all the rest of the administration and staff of this university, received me with great cordiality
and showed me round the whole building. From his words and
behaviour, I decided that we could view him as a true friend. He
promised me that in this year's year-book our students will not be
classified as Yugoslavs, as happened last year owing to the fact
that official and semi-official Vatican publications do not take into
account political changes that come about in time of war. In
order to avoid the cause of what has been so greatly deplored [in
the next year-book], there will be no indication of the student's
nationality next to his name, but only mention of the diocese to
which he is attached.

Mgr. Giorgio Madjerec, Rector of the Ecclesiastical College of S. Girolamo degli Illirici (St. Jerome of the Illyrians)

As we have already seen, the Croatian students (seminarists or
priests) attended the Istituto di San Girolamo, whose Rector was
Mgr. Giorgio Madjerec. When we read Rusinović's reports we would
think that at that time the College was a stronghold of Ustaše propaganda, and especially in virtue of its superior. Indeed we see him
lowering the Yugoslav flag so as to fly that of new Croatia in its
place, opening the doors of the Institute to Ustaše leaders passing
through Rome, celebrating the founding of the NDH and Pavelić's
name day with religious ceremonies, making every effort to obtain
audiences with the Pope for important representatives of the regime,
and so on. As for the *de facto* representative to the Holy See, he is
often invited to dinner, or to attend religious and civil ceremonies
officially sponsored by the Institute, and he continues to receive a
candle on 2 February of every year as the representatives of the
Belgrade government did before him, and so on.[138]

However, anyone who is at all aware of the principles adopted by the Secretary of State and the Congregation for Seminaries concerning the regular life of Roman ecclesiastical colleges (especially those for countries of mixed nationality) would hardly find this surprising, particularly when it is realized that Mgr. Madjerec continued to hold the same position for many years, even after the war. The instructions from the Holy See aimed at ensuring that the residents of these Institutes should live side by side in a peaceful and profitable way, and should avoid any political friction; any interchange of relations between them should be on a purely religious and ecclesiastical level. There is a scrupulous choice of names for the Institutes (rather than nationalist ones, they are names taken from the saints: Saint Jerome of the Illyrians in the case of the students from the various federated nations of Yugoslavia; Saint John Nepomucene for those from Czechoslovakia, and so on), and a scrupulous choice of colours. . . .

As for San Girolamo, or Saint Jerome, it is enough to recall the stormy events, immediately following the First World War, which only came to an end in 1929 with a compromise (the Holy See accepted the Yugoslav character of the Institute, and the Yugoslav government conceded the privileges of control previously enjoyed by the Austro-Hungarian Empire),[139] in order to doubt that the choice of its Rector had fallen on a fanatical nationalist. And indeed Rusinović's unbelievably blind optimism is belied (and partly explained) by reports from Fr. Wurster and from Lobkowicz himself. Here is what Fr. Wurster had to say on 12 June 1942:

> The istituto di San Girolamo should, as a matter of course, become a real support for us in our struggle to establish ourselves. But at present the situation in the Institute is such that this cannot feasibly come about. Indeed the relations between the Rector, Mgr. Madjerec, and the students—for the most part enthusiastically (and often imprudently) Ustaše—are untenable. Mgr. Madjerec is a careerist, with little civic courage. Despite this I think we could usefully exploit him. All the same it would certainly be better if his post were held by someone more energetic, and a sincere friend of ours.

It is true that Lobkowicz never mentions Mgr. Madjerec, but, reporting a meeting with Cardinal Fumasoni-Biondi, he puts forward, without realizing it, the most decisive argument for supporting

Father Wurster's opinion, rather than Rusinović's. Rusinović, too, had visited Fumasoni-Biondi, but he had not even noticed that the Cardinal was teasing him: he even hoped to make a good impression in his report by ironical remarks on the ignorance of the 'red pope'. On 20 March 1942 he wrote:

. . . Fumasoni-Biondi is a very distinguished person, but he knows our country about as well as I know New Guinea or somewhere like that. (Indeed) he did not know that relations between the Holy See and Croatia were still not established; at least that's what he said. But I believe him, because he asked me whether Antivari and Skopje belonged to Croatia or to some other State. N.B. He is the Cardinal Secretary [*sic*] of the Congregation of Propaganda Fide, under the jurisdiction of which belong the dioceses of Mostar, Sarajevo and Banja Luka, considered *in partibus infidelium*!

Cardinal Fumasoni-Biondi should in fact have been someone still more important for Rusinović: the protector of the Istituto San Girolamo. And if he had directed the conversation more cunningly he would have reached far less exhilarating conclusions; conclusions plainly hinted at in the following report from his successor, Lobkowicz (20 December 1942):

I paid a visit to Cardinal Fumasoni-Biondi, Prefect of the Sacred Congregation of Propaganda Fide, and protector of our Istituto di San Girolamo. His welcome was cordial too. We spoke mainly of the Institute. I noticed that the Cardinal has a very special idea of his role as protector. Indeed he stressed that he would be happy if the Institute could exist without any help from the Croatian government, and he is very anxious that things should continue like this, as he sees in this the best guarantee for the Institute's absolute independence. For this reason I think the Croatian government should find a way of showing that the Institute belongs to the Croatian people (by donating, for example, some gift or help). The Cardinal is very pleased with the Rector of the Institute, Mgr. Madjerec, and as for the misunderstanding between him and the students in the past, he excuses the students on grounds of their youthful impulsiveness and considers the matter forgotten.

If Madjerec was dear to the anti-Ustaše, Fumasoni-Biondi, there is much to doubt in his own feelings towards the Ustaše. In the situation in which he found himself—with most of the students ardent

nationalists—it was inevitable that he should manœuvre: and Rusinović shows that he did so admirably.

Among the diplomats accredited to the Holy See

For *de facto* representatives of a war government, and, moreover,
one that was duplicated by another representation from their own
country already regularly accredited to the Holy See, there was
another citadel to conquer: that of the diplomats. With the obvious
exception, though not a consistent one, of the diplomats of the
powers allied to the NDH, and of a few neutral powers. To be
honest, such contacts as are documented by the reports in our
possession do not reveal particularly sensational successes on the
part of Rusinović and Lobkowicz. The people with whom relations
were established in more than brief or formal meetings can be reduced to a short list of names: Sidor, Slovak representative to the
Holy See; Baron Apor, Hungarian representative; von Bergen and
von Weizsäcker, German; Ciano, Italian; Llobet, Argentine, etc.;
and we can add Mgr. Borgoncini Duca, nuncio to the Quirinal. But
even in these cases there were only one or two meetings, and usually
of little interest as far as relations between Croatia and the Holy See
were concerned. We shall quote the most significant, or the least
insignificant, of these encounters.

Rusinović-Sidor (report of 28 May 1942):

One day I asked to be received by the Slovak ambassador to the
Holy See, Sidor, as I had heard from a friend of his that he was
offended that I had not yet called on him. I think it is unnecessary to
describe the way in which he received me. Our meeting was that of
a Croat with a Slovak. We talked from ten in the morning until
three in the afternoon. That same day he should have gone to see
Maglione, but at midday he cancelled the appointment as he found
himself unexpectedly detained. He showed great interest in our
situation. . . . He has heard our enemies say that the Ustaše movement has no following among the people, and that it is made up of
a handful of men who have gained power by chance; and he was
delighted when I told him how things really stood. . . . He is a man
of great political knowledge, intelligent and serious-minded. In the
past he committed an error, but no one can deny that he is a true
patriot and has done fine work in the political field. We also talked

of our relations with the Holy See. He says it is unbelievable how many tales our enemies tell against us, and he advised me to pay more frequent visits to the Vatican as this is the only way to contradict the calumnies. Anyway the Vatican does not really know the facts. Slovakia's relations with the Holy See are not too good either. Just in these last days I have happened to hear criticism of Slovakia because of the barbarous treatment inflicted on the Jews. Despite this the Slovaks are trying to improve their relations with the Vatican as much as possible. Sidor completely understands our situation with regard to the Holy See, and sympathizes with our indignation about many things—all originating from the Vatican; but he warned me that the Vatican is slow to move when it comes to recognizing a new State and creating new diplomatic relations. As for him, he will do everything possible to further our cause and he asked me for frequent meetings. . . .

Lobkowicz-Ciano (report of 14 April 1943)

(Prior to this report, i.e. on 9 February, Lobkowicz had informed Zagreb of the appointment of the Duce's son-in-law as ambassador to the Holy See in these terms:

The appointment of Count Ciano as ambassador to the Vatican has caused a revolution in official Vatican circles. The main reason for this shock is the behaviour of the new ambassador's wife, who is very immoral. All the same, approval for this appointment was given a few days after it was asked for. People say that this appointment is the most important event in the recent political changes in Italy. Some people assert that the aim is to get Ciano inside the Vatican so as to be better able to carry out a special mission there. . . .)

Count Ciano was among the people to whom I had to pay a courtesy visit, although I did not expect to achieve anything important by it. I waited more than a week before I could be received. As soon as I entered his room his first gesture was to look at the clock. Given that my visit coincided with the Duce's return from Salzburg, I asked for clarifications as to the significance of that meeting. He replied: 'I have not yet had time to speak to my father-in-law' and added that he knew absolutely nothing. We also talked of the departure of the English Ambassador, Sir Osborne [*sic*] for London. Ciano made a disdainful gesture with his hand, and said that Osborne could not have been sent on any mission, and that he had really left for a period of rest. After five minutes he brought the meeting to a close, saying, and I quote: 'If you see Signor Pavelić, give him my regards. I know him well: he often came to see me to tell me his plans.' All in all, my impression was of someone not very serious-minded. During a reception at the Spanish Ambassador's I saw Ciano's wife dressed very informally, although the invitations said that evening dress should be worn. All those present were thoroughly put out by her appearance.

Lobkowicz-Llobet (report of 14 April 1943):

The Argentine ambassador, Llobet . . . continues to receive me with great cordiality. Although his government does not recognize us, he treats me as a colleague and introduces me as 'Croatian ambassador'. At my last visit he became especially communicative and told me a very significant fact. Four months ago he had had orders from the Argentine government to approach the Holy Father directly with a proposal for an Argentine mediation for peace. The Holy Father was visibly moved by it, but replied that he did not consider that the right moment had yet arrived for a peace move. Llobet thinks that there have been many changes in these last four months and that the right moment has perhaps come: he believes that Osborne's trip to London may have something to do with this. He is also of the opinion that the Salzburg meeting is not a coincidence. He says that in the Vatican no one knows anything about it. He states that, according to information available to Argentine military circles, the Russians have reached the end of their strength. . . . With regard to the Holy See, he says that it enjoys greater esteem than during the First World War.

Lobkowicz-Borgoncini Duca (report of 14 April, 1943)

Mgr. Borgoncini Duca, the Holy See's nuncio to the Quirinal, received me with affability, and was interested to see the books I gave him. I asked him how Italy's behaviour on our territory could be explained. He replied that it was important to make a clear distinction between Italy and the Vatican, since the latter does not identify itself with Italian principles and methods. I said in my turn that this theoretical difference does not help us, and that it even harms the Vatican, since there is the danger that some of our regions will abandon Catholicism. However he denied such an eventuality, supporting his view by a statement of Bastianini's. According to the latter the difference between the Croats and the Serbs is so great that it is out of the question to speak of the danger of a considerable number of Croats leaving the Church. He said that Bastianini was a well-meaning, intelligent person, to whom one could talk. We discussed the fact that the Italians support the Chetniks, which obviously cannot fit in with a policy of friendship and alliance with Croatia. Mgr. Borgoncini Duca replied that the Italians are deeply afraid of Pan-Slavism and that it is in their interest to keep disagreements between the peoples of the Balkans alive. Besides, Italian policy is directed by people who are ignorant of the nature of Balkan problems, and hence it is easy to understand the repeated mistakes that are being made in that area. I also brought up the fact that we have many prisoners in Italian concentration camps. He replied that he had paid personal visits to many of the camps where our compatriots are held, and that he has succeeded in getting the daily bread ration increased to 500 grammes. The difference between the two rations will be made up by the Vatican. Finally he expressed his pleasure at my presence in Rome, emphasizing the importance and delicate nature of my position. He promised to give me any help or collaboration that I might need. He declares he is a sincere friend of Croatia. Mgr. Borgoncini Duca has certainly great political influence and played an important part in the preparation of the Lateran Treaty, whereby an end was brought to the divisions between the Vatican and Italy.

Lobkowicz-von Weizsäcker (report of 13 July 1943):

I called on the German ambassador. He received me kindly, and told me he had already heard about me, and that he would be pleased to keep up relations with me. He asked me for information, and even my opinion of various important people in the Vatican, saying that he was new to the place and most ready to make use of my experience. We reviewed together all the College of Cardinals and all the other Vatican personalities, so he had his first information about many of them from me.

He said that he was very pleased by the way in which he had been received by the Holy Father. It is quite clear that the Pope is very sympathetic towards the German people, and that he remembers his period in Germany with pleasure.

His arrival has brought about no fundamental changes in the relations between Germany and the Vatican. There is no question of a *Richtungsenderung*. He said that the sole characteristic of the relations is patience. He personally would have been pleased to see such relations on a different basis. He says the Pope shows a good understanding of all the problems, and that he does indeed display great patience. He has noticed that not everyone in the Vatican is of the same opinion, and that some people adopt a less pacific attitude towards the Reich, as indeed does a section of the ecclesiastical world in Germany herself.

He said that the German government does not consider that the Pope's recent speech about Poland constituted an attack on Germany.

Then we went on to examine current political problems. I saw clearly that von Weizsäcker does not feel at all sympathetic towards the Italians. . . .

It is said that Fritz Menshausen, Councillor at the German Embassy to the Holy See, should give up his post. He should be replaced by someone in whom the party has absolute trust. Some say that this new man should keep an eye on Weizsäcker who belongs to the old personnel that was in charge of German foreign affairs before Hitler came to power.

The most curious aspect of the contacts that the two NDH representatives at the Vatican made with the diplomatic world centred round the Holy See is, undoubtedly, the chance meetings they had with several members of the Yugoslav Legation to the Holy See (resident in the Vatican) and the secret control they had over them. The information they managed to glean is not very exact, yet not without interest. Lobkowicz's first report in this context deals with an unexpected meeting with Mgr. Moscatello. It was written on 20 December 1942:

One of the most interesting meetings . . . was with Mgr. Moscatello, chargé d'affaires for the Yugoslav Embassy at the Vatican. We met in Cardinal Tisserant's antechamber. It could have been that the meeting was arranged by someone. I have known Mgr. Moscatello for some time, so the meeting was very relaxed. I took the opportunity of pointing out to him that his role was an awkward one, and that perhaps he should find a way of being more favourably disposed towards us. He was decidedly against this, claiming that as a priest he could not do such a thing, that he has always acted consistently, that because of his Croatian behaviour he has always been up against Belgrade, and consequently seriously inconvenienced. Now he lives like a hermit and has no relations with emigrants, not even with his own minister, Mirošević Sorgo. He said that the greatest misfortune for the Croats was their discord. I replied that his own attitude illustrated this discord, and he retorted that his attitude was 'another matter'. He stated that Dalmatia had been sold and that every sacrifice should have been made to prevent this. He agrees that no criticism can be levelled against the Poglavnik as a Catholic. From all this it becomes clear that Mgr. Moscatello pursues his own particular and individual policy. This office has undertaken to get complete information on the role and activities of the Yugoslav Embassy at the Vatican.

On 9 February 1943 Lobkowicz could report to Zagreb that the first steps to this end had been taken, and these were the results:

This office has managed to get a man into the Yugoslav Embassy as assistant to the first secretary, Kosta M. Čukić; and through him the following information has been obtained:

At present Čukić is in fact chargé d'affaires at the Yugoslav Embassy. He lives in the Vatican and very rarely leaves the city, and then only when accompanied by an Italian agent. He spends most of his time with the other 'imprisoned' diplomats, playing tennis and going to cocktail parties. He said that they approved of the previous Croatian representative at the Vatican [Rusinović] because unwittingly he was useful to the Yugoslav thesis. Now the situation has radically changed.

On the subject of the activities of the Yugoslav government in London, he says that he can find no parallel, not even in Serbia, a country with which Čukić seems to have direct contacts.

The last mail but one from London brought Čukić a whole suitcase (of medium size) full of letters. He claims that, all in all, England has no interest in the internal organization of Yugoslavia and that therefore, after the inevitable collapse of the Axis, the Serbs and Croats will have to find some mutually satisfactory agreement. He does not approve of Četnik activities and says that it is more important to conserve life and strength than to sacrifice them in the interests of a third party. Up till now both the Croats and the Serbs have erred, and to a certain extent he is glad that the Croats have exterminated the Serbs, because in that way the score is even and afterwards neither side will be able to reproach the other.

. . .

Mgr. Moscatello's role . . . seems to be exactly as we described it in our report N. 2/42 (VT 14/42 of 18 Dec. '42). Čukić said that he sees Moscatello very rarely, but that he expects him 'any day now'. From the way in which he spoke one could deduce that he is not very pleased with Moscatello's behaviour.

By chance Pétain's representative at the Vatican, Léon Bérard, was mentioned, and Čukić said that everyone in the Vatican laughs at him behind his back. This obviously refers to diplomats and not to Vatican personalities.

He also said that the Yugoslav government has great monetary funds at its disposal, and as for himself he boasted of possessing Swiss francs. At the end of the conversation he asked if *The Yugoslav Historical Archive* by Kukuljević and Saksinski could be obtained for him. He also asked for Croatian cigarettes, obviously in order to see whether the man we had planted was in touch with us. We hasten to say that the whole conversation was contrived in such a way as to exclude any suspicion that we were connected with it.

And here are some of the 15 points of a report sent to Zagreb by Fr. Wurster on 10 May 1943 (N. 42/43 VT, Report N. 6/42):

I have recently learnt from a reliable source various facts regarding the activities of the Yugoslav Embassy at the Vatican, and also some personal political opinions of Signor Kosta Čukić, secretary and chargé d'affaires of the Yugoslav Embassy at the Holy See. . . .

(1) Recently a regular link line has been set up between the Yugoslav Embassy at Berne and the Yugoslav Embassy to the Holy See. The link operates regularly every fortnight.

(2) The Yugoslav Embassy at Berne is now playing an important political role in the development of events. The Embassy is led by Sturm-Jurišić, brother of General Pantelija Jurišić. At the Berne Embassy Croatian citizens living in Italy and Switzerland are frequently to be seen. Members of the Embassy are prepared to give help and protection to any Croatian citizens who ask for it. They can issue passports with visas for Portugal and for transoceanic countries. Čukić claims that many important Croats living in Switzerland have tried to get into touch with the Yugoslav Embassy. Rumour has it that certain ministers in office are involved; and that the Berne Embassy has exact information on certain monetary transactions by very important Croatian figures (their names are mentioned) in Switzerland.

. . .

(9) According to the official information handled by the Yugoslav government in London, the number of Serbs killed amounts to 700,000. However, every member of the government is personally convinced that the figure is greatly exaggerated.

(10) People are becoming convinced that the partisan movement in Croatia is being mainly assisted by Serb and Slovene elements, and that in practice one cannot distinguish between Ustaše and non-Ustaše, inasmuch as it is more than evident that a large part of the Croatian people do not participate in the Ustaše movement. . . .

Fr. Agostino Gemelli

Before following the two Ustaše representatives through the maze of the Vatican, we shall stop and consider two meetings that Lobkowicz had with two important figures only partly, or only formerly belonging to the Curia. First, the President of the Pontifical Academy of Sciences, Fr. Agostino Gemelli, all powerful in the Vatican under Pius XII and even afterwards a personality of the front rank. The Rectorship of the Milanese Catholic University of the Sacred Heart which he had founded, as well as his scientific activity, obliged him to live mainly in Milan; but his numerous duties, either for the Vatican or for various State cultural organizations, brought him frequently to Rome. Lobkowicz, with his inseparable Jesuit shadow (Fr. Wurster), visited him and revealed in his report of 14 April 1943, the precise aim of his visit, namely to ask him officially— following a decision taken at a special meeting[140] mentioned in his previous report of 20 December 1942—to write the preface to the book *Croazia Sacra* (Sacred Croatia) then in process of being printed. A better choice could hardly have been made, not only because of his political commitment, but especially because of his international reputation as a scientist.

Gemelli [reports Lobkowicz] not only immediately agreed to write the preface, but he also offered to have the book issued in the series 'Vita e Pensiero' put out by his own publishing house. This would be advantageous for us, and the book would be reviewed in all the most important magazines. He promised that he personally would review it in the *Osservatore Romano*. . . . During our talk Gemelli was very cordial. He told me that Roosevelt had written to the Holy Father calling him *My dear old friend*, and of the tactlessness of Myron Taylor's wife in taking the Pope a present of a box of chocolates. He praised Professor Guberina, Lecturer in Croatian at Milan University, with whom he is engaged on a scientific work. He said that rarely had he met a better educated colleague. He did not say much about the general situation. He believes that there is nothing good to be expected from the English, while America might perhaps come up with something, because there is a strong group of intelligent and fairly influential Catholics. It is interesting to note that in the past he made a speech in Fiume in which he referred to the frontier of the barbarians coming as far as Fiume. Now he is certainly sympathetic towards the Croats. We must return the kindness that he is doing by publishing the book.

In fact, however, perhaps for practical reasons, the book was published in Rome, and in the Vatican at that, by the *Officium Libri Catholici*, that same year. Despite his promises, Father Gemelli did not write the preface; this was done by Cardinal Fumasoni-Biondi,[141] naturally in a different key, but nevertheless auguring a better understanding between Italians and Croats.

Archbishop Francis Spellman

There is no need for a special introduction for the Archbishop of New York. In any case Lobkowicz provides one in this report (6 March 1943):

Accompanied by the office secretary, Wurster, I was able to visit the Archbishop of New York, Spellman. As is known, Archbishop Spellman has been in Rome for about a fortnight. Numerous contradictory rumours circulate about him and the significance of his visit. The following information is undoubtedly correct:

Before his investiture as Archbishop of New York he was attached to the Secretariat of State under the present Pope: so he is a political figure. He was trusted by Pacelli, has travelled a great deal, and established many relations. He is very up to date, and is perhaps the first and only Catholic bishop to hold an air pilot's licence: he piloted a civil aircraft himself when on a tour of inspection in Alaska. At that time the newspapers all over the world talked of the 'flying bishop'. At present he is completely in President Roosevelt's confidence, since the President views him as the most eminent representative of Catholicism in North America, as well as a former close collaborator of the present Pope. Spellman is also chaplain to the Catholic troops in the American army.

On his way to Rome he spent two hours in Madrid with the Caudillo [General Franco]. The Spanish ambassador has promised me a detailed account of that meeting.

During Spellman's stay in Rome the Holy Father granted him four long audiences. No one knows what they talked about; it is obvious that there are things the Pope does not even confide to his Cardinal Secretary of State—as was the case over Taylor's arrival.

Spellman repeatedly declared to several people here that his trips are of a strictly religious nature, and that no back-stage politics are involved.

The Italian authorities adopted a very friendly attitude towards him. He had a body-guard of Vatican police, and only when he crossed Rome was he escorted by an Italian police car. He lived outside the Vatican, on the Janiculum, in the extra-territorial zone of the pontifical College 'De Propaganda Fide', also the site of the North American College.

After consulting the delegate Dr. S. Perić, I requested an audience with Spellman through an American canon here, a member of the Liberian Chapter, whom I have known for many years.

I received a telephone call from Spellman's own secretary and fixed a meeting for Tuesday, 2 March, at 8.30. We met at the arranged time at his place of residence. While waiting, Wurster managed to glance at the visiting cards lying on the table and to ascertain that many of them were from Italian personalities such as the President of the Court of Appeal, senators, and so on. I handed my visiting card as private chamberlain to the Pope. While we were waiting we heard the word 'Croatia' from the adjoining room where a lively discussion was taking place.

Spellman received us very politely and said straightaway: 'There's not much that you can tell me about your affairs that I don't know. I'm well informed on everything and know the Croatian question well. A few years ago I travelled through your country and even then the difference between Belgrade and Zemun, not to mention Zagreb, told me enough: there are two worlds. They cannot coexist.' We pointed out that the present State is now in a very special position in the context of its Catholicism and especially through its position between East and West; that the frontier on the Drina guarantees the maintenance of the Catholic position in that sector; and that the rebuilding of Yugoslavia would mean not only the annihilation of the Croatian people, but also of Catholicism and western culture in those regions. Instead of a western frontier on the Drina, we would have a Byzantine frontier on the Karavanke. Spellman agreed with these observations and added that President Roosevelt wants freedom for all peoples, and that obviously includes the Croats. He also said that he is personally doing all he can for us, but that we have many enemies and one person cannot achieve much against many. He is very pleased with the Croats in his diocese, both clergy and faithful. Then he repeated that he was well-informed about us, partly through the Archbishop of Zagreb's secretary, partly through Dr. Lacković who had visited him.

We gave him a copy of the *Grey Book* and also *Ustaše Principles* in Latin translation. He glanced at them with interest and asked if President Roosevelt possessed them. We replied that he certainly did not. So he said that we should give copies of them to Roosevelt's ambassador at the Vatican, Tittman. We replied that our State was at war with the United States of America, and that we could not consider relations of that kind; we had only turned to him in his capacity as Catholic bishop who had a large number of our emigrants in his care, that is to say as Catholic Croats and not as officials. Spellman was very understanding. He made it clear by his manner that he wanted to take the *Grey Book* and the one on Ustaše principles to President Roosevelt.

He was in a hurry because he had to attend a farewell audience of the Holy Father, and so had to bring our talk to an end. He came out with us to the car, and personally helped us on with our coats. He was more than friendly and was obviously sorry not to have more time with us. As we took our leave he said in English, 'God bless Croatia!'

The following day he left for Africa, and will then go on to Syria, Iraq and Iran.

Mgr. Arborio Mella, Maestro di Camera to His Holiness

At the head of the Curia, in the Vatican proper, it is possible to divide the people whom the two Ustaše representatives approached into three groups: the members of the Papal Court, lesser functionaries of the Secretariat of State (the heads have already been mentioned in the course of our study), and, finally, the cardinals.

The first group can be restricted, for our purposes, to the single figure of the Pope's maestro di camera, Mgr. Arborio Mella di Sant' Elia. The best portrait we have of him is one left us by himself in some memoirs he wrote about the popes under whom he had served.[140] There he reveals himself as a man of such simple and steadfast faith that it even outstripped, perhaps, his devotion to his sovereigns, boundless as that was. To find someone with whom to compare him we would have to go back to typical examples of Catholic hagiography, to a St. Maurus (disciple of St. Benedict) or a Fra. Juniper (disciple of St. Francis); with the difference that St. Maurus and Fra. Juniper were simple men living in a monastery or freely among mendicant friars, whereas Mgr. Mella came from noble Piedmontese stock and had a brother who held exactly the same position at the Quirinal.

So any temptation to explain his willingness to help the Ustaši representatives in terms of Machiavellianism would be mistaken. He saw in them no more than the predecessors of legal representatives of a probable new Catholic monarchy. Thus, having received a visit from Rusinović, not only did he return it but promised to call on him whenever he was invited. Meanwhile he tried his utmost to convince him 'of the love and the interest that the Holy Father felt for the Croats'. He explained why there could not yet be official relations, etc. But the most significant instance of his zeal came with the Papal audience of the Minister Simčić, whom he knew wanted to embark on a specifically political discussion. Protocol did not allow the Minister to take the initiative, and Mgr. Mella undertook to prepare the Pope in such a way that he would be the one to introduce the subject.

Mgrs. Sigismondi and Cippico

Among the lesser figures at the Secretariat of State, we have already mentioned, if only by name, Mgr. Sigismondi[143] and Mgr. Prettner-Cippico.[144] About the former we unfortunately have only the passage from Rusinović's second remaining report, already quoted. As for Mgr. Prettner-Cippico, he himself has revealed that he was chosen by Cardinal Maglione to help Rusinović as his mother was a Croat and he knew the country, its people and its language. He was supposed, by his attentions, to appease the Zagreb representative with regard to the establishment of diplomatic relations and the continual postponement of an audience with the Pope. And Mgr. Cippico, whose function in the Secretariat of State was that of assistant archivist, was truly tireless in his care of the Ustaše representative: he introduced him to his superiors, explained to him the rules of etiquette, acted as his spokesman with the Secretariat in moments of tension, accepted and returned his invitations to dinner, met him at the Illyrian College, encouraged him when he was down-hearted, and so on.

The ex-nuncios Micara and Felici

But the two Ustaše agents also came into contact with several nuncios, men who had lost their positions as a result of the war, and were now back in the Secretariat working humbly in the Office of Information—archbishops and former doyens of diplomatic corp though they were.

With one of these, Clemente Micara[145]—simultaneously nuncio in

Belgium and internuncio in Luxembourg until July 1940—Rusinović
had a meeting brought about through a friendship with his (Micara's)
nephew. Reporting on the contacts he had made, Rusinović praised
the prelate as someone well acquainted with the 'rights' of the Croats,
as he had been secretary at the nunciature in Vienna during the
First World War and subsequently in Czechoslovakia, and he added
that the prelate had 'a good opinion of the Croats'. Moreover he had
offered his services to Rusinović whenever he should need them in
the Vatican.

But the two NDH representatives needed more energetic and
powerful protectors. And suddenly, almost against all hope, they
discovered such a man in the ex-nuncio in Belgrade until 29 June
1941, that is until Germany expelled from the Serb capital all members of the diplomatic corps who had been accredited to the former
royal government. Mgr. Ettore Felici,[147] the nuncio in question, was
still officially accredited to King Peter, although he had been sent
back to the Vatican.

Despite this, Rusinović had no doubt that his political sympathies
(in Belgrade he had openly shown himself as favouring the military
regime of the extreme right) would lead him to uncompromising
support of the New Independent State of Croatia. Indeed, to judge
by the reports of the first Ustaše representative, Felici put more energy
than anyone else in the Vatican into achieving this support. Rusinović
never took an initiative without finding that Felici had forestalled
him. Indeed Felici was always ready to suggest to him ways of impressing his Vatican superiors: he advised him about papal occasions which Rusinović could not absent himself from without giving
a bad impression, he arranged useful meetings for him, taught him
the formalities most likely to impress the Pope, and so on.

Here are two very significant episodes: in March 1942 the *Osservatore Romano* mentioned Pavelić among the people who had sent the
Pope congratulations on the third anniversary of his coronation.
'That same day,' writes Rusinović, 'the nuncio Felici came to see
me in the afternoon to ask me if I was pleased by this, and how I
interpreted it. He maintains that, to a connoisseur of Vatican politics,
this shows already a certain recognition of the NDH'.[148] Two months
later Felici unexpectedly called on Rusinović: this time to ask him

'why the Poglavnik had not sent good wishes to the Pope, as the fact had been much commented on in the Vatican'.[149]

This prelate acted in the same way with Lobkowicz. 'I have seen the ex-nuncio from Belgrade again'—Lobkowicz informed his minister on the following 20 December—'who is still eagerly helping us in all sorts of ways.' Indeed his zeal sometimes amazed those who profited by it. 'Once', reported Lobkowicz, 'he went so far as to admit his conviction that the Vatican's restraint towards us is excessive.'[150]

Only Fr. Wurster seems to see the matter in a different light:

The tragic thing is that Signor Felici has installed himself in the Istituto de San Girolamo, where one whole floor has been put at his disposal, for which he pays, including meals, only 25 *lire* a day. On the other hand Signor Felici still deplores the end of Yugoslavia. For him Maček is a genius and his policy very much to his taste.

And in his report of 12 June 1942:

. . . the ex-nuncio from Belgrade, Mgr. Felici, is living at San Girolamo. He is a very shrewd man, but a bit mediocre as a diplomat, and he is sympathetic towards Maček. However, from various incidents it may be deduced that he would not be displeased to be sent to Zagreb as nuncio. We must consider him more seriously, because at the Vatican he is looked on as an expert in our affairs.

So, whether sincere and disinterested or not, Mgr. Felici's game was basically that of the Ustaše.

The Cardinals

Visits paid by the NDH agents to the cardinals were more or less formalities, even if they aimed at establishing a basis for winning them over to their side. Reports that have a bearing on this are always interesting as they help to penetrate the secret world of the political likes and dislikes of the Sacred College—always assuming that its members were interested in active politics, something less common than one would suppose. It is also true that some of the cardinals pretended to an indifference which they were far from putting into practice. We have seen this in the case of Cardinal Fumasoni-Biondi.[151]

But if it was possible to distrust the wily statements of the 'red Pope', only people who knew him very well could adopt the same attitude to *Cardinal Mercati*.[152] For anyone else it would have been a matter for surprise if this cardinal had noticed anything beyond his own bookshelves. When Lobkowicz presented him with the usual volumes of Ustaše propaganda, he had no idea that he had provided the cardinal with the best possible screen behind which to hide. Mercati seemed very touched by this attention, and childishly pleased with the gift. He kept on weighing the books, passing them from hand to hand, praising their tasteful bindings, the choice of type, and so on. And that was all.[153]

Could anything more be confidently expected from his colleague, *Marchetti Selvaggiani*?[154] The Pope's 'vicar' for the city and diocese of Rome had been a diplomat for the first thirty years of the century —among other things, nuncio in Vienna. But there was one difficulty: as Lobkowicz put it, 'he does not approve of the present government in Germany.' So no great hopes could be built on his support. However, Marchetti Selvaggiani showed a 'fair amount of interest' in Croatian affairs and even said he approved of the Drina boundary. But his last remark threw cold water on the whole matter: 'He said he doubted if we would succeed in this, especially if the Allies were victorious.'[155]

Besides those who were sympathetic and those who were indifferent, there were also those who were hostile, whether half-heartedly or totally. Take *Cardinal Pizzardo*, for instance.[156] According to Lobkowicz, 'He is known to be very ambitious. His name came up several times during the election of the present Pope. It is said he was one of the likeliest candidates'. Perhaps this cold allusion may be explained partly by the following:

> He [Pizzardo] thinks that the present map of Europe ought to be substantially changed. He is in any case convinced that the Croats should be separated from the Serbs. He tends to favour a Danubian Confederation as the solution to the central-south-east European problem.[157]

As for *Cardinal Pellegrinetti*,[158] Lobkowicz scarcely had time to pay him a visit and ascertain that 'he was not very much in favour of the Ustaše government' before the cardinal died. Lobkowicz should have found reason to rejoice about this, since, as the cardinal was one of the few 'who was fairly well informed about Croatia', it could be assumed that he would not exert an influence favourable to the NDH. Surprisingly, Lobkowicz wrote a very positive obituary:

> He knew the Croatian language very well and subscribed to many of our newspapers and reviews. He followed attentively all the changes in our writing and the purification of our language. Often when speaking to a Croat he would correct his way of expressing himself. He had read all the volumes of our encyclopedia so far published. As he died, he was praying in Croatian.

Why such generosity? Mainly, we think, because Pellegrinetti was a moderate and a realist. So much so that Rusinović had almost taken him for an ally. He had written to his friend the minister on 20 March, 1942:

> I have not had to exert myself too much with him because he knows the Serbs well and they are very dear to him! He spoke to me of their policy, of King Alexander and so on, for a whole hour, and he reminded me of Alexander's 'criminal actions'. In a word he could defend our cause to the Vatican better than many of us, as he knows our history so perfectly that I was amazed; and the Serbs have wronged him more than anyone else. He finished by saying that even if the accusations made against the Croats of persecuting the Serbs are true, anyone acquainted with the past could hardly be surprised: '*atrocities cannot be approved of, but they can be understood.*'

The four meetings with Tisserant

The Cardinal from Lorraine, Tisserant, had a very different character. He was the only non-Italian curial cardinal during the war, and indeed for many years before. He had much in common with his friend and colleague, Pellegrinetti. Like Pellegrinetti, he knew the Slav languages and literatures, was interested in the history of the East, and was a librarian—though Pellegrinetti, for reasons beyond his control, had only got as far as a diploma in paleography. Like Pellegrinetti, Tisserant owed the career that led him to his position as cardinal to an encounter with the librarian Ratti. It is strange that these two experts of the Slav world, and intimate friends of a Pope (Ratti) who was certainly not tortuous and knew nothing of diplomatic flattery, should have been, though in different ways, the most open adversaries of Fascist Croatia in the Roman Curia.

The reports of the Ustaše representatives' meetings with Tisserant are the liveliest and most fascinating part of the documents that have come down to us. In all, the Cardinal granted them four audiences: three to Rusinović and one to Lobkowicz. And we have an ample report of each. The first has an abundance of unnecessary detail: but, obviously, no other meeting had given the unfortunate Rusinović such a shock—especially as he had expected a very different welcome. The meeting had been arranged for him by Mgr. Sigismondi who must have given him a strange impression of the Cardinal, for when Rusinović reported to Zagreb on 8 February 1942, he wrote:

In a few days I shall have the opportunity to visit several cardinals who are on our side, and among them the French Cardinal Tisserant, who once upon a time was very sympathetic towards ex-Yugoslavia; but since Yugoslavia betrayed France, his sympathies have gone over to the Croats, and he explains his change of allegiance in terms of the punishment merited by Yugoslavia. He is a great friend of the Holy Father and his personal secretary [*sic*].

The Cardinal with the Michelangelo face, framed even then by his splendid Moses-type beard, with his stormy temperament—sometimes amiably ironical, sometimes impetuously aggressive—teased and baited his simple adversary with the feline cynicism of a cat playing with a captive mouse. His predominant characteristic, as it emerges from his words, is that of a Prince of the Church, a prince in ecclesiastical clothes, that is, but with profane and worldly judgments, for whom politics are almost everything and the world is divided exclusively into allies and enemies. The priest rarely emerges, but when he does his words burn like red-hot steel. They are the words that his Superior fails to say, the proud denunciations and open invective that he would have liked to hear on the Pope's lips, and for which he has waited in vain. Such words make the report unforgettable and extremely valuable. But we shall also quote the other reports in full, so as to make the man who spoke in such a way as understandable as possible, and so as not to withhold useful pointers to events in Croatia and the world of the Curia. The first report (of 6 March 1942—the audience took place on the 5th) is clumsily composed, as to style, punctuation, transitions from direct to indirect speech, and so on; so, all the more, does its fascination lie in its content. After mentioning the importance of the person he had visited (that he was Secretary of the Sacred Congregation for the Eastern Church of which the Pope himself was prefect), Rusinović begins:

Tisserant received me very affably, with exquisite manners. The conversation lasted an hour and a half, but it was completely different from any I have had with other important Vatican figures. He has the temperament of a politician rather than an ecclesiastic, he is open and polemical. Given the interest of his statements and theories on our situation, and the general situation of Europe and the world, I shall try and summarize the main lines for you. After the customary formalities, he began like this: 'Where do you come from, Doctor? Would you prefer to speak French or Italian?' 'If you will allow me, I shall speak Italian: I studied French at school but I do not know it as well as Italian.' 'Most willingly. I am French but have lived in Rome for many years (twenty-three) and am completely at home in Italian. Where did you learn French?' So I told him that I was a Dalmatian, that I had studied at Split, then at Zagreb, and so on. 'And how can you, a Dalmatian, represent Croatia? Do such things still happen in your political and public life? When the Italians have declared that Dalmatia is Italian and that the people who live there are Italians?' And he smiled maliciously and ironically. I must admit that I felt rather uncomfortable, not at all expecting questions of this kind. However, I recovered myself and replied roughly as follows: that except for an insignificant number of Italians, Croatians are the inhabitants of Dalmatia, a large number of whom were living in the other regions of Croatia before the formation of the NDH, and a good part of these emigrated from Dalmatia after the annexation. As for myself, I cannot see what obstacle there could be to my representing Croatia, even if I was a naturalized Croat and came from a completely different part of the world. 'But then how on earth were your great friends and allies, the Italians, able to take Dalmatia from you?' This was an even more agreeable question! And I embarked on a historical account of the Croats' arrival on the shores of the Adriatic, touching on all the ups and downs in Dalmatia's past up to the present day. I said that the Italians wanted Dalmatia on grounds of an alleged historical right and also for sentimental reasons, and finally to satisfy the Italian Irredentists who had launched a great campaign in Italy for annexing Dalmatia. This, needless to say, is very hard for us: the Poglavnik himself, in his first important speech in our liberated country, stressed that it was a genuine sacrifice. But, thank God, Croatia is now free, whereas up to a short time ago Croatia, together with Dalmatia, was in the direst slavery. Now we are a State and free in our own house: often even great countries have to renounce some most cherished part of their State and people for the sake of freedom, just as an individual, if it were necessary, would sacrifice his eye so as to keep his head. 'Are you free then? Aren't you doing exactly what the Germans want, like all the other European peoples today? And you call that freedom?' 'Forgive me, Your Eminence, but I cannot agree with you there. Croatia has its own frontiers, its own Head of State, its own government, its own army, its own diplomatic representatives: thus all the symbols of an autonomous and independent country. Croatia decorates her house to please the popular soul and the interests of the Croatian people, and there is no outside influence in all this. Besides, even if this were not so, even if what you said were true, that all the countries of Europe do what the Germans want, there would be nothing outlandish in our doing so too, given that a little country like ours wouldn't be in a position to resist such a giant, especially when States with 30 and 40 million inhabitants have not been able to do so. But this apart, what I told you before holds true: we are a free people in our own State. You, Eminence, know full well what a disastrous opinion ecclesiastical circles have of Germany in matters concerning faith; you consider Germany as the greatest enemy of every religion; but you also know that the Croats are Catholics and proud of being so, and do not hesitate to proclaim it in public, as when for instance, according to ancient tradition, the Poglavnik goes to church with all the government and the members of the Croatian Assembly to invoke the Holy Ghost for the opening of that Assembly. If we do what the Germans want, and for you they are the greatest enemies of religion, we would never dare do that.' 'Yes, your freedom is very similar to that of our Pétain. He too is free, but he has to give the Germans 80 per cent of our foodstuffs while at the same time the French population dies of hunger. This is true: I'm very well informed on these matters. But it is not all: the Germans also take 70 per cent of everything that arrives by sea from North Africa, and they do so immediately, in the port itself. Would you not have to do the same, even if you yourselves were without bread? . . . You are like all the other countries; that is to say, economically you are slaves; and without economic freedom there can be no political freedom.' I replied that the situation in France cannot possibly be compared with the situation in Croatia. . . . France was defeated in war as an enemy country, whereas Croatia unanimously sided with Germany and helped her to destroy Yugoslavia. The perennial dream of the Croatian people had been to resurrect the Kingdom of Croatia. Yugoslavia was a real prison for the Croats. Today we are on friendly terms with the Axis powers, and when we can, seeing that we are friends and allies, we give our friends what is available and help them in the fight against the common enemy, Bolshevism, against which we too are fighting.

'I know that the Croatian people longed for their freedom and they had a right to do so. No one could contest that right. (I understand that they moved against the Serbs at the most opportune moment) but, dear sir, your Fascist friends could not care less about your independence and your freedom, nor about the existence of the State of Croatia. I have learnt this straight from their political chiefs. Your king, the Duke of Spoleto, will never go to Croatia. He says he will not go to Croatia because he has been crowned king of a kingdom that doesn't exist as it is subject both to Germany and Italy. In Croatia everyone has more power than the Croats. That's how things are. And if you knew what the Italian authorities on the coast say about you, you would be horrified. According to them, you cannot imagine what is in store for you as you have never experienced it. Killings, fires, acts of banditry and looting are the order of the day in those parts. I don't know whether all this is true, but I know for a fact that it is the Franciscans themselves, as for example Father Simić of Knin, who have taken part in attacks against the Orthodox populations so as to destroy the Orthodox Church. (In the same way you destroyed the Orthodox Church in Banja Luka). I know for sure that the Franciscans in Bosnia and Herzegovina have acted abominably, and this pains me. Such acts cannot be committed by educated, cultured, civilized people, let alone by priests.' You can imagine how I felt on hearing all that enemy propaganda has said against us, and I was very surprised and showed my surprise to His Eminence concerning these falsities spread abroad by our enemies by answering all his points as well as I could. We do not take much interest in what individual Fascists say and think about us, for we know that their leaders who helped us to build up our country do not think that way. As for the rumours about our future king, Your Eminence, if you did not learn these things directly from him, allow me to doubt them, as such tales are rife. As for the destruction of the Orthodox churches I have heard nothing and therefore find the facts difficult to believe. In recent months I have been several times to Zagreb, and our government at such times gives us an exhaustive account of how things stand: so I think I would have heard of it. In any case I shall take the responsibility of investigating such facts and shall make a point of informing you. Acts of violence have indeed been perpetrated, but by the Orthodox on the Catholics, and perhaps here and there the Croatian Catholic element has been driven to react. The Italian soldiers who found themselves in an unknown area must have heard all sorts of things, but in an unknown area and without knowing the language they couldn't have ascertained with any certainty the real state of affairs. There are among them those who do not give their own people any cause for pride, so it is not surprising if they turn round and reproach us. Just as there are those among them who are not satisfied with the solution that has been reached because they wanted the whole of Dalmatia to be united to Italy. Not to mention the fact that there are Communists among them and others too who have different ideas from their leaders on how events should develop. At this point Tisserant interrupted me, saying: 'I know that the Italians are not kindly disposed towards you, and that therefore many tales will be told, but the case of Simić is well known to me, as well as the destruction of the Banjaluka Church, and the persecution of the Orthodox population. You must punish the authors of these crimes. What I told you about your future king I learnt from intimate friends of his who are absolutely reliable: they are frightened of Germany. After all, what is Italy compared to Germany? And what can she do without orders from Berlin? Look at the part she plays now, and imagine what it will be like after the war. If victory goes to the Axis powers what will Italy gain from it? Italy's position is such that she cannot do anything, and the situation will be even worse after the war. You must move with great caution in your relations with Italy, because Italy fully realizes that after the war Croatia will not be part of her vital space, but part of Germany's. And that is not all. You can be sure that Italy will lose Trieste and Fiume. This is absolutely certain, and she will also lose the whole of Dalmatia which she gained by the Rome negotiations. Dalmatia will go back to Croatia, and in exchange the Germans will perhaps leave part of Southern Dalmatia to the Italians.' At this point I put forward my doubts so that I could hear more on this topic, and I started maintaining that this was impossible, especially during the lifetime of the Führer and the Duce owing to the sincere ties of friendship between them. At this he laughed, saying that he was not surprised that these were my ideas on the subject, as my information came from people who have to support that point of view. But—he said —if we were able to enter official circles and gain their confidence we would hear exactly the same things as he relates. He learns all this from people who hold the highest positions in Germany: information that the diplomats of the German Embassy in Rome do not even dare to reveal. And he repeated this word for word: 'You can take it as an absolutely certain fact that Fiume and Trieste, with all the territory that stretches between them, will be German, and that Dalmatia will be Croatian, but included within Germany's sphere of influence. In international life there exist interests, not emotions. This is the rule for every politician and for every nation, and the Germans, with or without the Führer, will take no notice of the friendship that momentarily binds them.' I shrugged my shoulders to show that I could not believe these things and I didn't say anything more on the subject. Then the Cardinal wanted to hear about the history of Croatia during the last two decades, about relations with Austria, Hungary and Serbia. He wanted detailed information on all these points. But I will not trouble you with this, as I imagine you will not be very interested.

However, during the discussion we came to mention the Medjumurje. . . .

During our conversation we also tackled the problem of conversions. He seemed very interested in this, and I began to expound, on the basis of Draganović's book, the historical background to the religious situation in Croatia. But when I wanted to show that at one time Croatia, like Montenegro, had been a Catholic country, and that with the arrival of the Turks the Orthodox began to infiltrate into the Catholic parts of the country, and that finally under serious pressure many Catholics abandoned their own faith, some of them going over to Islam, some to Orthodoxy, he refuted me, saying that all this was new to him: he knew well the history of Christianity and there were no instances of Catholics of Latin rite going over to the Orthodox Church. He reminded me of the instance of Greece, which was in an identical situation to Croatia's with regard to the Turks: well, in Greece the number of Catholics remained identical to what it was before the arrival of the Turks. According to him only this is possible: that the Greco-Catholics passed over to Orthodoxy. As we could not agree, I asked him if he would let me prove my argument with a historically documented work, or with an *ad hoc* bibliography. He readily consented, and I promised to bring him Draganović, as he told me he read German as easily as French. Then we got up, but he wanted to go on talking, and started to ask me about our food problem. I told him what the position was and then he told me that the food situation in Europe was terrible, especially in Greece, where people are dying of hunger; but also in France, and even more in Belgium, as in Holland and Norway. In Poland he said that more than four million people have died up till now, from hunger or cold. He thinks that the situation is worst for the oppressed countries. In Poland there is petichial typhus, but the Germans will not allow medical aid because they need all the doctors for the troops on their various fronts, and in any case, the fewer Poles the better.

Then we started on the problem of Franco-German relations. I said perhaps it would be better for the French to make peace with the Axis Powers, as everyone expected them to. He replied that the French have been ready since the day after the capitulation, and still are; it is the Germans who want to destroy France completely, as Hitler described in *Mein Kampf*. In addition the French are paying 300 million francs a day. Neither the Italians nor the Germans want to make peace with France, and so it will continue until the end of the war: then Germany will be able to impose on France the conditions she wishes. Then he added that the relations between France on the one hand and the Italians and Germans on the other are very difficult, but that popular hatred is much stronger against the Italians.

To find out the Cardinal's ideas about the future of the war, I asked him when he thought it would end. He replied: if the Germans defeat the Russians within the year, one can anticipate that peace will be made between June and July 1943, but if the Russians hold out, and the war in Russia develops next winter, then it will go on for another three to four years, since England has four and a half million troops, with first-class equipment, who have as yet not been engaged in fighting, and they too will have to be defeated. But if the Germans conquer Russia, even that will not be impossible, though they will obviously suffer heavy losses. America will not play an important part in the war, contrary to what some people think but it is difficult to envisage how she will emerge from the war, given her geographical situation, her economic power, etc. I expressed doubts as to whether the Germans could continue to fight the Russians through next winter, saying that if they did there would be mutinies in the occupied territories and probably even revolution in Germany herself. I wanted to see what the Cardinal's reaction to such a statement would be, and this is what he said: Revolution in Germany is impossible because the Germans have food supplies for another three years; that others are dying of hunger does not interest them. And in the occupied territories no one is likely to cause a revolution since it is well known that corpses are not much good at fighting, and the occupied nations, with hunger, disease and other social ills, are very similar to corpses. He is absolutely sure that the Germans have food supplies for three years. A few months ago he had the opportunity of talking to one of the world's greatest economic experts who had explained to him and given him proof of Germany's economic organization.

So you see we talked of various things, even if the beginning of our meeting was far from pleasant. However, by the end he had become friendly and expansive, to such an extent that he was wishing our country and our people well. As I took my leave he told me to come and see him whenever I feel like it.

Well, I think I have told you the broad lines of everything that could be of interest to you. As for the minutiae, it is impossible to enumerate them and would serve no purpose. You can form your own opinion of him from what I have told you and so, not to take up more of your time, I shall end. Greetings.

At the second meeting (which must have taken place about a fortnight later, since he reports on it to Zagreb on 20 March), Rusinović was supposed to take Tisserant the book he had promised. But he managed to take something more (the thought of which was enough to make him climb the stairs of the Palazzo dei Convertendi with a sprightly step, like a victor enjoying a triumph in anticipation): the repudiation of some of the Cardinal's most serious accusations. But here is his account:

I again paid a visit to Cardinal Tisserant, to whom I had promised Draganović's book, as well as a reply to some of his allegations about the Croatian clergy, and the destruction of Orthodox churches by the NDH. I was lucky enough to meet in Rome some friars who could testify to the inaccuracy of the information about Fr. Simić of Knin, and about the destruction of Orthodox churches in Knin and Banja Luka. He was very surprised that I could prove to him that the Orthodox church in Knin is undamaged, and that the one in Banja Luka was hit by a bomb during the first days of war between the Germans and the Yugoslavs. These two facts dispelled 90 per cent of the accusations that he has heard from our enemies, and so the rest of our meeting was conducted on a very friendly level. The Cardinal already had a copy of Draganović, but he thanked me all the same, and I gave him another book—of Croatian short stories in French translation. He was delighted.

I can tell you nothing new about our last meeting as I have

already written you a report on it. However, as Tisserant is some-one who likes talking, he told me several interesting facts. The subject that interests him most is undoubtedly that of Germany and Italy. He has not changed his ew on the relations between these two countries. As he sees it, Germany has embarked on a war of life or death. After the Polish and French campaigns she tried to reach a compromise with England. With this end in view was Hess sent to England, as a friend of the English. He was sup-posed to persuade Churchill to undertake a mutual action against Russia, once the problems between the two countries had been solved. However, Churchill, thinking Hitler's offer had come his way too easily and fearing that the reason for it was Germany's weakness, informed Stalin of the matter. Stalin realized that the English would be more trustworthy than the Germans, so found it easier to decide to enter the war beside them and against Germany.

Despite the failure of his first attempt, Hitler tried once again to reach a peace with the English by sending Ribbentrop, last July, to Seville to persuade Franco to act as mediator between England and Germany; however, this initiative was also unsuccessful. Per-haps the English were mistaken in not accepting these offers, since it is obvious that Japan's great successes can be of no use to any people of the white race today. Germany had foreseen the danger and wanted to prevent it; nevertheless it is she who is to blame for everything that may happen in the future between Japan and Europe and the white race generally. Hitler has involved everyone in the same struggle.

He wanted to annihilate Russia as quickly as possible. He speeded up the war operations in every way with the object of getting as substantial a result as he could; he even wanted to occupy Moscow and Petersburg—in opposition to the plans of the Supreme Commander General Brauchitsch. The latter wanted to head towards the Caucasus and break up the Southern front. When Hitler's action failed, he blamed Brauchitsch who lost his position and was attacked and wounded by a member of the Gestapo. Six other Generals were wounded besides Brauchitsch, and no one knows what has become of one of them.

Then the Cardinal went on to speak of the danger of National-Socialism, not only for the Catholic Church, but for all the coun-tries of Europe, given that the doctrine was started by the famous Rosenberg, a Communist in Moscow until 1920, who does not recognize that small countries have a right to live. Anyway, this is by no means a new idea for Germany, as the doctrine was already well known to Hans Blucher and others.

The most recent changes in the Hungarian government are interesting too. Tisserant claims that the fall of Bardosi, and his replacement by Kallai, is the first concession made to Germany. Now the Germans will attempt to provoke more reforms in Hungary, so that despite Magyar opposition, National-Socialism will prevail and win. The Magyars are backward in solving their internal problems, and this makes it easier for the Germans to dictate laws; with the reforms that they are introducing, National-Socialism will inevitably gain ground in that feudal country.

This is all I have to say about Tisserant.

But Rusinović was deceiving himself in thinking that he had tamed Tisserant and shut his mouth for ever. The third meeting gave him an even greater shock than the first, and it is a great pity that he was too upset to do more than report briefly on a few of the topics discussed. Yet his excited phrases do not only disclose sensational data on the religious situation in Croatia, but also that Tisserant was so beside himself on account of their gravity that he inveighed against the Croats themselves (and not only the Ustaše), and went as far as to say that he preferred the Serbs. In Rusinović's eyes, of course, there could be no greater insult, and there is nothing surprising in his decision never again to visit such an exasperating man.

His report, written the day after the visit (28 May 1942), starts off with the worst:

On Wednesday 27th I paid my third visit to Cardinal Tisserant—my third and also my last. You already know from my previous reports who this man is and what his opinions are. But I was not so much struck by these this time as by his manner.

And after saying that he does not want to tire his friend the Minister with a detailed account, he goes on:

He says that the Germans recognized the Orthodox Church of Croatia when, together with us, they had killed off all the priests and when 350,000 Serbs had disappeared. He asks what cause we have to blame the Serbs when we ourselves commit worse crimes against them than they committed against us, although we are, as it were, more civilized and Catholic. In one single concentration camp there are 20,000 Serbs.

In the struggle against the Turks, the Serbs have given just as much as us to the West and to Catholicism, perhaps even more. The Croats have been called 'antemurale christianitatis' because they were Catholic. He knows what the Croats are like because of what they did in Lorraine. I had great difficulty in getting a word in edgewise. He went on to say that he had more sympathy towards the Serbs than the Croats. He is convinced that the Anglo-Saxons will come out victorious. As he sees it, the world situation today can be compared with 1918. He thinks that the war will end in the summer of 1943, but says that he could be mistaken because even in the last war the Allies were preparing for a victory in 1919 and it came in 1918. All that the oppressed nations have had to endure up till now will devolve on the Germans. Today others die, tomorrow it will be the Germans' turn. The Croats will fight the Serbs, the Hungarians the Rumanians, and we shall see who wins. In saying this he laughed cynically. As I have already said, I was dumbfounded, and decided not to pay him another visit as I am obviously wasting my time with him.

Rusinović's decision did not automatically bind his successor, who perhaps was not even aware of it. For Lobkowicz did in fact visit Tisserant towards the middle of December 1942. It must be said that he was very good at 'taking the punishment' (to us a boxing term), but then he was a cold man and much less passionate than his predecessor, all in all someone much better suited to be a diplomat than Rusinović. Tisserant poured cold water on everything he said, though perhaps exercising a little more formal restraint. Though the water was, if anything, more icy, Lobkowicz not only found it quite in order but thought it would be useful to remain in contact with such a formidable enemy (and he was not wrong). However, in the eyes of the Minister, Lorković, Tisserant overstepped the mark this time: where he (the Minister) had written in the margin of Rusinović's first report, 'Beware! Enemy!', he wrote this time: 'After such insults to Croatia, relations with Tisserant cannot be maintained.' But here is Lobkowicz's report (20 December 1942):

. . . he received me cordially, with marked kindness. We embarked on a long, sincere and frank discussion which clearly revealed the Cardinal's attitude, not only towards the State of Croatia and the present regime, but towards the Croatian people as such. (He said that at the time of the Thirty Years' War the Croats were already noted for their savagery, and that in his province, Lorraine, they had burned down several villages; they are generally viewed as a cruel people). The Cardinal said that he had read a book that had been given him by Dr. Rusinović and that in this book there seems to occur nothing but massacres and acts of violence. Here I must point out that certain books obviously have a powerful effect, and that books to be given as propaganda must be chosen with great care. The Cardinal is absolutely convinced that the Axis will be defeated and that Yugoslavia must be rebuilt. When I protested he agreed that ex-Yugoslavia had not been an ideal State formation, and blamed this on the influence exercised by France after Versailles on countries originally forming part of the Austro-Hungarian Empire. In Yugoslavia, as in Czechoslovakia and Poland, there had been too much emphasis on centralization, which was helpful for France but of no use to these countries. Therefore this experience must be taken into account when the new Yugoslavia is formed. It was obvious from our discussion that the Cardinal is resolutely against the Hungarians and the Italians. Among other things he called the Crown of Saint Stephen an illusion. On the subject of the help given by the Italians to the NDH rebels he answered that just as the Italians armed the rebels, so the Germans armed the Ustaše, with the result that the situation in Croatia is extremely confused. Concerning the Croatian Orthodox Church, he said that it has no importance, as it was established at the wish of the Poglavnik, and the same wish could make it disappear. He warmly recommended the diocese of Križevac to me, which comes under his jurisdiction. I replied that the clergy and faithful of Križevac are particularly oppressed by the enemies of the Croats. He said he knew that, but that some of the blame lies with the Croats. He then went on to express an opinion, commonly held at the Vatican, that Bolshevism represents a much less serious danger for the Church and for Europe than National-Socialism. I must add that Cardinal Tisserant is generally known as an Anglophile: but I maintain that it is useful to have contacts with him if only to keep informed. From the general climate of opinion among those in the know, one gathers that the Holy Father does not share Cardinal Tisserant's extremist viewpoint on politics.

Taken together, these last reports are of fundamental importance in proving that the Holy See was aware of the situation in Croatia. Tisserant does not use veiled terms and euphemisms with the people he is talking to, as do the Heads of the Secretariat of State, nor does he react to attempts at justification by giving way and professing to be grateful and satisfied by 'exhaustive and valuable explanations'. On the contrary, he resolutely refutes arguments, while still leaving room for convincing documentation to prove him wrong. He is certainly a more active politician than his colleagues in papal diplomacy, but at the right moment he is more consistent than they are in carrying out his responsibilities as a Christian and a priest. Here too, as in other matters, he does not waste his time (like Cardinal Pizzardo, for instance) in pointless romantic idealizations directed to resurrecting an irreversible past or the utopia of an independent Croatia—which would be equivalent to a powder-magazine ever ready to explode in the heart of the Balkans. Especially after all that has happened, he believes, realistically, that the future of Croatia will only make sense within the context of a re-created (though perhaps more decentralized) Yugoslav federation. And in the field of religion he pursued not only a Catholic line of thought, but an ecumenical one. When he defends the Eastern Catholic Church's cause, we can say with certainty that he is speaking as the person in charge of the corresponding Ministry in Rome; but when he defends the Orthodox (and he is the only one among all the people mentioned in these reports to do so) he is speaking more than as a Catholic: as a man and a religious in all the breadth of both words.

These reports are of exceptional value not only because they prove that the Holy See knew about the situation in Croatia as early as March 1942 (was able to distinguish the purely civil struggle from the religious one, was aware of precise episodes, and of individual people involved) but also because they rule out the possibility that Pius XII did not know what was going on. Even if Cardinal Tisserant remained more or less in isolation throughout the war, this cannot and must not be taken to mean that the Secretary of the Eastern Congregation (the Cardinal) never met its Prefect (the Pope). His scheduled visits to Pius XI happened twice a month, and they went on similarly under Pius XII, as various volumes of the *Annuario Pontificio* bear witness. It does not follow that they were reduced during the war, nor are there reasons for thinking that this was so; but even supposing that it was so, the visits could not have been so drastically reduced as to make it impossible for Tisserant to report to the Pope on the things with which he so violently reproached the Ustaše representatives.

NOTES

Foreword

1. Cf. J. Nobécourt, '*Le Vicaire*' *et l'histoire*, Paris, 1964.
2. Hochhuth had many precursors, e.g. Emmanuel Mounier in *Le Voltigeur*, 5 May 1939; Bernanos in *Le Chemin de la Croix-des-Ames*, Paris, 1948; Ernesto Bonaiuti, *Pio XII*; Giovanni Papini, *Celestino VI*; well-known comments by Camus, Mauriac and others; and further comments that followed the publication of *The Representative*. There was a substantial polemic.
3. Published in the *Osservatore Romano*, 9 April 1959.

Introduction

1. Pius XII: address to the Sacred College, 12 March 1939.
2. Pius XII: encyclical *Summi Pontificatus*, 20 October 1939.
3. Pius XI: encyclical *Ubi arcano Dei*, 23 December 1922.
4. F. Pellegrino, S. J., *Civiltà Cattolica*, 19 July 1941.
5. Luigi Salvatorelli, *La Politica della Santa Sede dopo la guerra*, Milan, 1937.
6. *Civiltà Cattolica*, 5 July 1941.
7. *Loc. cit.*

Part One

1. Cf. F. Charles-Roux, *Huit Ans au Vatican*, Paris, 1947.
2. Cf. Pius XII's words to the new Belgian ambassador, 14 September, and to the new Lithuanian ambassador, 18 September.
3. From the speech by the Lithuanian ambassador, 18 September.
4. The treaty relative to the division of Poland was signed by Germany and the USSR on 28 September 1939.
5. Pius XII: encyclical *Summi Pontificatus*, para. 10.
6. *Ibid.*, para. 31.
7. *Ibid.*, para. 39.
8. And in fact Germany took no reprisals against the Papal encyclical. Cf. Saul Friedländer, *Pie XII et le III Reich, Documents*, Paris, 1964.
9. *Summi Pontificatus*, para. 40.
10. 30 November 1939.

11. The French and English, on the night of 7–8 April, had in fact laid mines in Norwegian waters, giving rise to a solemn protest from Oslo.

12. Cf. Pius XII's words to Dino Alfieri, new Italian ambassador to the Holy See (7 December 1939).

13. Had not Poland profited by the German aggression against Czechoslovakia to annex the territories of Teschen and Tristadt?

14. The Casablanca decision was taken by Churchill and Roosevelt in January 1943. Pius XII, through the intermediary of Mgr. Kaas and Archbishop Spellman, sent Roosevelt a note expressing disagreement and regret (cf. J. Nobécourt, *op. cit.*, p. 238).

15. Christmas broadcast, 1944, para. 14.

16. Cf. the Frankfurt trials, 17 August 1964.

17. Cf. the Limburg trials, February 1964.

18. Cf. the Munich trial of SS official Karl Wolf, August 1964.

19. Para. 3.

20. Para. 19.

21. Para. 21.

22. Paras. 22 and 23.

23. Para. 29.

24. Para. 30.

25. We are not forgetting the pontifical discourse of 2 June 1943, but a careful reading of this reveals not only tortuosity but also an irritating balancing of terms.

25 *bis*. Cf. *Ecclesia*, the Vatican Office of Information, September 1942; *L'Attività della Santa Sede*, vol. I. Vatican City, 1942; *L'Opera della Santa Sede per la pace nel primo anno di pontificato di Pio XII*, Catholic Institute, Milan, 1940; *La Chiesa e la guerra. Documentazione dell'opera dell'Ufficio Informazioni del Vaticano*, Vatican City, 1944.

26. Jesuit historian, born 10 April 1887, ordained 1917. In 1930 he became professor of ecclesiastical history at the Pontifical Gregorian University.

27. Rome, 1960.

28. Rome, 1962.

29. *Pio XII parla alla Chiesa del silenzio*, Milano, 1958.

30. *La vera storia e 'il Vicario' di R. Hochhuth*, 6/VI/1964.

31. Fortunately this was possible, as Cardinal Montini, now Paul VI, in his letter to *The Tablet* had not gone into the matter of Pius XII's knowledge of the facts.

32. Appointed 22 May 1940 in succession to Charles-Roux.

33. Cf. *Osservatore della Domenica*, 28/VI/1964.

34. This created difficulties for the Holy See which had to move ten families of employees out of the Palazzo del Tribunale to a building outside Vatican City so as to make room for the diplomats.

34 *bis*. Cf. the remark of Prince Lobkowicz (Ustaše representative to the Vatican between 1942 and 1943), speaking of the first secretary of the Yugoslav Embassy to the Holy See, Kosta Čukić, 'he lives in the Vatican and seldom goes out into the city and only if accompanied by an Italian policeman'.

35. Finland sent its representative to the Holy See on 10 July, China on 23 October, and Japan on 30 March 1942.

36. On the communications between the Holy See and Belgium, cf. *Le Cardinal van Roey et l'occupation allemande en Belgique, actes et documents publiés par le chanoine Leclerq*, Brussels, 1945.

36. *bis*. Cf. the interesting report of Prince Lobkowicz reproduced in its entirety in the *Appendix* to Part III of this book.

37. Galeazzi, a close friend of Archbishop Spellman, made another trip to the USA at the end of 1941. Cf. S. Friedländer, *Pie XII et le III Reich, Documents*, Paris, 1964.

38. The most powerful semi-official men at the Vatican at this time were Mgr. Kaas, Fr. Leiber, Fr. Pfeiffer, Mgr. Hudal, etc., the German *éminences grises* of the Sacred Palaces and the Curia.

39. Concerning Fleischmann and Kästner, cf. L. Poliakov, *Le Bréviaire de la haine, Le III Reich and les Juifs*.

40. Paris, 1955.

41. J. Nobécourt, *'Le Vicaire' et l'histoire*, Paris, 1964.

42. R. Hochhuth, *The Representative*, London, 1964.

43. Cf. Leone Algisi, *Giovanni XXIII*, Turin, 1959, especially chap. VI (The Turkey of Atatürk) and the letter to von Papen of 4 August 1944 (*Appendix*).

44. Concerning Dachau, for instance, there were sayings such as, 'O God, make me dumb so that I shan't be sent to Dachau,' and on 11 November 1938 Nazis demonstrating in Munich against Cardinal Faulhaber shouted, 'Send the traitor to Dachau!'

45. The Allies naturally did all they could to inform the Germans of these enormities. Besides broadcasts (from the middle of 1942 onwards) they made use in 1943 of leaflets dropped from bombers. However, these means may not have been all that efficient as broadcasts were constantly jammed and leaflets would have been immediately picked up.

46. Cf. *Il Giorno*, Milan.

47. Cf. *Papers concerning the treatment of the Nationals in Germany 1938–39*, published in Great Britain on 31 October 1939 and based on the findings of British diplomats, consuls, etc., in Germany. It contained documentation on Buchenwald and Dachau.

48. Concerning Gerstein, cf. L. Poliakov, *op. cit.*, and R. Hochhuth, *The Representative*.

49. Alfred Wetzler was present at the Frankfurt trials in 1964 and provided the court with 'the translation into English of his report on the mass killings by gas in Auschwitz, written in German directly after his escape from that camp on 7 April 1944.' He told the court that he gave a copy to the apostolic nuncio [*sic*] in Prague who in his turn sent it to the Pope. 'At that time,' said Wetzler, 'we hoped that the Pope would make the report public and brand the Nazi atrocities against the Jews; but we never heard anything from the Vatican.'

50. *La Santa Sede e gli ebrei della Romania durante la seconda guerra mondiale* in *Civiltà Cattolica*, 2 September 1961.

51. Cf. the article by A. Martini, *La Vera storia e 'il Vicario' di Rolf Hochhuth*, in *Civiltà Cattolica*, June, 1964.

51 *bis*. Said by Mgr. Tardini in his commemoration of Pius XII in the presence of John XXIII, 1959.

52. Cf. *Documentation Catholique*, 2 February 1964.

53. Between October and December 1939 the Germans planned the 'Jewish reserve' of Lublin and publicized it in the press. Immediately a series of convoys from Vienna, Prague and Stettin began moving towards that 'reserve'.

54. Cf. Fr. Martini's article, already quoted, in *Civiltà Cattolica*, June 1964.

55. *Civiltà Cattolica*, June 1964.

56. Camillo Cianfara, *The War and the Vatican*, 1945.

57. *Foreign Relations of the U.S.*, III, 1942, pp. 772–5.

58. *Ibid.*, pp. 776–7.

59. Cf. Eberhard Jaeckel of the University of Kiel, *Zur Politik des Heiligen Stuhls im zweiten Weltkrieg*, in 'Geschichte in Wissenschaft und Unterricht', January, 1964.

60. In an interview on 27 March 1964, Tisserant said that the encyclical he had in mind was not to be addressed only to the Germans 'but to all those who are subjected to commands, to a collective morality'.

61. In the interview of 27 March 1964, Tisserant said that when the ideas expressed in his letter failed, he had a few talks with the Pope to find out whether he was influenced by the philo-Fascist elements in the Curia who were trying to avoid the publication of anti-German declarations.

62. Before this collective pastoral, a strong anti-Nazi declaration had been made by Cardinal Mundelein of Chicago which had also aroused diplomatic protests from Germany to the Vatican.

63. Cf. Fr. Martini's article in *Civiltà Cattolica*, June 1964.

64. Cf. *The Tablet*, London, 29/VI/1963.

65. Cf. Fr. Dezza, rector of the Gregorian University, article in *Osservatore della Domenica*, 28 June 1964; and Mgr. Pirro Scavizzi, article in *La Parrocchia*, May 1964.

66. See *Documentation Catholique*, 2 February 1964.

67. Cf. Werner Stephan, *Joseph Goebbels—Dämon einer Diktatur*, Stuttgart, 1949; and Fr. Riquet, S.J., *Dal Vicario al capro espiatorio* in *Osservatore della Domenica*, 28/VI/1964.

68. Eugen Kogon, *Der SS-Staat. Das System der deutschen Konzentrationslager*, Munich, 1946.

69. J. Toulat, *Due cardinali di Francia, due protettori degli ebrei*, in *Osservatore della Domenica*, 28/VI/1964.

70. Cf. *Civiltà Cattolica*, 6 June 1964.

71. For discussion of all this, cf. J. Nobécourt, *'Le Vicaire' et l'histoire*, pp. 232 *et seq.*

72. A. Giovannetti, *Venti anni fa* in the *Osservatore Romano*, 2/II/1964.

72 *bis*. Cf. S. Friedländer, *op. cit.*, p. 159.

73. The German Catholic writer, Theodor Haecker, wrote in his diary for 14 June 1940: 'The prophetic voice of the Church has fallen silent as if

her prophetic function had come to a stop. Is even this part of the evil of the times? Each of us has to grope his own way, abandoned and alone. . . .'

74. Jacques Nobécourt, *op. cit.*

75. Cf. Albert Wucher, article in *Sudeutsch Zeitung*, 19/IV/63; Gordon C. Zahn, *German Catholics and Hitler's War*, London, 1963; Guenther Lewy, *The Catholic Church and Nazi Germany*, New York, 1964.

76. Simon Wiesenthal, the well-known director of the Centre for Jewish Documentation, who agreed to the capture of Adolf Eichmann. He is an architect aged 56, born in Poland, and survivor of six concentration camps.

77. Cf. the findings of Simon Wiesenthal.

78. Cf. Mgr. A. Giovannetti, *Il Vaticano e la Guerra.*

79. He met Wilhelm II at last on 29 June 1917.

80. Cf. Riccardo Galeazzi-Lisi, *Dans l'Ombre et la Lumière di Pie XII*, Paris, 1960.

81. Cf. his well-known words to the ambassador, Dino Alfieri, on 14 May 1940. Alfieri paid a farewell visit to him on being transferred from the embassy to the Holy See to the embassy in Berlin. Cf. A. Giovannetti, *op. cit.*

82. The cardinals thanked the Pope but without exception said they would follow his destiny. The panic amongst the ambassadors who had taken refuge in the Vatican came when they were notified by the Secretariat of State about the ever-increasing rumours of a possible transfer of the Pope to Germany. The Vatican even increased the number of the members of its armed forces and armed part of its troops with automatic rifles. The audience in which the German ambassador asked the Pope what his attitude would be if he were eventually 'given hospitality' in the Third Reich would seem to have occurred on 5 February 1944.

83. Cf. Fr. Leiber, *Pius XII* in *Stimmen der Zeit*, November 1958.

84. Cardinal Tisserant was also convinced of this and said so in an interview (*Vita*, 8 April 1964).

85. Cardinal Tardini, *Pio XII*, and A. Giovannetti, *op. cit.*

86. The letter referred to three small hard-working peaceful nations being attacked without reason. The Pope said he was obliged to raise his voice once more to deplore injustice and iniquity.

87. Cf. *Vita*, 8 April 1964.

88. Cf. the *Osservatore della Domenica*, 28 June 1964, a special number devoted to the defence of Pius XII.

89. Cf. *Documentation Catholique*, 1964.

90. Cf. von Weizsäcker (his memoirs were published in 1950), Sir D'Arcy Osborne (*The Times*, 20 March 1963), Haggelof, the Swede (29 September 1963), Grippenberg, Finnish ambassador to the Holy See (5 December 1963), and Kanayama, now Japanese ambassdor in Chile, who was a member of the Japanese team at the Vatican during the war (cf. the *Osservatore Romano*, 5 August 1964).

91. *Op. cit.*

92. There were, however, numbers of notes of protest on religious grounds which were less well known than political protests.

93. Cf. *Vita*, 11 August 1960.

94. To Dino Alfieri on 13 May 1940: A Giovannetti, *op. cit.*

95. Cf. P. Duclos, *op. cit.*

96. But one of the most disagreeable examples of Pius XII's silence was at the time of the massive air attack on London throughout the summer of 1940.

97. Cf. Tittman's telegram to Washington on 6 October, 1942, in *Foreign Relations with the United States, 1942,* III.

98. Hochhuth's moral portrait of Pius XII is not so much an effort at interpretation as an attempt at caricature.

99. Especially by J. Nobécourt and S. Friedländer.

100. According to Friedländer he was also influenced by his Secretary of State, Cardinal Pacelli, so far as Germany was concerned.

101. Made by Pius XI to some Belgian pilgrims on 6 September 1938.

102. Whereas Mussolini was indignant and ordered Vittorio Cerruti, the ambassador in Berlin, to protest to Hitler (cf. Cerruti, *La Stampa,* 12 September 1945).

103. This encyclical only mentioned the Jews so as to defend the sacred books of the Old Testament which are revered in common with the Catholic Church; worse, it referred to them as 'the people who were to put Him (Christ) on the cross'.

104. Or better, substantial extracts in the letter to the Italian episcopate on 6 February 1959.

105. S. Friedländer shows that the despatches sent by the German embassy at the Holy See to Berlin immediately after the election of Pius XII were favourable to Pacelli. Probably Pius XII considered that the German foreign minister, von Ribbentrop, was inclined to improve relations with the Holy See but he was also aware that Goering, Goebbels and Himmler had more influence on the Führer. Mgr. Kaas was certainly the most hated of the Pope's German counsellors.

106. *Stimmen der Zeit,* November 1958.

107. Cf. *Osservatore della Domenica* of 28 June 1964, and the work of the Italian Catholic pamphleteer, Rosario F. Esposito, in his *Processo al Vicario,* Turin, 1964.

108. Martini in *Civiltà Cattolica,* 6 June, 1964.

109. The text (not verbatim) is taken from A. Giovannetti, *Il Vaticano e la guerra.*

110. *Ibid.*

111. It will be remembered that concerning the audience Pius XI gave to Chamberlain and Halifax, *The Church Times,* expressed itself warmly and ecumenically. Cf. *Civiltà Cattolica,* 1939, I.

112. 'Nor do we wish to pass over in silence our deep emotion of gratitude . . . for the good wishes of those who, though they do not belong to the visible body of the Catholic Church, have not forgotten . . . all that unites them to us either in love of the person of Christ or belief in God.'

113. Cf. the article by the editor of the *Osservatore Romano,* 4 November, 1956.

Part Two

1. Cf. Naujoks's account in *Der Spiegel* at the end of August 1964.

2. Warsaw fell on the 27th but the Hela peninsula held out until 2 October.

3. Every district was administered by a *Distriktschef* under the *Generalgouverneur* stationed at Cracow. The only *Generalgouverneur* was Hans Frank who was eventually hanged at Nuremberg on 16 October 1946. His secretary of state, or *Stellvertreter*, was Dr. Buehler. But until May 1940, his *Stellvertreter* was Seyss-Inquart. The latter was Governor of Holland until 1945. He was executed at Nuremberg.

4. According to the *Handbook of Central and East Europe*, 1938, Zurich, in that year 64·9 per cent of the Poles belonged to the Latin Catholic rite; 10·4 per cent to the Greco-Catholic rite; 11·8 per cent were Orthodox; 9·8 per cent were Jewish, and 3·1 per cent were Protestant.

5. Of course the Germans took care to annex the richest areas and those most interesting from the tourist point of view.

6. We shall be revealing our sources later.

7. Those of Chełmno, Katowice, Łódź, Plock, Włocławek, etc.

8. The picture of the situation in the western areas annexed to the Reich was as follows:

Archdiocese of Gniezno: Titular, Cardinal Hlond, absent in Rome; vicar-general, Canon E. van Blericq, under house arrest.

Archdiocese of Poznań: Titular, Cardinal Hlond, absent in Rome; vicar-general, Bishop Dymek, under house arrest.

Diocese of Chełmno—vacant: Ordinary, Mgr. St. Okoniewski, absent in Rome; vicar-general, Bishop Dominik, forcibly absent in Danzig.

Diocese of Katowice: Ordinary, Mgr. Adamski, free only at his headquarters; auxiliary Bishop Bieniek, resigned.

Diocese of Łódź: Ordinary, Mgr. Jasinski, under house arrest; auxiliary, Bishop Tomczak, in concentration camp.

Diocese of Plock: Ordinary, Mgr. Nowowiejski, expelled; similarly expelled auxiliary Bishop Wetmanski.

Diocese of Włocławek: Ordinary, Mgr. Radonski, absent at Budapest; vicar-general, Bishop Kozal, in concentration camp.

Shortly afterwards the situation deteriorated: the two bishops of Plock finished in a concentration camp; Bishop Adamski was transferred to the General Governorship, etc.

9. *Sklavenvolk* = slaves, *Herrenvolk* = masters.

10. We are omitting, amongst other things, what concerns the Western areas annexed to the Reich, except for information which is not contained in Documents A and B.

11. The author begins by an affirmation of his objectivity.

12. We omit a polemical part concerning a supposed interview with Archbishop Gall of Warsaw.

13. Article III. For the text of the Concordat cf. *Acta Apostolicae Sedis*,

XVII, 1929, and *Raccolta dei Concordati*, etc., ed. by A. Mercati, Vol. II, 1915–54, Rome, Vatican, 1954.

14. Lorenzo Lauri signed the Concordat which had been prepared by his predecessor, Ratti. A Roman, he was nuncio at Warsaw from 1921 to 1926.

15. Francesco Marmaggi, also a Roman, made Cardinal in 1935, was nuncio in Warsaw from 1926–36.

16. Cf. *Osservatore Romano*, 11 June 1936.

17. Mgr. Filippo Cortesi was a Sicilian. He died in 1947 near Rome and was still nominally nuncio in Warsaw.

18. There is no trace of this agreement in the *Raccolta dei Concordati* mentioned above.

19. A.K., 9 January 1942—K.G., Office VI, Information Section, 203/VII-46.

20. Cf. Giuseppe dei Marchi in *Le Nunciature Apostoliche dal 1800–1956*, Rome, 1957, and *L'Invasion allemande en Pologne, documents receuillis par le Centre d'Information et de Documentation du Gouvernement polonais*, Paris.

21. Cf. A. Giovannetti, *Il Vaticano e la guerra*.

22. *Ibid.*

23. *Ibid.*

24. The Reich Government also refused all requests to send 'pontifical missions for aid'.

25. See S. Friedländer, *op. cit.*

26. Cf. '*Klechy*' *w obozach smierci* (Priests in death camps) published in Polish by the authorization of the headquarters European Command, civil affairs division. Eight hundred and fifty-one priests died in the famous camps.

27. The Italian title is *Pio XII e la Polonia, 1939–1949, discorsi, lettere, commenti*. Published in Rome by Studium, edited by the Ass. of Refugee Intellectuals in Italy with financial help by the Ford Foundation. Preface by C. Papée.

28. See the documents in *Appendix I*, and A. Martini, *Civiltà Cattolica*, 5 May 1962.

29. S. Friedländer, *op. cit.*

30. *Ibid.*

31. *Ibid.*

32. Mgr. Aloisi-Masella, nuncio in Brazil, and Mgr. Micara, nuncio in Belgium.

33. Orsenigo, born 1873, was a Milanese, promoted by the Milanese, Pius XI. He served in the papal diplomatic service and succeeded Pacelli in Berlin. After the collapse of Nazism he was sent back to Eichstätt in Germany with the aim of guaranteeing the continuity of the Concordats. But as ex-nuncio to Nazi Germany he was anything but welcome in various circles, and his personal situation became still worse.

34. The city of Fulda. In the cathedral the tomb of St. Boniface, the apostle of Germany, is preserved. It is the seat of the principal German Episcopal Conferences.

35. The German bishops asked Pius XI for an encyclical on the religious situation in their country on 18 August 1936 at their annual meeting at Fulda. Cardinal Pacelli subsequently invited to Rome Cardinals Bertram, Schulte and Faulhaber, and Bishops von Galen (of Munster) and von Preysing (of Berlin). Faulhaber played a big part in drawing up the encyclical. Cf. A. Martini, *Civiltà Cattolica*, 5 December 1964.

36. See text, p. 171.

37. Cf. *Osservatore della Domenica*, 28 June 1964, and the memoirs of Franciszek Korszynski, Bishop of Włocławek, who was a prisoner at Dachau during the war.

38. A. Giovannetti, *op. cit.*

39. He was appointed to this archdiocese on 24 June 1926 and received the cardinal's hat a year later. He returned to Poland on 4 March 1946 and succeeded Cardinal Kakowski to the see of Warsaw. He died in Warsaw on 22 October 1948.

40. Cardinal Kakowski had been Archbishop of Warsaw since 1913. In 1919 he consecrated the new nuncio, Ratti, as bishop in the presence of twenty-two Polish bishops and the President of the Republic. On 15 December of that year he was made cardinal.

41. Pius XII received Hlond on 21 September and the delay was significant. We know for certain that the audience was frigid. Pacelli was not often severe; when he was, it was unforgettable. Only a minority of the members of Hlond's diocese had fled though they had no moral obligation to stay. Hlond cannot have been unaware of paras. 1 and 2 in canon 338 of the code of Canon Law.

42. Cf. A. Giovannetti, *op. cit.*

43. This and other pieces of information which derive from the written account of the bishop's trial were courteously provided by a Polish collaborator. The present author, however, had no time for verification.

44. There is a clandestine piece of information contained in a report sent to London by the Delegatura on 30 March 1944 (DRRP-Office of the Presidium-Mail to the government; 202/I-40).

45. Dated 23 January 1941; 1 January 1942; 30 May 1942; 11 January 1943; 11 February 1944; and 12 April 1945.

46. Born 14 May 1867. He studied in Poland, Austria and Rome; was responsible for various good works as Archbishop of Cracow: founded hospitals and sanatoria, hospices for poor students, rest-houses for aged priests, etc. He strengthened the 'Caritas' organization and promoted the foundation of the Polish college in Rome. He died on 23 July 1951 and was buried in the castle of Wawel.

47. See A. Martini, *Silenzi e parole*.

48. Mgr. Romuald Jalbrzykowski and Mgr. Boleslaw Twardowski.

49. For instance Pius XII's letter to Hlond, dated 11 February 1944, was written eight days after the Cardinal's arrest by the Germans.

50. They were almost certainly in concentrated form and at least excluded news of a delicate nature on the behaviour of the bishops and the clergy.

51. Later on we shall find some unflattering comments about him in

several clandestine reports. These we cannot guarantee but in any case they are not of a nature to cast aspersions on his report's objectivity.

52. On 1 July 1940, Bucharest formally renounced the Franco-British guarantee of 1939 and on 10 July left the League of Nations.

53. Cf. General Roatta, *Cento Milioni di Baionette, l'esercito italiano in guerra dal 1940–1944*, Milan, 1946, and General Giovanni Messe, *La Guerra sul fronte russo*, Milan, 1947.

54. Alceo Valcini, *Il Calvario di Varsavia*, Milan, 1945.

55. *Ibid.*

56. *Vita*, 15 April 1964.

57. *Ibid.*

58. He patented two of his inventions, an electric brake for trams and an automatic signal for trains, 'so as to save so many poor people,' as he put it.

59. *La Parrocchia*, Rome, May 1964.

60. Article already quoted (Martini).

61. The Embassy secretary, Mario di Stefano, was able to go back to Warsaw and stay there despite opposition until 18 March 1940. The negotiations to establish the royal mission lasted almost two years and was the outcome of real *entêtement* on the part of the Italian Ministry of Foreign Affairs. Von Ribbentrop wanted no witnesses in Poland, above all no Italian witnesses, given their 'compound allegiances' (with the Holy See).

62. L. Frassati, *Il Destino passa per Varsavia*, Bologna, 1949.

63. *Ibid.*

64. *Ibid.*

65. *Ibid.*

66. *Ibid.*

67. *Ibid.*

68. She was also the sister of Pier-Giorgio Frassati who died when still young but was so famous for his virtue that numbers of hagiographies were devoted to him.

69. L. Frassati, *ibid.*

70. *Ibid.*

71. Fr. Wladimir Ledochowski (1866–1942) was from 1915 until his death the 26th General of the Society of Jesus. His uncle was Cardinal Miecislao (who had challenged Bismarck), his sister Maria-Teresa was the foundress of the sodality of St. Peter Claver; his sister Julia was the foundress of the Ursuline Sisters of Jesus in Agony; his younger brother remained in the world, took up a military career, and became a general.

72. Frassati, *ibid.*

73. *Ibid.*

74. *Ibid.* Mgr. Gall (1865–1942) was ordained bishop in 1918 and from 1933 was the first auxiliary of Cardinal Kakowski. Mgr. Szlagowski, born in 1864, was professor at Warsaw university and one-time rector and had been second auxiliary of the archdiocese since 1928. He seems to have distinguished himself during the Warsaw rising in 1944.

75. Gawlina was born in Silesia in 1892 and died in Rome in 1964. He

fought with the German army in the First World War and was ordained priest in 1921. He became military bishop in 1933. After the Second World War he stayed on in Rome as spiritual leader of Polish emigrés throughout the world. He played a part during the first two sessions of the Second Vatican Council, but died at the beginning of the third session.

76. Cf. *Osservatore della Domenica*, 28 June 1964.

76 *bis*. Casimir Papée was born in 1889 and occupied many posts in the Polish foreign service. He retained his position as Polish ambassador to the Holy See on behalf of the Polish governments in exile until December 1958. Since then he has been listed in the *Annuario Pontificio* as 'agent of embassy affairs' and is no longer recognized as doyen of the diplomatic corps to the Holy See.

77. Cf. S. Friedländer, *op. cit.*

78. Since 4 February 1960 he has been nuncio in Berne.

79. The Foreign Ministry of the Polish government in London wrote to thank the Pope for this appointment on 23 June 1943, though it was an unwelcome one.

80. In his preface to his book, Papée admits that many documents remain in the archives and wait for the future.

81. Here are a few: *L'Invasion allemande en Pologne*, Paris, April 1940 (with a preface by Herriot); the series of *Documents relating to the adminis-tration of occupied countries in Eastern Europe*, pub. by the Polish Informa-tion Centre in New York. We have read five pamphlets in this series. Another useful book is Jan Ciechanowski's *Defeat in Victory*, New York and Zurich, 1948.

82. Papée, *op. cit.*

83. There is no record of the appointment of Breitinger in the *Annuario Pontificio*.

84. Cf. Papée's report of 12 October 1942, p. 206.

85. The three documents were handed over by the Polish government in London to the Delegatura during the war, and are now in the Archivum Zakladu Historii Partii (AZH P-202).

86. Mgr. Valentine Dymek, auxiliary Bishop of Poznań, at his post but under house arrest.

87. *Raccolta dei Concordati, etc.*, ed. cit.

88. Cf. *Osservatore Romano*, 26 September 1945.

89. On the Polish clandestine organization see *Polskie Sily Zbrojne w II wojnie swiatowej, tom. III, Armia Krajowa* (The armed Polish forces in World War II, vol. III, A.K.) published by the General Sikorski Historical Institute of London in 1950.

90. On 18 June 1940 the government in exile declared that it looked on the inter-party committee as representative of the nation and that the commandant at the head of the ZWZ had the obligation to consult it in all important matters.

92. L. Frassati, *op. cit.*

93. In a long conversation on 13 July 1964 at Jastarnia, in the Hela peninsula, where he was on holiday.

94. A.K.-K.G., Office VI, Information Section: 203/VII-46.

95. D.R.R.P., Office of the Presidium, Despatches from the government 202/1-2.

96. *Ibid.*

97. *Ibid.*

98. *Ibid.*

99. *Ibid.*

100. D.R.R.P., Office of the Presidium, Despatches to the government: 202/I-6.

101. D.R.R.P., Office of the Presidium, Despatches from the government: 202/I-4.

102. Mgr. Eugene Baziak, in the *Annuario Pontificio* of 1939, figured as the auxiliary bishop of the Metropolitan of the Latin rite of Lwów, Mgr. Twardowski.

103. Mgr. Radonski was bishop of Włocławek from 1929. In 1940 he was in Budapest.

104. The name is indecipherable except for the end.

105. D.R.R.P., Office of the Presidium, government mail: 202/I-40.

106. 'You have offended the community of the German people and therefore you have lost their confidence. We have no place for you.'

107. Translated in the text.

108. This was the name for Poles who had accepted German citizenship.

109. The famous Warsaw prison, destroyed during the Warsaw rising.

110. Cf. L. Poliakov, *Bréviaire de la haine, III Reich et les Juifs*. This gives further evidence, touched on occasionally in these reports, about the anti-Semitism which was characteristic of Polish Catholics and their clergy.

111. It can be imagined how scandalous this seemed to the ultra-Catholic mentality of Polish Catholics.

112. The re-opening of the seminaries did not mean that fresh novices could be admitted, but simply that those already enrolled could finish their course. After which the seminaries automatically emptied.

113. Triduum of solemn exposition of the Blessed Sacrament.

114 & 115. In the original book these phrases occurred in German in the text, but here they have been translated [Trs.].

116. Mgr. Sigismondo Kaczynski, author of the report referred to by us as Document 3.

117. D.R.R.P., Department for Internal Affairs, reports on the situation: 202/II-6.

118. D.R.R.P., Office of the Presidium, government mail: 202/34.

119. Cf. note 104.

120. A.K.-K.G., Headquarters, Office VI, Information Section: 203/VII-46.

121. *Rada Glowna Opiekuncza* (General Committee of Aid): the only organization for aid allowed by the Germans. It had two main centres, in Cracow (administrative) and Warsaw. It disposed of the help from the Holy See and from the American Red Cross through the Geneva Red Cross. The president for a short time was J. Radziwill, then Adam Konizier who was in contact with Sapieha.

122. The largest Catholic charitable organization, under the bishops.

123. The *Falanga* was a Nazi political movement founded by Piasecki in Poland before the war and from which he later dissociated himself.

124. D.R.R.P., Office of the Presidium, government mail: 202/1-32.

125. In the text the word is *ksiezy*, which in Polish is prefixed to the name of any ecclesiastic irrespective of his grade (cardinal or priest). It is a term used mainly by the laity, less expert in making distirctions in ecclesiastical grades.

126. Delegatura Rzadu = Delegatura of the government.

127. The reader may usefully compare this text with an extract from a report (n. 6/42) sent to his collaborators by the Minister for Internal Affairs of the Polish government in London (23 December 1942): 'The behaviour of our bishops is not uniform. Some want to conserve what is most important for religion, and above all the seminaries. These bishops avoid making statements in public, Archbishop Sapieha and Twardowski, Gall, Lukomski, Barda. Another group of bishops seeks a *modus vivendi* with the occupying power and is even prepared to make some compromises. . . . This attitude is severely criticized by the people. Public opinion is full of admiration for the dignified attitude of the Metropolitan Sapieha, whom it considers the best. Archbishop Gall's health gives cause for anxiety and one must be prepared for his probable death. Archbishop Jalbrzykowski of Wilno is behaving well and adminstered his diocese with admirable strength of will in spite of his grave illness. Last March he was transferred to Mariampol where he is interned. Bishops Adamski and Sokolowski must be dealt with separately. The first for his behaviour in Silesia, the other in the diocese of Podlasia (Siedlce), have cast grave doubts on their attitude towards the Polish State and Nation. . . .'

128. R. Hochhuth, *The Representative*.

129, For instance in an article on 12 December 1940 concerning a booklet entitled *La Germania e il culto cattolico in Polonia* (Germany and the Catholic religion in Poland).

130. A. Martini, *Silenzi e parole* in *Civiltà Cattolica*, 5 May 1962.

131. See p. 385 of this book.

132. For instance on 8 July 1942; but Cardinal Hinsley often spoke on the BBC, wrote to *The Times* (17/III/1943), and contributed the preface to *The Persecution of the Catholic Church in German-occupied Poland* (1941) and other books on the same subject.

133. Cf. C. Papée, *Pius XII a Polska*.

134. *Ibid.*

135. *Ibid.*

136. *Ibid.*

137. *Ibid.*

138. See *Documentation Catholique*, 2 February 1964.

139. This was Professor David L. Hoggan: his book runs to 900 pages.

140. S. Friedländer, *Pie XII et le III Reich*, Parish, 1964.

141. There seems no denying that there was some personal friction between Pius XII and Colonel Beck. G. Bonnet has referred to Beck's

megalomania in his memoirs (*Defense de la Paix*, Geneva, 1948). See also Charles-Roux, *Huit ans au Vatican*, Paris, 1947.

142. S. Friedländer, *op. cit.*

143. A Giovannetti, *op. cit.*

144. This came to light during the Nuremberg trials and was published in 1947 by M. Maccarone in *Il nazional-socialismo e la Santa Sede*, Rome.

145. S. Friedländer, *op. cit.*

146. In the article already quoted.

147. S. Friedländer, *op. cit.*

148. *Osservatore Romano*, 15 October 1939.

149. C. Papée, *Pius XII a Polska*.

150. *Ibid.*

151. This document is at the 'Centre de Documentation Juive Contemporaine'.

152. Quoted by S. Friedländer, *op. cit.*

153. C. Papée, *op. cit.*

154. *Ibid.*

155. *Ibid.*

156. S. Friedländer, *op. cit.*

157. See *Documentation Catholique*, 2 February 1964.

157 *bis*. Sibilia's remark is to be found in a report of 10 June 1943 to the Zagreb Minister of Foreign Affairs; Weizsäcker's in a report to the same Minister on the following 13 July.

158. S. Friedländer, *op. cit.*

159. *Op. cit.*

160. L. Frassati.

161. In fact diplomatic relations between Yugoslavia and the Holy See came to an end.

162. The actual words of Rzepecki.

163. A. Martini, *Silenzi e parole*, in *Civiltà Cattolica*, 5 May 1962.

164. C. Papée said in *Pius XII a Polska* that for these reasons the letter should have been omitted from the *Acta Apostolicae Sedis*.

165. In a letter of 28 August 1942 Sapieha said that in that period the Poles were 'subjected to even more atrocious afflictions' and that 'the enemy's present hatred is worse than anything one could imagine or express'.

166. The varying points of view of Sapieha, Radonski and Szeptyckyi are to be found in Fr. Martini's article quoted above.

167. Concerning Lobkowicz, see Part III of this book (the Case of Croatia).

168. A report from von Bergen to the Wilhelmstrasse on 24 May 1941 quoted by S. Friedländer, *op. cit.* In September 1942 Papée united himself with the initiative taken by the Brazilian ambassador backed by his colleagues from Great Britain, Belgium, Yugoslavia, Latin America, and by the representative of the USA President. On the following 9 October Papée said to Maglione: 'Given the vastness of the persecution of the Church in Poland, could not the Holy Father say something in defence of that country?'

169. D.R.R.P., Office of the Presidium, despatches from the government (in London).

170. *Ibid.*

171. C. Papée, *op. cit.*

172. *Ibid.*

173. S. Friedländer, *op. cit.*

174. D.R.R.P., Office of the Presidium, government mail, 202/I-40.

175. *Ibid.*

176. In Italian in the text.

177. D.R.R.P., Department of Internal Affairs, reports on the situation: 202/II-6.

178. A.K.-K.G., Office VI, Information Section: 203/VII-46.

179. Cf. note 177.

180. D.R.R.P., Office of the Presidium, government mail: 202/34.

181. Cf. note 179.

182. There were about 1,400 clandestine publications in Poland (1,193 in Holland, 1,106 in France, etc.). We know of 1,123 titles, but of course many were mere leaflets and had a very short life. See *Katalog Polskiej Prasy Konspiracyjenj, 1939–1945*, Editions of the Ministry of National Defence, Warsaw, 1962.

183. A.K.-K.G., Office VI, Information Section, 203/VII-49.

184. Organ of the organization of the same name (Peasants' Struggle), linked up with KOP, right-wing organization of ex-army officers. Published in Grojec between 1940 and 1942.

185. A.K.-K.G., Office VI, Information Section, 203/VII-50.

186. Famous sixteenth-century preacher.

187. A.K.-K.G., Office VI, Information Section: 203/VII-50.

188. Weekly of the S.Z.P. (*Zwiazek Syndykalistow Polskieh*, association of Polish syndicalists). Tendency: left-wing socialist.

189. Here *Sprawa* touches on one of the most complicated and difficult points in nationalistic Catholicism and Catholicizing nationalism in Poland. Poland has never maintained that she is a bridge between East and West, but that she is a forward bastion as regards religion. Hence her struggle even against eastern forms of Catholicism. This obviously derives from a complex of weakness about the neighbouring Orthodox colossus. But hatred of Orthodoxy is nothing but terror of Russian power. On her side, Rome has always kept alive as a point of honour the aim of winning over the immense territory of Russia to Catholicism.

190. Occasional periodical of the WRN (Liberty, Equality, Independence) which came out in Warsaw between 1940 and 1944. WRN was a socialist organization of the right.

191. Organ of *Polski Zwiarek Wolnosci* (a movement of Pilsudski's followers). Published in Warsaw between 1940 and 1944.

192. Born in 1348, died in 1434.

193. 1058–1080. He killed a bishop who opposed his will.

194. A.K.-K.G., Office VI, Information Section: 203/VII-50.

195. 'Food and Defence' was the Polish motto during the 1794 rising. Organ of the Popular Movement (SL) and of the Chtopskie Battalion (of

peasants). Tendency: centre-left. Published in Warsaw between March 1942 and June 1944.

196. Famous nineteenth-century Polish poet.

197. A.K.-K.G., Office VI, Information Section: 203/VII-50.

198. Organ of the organization of the same name of right-wing socialist tendency. Published in Warsaw between 1940 and 1944.

199. D.R.R.P., Information and Press Department. Resumé of the weekly press: 202/III-80.

200. D.R.R.P., Information and Press Department. Review of the illegal Polish press: 202/III-87.

201. Organ of the National Confederation.

202. Organ of the same.

203. Cf. note 199.

204. Cf. note 199.

205. Right-wing socialist paper which came out in Warsaw between 1940 and 1944.

206. Cf. note 199.

207. Cf. note 199.

208. News-sheet of the OPW (*Oboz Polski Walczacej*—Battlefield of Poland) of the Sanacja group. It was devoted to Polish culture. Published in Warsaw between III/1943 and IV/1944.

209. Cf. note 199.

210. Organ of the SN (*Stronnictwo Narodowe*), movement of the clergy, the landed gentry and the petit bourgeoisie: a movement of the right. Published in Warsaw between 1940 and 1945.

211. We do not know whether the gospels with attached prayers in writing 'for Polish emigrés and prisoners and Poles dispersed throughout the world', published in 1942 by the Vatican, was introduced into Poland. In the beginning of the volume a dedication in long-hand by Pius XII was reproduced: To the 'dear sons and daughters of the Polish nation'. In the *Appendix* papal speeches and messages to the Poles were collected as well as a list of offerings in money and kind which the Holy See had despatched to Polish prisoners and emigrés in all parts of the world.

212. Cf. note 199.

213. D.R.R.P., Information and Press Department. Review of the clandestine Polish press, 202/III-87.

214. A. Martini, *Silenzi e Parole*, etc.

215. L. Frassati, *op. cit.*

216. Cf. the Roman monthly, *La Parrocchia*, May 1964.

217. D.R.R.P., Office of the Presidium, government mail, 202/I-40. (It is almost certainly dealing with the same news referred to in WRN 19 September 1942).

218. C. Papée, *op. cit.*

219. Of the OPW mentioned in note 208. Published in Warsaw between 1941 and 1944.

220. D.R.R.P., Information and Press Department, weekly digest of the press, 202/3-80.

221. *Ibid.*

222. Organ of the Polish Popular Party (Communist party) appearing in Warsaw from 1942 to 1944.

223. Cf. note 220.

224. From *Civiltà Cattolica* of the time.

225. C. Papée, *op. cit.*

226. *Ibid.*

227. Cf. note 224.

228. All the documents contained in these appendices derive from the archives of the Historical Section of the Party (PZPR) of Warsaw. They were, so to speak, 'fished out of' material being set in order.

229. The three documents A, B, C, of this first *Appendix* are collected in the Polish original in a kind of folder entitled, *The Holy See and the Defence of the Rights of Polish Catholics. Some documents (1941–1942)*. So far as we know only the second of these documents has seen the light in Maccarone's book, *Il Nazional-socialismo e la Santa Sede*.

230. I.e. at the request of the Polish embassy to the Holy See under Casimir Papée.

Part Three

1. These and other unpublished details were recounted by Cvetkovic himself in the *Figaro*, 4 April 1960.

2. On Ante Pavelić, cf. Šime Balen, *Pavelić*, Zagreb, 1952. Here we will only recall his last period. He managed to escape to safety when the NDH collapsed in 1945—he remained shut up in a convent in Salzburg, Austria, till the spring of 1948. Then he was able to move to Rome though scarcely changing the rules of the cloister (he lived as a guest of the Collegio Pio Latino Americano under the pseudonym of Fr. Gomez.) Next year the Ustaše priest, Krunoslav Draganović, enabled him to reach the Argentine where Peròn had offered him hospitality. Those years spent at Buenos Aires were Pavelić's last years of freedom. The fall of Peròn, his protector, obliged him once more to take to a semi-clandestine life, until an attempt to kill him on 10 April 1957 (the sixteenth anniversary of the foundation of the NDH) made it seem advisable to go to San Domingo da Trujillo and then to Madrid. He died in Madrid at the Hospital Aleman on 28 December 1959 at the age of seventy.

3. Pavelić was also helped by Horthy's Hungarian regime.

4. As soon as the news of the king's murder reached Rome, the Ustaše being trained in a barracks at Borgotaro were immediately despatched by Mussolini to the Italo-Yugoslav frontier. At the same time various correspondents of Rome newspapers were sent to Belgrade to describe at close quarters the stages of what the Duce believed to be the imminent disintegration of the country.

5. A certain deputy from Montenegro, Račić, drew a pistol and shot a number of times at Radić. Radić was gravely wounded, three other Croatian deputies were killed, and yet three more wounded. Radić died several days later.

6. The article takes up four small-type pages.

7. To end the year of celebrations in 1942, a big national pilgrimage to Rome had been planned. One thinks of the spiritual enthusiasm accumulated with such laborious preparations.

8. Published in the miscellany, *Croazia Sacra*, Rome, 1943. It was also published separately as an off-print and distributed.

9. See also Fr. Cherubino Seguic. *I Croati. La loro Missione storica durante 13 secoli. Studio etnografico storico*, Rome, Istituto Grafico Tiberino, 1941.

10. Of course Pius XII was referring to the hopes arising from Croatia's new autonomy; at that time he obviously could not foresee what would happen under the Ustaše.

11. The allusion is to the Yugoslav national Church which emerged in 1923 through the association of a few members of the Catholic Church with the Old Catholics. Its first bishop was the ex-canon of Spalato (Split), Marko Kalodjera, who took up residence at Zagreb (Agram). But his irregular behaviour ended by causing a schism. Only a third of the associates (some 15,000 out of 50,000) remained faithful to him. In 1933 even the Union of Utrecht (Old Catholics) broke with him. In 1934 the 80-year-old priest Ivan Cerowski was elected bishop, recognized by Utrecht, and consecrated.

12. In his appeal to Pius XII on 18 May 1943 about which we shall have more to say, Stepinac, Archbishop of Zagreb, upheld the same thesis. Cf. *Sudenje Lisaku, Stepincu, Saliću i Družini, Ustaško-Križarskim Zločincima i Njihovim Pomagačima*, Zagreb, 1946.

13. *Hrvatska Stráža* (the Croatian Guard) organ of the episcopate, published various articles between 1939 and 1940 which hoped that Croatia would experience what had happened to Slovakia when Czechoslovakia was dismembered. The *Katolički List* of the Zagreb curia maintained in no. 5 of 1940 that Catholics could be good Nazis and quoted *Mein Kampf*.

14. Their forerunners were the 'Hrvatski Orlovi' (Croatian Eagles) founded in 1920. Cf. *Croazia Sacra*.

15. There were two metropolitan dioceses in Croatia, Sarajevo with four suffragans, and Zagreb with four suffragans. Hence the Ustaše bishop was not only autonomous but almost on the same level with Stepinac.

16. In this pastoral Stepinac saw 'God's hand in action' in the creation of Croatia. He added that he called on the clergy to uphold the new state, not only as Croats 'but also as representatives of Holy Church'. Then he called for prayers for the Poglavnik and ordered a 'Te Deum' to be sung in all churches in the presence of the authorities and the people.

17. The Minister of Justice and Religion, Puk, said on 25 February 1942, in the Croatian Sabor (parliament) that the Ustaše government had deprived this Church of its rights and closed it.

18. The national Serb Orthodox Church was the outcome of the union proclaimed on 30 June 1920 of all the Serbian Orthodox Churches in the Kingdom of Yugoslavia. On the Serbian Orthodox Church cf. C. Crivelli in *Civiltà Cattolica*, 17 January 1942. This article contains no reference to the contemporary situation.

19. The frontiers were fixed, with specific agreements, later: on 13 May with Germany, on 18 May with Italy, on 7 July with Serbia and on 27 October with Montenegro.

19 *bis*. See Hory-Broszat, *Der Kroatische Ustascha-Staat*.

20. N. LV, 87-Z, p. 1941. The signature is that of the Poglavnik, countersigned by Dr. Mile Budak, Minister for Religion and Education. Cf. Sima Simić, *The Change of Religion among the Serbs during World War II*, Titograd, 1958.

21. N. 42. 678-B-1941. Cf. Sima Simic, *op. cit.*

22. The Minister Puk said in his turn at Sisak on 2 June 1941: 'They [the Serbs] came as guests and now our hospitality is finished.' (*Hrvatski Narod*—The Croat People—4 June 1941).

22 *bis*. Cf. Hory-Broszat, *Der Kroatische Ustascha-Staat*.

23. Cf. Sima Simić.

24. *Op. cit.*

25. Yugoslav polemists have blamed Stepinac and his colleagues for communicating all the government documents to the clergy without contesting them in their comments. But here there seems some exaggeration.

26. N. 46.468/1941. Cf. Sima Simić.

27. Dr. Mirko Puk for the Ministry of Justice and Religion; Dr. Artuković for the Ministry of the Interior; Lorković for the Ustaše command; and Curić for the State Office for Economic Renewal.

28. The oath was taken by Ustaše chaplains before two candles, the crucifix, the Koran, a dagger and a revolver.

29. Cf. Sima Simić, *op. cit.*

30. *Op. cit.*

31. The *Glagoljica* is ancient Croat writing.

31 *bis*. Cf. *Tajni Dokumenti, op. cit.*

32. The 'Kuna' was the new Croat unit of currency started by the NDH. It had a fixed relation to the Italian lira.

33. Dr. Rusinović wrote in his report of 9 May 1942 that the recognition of the Orthodox Church was welcomed in the Vatican. In the Vatican view it would be necessary to found Greco-Catholic centres in regions where there were Orthodox and confide the whole business to Dr. Simrak. The Vatican, like Stepinac, viewed conversion to the Eastern Catholic rite as the easiest and shortest path to reunion.

34. The Četniks were Serbs commanded by Mihajlović who had not accepted the surrender of 15 April 1941. They fled to the mountains and for the most part supported the monarchy. They were guerrilla fighters.

34 *bis*. Cf. the report by Fr. Antun Wurster to the Zagreb foreign ministry, 10 May 1943.

35. These and other letters were used by the defence at Stepinac's trial.

36. We see an example of this in the text of a leaflet printed by the press of the Bishop of Djakovo and distributed in the second half of May 1941.

37. Stepinac asked the Poglavnik for houses and land for the Trappist monks of Reichenburg who had been driven out by Hitler and taken refuge with their Trappist brethren at Banja Luka.

38. 'Your Excellency. Dr. Ivan Šarić, Archbishop of Sarajevo, some time ago asked for and obtained as a gift from the Croatian government certain properties formerly belonging to a Jew of Hungarian origin. Some members of the clergy and some citizens of the archdiocese in question have judged the affair badly, have informed me and asked me to intervene. Therefore I proposed to Dr. Antonius Filpanović, then minister of the treasury, that he should be kind enough to exchange those properties belonging to the Jew for others or for a sum of money to be assigned to Archbishop Šarić. Dr. Filpanović kindly agreed to this but shortly afterwards was stricken by a serious illness and had to leave his post. So I implore your Excellency to be so kind if possible as to complete the business according to my desires . . . Marcone. . . .'

38 *bis*. This letter is preserved among the appendices to the 4th volume of Stepinac's *Diary*.

39. In July 1941 Stepinac protested to Puk against his accepting young priests as members or officers of the Ustaše party. On 4 February 1942 Stepinac reminded the clergy of his circular sent out in 1938 forbidding priests to stand in elections. In a special letter he justified his decision that his priests should be excluded from the Party and the Sabor.

40. Cf. the pastoral letter of the Yugoslav Catholic bishops drawn up at the plenary episcopal conference in Zagreb on 20 September 1945. The whole text is to be found in *Civiltà Cattolica*, 17 November 1945.

41. The Franciscans distinguished themselves outstandingly in these enterprises and went on doing so even after the war—Medić, who a few years ago committed a crime of violence against the Yugoslav embassy in Bonn, was a Franciscan. Their distinction is partly explained by their numbers and partly by the violent traditions of their agelong resistance, especially in Bosnia, against Turks and Orthodox. In 1942 they had five provinces in the NDH with 54 convents, 213 parishes, and 800 priests. If we remember that there were fewer than 1,800 diocesan priests we see that out of every three priests in Croatia two were secular and one was Franciscan.

42. Cf. V. Gorresio, *La Guerra dei Poveri: in Tempo presente*, May 1958.

43. The article appeared on 18 September. The news was confirmed in another article on the 21st.

44. He was born in Turin in 1900, was an air-pilot in the First World War, and awarded a silver medal during the Abyssinian war. He married Princess Irene of Greece in 1939. King Victor Emmanuel appointed him King of Croatia on 18 May 1941. The evening before he had been received in private audience lasting over forty minutes by Pius XII. Even today we do not know how Pius XII influenced the prince. Pavelić met him at that period and also subsequently did everything he could to persuade him to be crowned. On 18 March 1942 Aimone assumed the title of Duke of Aosta after the death of his elder brother Amadeo di Savoia Aosta.

45. In the discussions that took place at Monfalcone on 7 May 1941 between Mussolini and Pavelić in Ciano's presence, it was reconfirmed that Croatia was in the Italian sphere of influence. But the Italians only occupied south-west Croatia. In the spring of 1942 the Italian troops,

however, were in operation against the partisans in Eastern Bosnia and Herzegovina.

46. Mgr. Prettner-Cippico, who was attached in those years to the archives of the Secretariat of State and who had the task of helping the Croatian representatives in view of his knowledge of the language, has recalled the comings and goings of Italian military chaplains stationed in Croatia.

47. Mgr. Marcone was in Križevci on 18 August 1942 for the consecration of Mgr. Simrak, and at Mostar on 4 October of the same year, for that of Mgr. Petar Cule; in 1943 towards mid-April he was again at Mostar, on the 20th of the same month at Sarajevo, then in Slovenia; on 30 May he was at Djakovo, then at Osijek, Vukovar (as guest of Prince Erwin Lobkowicz) and so on.

48. Mgr. Stepinac, for example, was in Rome at least three times, in 1941, in April of 1942 for twelve days, and in 1943 (from 26 May to 3 June); Mgr. Srebrnić, Bishop of Mostar, from 30 May to 6 June 1943; Mgr. Burić of Senj for a few days in the June of 1943, etc.

49. Here, for example, is what Lobkowicz wrote (10/VI/1943) about Bishop Cule of Mostar: 'He has left the impression of a very thoughtful, well-intentioned and balanced person, and we can certainly suppose that his reports spoke in favour of Croatia.'

50. Envoy Extraordinary and Minister Plenipotentiary of Yugoslavia to the Vatican from 31 March 1937 was Dr. Niko Mirošević Sorgo, but as he was absent from Rome from 1941 the *de facto* regency of the legation passed automatically to the most senior official, Dr. Nicola Moscatello, a man who fulfilled many roles. As is seen in the *Appendix*, the situation seemed a bit confused to the Ustaše representatives at the Vatican.

51. 6 October 1946.

52. Cf. A. Giovannetti, *Pio XII parla alla Chiesa del silenzio*, Milan, 1958.

53. Or rather, by his substitute, as Dionisio Njaradi, the Ordinary since 1920, died on 4 April 1941. Mgr. Simrak succeeded him in April 1942, and after he was condemned to death (commuted through Stepinac's and Marcone's intervention) the diocese was administered by Apostolic Administrators.

54. Cf. Sima Simić, *op. cit.*

55. *Op. cit.*

56. *Op. cit.* Maglione's letter was communicated to the bishops of Croatia by Abbot Marcone, 27 March 1942.

57. 'Among the diplomatic corps enclosed within the walls of the Vatican we have many enemies. And they recount *urbi et orbi* endless stories about banditry in Croatia. I have heard that 8,000 photographs have been collected as documentation to prove acts of violence committed by the Ustaše against the Serbs' (9 May 1942).

58. Fr. Cherubino Seguic had long been a Ustaše sympathizer and was about eighty in 1941.

59. His *Diario* is called *Nei primi mesi della fondazione del NDH. La mia missione in Italia, 7–24 September 1941*. Only 100 confidential copies

were published. One copy is preserved in the university library of Zagreb (N. 179248, Section 147).

60. Cf. *Tajni Dokumenti.*

61. Report by Rusinović, 4 March 1942.

62. *Ibid.*

63. Report by Rusinović, 6 March 1942.

64. Report by Rusinović, 27 March 1942.

65. That is to say, the majority. In all likelihood there were exceptions who were pro-Yugoslavia. Mgr. Bauer, Stepinac's predecessor, was of this latter view.

66. Pavelić seems to have asked that he should be removed on three occasions. We are broadly in agreement with what Fr. Cavalli said about Stepinac in his article on the trial in *Civiltà Cattolica,* 7 December 1946.

67. Cf. note in the *Osservatore Romano,* 11 October, 1946.

68. The signatories were really only four, but they maintained that they had the authorization of those absent.

69. Quoted by Fr. Cavalli, *Civiltà Cattolica, art. cit.*

70. Report by Rusinović, 9 May 1942

71. Hopes perhaps deriving from despatches about the military operations undertaken first by the Croatian army and the Germans, and subsequently by the Italians against the Četniks and the Communists.

72. Report by Lobkowicz, 10 June 1943.

73. Cf. the article commemorating Stepinac in the *Osservatore Romano,* 12 February 1960.

74. For instance, cf. the report by Lobkowicz of 13 July 1943.

75. When relations between Yugoslavia and the Holy See were broken in December 1963, quite unjustified denunciations were made against Stepinac, e.g. by the Foreign Minister, Kardelj, to the Belgrade House of Deputies. Absurd accusations were made in pamphlets against Stepinac at the time of his trial.

76. Palmiro Togliatti, after a visit to Yugoslavia, wrote in the Italian Communist paper, *Unità,* 7 November 1946, that Tito had told him that he had warned the chief of the Belgrade nunciature, Mgr. Hurley, that he had full proof of Stepinac's collaboration with the Germans and with the Ustaše, and had asked him to urge the Vatican to avoid a trial by withdrawing him.

77. The Holy See is not in the habit of withdrawing its bishops for debatable political reasons. The case of Mindszenty is just as eloquent as that of Stepinac. In France De Gaulle wanted thirty Pétainist bishops to be retired. The papal nuncio, Roncalli (later John XXIII), managed to reduce this number to three. But Roncalli's predecessor, Mgr. Valeri, was obliged to return to Rome.

78. L. Poliakov, *op. cit.*

79. A. Martini, *op. cit., Civiltà Cattolica,* 5 June, 1964.

80. M. Roatta, *op. cit., Cento Milioni di Baionette.*

81. V. Gorresio, *La Guerra dei Poveri, op. cit.*

82. *Ibid.*

83. Report by Rusinović, 4 March 1942.

84. The word 'Auditor' seems inexact.

85. We have quoted the text of the photostat of the document from *Tajni Dokumenti*.

86. See note 50.

87. Mgr. Giuseppe Ramiro Marcone was born in 1882. At a young age he joined the Benedictine Congregation of the original observance of Monte Cassino as founded in 1872. This was why he wore a white habit. He died in 1952.

88. Dr. Nikola Rusinović was born in 1907 in the province of Spalato (Split). He studied medicine and became a doctor but soon had to emigrate owing to his Croat nationalism. He joined Pavelić's Ustaše abroad. When the NDH was set up he joined the diplomatic service and for a short time was ambassador in Bulgaria. His next move was to Rome as counsellor to the Legation to the Quirinal and at the same time plenipotentiary to the Vatican. He returned to Zagreb halfway through 1942 but in May 1943 the NDH appointed him Consul-General at Munich. After the war he emigrated to the United States where he is a practising doctor.

89. Prince Erwin Lobkowicz was born in Prague on 28 February 1887. He was a former chamberlain of the imperial court of Austria and became private chamberlain *di spada e cappa* under Pius XI and was confirmed in this position by Pius XII. He was appointed to represent the Zagreb government to the Holy See on 31 July 1942. He planned to continue his mission even if Rome was occupied by the Allies. But, with the fall of Fascism and the armistice of 8 September, his plans were irrevocably upset. In Zagreb he was given out as dead even before the end of the war. But he continued to be listed among the private chamberlains in the Vatican until 1958. He has three daughters and is related to the royal house of Bourbon-Parma.

90. The Ustaše ceased to be represented in approximately the summer of 1943. But Marcone stayed on in Zagreb after the occupation of the city by Tito's troops. When Rome was liberated by the Allies his activities were suspended and subsequently they ceased when the NDH was dissolved. In the months that followed efforts were made to renew diplomatic relations with the emerging Yugoslavia. As a result Mgr. Patrick Hurley, an American, was appointed as head of the nunciature in January 1946.

91. Cf. Report by Rusinović, 8 February 1942, and report by Lobkowicz, 10 October 1942.

92. Report by Lobkowicz, 20 December 1942.

93. Report by Rusinovic, 28 May 1942, etc.

94. Report by Lobkowicz, 10 June 1943.

95. Antun Wurster was a Jesuit, and in 1935 the royal Yugoslav government refused to give him a passport owing to his pro-Ustaše activities. Fr. Wurster was sent to Rome as informant in December 1941 or at the latest in January 1942. His reports discredited Rusinović possibly to prepare the way for Lobkowicz who had promised him that he would be made secretary in his office.

96. Report by Lobkowicz, 14 April 1943.

97. Report by Lobkowicz, 9 November 1942.

98. Though the delegation to the Pope was headed by the auxiliary of Zagreb it included political and ecclesiastical men who had come to Rome to the Quirinal to offer the crown of Zvonimir to the king-designate of Croatia.

99. Report by Lobkowicz, 18 May 1943.

100. Report by Rusinovic, 5 June 1942.

101. *Ibid.*

102. The diocese of Djakovo was vacant owing to the resignation of its incumbent, Mgr. Aksimović, who had been bishop since 1920. Negotiations about a successor lasted a long time and the war ended before they did. In 1950 the Holy See made him Apostolic Administrator of this diocese and he died in 1959.

103. Of these three only the third, Mgr. Seper, became a bishop, but not till 1954, and then as coadjutor *sedi datus* to Stepinac, debarred. He became Archbishop of Zagreb on 5 March 1960, and Cardinal on 22 February 1965.

104. Cf. Lobkowicz' report of 14 April 1943.

105. It is probable that it was decided to deal with these two dioceses in terms of their peculiar difficulties; the first had to be protected from Franciscan fanaticism (cf. Tardini's opinion in the report referred to above) and the second from persecution sustained by the Uniates, given their Byzantine rite.

106. Report by Lobkowicz, 10 June 1943.

107. *Diario*, mentioned in the bibliography.

108. *Ibid.*

109. Report by Rusinović, 4 March 1942.

110. Report by Lobkowicz, 9 November 1942.

111. Rusinovic was officially posted at the Quirinal so the meaning is, 'for me, as for our other colleagues in the Legation to the Quirinal'.

112. Report by Rusinović, 8 February 1942.

113. Report by Rusinović, 4 March 1942.

114. Report by Lobkowicz, 14 April 1943.

115. *Ibid.*

115 *bis.* At first they regarded them with hostility, but this gradually changed. For instance Lobkowicz wrote about Montini on 20 December 1942, 'Perhaps he has some feelings of sympathy for us, at least in this last period. . . .'

116. Report by Fr. Wurster, 12 June 1942.

116 *bis.* Reports by Rusinović of 22 February and 25 March 1942, etc.

117. Report by Rusinovic, 27 April 1942.

118. Report by Lobkowicz, 9 February 1943.

119. This word was used by the three heads of the Secretariat of State.

120 Report by Lobkowicz, 10 June 1943.

120 *bis.* This is apparent from all their reports. For them Marcone was a reliable and trustworthy man.

121. We deduce this from what Fr. Seguic wrote in his *Diario*.

122. Fr. Giuseppe Masucci was born on 15 July 1906. As a boy he entered the Abbey of Montevergine where Abbot Marcone taught him

philosophy. He studied theology and canon law in Rome. Subsequently Marcone sent him to England where he completed his studies to teach English. On returning to Italy he was made Rector of the Benedictine College, professor of Canon Law at the abbey, teacher of religious instruction and English at a lycée, and master of novices, etc. In Zagreb he was also chaplain to the Italian colony and blessed ensigns, etc.

123. Usually representatives of the Holy See are characterized by their reserve. Marcone's behaviour was very different.

124. From the *Diario, op. cit.*

125. Report by Lobkowicz, 9 November 1942.

126. Report by Lobkowicz, 9 February 1943.

127. Report by Lobkowicz, 14 April 1943.

128. Cf. *Tajni Dokumenti.*

129. Not all the Ustaše leaders went to the Vatican. For instance Marshal Kvaternik, head of the Croatian armed forces, spent ten days in Italy in 1942 and did not call on the Pope, nor did the Minister for Industry and Commerce who visited Rome in April of that same year.

130. Report by Lobkowicz, 20 December 1942.

131. E.g. 'anyone who cannot use a knife to tear a child from the bowels of its mother is not a good Ustaše'.

132. Quoted in the report by Lobkowicz, 13 July 1943.

133. Report by Lobkowicz, 9 February 1943.

134. Mario Luzi, born in Florence in 1914, is a writer, poet and essayist as well as journalist.

135. Pio Bondioli, born in 1890, also published one or two interesting works on Catholic regions and organizations in Lombardy. He was author of *Manzoni e gli amici della verità*. He is now dead.

136. Report by Rusinović, 10 March 1942.

137. Conte di Sanguineto. He held this post for more than forty years and was finally retired by Pope John XXIII in 1960.

138. Report by Rusinović, 8 February 1942, and subsequent reports.

139. See the essay by Mijo Tumpić in *Croazia Sacra*, Rome, 1943, and the polemical chapter devoted to this college by Frane Barbiere in *Crna Internacionala.*

140. The meeting was called for the printing of *Croazia Sacra*. There were present: Lobkowicz, Fr. Wurster, Dr. Magnino, counsellor to the Italian Ministry of Public Education, Prof. Spalatin, Reader in Croat language at the University of Rome, and Ivo Lendić, Rome correspondent of *Croatia.*

141. In the form of a letter to Prof. Draganović, the organizer of this important miscellany. Fr. Draganović's political faith is widely known. After the war in Rome and in Europe he was almost omnipotent as saviour and protector of the most notorious Ustaše. He stayed for years in Italy and then seems to have retired to Germany. He returned to Yugoslavia in 1968, apparently voluntarily, and no proceedings have been taken against him for alleged complicity with the Ustaše.

142. *Istantanee inedite degli ultime quattro papi*, Modena, 1956.

143. Mgr. Pietro Sigismondi was born in 1908. During his diplomatic

career amongst other things he was secretary to the apostolic nunciature in Paris. After some years at the Secretariat of State he was appointed Apostolic Delegate in the Belgian Congo and Ruando Urundi in 1949. He is now the secretary of the Propaganda Fide in Rome.

144. Mgr. Prettner-Cippico originates from the diocese of Trieste. After studying in Rome and at the Pontifical Ecclesiastical Academy, he entered the Secretariat of State. After 1948 his name was struck off the lists in the *Annuario Pontificio* as the result of severe accusations which threw an equivocal light on various financial activities of the Holy See during the war and involved other Vatican personalities. He was laicized by Pius XII who never forgave him for being the excuse for the Communists' campaign of denigration against the Holy See on the eve of the Italian elections in 1948. John XXIII restored to him permission to celebrate Mass privately after the civil tribunals had thrown light on his activities.

145. Clemente Micara was born in 1879 and died in 1965. From 1909 to 1948 he was abroad in the Vatican foreign service. He was made Cardinal by Pius XII in 1946 and was Vicar for the city and diocese of Rome.

147. Mgr. Ettore Felici was born in 1881. After a brilliant career as a student he taught in seminaries and in 1916 joined the Secretariat of State. In 1920 he was at the new nunciature at Belgrade and four years later in Lisbon. He rose to the position of chargé d'affaires in Chile and in 1938 was transferred to Belgrade. He was made nuncio to Ireland in 1949 and died at his post in 1951.

148. Report by Rusinović, 20 March 1942.

149. Report by Rusinović, 28 May 1942.

150. Report by Lobkowicz, 9 November 1942.

151. Cardinal Pietro Fumasoni-Biondi was Apostolic Delegate to India from 1916–1919, first Apostolic Delegate to Japan until 1923, and ended his diplomatic career as Apostolic Delegate to Washington. He was in charge of Propaganda Fide from 1933 onwards. He died in 1960.

152. Cardinal Giovanni Mercati was born in 1866 and died in 1957. He was made a cardinal by the librarian pope, Pius XI, in 1936, and was given the post of librarian and archivist for Holy Church.

153. Report by Lobkowicz, 14 April 1943.

154. Cardinal Marchetti Selvaggiani was born in 1871. He worked at the apostolic delegation in Washington and at the Secretariat of State. During the First World War he was at Berne, in 1918 he was sent to Venezuela, in 1920 he was made nuncio in Vienna. He was secretary of Propaganda Fide for seven years before he was made a cardinal in 1939. He died in 1951.

155. Report by Lobkowicz, 4 April 1943.

156. Cardinal Pizzardo was born in 1877. He was one of the best-known of the Holy See's diplomats. With the exception of three years passed in Munich from 1909 to 1912, he spent his life in Rome. He was made a cardinal in 1937 and under the pontificate of Pius XII he was one of the most powerful men at the Curia (he was Secretary of the Holy Office,

Prefect of the Sacred Congregation of Seminaries and Universities, etc.).

157. Report by Lobkowicz, 10 June 1943.

158. Cardinal Ermengildo Pellegrinetti was born in 1876 and died in Rome in 1943.

BIBLIOGRAPHY

A. Source-books

Parts Two and Three of this book are based to a large extent on information culled from documents so far unpublished (as regards Poland) and only partly published and almost entirely unknown (as regards Croatia).

1. *Polish Documents*

The reader will find information about the Polish documents in the text and the notes. The author has only used a third of all the material he unearthed in Warsaw; another third was left in the archives as superfluous.

2. *Croatian Documents*

(a) We have taken the official acts of the Ustaše government and the Croatian bishops on the question of the conversion and re-baptism of the Orthodox mainly from the work of Sima Simić (see secondary sources). Simić is an Orthodox Serb and his judgments are certainly not objective, especially as regards Stepinac and the Croatian bishops. But he is scrupulous in reproducing documents and even includes in their entirety those that contradict his own thesis.

(b) More important are the official reports sent to the NDH government by the Ustaše representatives to the Holy See. We have ten reports by Rusinović, fourteen by Lobkowicz and three by Wurster. These documents were found among other material in the archives of the Ministry of Foreign Affairs in Zagreb—material that for some unknown reason the Ustaše failed to destroy or take with them in their flight to Austria at the time of the collapse. The material (trunks of it) was handed over to Archbishop Stepinac by the Minister Alajbegović to be kept safely in view of their (the Ustaše's) possible return (according to the charge made by the Communist authorities at the time of the Archbishop's arrest), or simply to be kept safely (according to Stepinac himself, who said that he notified the new authorities of the material's existence at once, as soon as Zagreb was occupied by Tito's army).

(c) In the course of our study we have made several references to Stepinac's *Diary*. It is a manuscript bound in five volumes, beginning on 13 May 1934 and ending on 13 February 1945. The *Diary* records all the events in the Archbishop's life during that period. It was drawn up by himself and also by members of his household. The author had no time to study it in its entirety and has limited himself to a few quotations. In particular he has made use of some of the documents attached to Vol. IV, such as Stepinac's report to Pius XII, and Abbot Marcone's letter containing the directives of the Holy Office on property expropriated from the Orthodox and offered to the Catholic Church.

B. Secondary Sources
(the essential ones, excluding articles)

1. *Part One: General*
   (a) Catholic authors:
   Michele Maccarone, *Il Nazional-socialismo e la Santa Sede*, Rome, 1947.
   Alberto Giovannetti, *Il Vaticano e la Guerra* (*1939–1940*), Vatican City, 1960.
   (b) Uncommitted authors:
   Jacques Nobécourt, '*Le Vicaire*' *et l'Histoire*, Paris, 1964.
   Saul Friedländer, *Pie XII et le III Reich*, Paris, 1964.
   Also, of course, *Acta Apostolicae Sedis* for Pius XII's speeches and documents, etc.

2. *Part Two: The Case of Poland*
   Apart from the works mentioned for Part One:
   (a) On the Catholic Church in Poland on the eve of, and during, Second World War:
   Władzimierz Gsovski, *Church and State behind the Iron Curtain*, New York, 1955.

The Persecution of the Catholic Church in German-occupied Poland, London, 1941.

And various official collections of documents on occupied Poland.

(b) On the clandestine Polish State in Poland occupied by the Germans:

Polskie Siły Zbroine w II wojnie światowej, vol. III: *Armia Krajowa* (The Polish Armed Forces in World War II: vol. III: the National Army), London, 1950.

Jan Karski, *Story of a Secret State*, Boston, 1944.

(c) The Holy See and occupied Poland (1939–1945):

Pius XII a Polska (Pius XII and Poland, 1939–1949, speeches, letters, comments) edited by Casimir Papée, Rome, 1954.

3. *Part Three: The Case of Croatia*

(a) On Croatia in general and her historic 'mission':

Croazia sacra, Rome, 1943, miscellany.

The Croatian Nation, edited by A. F. Bonifačić and S. C. Mihanović, Chicago, 1955.

Jere Jareb, *Pola Stoljeća Hrvatske Politike* (Half a century of Croatian Politics), Buenos Aires, 1960.

(b) on the NDH:

Works by non-committed writers:

Ladislaus Hory-Martin Broszat, *Der kroatische Ustascha-Staat, 1941–1945*, Stuttgart, 1964.

Rudolf Kiszling, *Die Kroaten. Der Schiksalsweg eines Sudslavenvolkes*, Cologne and Graz, 1956.

Works by Titoist writers:

Viktor Novak, *Magnum crimen*, Zagreb, 1948 (1,124 pp.).

Various authors: *Les systèmes d'occupations en Jugoslavie, 1941–1945*, Beograd, 1963.

Works by writers in exile:

Marko Sinovčić, *NDH u svietlu dokumenta* (the NDH in the light of the documents), Buenos Aires, 1950.

Ivan Meštrović, *Uspomene na političke ljude i dogadjaje* (Memoirs of political men and experiences), Buenos Aires, 1961.

(c) On the religious policy of the NDH:

Suđenje Lisaku, Stepincu, Saliću i družini, ustaško-križarskim zločincima i njihovim pomagačima (Trial of the Ustaše delinquents and crusaders, Lisak, Stepinac, Salić and their collaborators), Zagreb, 1946.

Dokumenti o protunarodnom radu i zločinima jednog dijela katoličkog klera (Documents regarding actions against the people and crimes committed by part of the Catholic clergy), edited by Joža Horvat and Zdenko Štambuk, Zagreb, 1946.

Tajni Dokumenti o odnosima Vatikana i ustaške 'NDH' (Secret documents on the relations between the Vatican and the Ustaše NDH), Zagreb, 1952.

Sima Simić, *Tudjinske kombinacije oko NDH* (The Designs of Foreigners on the NDH), Titograd, 1958.

Sima Simić, *Vatikan protiv Jugoslavije* (The Vatican against Yugoslavia), Titograd, 1958.

Sima Simić, *Prekrštavanje Srba za vreme drugog Svetskog rata* (The Re-baptisms of the Serbs during the Second World War), Titograd, 1958.

Finally we quote the following works, but mainly so as to point out their extremely tendentious nature:

Hervé Laurière, *Assassins au nom de Dieu*, Paris, 1951.

Avra Manhattan, *Terror over Yugoslavia, the threat to Europe* London, 1953.

Edmond Paris, *Le Vatican contre l'Europe*, Paris, 1959.

INDEX

Adamski, Mgr. Stanilsas, 181, 184–5, 404
Aimone of Savoia-Aosta, Duke, 302, 325, 411
Aksimović, Mgr., 415
Albania, 36
Alexander, King of Yugoslavia, 261, 378, 408
Alfieri, Dino, 393, 396, 397
Algisi, Leone, book by, 394
Aloisi-Masella, Mgr., 399
Anders, General, 241
Angers, 143, 158, 159
Antonescu, General, 347
    Jews and, 59
Annuario Pontificio, 324, 391, 402, 403 417
Apologetische Rundschau, 356
Apor, Baron, 363
Attività della Santa Sede, L', 44
Austrians, 78
    Anschluss, 51, 78, 94
Axis Powers, the, 13, 34, 53, 56, 70–1, 82, 90, 235, 259, 346, 382, 385

Bačić, Dr. Vilo, 334
Baclas, C., 67
Baltic States, the, 35
Barthou, Louis, French President, 261
Bastianini, —, 365
Baziak, Mgr. Eugene, 175, 463
Beck, Colonel Joseph, 158, 203, 404–5
Belgium, 35
    German invasion, 35, 87–8, 396
Benedict XIV, Pope, 15
Benedict XV, Giacomo della Chiesa, Pope, 22, 85, 93, 94, 139, 144
Bérard, Léon, 368
Bergen, — von, 79, 138, 204, 205, 212, 254, 363, 405

Berlin:
    Nunciature and Nuncio in, 51, 60, 136–7, 146
    see also Orsenigo, Mgr.; Preysing, Mgr. von
Berliner Boesenzeitung, 124
Bernardini, Mgr., Nuncio, 61
Berne, 51
Berning, Bishop, 178–9
Bertram, Adolf, Cardinal, 62, 137, 139–40, 147, 161, 166
Bessarabia, 35, 43, 92
Bieniek, Mgr., 181
Blericq, Canon Edward van, 112–13
Boehm, Mgr., 307, 333, 353–4
Bondioli, Pio, 353, 416
Bonnet, G., book by, 404–5
Borgoncini Duca, Mgr., 318, 363, 365–6
Bralo, Rev. Božidar, 298
Brasse, Canon, 113
Brauchitsch, General, 387
Brazil, 399
    ambassador of the Holy See in, 68–9
Breitinger, Rev. Hilarius, 160, 161, 162, 164, 165, 166, 402
Breslau, Archbishop of, *see* Bertram, Adolf
Budak, Mile, 277, 410
Buehler, Dr., 398
Bukovina, 35, 43, 92
Burić, Mgr., Viktor, 289, 412
Burzio, Mgr. Giuseppe, 58–9, 60

Canaris, Admiral, 54
Cardinals, the Sacred College of, 376ff.
Casablanca Conference (1943), the, 37, 393
Casertano, Raffaele, 320
Cassulo, Mgr. Andrea, Nuncio, 59–60

423